PURE GOLDWATER

JOHN W. DEAN
BARRY M. GOLDWATER, JR.

palgrave
macmillan

Excerpts of letters, diaries, testimony, and speeches by Barry Goldwater are from the Arizona Historical Foundation/Documents from the personal and political papers of Barry M. Goldwater/MS FM MSS #1, and are printed with permission.

Photograph that appears on page viii: © Gittings; Goldwater Family Foundation, is printed with permission.

Photographs that appear on pages 6, 16, 51, 70, 76, 104, 136, 148, 193, 340, and 361 are from the Arizona Historical Foundation and are printed with permission.

Photographs that appear on pages 3, 8, 24, 26, 27, 30, 38, 42, 46, 55, 88, 115, 158, 189, 190, 225, 261, and 276 are from the Goldwater Family Foundation and are printed with permission.

PURE GOLDWATER

First published in hardcover IN 2008 by PALGRAVE MACMILLAN in the U.S.— a division of St. Martin's Press, LLC, 175 Fifth Avenue, New York, N.Y. 10010.

Where this book is distributed in the UK, Europe, and the rest of the world, this is by Palgrave Macmillan, a division of Macmillan Publishers Limited, registered in England, company number 785998, of Houndmills, Basingstoke, Hampshire, England RG21 6XS.

PALGRAVE MACMILLAN is the global academic imprint of the above companies and has companies and representatives throughout the world.

ISBN: 978-0-230-61133-7

Library of Congress Cataloging-in-Publication Data

Goldwater, Barry M. (Barry Morris), 1909–1998.
   [Journals. Selections]
  Pure Goldwater / John W. Dean, Barry M. Goldwater, Jr.
     p. cm.
  Based on the unpublished journals of Barry Goldwater.
  Includes index.
  ISBN-13: 978-1-4039-7741-0 (hardcover)
  ISBN-10: 1-4039-7741-0 (hardcover)
  1. Goldwater, Barry M. (Barry Morris), 1909–1998—Diaries. 2. Goldwater, Barry M. (Barry Morris), 1909–1998—Correspondence. 3. Legislators—United States—Diaries. 4. Legislators—United States—Correspondence. 5. United States. Congress. Senate—Biography. 6. Presidential candidates—United States—Biography. 7. Conservatism—United States—History—20th century—Sources. 8. United States—Politics and government—1945–1989—Sources. I. Dean, John W. (John Wesley), 1938– II. Goldwater, Barry, 1938– III. Title.
  E748.G64A3 2008
  973.92092—dc22   2008003318

A catalogue record of the book is available from the British Library.

Design by Scribe, Inc.

First PALGRAVE MACMILLAN paperback edition: October 2009

10 9 8 7 6 5 4 3 2 1

Printed in the United States of America.

We will be known forever by the tracks we leave.

—a Native American proverb
favored by Senator Goldwater

CONTENTS

Preface   ix

PART I
THE EARLY YEARS

Chapter 1   The Boy Who Became the Man   3
Chapter 2   Journals and Opinions   15
Chapter 3   A Break from Business to Explore Arizona   23
Chapter 4   Military Life   45
Chapter 5   Political Beginnings   67

PART II
THE SENATE YEARS: 1952–1965

Chapter 6   The First Senate Campaign   75
Chapter 7   Learning How Washington Worked   87
Chapter 8   Playing on the National Stage: 1959–1963   103

PART III
AFTER THE 1964 PRESIDENTIAL RACE

Chapter 9   Setting the Record Straight   139
Chapter 10   Seeing the World and Spreading the Word   177

PART IV
NIXON AND WATERGATE

Chapter 11   Recalling Nixon   197
Chapter 12   Nixon's Presidency: First Term   213
Chapter 13   Nixon's Presidency: Second Term   255
Chapter 14   Watergate   275

PART V
ON THE ISSUES

Chapter 15   American Foreign Policy   331
Chapter 16   Domestic Issues   341
Chapter 17   Retirement Years   365

Epilogue   373
Chronology   379
Acknowledgments   389
Index   393

PREFACE

Today, public opinion of former Senator Barry Goldwater of Arizona is not unlike that of former President Harry Truman of Missouri in that people across the political spectrum appreciate his candor, role as a public official, and contributions to his country. Whether you agree or disagree with Goldwater's and Truman's positions, you can admire the manner in which they conducted the business of government and of themselves as public servants. In short, Goldwater's legacy and life transcend partisan politics. Accordingly, we hope that this material will be of interest to people of all political persuasions—anyone interested in American history and concerned with contemporary American politics—because it reveals like no other the life, times, and thinking of a political figure whose devotion to politics and public service was iconic if not exemplary. Better yet, he was a unique political personality who lived life to its fullest and from whom we can learn more about ourselves by examining that life—*as he saw it*. In doing so, he has invited others to know the person we knew and as we knew him.

We emphasize those words above because this is not a book by John Dean and Barry Goldwater, Jr., about the late senator; rather we are merely the initiators, organizers, and implementers of this project. In fact, this is a book by Senator Goldwater about himself, although he did not write it for publication. Throughout his adult life he paused from time to time—albeit on an irregular basis, yet with sufficient frequency to create a meaningful collection—to gather and share his thoughts and put them down in written form. He started a private journal when his first son, Barry, Jr., was born. He continued to make entries in his journal as his other children arrived, sharing thoughts about business and life for their benefit, and to clarify his own thinking.

As he explored the mountains and deserts of his much-loved Arizona, or visited the Indian reservations throughout his state about which he was deeply fascinated, he carried both his camera and a portable typewriter to record his impressions of his state's rugged beauty and his appreciation of the people who had occupied its land long before white people had arrived. When he went abroad to serve in World War II, he continued sharing his experiences and thoughts in his letters and in a journal. As his political beliefs were developing, he recorded them in his journal, and occasionally in guest editorials and radio addresses. And when he entered public life, he periodically paused to record his reactions and feelings. In addition, throughout his long public career as an elected official he made a point of personally responding to his constituent mail and other important correspondence, as well as reporting to his family as he traveled the world. Also, we have located a rather extraordinary source of material about the senator: his three days of sworn testimony about himself when he filed (and won) a defamation lawsuit to deal with false assertions made about him during his 1964 presidential bid. These materials are the sources of this book.

This is not, however, a belated autobiography. It is more a scrapbook of important thoughts; it is more nuggets than narrative. Still we think the collected material provides a most revealing view of Goldwater. This is not the material polished by speechwriters or staff, not the words of ghost writers or coauthors; rather this is material directly from Goldwater himself. At times, when circumstances permitted, his words were well chosen and professionally written. Other times, which was most of the time, he was rushed, so the material is raw and real, unpolished but informative. When we found this material—most of it at the Arizona Historical Foundation—it struck us as pure gold, and more appropriately, pure Goldwater. It is the voice of a man we knew—at times "the happy malcontent," as one commentator described him, and more often simply a man who enjoyed the hell out of doing whatever he was doing.

As such, it offers not the view of a biographer, who by definition filters a subject through his or her own outlook or agenda, or even an autobiographical view—for Goldwater produced several autobiographical works working with other writers, and though they are excellent, they are more filtered, restrained, impersonal, and distant than the material we found. We believe this material, which was not written for publication (although he left it behind knowing others might be interested in it), is far more intimate and revealing that his cowritten autobiographical works. Simply stated, this is a collection of material that reveals the heart and soul of a political figure who remains important to this day. But before turning to this material we should provide a bit more background.

In assembling this unpublished material we were very aware that we were gathering the words of a man who was the longtime friend to one of us and the father of the other. This situation could easily produce hagiography, although that is not our intent, nor do we believe (given the autobiographical nature of the material) that it is by definition possible. But our conflicts of interest and credentials need to be mentioned briefly. For over fifty years—since we first met in our early teens at Staunton Military Academy, a private secondary school in Staunton, Virginia (from which Senator Goldwater graduated as well, but which is no longer in existence)—we have been close friends.

We both pursued early careers in public service in Washington, DC, largely because of the influence of the senator, not because he suggested it to either of us, but because we both saw what he was doing with his life and why he was doing it. He made service in Washington, DC, appealing, if not a high calling. Our admiration and respect for the subject of this work, the love of a son for his father, and the fraternal affection one has for a good friend, in addition to our own careers in government, we submit uniquely qualifies us for this project, because we remain curious about this man who so influenced our lives as he did his nation; we feel we are able to recognize material that is both revealing about him and relevant today; and we are able to bring our own enthusiasm for the importance of knowing this man as we knew him to this undertaking. As we explain in the acknowledgments, we have been assisted greatly in this project by other members of the Goldwater family (by which we mean both consanguinity and affinity, both literally and figuratively—to be very Bill Buckleyesque about it) as well as by the staff of the Arizona Historical Foundation, the able people who are the keepers of the Goldwater papers.

At times the senator's handwriting required translation; his typing makes it obvious that he never attended secretarial school, not to mention that he used his portable typewriter when camping or traveling, often in less than ideal circumstances. This, for example, from a July 30, 1939, journal entry: "This typing is a mess. I am cramped over a box of canned food with one leg wrapped aroind [sic] the gear lever and the other braced against the steering post." Later, when he turned to dictation, it was transcribed by others. Accordingly in gathering "pure Goldwater" material, typos have been corrected, abbreviations spelled out, and appropriate punctuation added, plus occasionally very minor editorial clarifications have been made (as the senator would have done himself if he had ever published the material). Occasionally, we have corrected the syntax of sentences, or sorted out convoluted statements that can easily occur when dictating, or replaced an unduly repetitive word, which can also happen easily in a lengthy and typically interrupted dictation, but we have not changed the substance nor, we believe, his style. We have also copyedited the material to make it uniform since many different people typed his dictation over many years, and rather than bracket this material, we have simply made the appropriate changes, including material in the trial transcript from the defamation lawsuit the senator filed against Ralph Ginzburg following his 1964 presidential race.

Because not all the material we discovered is particularly relevant today, or of general interest, we have included only portions of many documents, or used ellipses to trim the material down (particularly his trial testimony, which exceeded 150,000 words), while we have reproduced other documents in full. We have also dropped salutations on letters. The amount of available material related to key events is also uneven. For example, there is almost no first-person material regarding his 1964 bid to become president of the United States, though, to our surprise, there was a great deal of personal material relating to Richard Nixon and Watergate. All the documents from which we have drawn can be found at the Barry M. Goldwater Collection at the Arizona Historical Foundation, and we have not drawn from all documents, rather only those we believe tell the reader something about the man who wrote them.

To provide context, we have assembled a chronology of his life, because the first-person material we have selected is far from a narrative of his life and career, or even any part of it. In fact, the material is at times frustratingly incomplete. Yet it is a fresh sketch, or self-portrait, of its author. We have organized the selected material into five parts, which are roughly chronological (although there is some overlap): Part I—The Early Years; Part II—The Senate: 1952–1965; Part III—After the 1964 Presidential Race; Part IV—Nixon and Watergate; and Part V—On the Issues. The content of this book has been controlled by the varying amount of new first-person material we discovered. To the degree necessary, we have provided brief editorial notes in brackets in text of the senator's material (and occasional footnotes) to explain the selected material, to note its significance and identify people. In the process, we have attempted to provide the bare bones of a narrative. Our aim, however, is to let the senator's words speak for themselves.

Finally, a last thought on why Barry Goldwater matters, aside from his being a historical figure and an interesting personality. Basically, it is because of the way he viewed others and his work. Today, we are a politically divided nation: red and blue states, conservatives and liberals, Republicans and Democrats. Divisive issues—such as war, abortion, gay marriage, guns, and immigration, to name only a few—are too often debated in shrill voices of activists shouting at each other across a growing political gulf, where no one can be heard. Politics—technically, "the art and science of governance"—has morphed into its lesser form of war by other means. Politicians spend far more time battling each other than looking for solutions to America's problems.

Political rancor, of course, is not new to our capital for it comes and goes. But contemporary political acrimony has been magnified and has grown increasingly pervasive, given the information age we live in with 24/7 news cycles and an omniscient news media that thrives on conflict. Political consultants coach and encourage their candidates to exploit, exaggerate, and exacerbate our differences to win election contests, because it works. When campaigning they rely on poll-tested messages, work to stay on message, and spin the truth when they fall off it. Once in office, incumbents never stop campaigning for reelection, leaving little distinction between governing and campaigning. Well-heeled special interest groups roam the corridors of power in Washington, DC, not too subtly corrupting the processes of government with their moneyed influence. Because many elected officials must devote so much more time to raising money, they have little time to think about government.

Goldwater rejected these approaches to elective office and governing, all of which emerged while he was on the national stage. His basic beliefs all build on the importance of individual freedom and, even more important for an elected official, the overriding need for honesty in public service. Without the latter, he did not believe there were effective ways and means to truly promote and protect American freedom. He has been described as "an American original." He could be described as a model as well. Not that he was even close to perfect, but as the words that follow show, this man of the twentieth century, who sought to move forward by relying on the proven wisdom and principles of public service developed in the nineteenth century, left us with a legacy of a courtly conservatism that perpetuated and emulated the best behavior of the past to address the problems of the present and future. His way of thought, his style, and his reliance on timeless wisdom and eternal truths should not be forgotten in the twenty-first century.

In addition to sharing himself in this material, he provided a good bit of historical information that he never mentioned to anyone. In fact, his children were unaware that President Nixon promised him the ambassadorship to Mexico—which he would have loved—but he did not let this promise interfere with the withdrawal of his defense of Nixon during the Watergate scandal. Nor did he tell anyone in his family (other than possibly his wife) that President Ford asked him to be his vice president when he became president, an offer that Goldwater refused. These are only a few of the historical nuggets we discovered, but we think it best for the senator to tell his own story.

John W. Dean
Barry M. Goldwater, Jr.

PART I

THE EARLY YEARS

CHAPTER 1

THE BOY WHO BECAME THE MAN

F rom a young age Barry Goldwater knew what interested him: radio
and electronics, photography and flying, the military and his family's
department store business, and public service, which began with the
military and proceeded into politics. Along the way he met the love of his life,
Margret "Peggy" Johnson, who would become his partner and the mother of
his four children. Goldwater's interest in those who were experts in the matters that interested him was documented in his letter to Thomas Edison.

A young Barry Goldwater.

Letter (1923)

This letter was sent by a fourteen-year-old Goldwater to inventor Thomas Edison. The director of the Thomas A. Edison Papers at Rutgers University discovered this letter in 1989 and sent a copy to the senator.

Dear Mr. Edison,

I wish to congratulate you upon your great success in the past years and hope that your future years may be as fruitful. I am very interested in electricity and radio. I operate a radio station here of ten watts power under the call—613 P I. I have studied electricity since I was a little kid and am going to keep it up until I am an old one.

Recollections (Undated)

To provide an overview of Goldwater's early life, we have selected a recollection that he dictated (which we believe was done in the mid-1970s) but did not date. We have slightly condensed it.

My father was a great lover of boxing, and it was a strong sport in Phoenix with some of the top professionals fighting here. I'll never forget one time when Paul Fannin [later governor of Arizona and senator] and I were young men and we went to watch a professional boxer work out. I think his name was Kid Parker. Both Paul and I had taken boxing lessons and because we were big kids Parker asked if we would like to step in the ring and trade a few whops. Paul did, and after one round got out. I climbed in the ring and very mistakenly hit him, and he hit me back so hard my head turned around. I tried to get out of the ring but he wouldn't let me leave until the bell rang, and when it was over he said, "Sonny, don't ever do that again." And I never did.*

The first time I became interested in flying must have been around 1917 or maybe earlier when the first airplanes showed up at

---

* *Swimming, track (a javelin thrower), and football (center) were Goldwater's sports, not to mention respectable golf and tennis games. He would later ruin his knees playing semi-professional basketball in Phoenix.*

the annual state fair. They would do whatever stunts they could, with people walking on the wing, or standing on the top of the wings, and even though I was very young, I was thrilled by it. During World War I, the exploits of our pilots got my attention, particularly Frank Luke, Jr., who I remember being in high school here; he was decorated with the Congressional Medal of Honor after destroying some twenty-seven enemy balloons during World War I. One day in 1928 I was walking down Central Avenue in Phoenix and passed R. D. Roper's automobile showroom, where they had an airplane, so I went in and looked at it. It was a Great Lakes Trainer and was selling for $2,500—a lot of money then. The salesman said if I went out to what they called the airport, I'd find Jack Thornburg who would be glad to teach me how to fly. Well, I went out and met Jack. He had a Great Lakes Trainer and the airport was merely a dirt strip. So I started taking lessons. After ten very pleasant hours I soloed one morning. I did all of my flying in the morning before going to work and my mother wondered what I was doing getting up so early and leaving. In fact, I think she thought that I had a girl, but she didn't learn about my flying until after I had my license and there appeared a little notice in the newspaper. I was still very interested in radio and I thought I could combine my radio interest with my flying interest, possibly doing something about developing or improving air-to-ground communications. I never did, however, because Herbert Hoover, Jr., got interested in this too and rounded up all the patents.

CIVIC AFFAIRS AND THE FAMILY BUSINESS

Recollections (February 5, 1977)

When my freshman year in college ended [and my father passed away] I elected not to continue at the University of Arizona but went into the family business in Phoenix which was at that time a store employing about fifty-five people and doing an annual volume of about $350,000 [approximately $4 million today]. The business was located

The grand opening of a Goldwaters department store in Scottsdale, Arizona, with an antique car parked in front.

in downtown Phoenix and it was the first reinforced steel concrete building built in Arizona.

I had worked in the store as a boy. I remember doing janitor work and one Christmas I was Santa Claus and then I remember the first job I had on the delivery truck being a helper. The first delivery we made was to a whore house on Gold Alley and it was for $88 and the madam paid it off in silver dollars and it was such a heavy pile of money we had to come back to the store and get rid of it. I started literally at the bottom in the piece goods section where I learned the different fabrics, how to tell them apart and what they were used for. After that I worked in every department in the store except corsets and shoes. My education was furthered by working a year in New York during the depression in our office at Frederick Adkins on 42nd Street. I gradually worked my way up until I was merchandise manager of ladies ready-to-wear and enjoyed it immensely. I also designed several innovative things like denim skirts and shirts, branding iron prints, and probably the most successful, monetary wise, was the "antsy pants," which consisted of white men's shorts with large red ants printed on them.

The business continued to grow, although during the depression years—and I would say the first five years were the most severe—the business didn't make any money but it didn't lose any either. In fact, we were able to maintain our employees and our salary scale. I was elected president of the board in the late 1930s and continued to serve in that capacity until I left to join the army air corps in the middle of 1941.

FALLING IN LOVE WITH PEGGY AND THE FAMILY

Goldwater hadn't planned to fall in love and marry until his late twenties, but the dapper young president of Goldwater's Department Store met the love of his life one morning when she came into the store with her mother. Here Goldwater recalls it all with a touch of humor and the usual truth.

Recollections (September 22, 1984)

Fifty years ago today Peggy became my bride and I'm sure all who know her agree—that in your heart you know I was right.* I have to admit that I was the one who did the chasing, and I made more promises than Vice President Walter Mondale. At least it shows I was consistent. Even in those days, I believed that extremism in the pursuit of giving up my liberty was no vice.** Before I go any further, Peggy has asked me to make it very clear that while we've been married for fifty years, when we got married she was a child-bride. And I go along with that because I found that on this issue, it's a lot better to be a conservative than to have a conscience.***

---

* *Goldwater's 1964 presidential campaign motto was "In Your Heart You Know He's Right."*

** *Goldwater's 1964 acceptance speech at the GOP National Convention included a statement that became highly controversial when taken out of context: "I would remind you that extremism in the defense of liberty is no vice. And let me remind you also that moderation in the pursuit of justice is no virtue." To see the statement in context, see http://www.washingtonpost.com/wp-srv/politics/daily/may98/goldwaterspeech.htm.*

*** *This allusion, of course, is to his 1960 classic book,* The Conscience of a Conservative.

Barry and Peggy married on September 22, 1934, in Muncie, Indiana.

I have a tendency to speak my mind—sometimes in no uncertain terms—but Peggy has always been an ever-present moderating influence. A lot of people are aware that I've had some troubles with my hip in recent years—but my hip problem wasn't caused by any of the reasons you may have read about. I think it was caused by fifty years of Peggy kicking me under the table and saying, "Barry, that's enough." If she wasn't twenty feet away, I'd be getting it right now as I dictate these recollections. Peggy's real challenge is going to come in 1987 after I've retired from the Senate. I'm sure that every woman knows the classic definition of retirement: It's when you have half as much income and twice as much husband. A good marriage is when you say, "How do I love thee, let me count the ways"—and you reach for a calculator. Peggy doesn't need a calculator.

Everything has to start someplace. Each of us came into this world as a little baby. Then each of us started our way through life doing almost what came naturally but also what came from the guidance of other people. I'll never forget my father telling me one time, "Son, I was forty-two years old when I got married and that was eight years too soon." So, I grew up with the feeling that a man had to be a little bit off his rocker if he got married too young. And then one day, a very attractive woman came into my store with a very, very beautiful younger person with her. The older woman was Mrs. Ray Johnson from Muncie, Indiana, who had come out to Phoenix for her husband's health and the attractive young lady was her daughter, whose name I very quickly found was Margaret.

You see, in those days, when I ran the store, you won't believe this, but I used to show up in striped trousers, a black coat, sometimes a cutaway, with a stiff white collar, tie and even, at times, a red carnation. You see, storekeeping in those days was a source of great pride and that's something I had in my business. In fact, I still have great pride in the fact that I was once what we laughingly called a "rag peddler."

My interest in the young lady from Indiana grew and grew and I soon found myself in love but I didn't sense any reciprocal feeling on her part. This went on for over two and a half years, and finally one New Year's Eve, when I was visiting her in Muncie, Indiana, I got her in a telephone booth and I said, "Now look, Peggy (I had grown intimate by that time—I called her Peggy), I'm running out of money and I'm running out of patience. Either you are going to marry me or not and I want to know right now." Well, she said yes. Now that was a New Year's Eve, and very shortly thereafter, in fact, in the next week she sailed from New York on a round-the-world trip with her mother.

But to go back a bit, in those two and a half years, I would travel to New York to do business for the store, and stop off to see her, either in Indiana or up in Charlevoix, Michigan, where her family had a summer home, or in New York where she studied and worked for a while as a designer. But I didn't get to see enough of her, and when I told her I was running out of patience that was not exactly true, but when I told her I was running out of money, that was true then and it's never quite ceased being true.*

---

* *Goldwater's son Michael has observed that the fact that his father left politics poorer rather than wealthier is both the exception to the rule and a testament to his honesty.*

I chased her as no woman had ever been chased before. I remember one trip she made out to Arizona. I had presents waiting for her at each stop of the train, like a crate of apples with a note saying, one of these a day will keep the doctor away, because there was a doctor's convention on the train she was on. Another stop, flowers and things like that because when you were traveling by train, you had many places to stop and time to make such deliveries, so I arranged to have them made as she crossed the country.

Well, as I was saying, as soon as she agreed to get married, off Peggy went around the world and so I wrote her letters every day and mailed them ahead to her various ports of call with instructions of where she should read them, like in front of funnel, or up in the bow, or on the stern, or on the bridge, etc., and that got her around the world, I think, rather safely because I was worried that some jackass might meet her and I would never see her again.

I couldn't give her a ring when I wanted to because it all happened so fast, so I mailed it to her so she would have it on her arrival from her around the world trip when she got into New York. The ring was the wedding ring of my grandmother. It was a diamond-cut yellow diamond, about a carat and a half, I think, and, while there wasn't much family tradition, we sort of made one that the first male in the family to marry would have access to that ring. So, sure enough, when Mike married Connie, he was the first to get married so Connie now has the ring. I don't know what she has done with it. It may be that little bright thing in her naval.

Peggy and I planned the wedding for September 22nd to be held in Muncie, Indiana. Peggy was a Baptist, I was an Episcopalian, and bless her soul, she changed her church to coincide with mine. So on the appointed day we were married in a beautiful little church that still stands in Muncie. My brother Bob was my best man. Every man in the wedding was a member of the Sigma Chi Fraternity and they included Ray Johnson, Peggy's brother, and Bucky Harris, one of my oldest and best friends. I think the only bad thing I did during the whole ceremony was when I kissed her after the minister gave me permission to, I gave her a pat on the ass, which has always been customary with me when I kiss a girl. I don't know why that ever started but it just seems okay to do something with your right hand and that was sort of natural.

We took our honeymoon to Mexico City but before that, I'll never forget Uncle Morris coming to the wedding. I went down to the train to meet him and there he was, walking up and down the platform. He'd gotten in a little earlier and didn't tell us, and at that time he would have been about eighty-five years old, with that great big mustache he had. But the waiting didn't bother him. Well, anyway, I planned to take Peggy to Mexico City by car and we drove to Laredo, Texas, crossed the river and drove down to Monterrey where I was told that it was possible to reach Mexico City by car, but it might take a month or two months even, and it would require a team of horses for about half the distance because no automobile could traverse the terrain. The road goes up a very, very steep mountain on the Gulf of Mexico side of Mexico, and they just told us it was impossible so we went back to Monterrey and had a most enjoyable day.

The day consisted of visiting the local brewery, where we drank our fill of beer, then a visit to a liquor store because you couldn't buy liquor in the United States then. So we proceeded to walk up and down the aisles in the liquor store, viewing the white tables loaded with bottles, sampling the ones we wanted and ordering each bottle we wanted. To identify it, we wrote our names on the label. It was an easy idea. We gave them 50 percent of the purchase price at the store and when we picked up the bottles in the United States, we agreed to pay the other 50 percent. Well, we got on the train, both of us about half smashed, and the first thing I did was lose the ticket, but after a couple of more drinks, I located it, wrapped around a bottle of brandy.

This is hard to believe, but we stayed at the Ritz Hotel in Mexico City, and the room was two pesos a day and that's when the peso was worth about fifty cents. So, we lived in luxury, real luxury, because I had a total of six hundred dollars in my pocket to take her on a honeymoon, and six hundred dollars today in Mexico City might get you one tortilla, one taco and a cot with no covers.

We headed back to the United States and picked up our car in Monterrey, drove back into the United States, went into a bar in Laredo where we were to get our booze, and gave the proper sign; I was told that a man would meet me at three o'clock by the railroad station and, sure enough, he was there. He directed me to drive out into the desert not too far from the Rio Grande River, and pick up the rest of the booze, and I said, well, that's either goodbye to the booze or hello. But in about an hour, here he arrived with a couple of other Mexicans, dragging two wet bags filled with our bottles which we checked, and each one had our name on it. Now, in those days, carrying whiskey around the United States was risky so I carefully took the spare tires apart and hid the whiskey in the spare tire compartment and we got home okay.

We had a wonderful time on our honeymoon. I visited old friends there with whom I had gone to military school. Friends that still live there that I see once in a blue moon. When we arrived in Phoenix, we didn't even have a place to stay so I found an apartment called The Edana on First Street and Fillmore and I paid $100 a month for a one-bedroom, one-bathroom, and kitchen apartment. We lived in that apartment for I guess about a year and then we moved over into Palmcroft were we rented a house and I think we paid $150 a month. It had a swimming pool but it was always dirty so we never used it. I built my first cooling system at that house but it put more water into the house than cooling, so it wasn't much good. Every marriage consists of a husband who comes up with a bright idea, kids who say it can't be done, and a wife who does it.

I don't think anybody ever dreamed the marriage would last very long. But the marriage has been long, and both happy and unhappy. I say unhappy because I've been away from Peggy a lot of the time: World War II, politics, business and so forth. But maybe absence makes the heart grow fonder and maybe it's one of the reasons we've stayed together and stayed so close.

Our first child, of course, was Joanne, born in Phoenix (January 18, 1936). The second child was Barry, born in a hospital in Los Angeles (July 15, 1938), the night that his grandfather, Peggy's father, Mack Johnson was killed running into a lamppost at the end of Wilshire Boulevard in that city. Mike was the next one, born in Phoenix (March 15, 1940). The last was Little Peggy born in La Jolla, California (July 27, 1944). I found out about Little Peggy's arrival in Abadan, Iran, when I was flying an aircraft through there heading to Cairo, Egypt. I had stopped to intercept any mail that might be going to my headquarters in India, and in the pile of letters there was one from Peggy, telling me of Little Peggy's arrival. I didn't get to see her for several months, however, when I was inadvertently and only briefly called back home by an erroneous cable.

I had joined the military before we were married, when I went into the Infantry Reserves at the age of twenty-one in 1930, as a Second Lieutenant. As World War II approached, since I had my pilot's license, I wanted to go in the Army Air Corps but I couldn't pass the eye test; so, I went on duty with the Air Corps as an Infantry Officer, but I swore that I was going to fly and, again, Peggy told me if that's what I wanted to do, go ahead and do it. I knew I could see fine with my glasses so with a little help, including taking a lot of flattering pictures of other pilots, I qualified and became a service pilot. Later I qualified as an army pilot and, of course, I'm now a retired Major General and a command pilot with a hell of a lot of flying time.

To my surprise the war dragged on and on. When I volunteered to go on active duty in August of 1941, I did not really think we'd go to war so I figured I would be away from my business only a year at most. But I was wrong. I didn't get out of the service until late 1945, after having served first in the training command, teaching fighter gunnery, and then in the ferrying command at Wilmington, Delaware, delivering airplanes to England, Scotland, across the South Atlantic to North Africa, and eventually I wound up in India and China flying across the hump.

I am not sharing all this history because we are getting older. To the contrary, a few years ago Peggy started wearing blue jeans and I bought a Honda motorcycle. Five years ago she dyed her hair blond and I took vitamin E shots. Last month she got a face-lift and I got a hair transplant. And that's the way it's been through the years—just the two of us, side by side, growing younger together. But let me share a little more history.

When the war ended and I came home, I had no idea of ever getting into politics, and it wasn't until Harry Rosenzweig, the best friend I ever had in my life, talked me into running on the Phoenix city charter government ticket with him and neither one of us thinking we had a chance in hell of getting elected, and darned if we didn't lead the ticket. Well, that got me into politics and that's another sad story because Peggy was always unhappy when I left the store to enter politics and, to tell you the truth, I have missed it ever since I left it. Although I am sure I would have retired many years ago had I stayed at the store and I doubt I would have been around now.

I must say that the biggest disappointment in my whole life has been the fact that I wasn't around during the years of the war and after I went into politics to help raise the children. This fell on Peggy and I think she did a wonderful job. I remember so fondly the few years we had together right after the war before I entered politics, when we owned the "Green Dragon"—an ugly green Chevrolet station wagon that had a trailer that converted into sort of a tent and beds, and I'd take the kids at least once a month, and sometimes more, to see all the beautiful spots in Arizona that my mother had shown me when I was growing up—the places I hope my kids would do the same for their children. Although, sadly, I don't know if it's as safe as when we did it and we used to just pull off the road and pull out the bedrolls and go to sleep. Who'll ever forget the night Mike, trying to be a real cowboy, heated a rock and put it in his bedroll to warm it, but the rock got so damned hot the bedroll caught on fire. [Barry put out the fire with a bucket of cold water, and Mike had to sleep in the bedroll.]

Those were some of the finest days and nights I ever spent in my life and what I missed in my life was the opportunity to spend more time with all my children. As for being a lousy father, I have to plead guilty. I do hope, so much, to be a good grandfather, or Paka, as the Indians refer to their family elder, to all of the grandchildren, who now number ten. I want to take them camping. That's the major reason I'm not going to run for re-election at the end of my term, in two years. I want to come home, enjoy my wife, my children and all of my grandchildren as they're growing up.

CHAPTER 2

JOURNALS AND OPINIONS

A few months after the birth of his second child and first son, Barry, Jr., Goldwater sat at his typewriter to make his first entry in his private journal; he called it "Me, Barry Goldwater." The entries that followed were irregular, but he returned to the journal again and again in one form or another for almost sixty years. His first urges to record his thoughts coincided with an invitation from the Phoenix Gazette to submit guest editorials on subjects of his choice, which became an annual spring event between 1935 and 1941. In addition, he was invited to give radio addresses on a broad range of topics on the local stations. Early journal material was personal and family directed; early editorials and radio commentary were publicly oriented. A sampling of both follow.

Journal Entry (September 1, 1938)

I am twenty nine years of age. Half way between twenty nine and thirty to be exact and at this particular moment I am possessed of a notion that has not been unfamiliar to me in the past. It is the god damned fool notion that from time to time I should sit myself down to some real serious recording of my feelings, thoughts and actions at different periods of my life. Why I can't say exactly, except that maybe someday my son might read this, or these series of blighted jottings of mine, and in a measure profit by my experience. To establish this reason as one of better judgment I might say here that my father died when I was about twenty and his leaving me meant that I must face a world of business without his wise counsel. Having gone through many years since his death without that word of his that would have meant what a hand is to a drowning man, I can safely say that I am not the least bit irrational when I hope that in the event of my not being here when my son or sons reach the age I was when he left me, that these papers will in some safe fashion guide them.

He proceeded to explain that the most valuable lesson his father taught him was "that all men were and are created equal." Then he added,

My father gave me this outlook on life. His ever ready smile and cheery hello, his absolute regard for the other fellow even at a loss of advantage for himself, his being ever ready to help a friend and even search for a friend in need, his understanding of the human race, and his invaluable ability to estimate a true friend formed the nucleus for a training that I can say that I think I have in a way absorbed. I say this without a feeling of braggadocio for I hope that this one trait of mine will be my son's. In fact, I can say that this is the one statement that I will make now that in the years to come I will not have to retract. I love my fellow man be he white or black or yellow and I am vitally interested in his well being, for that well being is my well being. To lose sight of

Left to right: Joanne, Barry, Sr., Barry, Jr., Mike, Peggy, Sr., and Peggy, Jr.

this is to lose that inestimable pleasure that comes from walking down the street knowing that the man you meet likes you or at least knows well of you. I say again that it is not conceit that prompts this remark but pride in one's association with one's fellow man.

Guest Editorial: "A Fireside Chat with Mr. Roosevelt" (June 19, 1937)

My friend: You have, for over five years, been telling me about your plans; how much they were going to do for me; how much they were going to mean to me. Now I want to turn around and ask you just what have they done that would be of any value to me as a businessman and a citizen?

Your plans, if I recall 1932 correctly, called for economy in government and a reduction in taxes. In five years you have spent more than this government of ours spent in its entire history before 1932. In five years my taxes have increased over 250 percent and I fear greatly that "I ain't seen half of it yet."

You had the very commendable plan of bettering the conditions of the working man. Have you done that? Well I wonder. True, hours are shorter, which is fine, but wages, well wages have been raised hourly but the working man is working less hours due to an industrial condition that your plans alone have caused, so the working man is making about the same, or a little less, than he did before. The worst thing about your labor plan has been that you have turned over to the racketeering practices of ill-organized unions the future of the working man. Witness the chaos they are creating in the eastern cities. Witness the men thrown out of work, the riots, the bloodshed, and the ill feeling between labor and capital and then decide for yourself if that plan worked.

You were confronted with a staggering number of unemployed when you took over in 1932. You immediately set up boards numerous enough to tax the entire run of the alphabet to name them in an effort to stamp out this evil. But in spite of your plans we still have just about as many unemployed in our midst as we did back in 1932.

Somewhere in your planning you thought it necessary to jump down the throats of everyone in business and where has it gotten you?

No place. Instead of the businessman having confidence in you today, he distrusts you and fears your every utterance.

Now you are going to prime the pump—but are you? Isn't that money really going to prime a few votes? Will it get into channels of business or will it get into weak districts?

Now, these are but a few of the things that go through my mind as I think of you. I, as a businessman and citizen, am very interested in the queer antics of those in Washington. I would like to know just where you are leading us. Are you going further into the morass that you have led us into or are you going to go back to the good old American way of doing things where business is trusted, where labor earns more, where we take care of our unemployed, and where a man is elected to public office because he is a good man for the job and not because he commands your good will and a few dollars of the taxpayers' money? I would like to know because I like the old-fashioned way of being an American a lot better than the way we are headed for now.

Guest Editorial: "Scaredy-Cat Businessmen" (June 23, 1939)

The biggest man in this country is afraid of his own shadow. He is the American businessman. He is the man who condemns, and sometimes justly so, the politician over his luncheon tables and his desks and in other very private conversations, but never in the open where his thoughts and arguments would do some good toward correcting the evils to which he refers in private conversations. Now, in my contacts with men who are engaged in the running of our different divisions of government, I have found them to be a good average class of Americans. Some of them, to be sure, fall below the average, but the majority are just like the businessman from whom they receive such behind-the-back criticism. They are possessed of intelligence, ambition and ability. They are interested, like the businessman, in keeping their jobs. It does not seem impossible, therefore, that if the American businessman rose and spoke his thoughts and beliefs in public, or addressed them to the supposedly offending public official, that the situation could be ironed out or, at least, that steps could be taken in a corrective direction.

Take taxes and waste in government. There isn't a businessman in this country today that does not fear the future status of our rising tax figure, yet he confines his suggestions for correcting the situation to his intimates who will agree with him. While his logical, businesslike criticisms are going into a sympathetic ear, the minority groups who are causing these tax increases are wagging their tongues where they will do the most good: in political offices. Naturally the politician, anxious to remain so employed, satisfies that group whose pleas he hears, and up go taxes. Remember, too, that this country is governed for the good of the majority and if the minority seems to be majority . . . well, government is done.

Mr. American Businessman fears to speak his mind in discussion at his luncheon club for fear of argument among members. Similar discussions at his Chamber of Commerce and his trade boards are taboo because "We shouldn't enter into politics." Now if businessmen who pay the cost of government shouldn't enter into that which is causing those taxes to mount, how will those who control the rate of ascent know the businessman's feelings and consequently do something about it?

One of the ablest politicians this state ever had classified all businessmen to me as "Political Cowards," and said, in the same breath, that they were the greatest potential powers in the country. If Mr. American Businessman just keeps his remarks to himself for a few more years he will have nothing to fear, for then he will be a minority and maybe have a chance to grow into a minority majority!

Radio Address: Community Chest Drive (October 25, 1939)

As president of the Community Chest in 1938 and 1939, Goldwater set new records for fund raising. This radio address is representative of the approach he employed, not to mention his feelings about the importance of charity.

You are living in a city that affords you a living to the good extent that you are classed second in this country in the amount of money you have to spend and do spend. You are living in a city that by virtue of its greatness grows in population by double every ten years. You live in a city that has a future both for you and for your children. Next to being an American the most fortunate thing that has ever happened to you is that you live in Phoenix and Arizona. Yes all these things are very rosy but let us look at the other side of the picture.

Are you proud of a condition that through the lack of your support has resulted in the closing of the women's shelter at the Salvation Army? Wouldn't you like to do something about the condition that again through the proper support of the Community Chest has resulted in one doctor taking care of over three thousand venereal cases in just one section of this city? Here in this great area of plenty do you realize that because the Chest hasn't had enough money on which to properly operate we have to serve meals to those in need that average less than seven and a half cents per meal, while in the slums of New York similar meals cost an average of over ten cents? While you are insuring your economic future and likewise that of your children don't you think it well to think of the social future of the people with whom you are and will be surrounded? What about those children who aren't as fortunate as yours? Do you want them to grow up believing in the Christian American way or do you want them to grow up hating the system that made them what they will be without your help? Give to the Chest so that the Chest may give to agencies that will develop the character that lies in those children—it means that your own children will have a good chance of growing up never knowing about the social problems we have today, for today the important person is the one who through no fault of his own winds up classed as an unfortunate.

This Community Chest of yours has fifteen agencies, all of them doing a separate job in the caring for the less fortunate. This Community Chest of yours does in one drive what it would take fifteen separate drives to do. It cuts the expense of administration to the bone allowing ninety-four cents of your dollar invested in the Chest to go *where* it should . . . to the person we want to help. The Community Chest needs your support. Help us remove the one blemish from our civic record—that of being the second lowest per capita givers in the United States, join the thousands who have already indicated their desire to see this Chest drive through by saying, "I WILL."

Journal Entry (April 22, 1939)

Given the loss of his father while in his first year of college and his father having spent considerable time traveling during his early childhood, Goldwater's Uncle Morris—for whom he had been named—was an important figure throughout his life. If he had a role model, it appears that it was Morris Goldwater.

That moment in my life has come and although I always knew it would come still it has left me a bit at a loss and quite a bit sad. Uncle Morris passed on to his final reward last week. He was one of those men I will be sorry for my sons not to know but they can't help but know something of him for the esteem that Morris was held in by every person in this country. That can't soon wear off and my sons will hear of him even when they grow up. I am sorry they will not be able to know him as I have because knowing and working with him has been one of the better things that have happened to me. He was one of those men that just don't happen every day or every year. He was one of those people that the good Lord just can't turn out so easily, but yet the Lord allows one or two in a lifetime to pass our way to better the world we live in. My pride in being his nephew will always be great.

I never knew till his passing just how much pride was contained in my feelings. I always knew that in his passing would go the last of the great Goldwater men that have made this state but I never quite felt that so strong as when I saw him for the last time. He looked so peaceful and so content and he seemed to radiate to me that I must keep his name forever honored and forever respected. I looked at him there and for the first time I realized just how impossible it will ever be for me to be what he has been. I realized that what he was will probably never be seen again in man but then I have the thought that even my trying will make a better man of me, and if I can impress my sons of the greatness he has given his name I feel sure that in their respect for him and what he asked of me in his last letter will be done. He wrote, "I think, I have kept the name of Goldwater clean and respected in this state. Don't do anything ever to change it." Signed, "Morris Goldwater."

CHAPTER 3

A BREAK FROM BUSINESS TO EXPLORE ARIZONA

F rom childhood Goldwater had loved to explore Arizona. For him, hiking the rugged mountains and meeting the native people as well as the old-timers who know it all best was a from of relaxation. When weary from overworking in business, Peggy would insist he take a break. He often recorded what he saw and who he met. The excerpts below are a typical outing.

Journal Entry (July 30, 1939)

Today has been the start of my vacation—long planned but also long put off. If I weren't afraid of literary pilferage I would call it "my" kind of day because it has been that in every sense of the word.

I left Prescott this morning and drove for the first time that I can remember in a slow and sensible manner. I haven't driven faster than thirty miles an hour all day and as a result I have seen a lot of country that I never saw before and enjoyed it. The day was too murky for good photography so I will retrace part of my route on the way home, for there are some of Arizona's lakes that I need in my collection of pictures.

The more that I see of this state of mine the happier I become with my lot. It's ever changing beauties and the seeming endlessness thereof enthrall me. Every mile brings something new and something I will remember forever. I am thankful tonight for many things: my

Barry, Sr., with a 16mm camera, taken at the Grand Canyon by wife Peggy.

wife who so graciously allowed me to leave her even though I hate that ordeal worse than anything on this earth, my business that goes on so well without me, the people who work for me who want me to do this. Hell, I even am beginning to be thankful I got myself into such a stew that this trip became a necessity.

Tonight I am camped within view of the San Francisco Peaks and their beauty has been augmented by a lovely orchid gold sunset. To the east lie the Painted Desert and my Indian country. It is dark out there with a large golden moon just peeking through a blanket of clouds. The road I am near hasn't offered but one car all day so the night should be quiet. I am purposely avoiding all roads that even smell of traffic. Now that it is dark I can see beacons flashing, so I must be about under the route of TWA. An airplane or two through the night won't make a tinkers damn to me.

It is good to get off from things. I already feel the good about it and if this is a forerunner of what is to be, I will have to be chained when I get home. Listened to the news today and didn't give a damn what Hitler said or what Chamberlain thought of it or what FDR was thinking up. How wonderful the world would be if all those people were with me on a vacation and a long one at that.

This typing is a mess. I am cramped over a box of canned food with one leg wrapped around the gear lever and the other braced against the steering post. Tonight I sleep so I might as well get that going as the sun will awaken me very early. Goodnight.

Journal Entry (August 1, 1939)

This was indeed a wonderful day, a day like I wish all days were, a day in which I did lots yet did little, saw lots and yet saw but little, and lived a lot yet lived but one small part of my life. The sun woke me early but I didn't see its call until its rays grew hot enough for me to consider getting under way, which I did about 8:00 AM. My camp near Richardson's Pass was, as I surmised, right under the TWA airline and their ships passed and re-passed all night. I had camped quite near Highway 66 and after a short drive I reached a road and followed it as far as Two Guns on Diablo Canyon. From there I drove to Leupp which has an Indian school on the Little Colorado. I left Leupp for Dilkon, why I will never know, other than the spirit of this trip is to roam. That road held little of interest so after passing Elephant and Pyramid Buttes, photographing them, I then headed north to Polacca.

Polacca is at the foot of First Mesa and an inquiry there told me that Walpi was but a few miles drive. What happened there makes it a most interesting Hopi village; for the Hopi are tough bargainers I found out when I wanted to take their pictures. They know only one word and that is "dollar." . . . But I did get some wonderful shots though and I am most happy about it because they will add greatly to my collection.

Leaving Polacca behind, I journeyed to Keams Canyon which has another school and hospital. I stopped in Mr. Haldiman's general store and bought a wash bowl and another canteen. While there, his son started a fire in the wash in front of the store and there being a high wind it was not long till the bridge was burning gaily. I went underneath it with a fire extinguisher and by the grace of God got the thing out. That was good deed number one for the day.

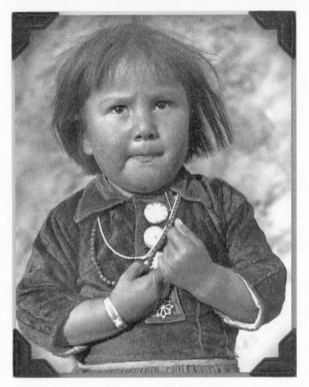

Hopi child, 1959. Barry, Sr. recalls, "This little bucket of fire was the daughter of Mr. Potter, a Hopi who lived at the Grand Canyon at the Indian Shop. The one right across from El Tovar. When she would see me coming, she would run up to me and want me to take her picture."

From Keams Canyon I went to a place that I, like many others, have read about but few have ever seen. That is the ancient city of Awatobi. It has been hidden by hills of sand and rock for centuries but during the past few years the Peabody Institute has been digging there and they have unearthed not only the old village and church but many objects that will add greatly to the knowledge of this section. I met there a Mr. and Miss Davis from Harvard and the Institute, and they were very kind to me. I also discovered my two water bags and a canteen that had dropped from the back of my station wagon on the rough road approaching the Institute's camp. It cost me a dollar a piece to retrieve them from the Indians. Leaving the camp I came upon two women whose car was stuck in the sand. With the help of other men, among them a Mr. Druel, we got them out and then I followed them to the main road to help again if necessary. That was good deed number two.

By now it was getting late so I drove till I found this lovely spot to spend the night. On the way I did give an Indian the valve cap from my spare tire and helped him pump air into his flat tire. That was good deed number three. Being out of good deeds I am going to give myself one in the form of a long night's rest here on the side of Steamboat Canyon. Goodnight.

Journal Entry (August 2, 1939)

This morning's sunrise was gorgeous. But it was the low call of a bull that awakened me so I rose up in bed to look out on one large bull running towards another large bull. I thought I was about to witness a serious bull fight but they sort of shook hands, in bull fashion way, and walked off shoulder to shoulder. Then over on the hillside I heard a small Navajo girl herding her flock singing to it. Shining on all this

Navajo maidens, 1956. According to Barry, Sr.: "I call the girl on the right the spinner because she has a handspindle in her hand. She spins the raw wool into threads the other girl will use to make the rug with. This was taken up on the Navajo Reservation."

was the rising splendor of a magnificent sun. For breakfast, I cooked three of my six eggs because I didn't want them spoiling on me and plus a few extra pieces of my large supply of bacon (for the same reason).

At noon I went over to Window Rock. The Window truly intrigued me just like I imagine it does most everyone and of course the first thing I wanted to do was to go up to it.* This, I suspect is instinct at work born of sight of this picturesque opening. The climb up was quite difficult but the sight and pictures made it worth the effort. Coming down I managed to slide half the way and wear a hole in my pants and the backs off my boots.

Fort Defiance was next and there I ran into Mr. Owens, who I had met last year at Navajo Post in southern Utah. Driving over the Chusca Mountains I traveled through the heaviest stand of timber I have ever seen in this or any other state. How many millions of feet of lumber stands up there God only knows and I hope he keeps it a secret and never lets man have a hand on it. Arriving at Chinle rather late in the afternoon I decided to stay over night and see Canyon De Chelly in the morning. Cozy McSparron runs a ranch there so I put up with him. A bed felt as good in comparison as did the home cooked meal and when a warm bath was tossed in with all that, the combination was too much and the result was a fine night's sleep.

Journal Entry (August 2–3, 1939)

After years of hearing about it I finally saw and went through the various canyons that make up Canyon De Chelly. Cozy McSparron drove me through in his car with the large tires that make the sand feel and act like an asphalt road. His acquaintance with the Indians made it easy for me to get very good pictures of them and I am looking forward to their development for some excellent reminders of a most enjoyable day. I forgot to mention it yesterday but Cozy McSparron

---

* Window Rock is the seat of government for the Navajo Nation, the tribal government of the largest Native American tribe in the United States, and "the Window" is a great round opening in the rock.

has the quaint and amusing custom of shooting an arrow into the ceiling each New Year's Eve. In this fashion he is able to keep track of the years he has spent on the reservation. There are now twenty-seven arrows stuck into the ceiling of his living room.

Journal Entry (August 4, 1939)

This was fit to be a day—and what a day it has been. Somehow every once in a while the Lord sneaks in a day on me that no one else will have and this has been one of them. I went down the mountain through Lukachukai and over to Round Rock which is one of the closest posts on the reservation. It gets its name from two round rocks about ten miles distant by road. Of course my road-map nose got me into it but I went over to the rocks and found that there were no roads there. This only added to my desire to see them so I made my own road. Now I will say that in spite of what followed I have never seen such an inspiring rock formation like this and something should be done to bring it to the attention of every tourist that gets this far west. Well I photographed the damned things from stem to stern and gawked at its beauty and thumped my chest and said how great it was to be alive.

Journal Entry (August 5, 1939)

I had a dandy night's sleep even though a horse was nibbling right outside my window all night. No bugs, no mosquitoes, no nothing but the sandman and he really went to work on me. I slept rather late, till 7:00 AM. I got up had my breakfast of tomato juice and then went over to fill my water bags.

The Indians were there at the water tank with horses and sheep and it was too interesting a picture for me to pass up either with my camera or my desire to know these people better. I helped one Indian siphon some water into his tank but I wasn't very successful with my efforts. I finally, after much sucking, had him fasten the hose to a nozzle and fill it that way. They got a great kick out of my camera and as a result I got some good pictures (I hope).

The road to Sweetwater is over rock and not very good but passable and interesting from the standpoint of the many colorful small canyons one passes. Sweetwater is a small trading post nestled in a crook of a canyon and one can't see it until one is right on it.

Leaving Sweetwater there is a very good desert road that goes within good sight of the Carrizo Mountains. Teec Nos Pos was the next post and there I got directions for the route to Four Corners. This is the only place in the United States that is common to four state corners and all that is there are a small concrete monument and an old ruin a few yards distance. It is on top of a hill covered with volcanic fragments and within sight of the San Juan River. The location is as barren a place as one would imagine and hotter then hell. I took my own picture with a part of me in each state, had lunch, drove around the monument, and started back over the road I had just come over.

Now I have seen God forsaken places in my life but I swear that I have never seen anything like the desolation that exists at Mexican

Church Rock, 1938. Barry, Sr. notes, "On the way into Kayenta I got a picture of Church Rock that should be a beauty. The clouds were black behind it and the sun was most bright on its tannish white front."

Water trading post. There is one house, the post, and a corral and miles and miles of barren rock. The road to Dennehotso goes over this rock for about eighteen of the twenty-three miles and it is slow going at the best. I imagine that a night trip over this road would be a lulu as the only way you can tell if you are on the road is by stone markers and some small catches here and there.

As I left Dennehotso I began to run into deep chuck holes someone had made by being stuck too often and this person got a good cussing from me for his efforts. I soon came upon the object of my wrath who was stuck again. And who should it be but Max Keighley out taking pictures for his new book. His left front wheel had been knocked back on the spring until each front wheel was going in a different direction and the steering wheel wouldn't budge them. By jacking up the left side and fastening a rope to the axle, tying the other end to my car, and then driving off real fast, I pulled the wheel back straight and he drove off. I met him later at Kayenta. On the way into Kayenta I got a picture of Church Rock that should be a beauty. The clouds were black behind it and the sun was most bright on its tanish-white front.

In Kayenta I met the Wetherills and meeting them is something I have long wanted to do. They are as much a part of the history of this country as are the Indians themselves. John Wetherill was the discoverer of every major archeological and geological item in this section so meeting them was very much a pleasure and a privilege. I stopped the night with them and here I sit in an old adobe room beating this out by the light of a lamp. I look forward to tomorrow and Monument Valley.

Journal Entry (August 6, 1939)

They get up early here in Kayenta. Someone beat my door down at six and I was up in a hurry for I knew that any one that got up at six wasn't fooling when they said breakfast would be at seven. This was the first breakfast that I had had that wasn't out of a can except the one that I had at Chinle and I ate like a horse. It was good that I did this, for instead of getting through with Monument Valley and being back at one in the afternoon it was nearly seven in the evening when

I finally did get home. I took Max with me as he wanted pictures and his car certainly wasn't in any condition to go even around a tree let alone all the way up through that sand. We started out and saw the routine monuments and then took a side road and by driving like hell in second gear we got through the sand. . . .

Back at Kayenta we had dinner and met Mr. and Mrs. Russ Montgomery, an architect from Los Angeles who is an outstanding authority on Franciscan architecture. He was most interesting in his descriptions of the churches at Awatobi. Mr. Wetherill* joined in and, as I hoped, a good discussion ensued and for once I kept my big mouth shut and listened. He told of some of his experiences and of the early days on the reservation. I understand from Mrs. Wetherill that she has written a book on the life of a Navajo and I earnestly urged her to have it published as an authoritative work like that is lacking.

Now to bed for a good night's sleep before these early birds tear down my door.

Journal Entry (August 7, 1939)

Well this day allowed me the pleasure of seeing an old ruin I have wanted to see for a long time: Betatakin [John Wetherill was the first white man to see Betatakin Ruins in 1909]. I am saving Keet Seel for another trip.** Saving Keet Seel, however, is the result of my not feeling like a fifteen mile hike. The trail to Betatakin is a very good one and only steep for the first half mile. It is a trip that is well worthwhile and one I want to make again some time. . . .

From the ruins at Betatakin I went to Shonto, and then over to Inscription House for gas and over the road that is so bad that the sheep won't use it. Finally, I went to Bill and Katherine Wilson's at

---

* *Background information on John Wetherill is found at http://wetherill-family. com/john_wetherill.htm.*

** *Goldwater is referring to a complex of three well-preserved and elaborate prehistoric cliff dwelling communities near the town of Kayenta in northeastern Arizona, located on the Navajo Reservation. The three sites are Betatakin (the Navajo word for "Ledge House"), Keet Seel ("Broken Pottery"), and Inscription House.*

Rainbow Lodge, where I plan to stay until Friday or Saturday and do nothing but sleep and eat and grow lazy. Bill and Katherine are their usual sweet selves and I can't begin to write the good it does me just to be around two real people like them. So in the spirit of eating I am stuffed, and in the spirit of sleep I now go to bed.

Journal Entry (August 8, 1939)

This day I did what I said I would yesterday. I slept, read and ate and did nothing else. Tonight we all played checkers but it is a game for two. So here it is nine thirty again, and I am tired and ready for bed. If this keeps up I will have to be tied down when I get home. PS: I forgot two things. One, I washed all my clothes today; and, two, I went back up on the hill this evening and watched the sunset. The clothes were dirty; the sunset very pretty; and I enjoyed both.

Journal Entry (August 9, 1939)

Another lazy, lazy day at Rainbow. Didn't hear the birds peep till ten thirty and then it took some time to get all six feet of me in a mood for getting up. Bill and Ernie were down working on the trail and I thought I might as well help them but just as that thought came to me they rode up so I was prevented from working.

Just before noon Red Shirt Indians with sheep and goats came by for water so I took my camera and some cookies for the kids tending the flocks and went to watch them. The herd figured that I wanted one of their keepers so they sort of shied away from me. Their dogs are the funniest looking creatures on four feet but they proved their efficiency by barking at me and their teeth didn't look like they were fooling. So I proceeded on down the hill to where a Navajo boy was fixing his saddle. I gave him some cookies and he sort of laughed and rode off, but I did get a picture of the herd coming by and I hope it is good. The flocks of the Navajos interest me because they are their chief means of sustenance and one of the yardsticks of their wealth.

This afternoon I rode a mule over to the Red Ruins about two and a half miles away. They are large ruins but no one seems to know anything about them and I guess it is just as well. People seem to know too damned much about what has happened not enough about what is a happening nowadays.

Journal Entry (August 10, 1939)

Well today I didn't get up till nearly eleven and, by-the-junks, as Bill would say, I don't know how I will get along after this with less than my twelve hours sleep or more. Nothing much happened today. Bill and I rode over to the edge of Navajo Canyon and then over to Navajo Post on the north side of the mountain where we phoned Peggy. She wasn't home but all I wanted to tell her was that I would be home on Saturday and to have something for me to eat. I guess I don't function so well without her and I am getting to the place where I miss the hell out of her and the kids so I had better be getting home.

Journal Entry (September 30, 1939)

Goldwater much preferred writing about his travels than his work, yet from time to time he did make entries he thought might be of interest to his sons when they would one day take over the family business.

Now it has been some time since I have written anything to this journal about business but the truth is that there hasn't been anything about which you might want to know, but—well I'll tell you.

It seems that since the beginning of time men have had to fight one another as nations every once in a while. This condition is a sad commentary on the state of the civilized world but then better men than I have said the same damned thing and still every twenty five years or so some ruler gets huffy at another ruler, or some country wants a bite out of a smaller country, and the boys go to it. That war is hell no one will deny but men won't do anything about getting along with one another in this world so let's accept the fact and wonder how we fit into the picture. When the last war [World War I] started I was too small to care much about rising costs, profiteering and the other commercial attendants of war. It is different now. I am at the head of my business and when Adolf started this one I was very interested in what way prices were going and how fast they were going to get there.

We sat around here and talked about it and the more we talked the more bewildered we got so I went to New York to find out what they knew. Well it didn't take a long time for me to ascertain that they were as befuddled as I was so I just sat around and thought about it. Thus far I am sure of one or two things and I pass them on to you. First do not get excited in a crisis like this. Be calm. THINK. Act slowly and when you act be sure. There will be an effort on the part of the wholesale element of this business to rush you into orders for merchandise that you normally would not buy. Don't be afraid to stick by the decision that I know you will make, which is to buy as you need things regardless of the increase in price you will have to pay. Remember that when you have to pay more the customer will have to pay more to you for the merchandise. You are not "in the gambling business" you are a merchant. Don't forget that. Buy when you need it as you need it in the amounts you need at the market prices then mark it accordingly. Don't profiteer. The surest way to lose customer confidence at a time like this is for you to mark your goods too high for your consumer's pocketbook. They become resentful and customers are too hard for you to get for you to endanger the pleasant relations I know you will have with them.

Journal Entry (December 23, 1939)

This has been our most successful Christmas season and one long to be remembered. Its success has been made possible by the cooperation of everyone here and the future now seems rosier than ever before because the confidence in what we are trying to do is more apparent every day.

I feel sure that with another year we will again remark that it is the best ever, as we have done this year. True, government taxes have curtailed profits but then they will always do that and I feel it is a lame crutch to use as an excuse not to show net profit at the end of the year.

To do so requires initiative and originality but I still believe that there is enough of that to go around, and that every man gets his share of the whole based on what his efforts deserve. But try as one may the net profit diminishes with the years, and it will continue to do so as long as we have a government that encourages laziness and waste—but enough of that.

The Christmas season always makes me want to reiterate what I have always preached to you that the love of one's fellow man can be the strongest thing in your life outside the love you will have for your wife. It is warming to realize that something you have done some time in the year has made someone happy. It is good to know that someone likes you for what you have done for them and not for what you could do for them. Always appreciate others in life before they need you, no matter what your circumstances, and it will add riches to your life.

I have nothing more to say to you tonight, except that I will enjoy nothing more this Christmas than watching your curly hair as you toddle around on your bowlegs and strong body to play with your new toys. I see you in years to come as a worthy successor to your name that I pray will be made worthy of my efforts of further perpetuating it by what I still plan to do during my life. It is tough following that little man with the big moustache, your Uncle Morris, but then who knows, I may leave to you a name that is blemished. But I can tell you now it will never be more revered than it is now because of your grandfather and your granduncle, who are up there playing casino with the Lord and probably beating him out of his wings and his favorite harp.

Journal Entry (March 16, 1940)

This day is better than any other days in the year because yesterday your brother Michael was born. We called him Michael Prescott Goldwater because my grandfather was named Mike and I love Prescott the city and it also is my brother-in-law's name, which takes care of two birds with one whack. We didn't get home till two thirty in the morning and at five your mother awakened me and said some thing was going to happen so to the hospital we went, and by golly at nine fifteen Mike came along and I'll tell you right here that he is a damned sight better looking baby than you or your sister were. So now I have two of you boys to write for so after this when I say "you" it means you both.

You both are lucky in having a brother. I have had one all my life and there can't be a closer or a finer association between men than exists between brothers. I need not tell you of this for you will both find it out, the feeling that come what may there is always someone who will, in spite of any petty differences, always fight for you. . . .

This city [of Phoenix] is growing fast, sometimes, I think, too fast for its own good. We have reached a point where we must ask ourselves questions about ourselves, like where do we want to go? How do we want to get there? Maybe we must have horse racing and gambling but I don't think so. Maybe we should have tax free homes that people holler for but I don't think so and by God I'll say so to anyone. That is something neither of you should ever be afraid to do: say what you think if you think what you believe is right. You never will succeed telling the other fellow what he wants to hear, even if speaking your thoughts might get you some criticism, it will get you far more praise. A courageous man is respected not so much for his thoughts or his actions but for his courage in presenting his thoughts and doing his job. I hope to see gambling wiped out here, including race tracks. I hope to see the tax evil corrected but those things will not come from a namby pamby attitude of the businessman; it will come, just like such reforms will come in your time, from the fearless united action of men who are willing to sacrifice a little time and a lot of guts.

Journal Entry (May 6, 1940)

On Monday, May 6, 1940, I started out to show Bill Saufley [vice president of Goldwaters] and Bob King [marketing director] that portion of Arizona that lies in the northwest and north-central, areas that few people know about. I did so to attempt to convert them to disciples of its beauties.

We drove up through Prescott and Flagstaff to Cameron and then the fun began. These fellows were just like everyone else who has never seen this beautiful country to the north of Highway 89 past Cameron.

Barry, Sr., guiding a flatiron boat down a rapid in the Grand Canyon, 1940.

It took us many hours longer than it should have to get from Cameron to our destination because we repeatedly stopped to take pictures and for them to marvel at the colors and the clouds and the rocks contrasted with the amazing blue of the sky. . . .

The next morning, Tuesday, we started early down the trail to Rainbow Bridge. Every turn and every new canyon we would top the previous and bring exclamations of amazement and wonder from my two companions. The climax to the trip is, of course, after climbing many thousands of feet through several canyons, when one comes out into full view of Cliff Canyon and its 2,400-foot drop in less than a mile and a half of trail. The view from this summit is without parallel in the world, if my limited knowledge of the world means anything. It is too big to describe, it is too big to picture, and its colors are too beautiful to believe. . . .

The next day, Wednesday, we headed down to the Colorado River through Bridge Canyon and Forbidden Canyon. After a leisurely lunch on the banks of the swollen Colorado, we made our way back up the

Forbidden Canyon and let the mules go at the Narrows. The Narrows is a small canyon where Bridge Canyon empties into Forbidden Canyon, possibly one hundred yards long, the course of which resembles a slight "S" and the width of which is never more than thirty or forty feet. The floor of The Narrows is solid rock, so once again we took off our clothes and scampered around through the pools in this canyon and then lay out on the hot sand on the side of Forbidden Canyon.

Thursday morning, again early, we started up the trail and immediately upon reaching the Lodge, we started out in the car for Mexican Hat via Shonto Springs, Kayenta, and Monument Valley. Needless to say, Monument Valley astounded not only my guests but once again myself though I have seen it many times. . . . Arriving at Mexican Hat Lodge in Utah after sundown, we looked up Norman Nevills, with whom I am going down the Colorado River this summer. He suggested an early boat trip of about four to five miles down the San Juan River to Goodridge Bridge. Naturally we were all enthused over this, so the next morning early out to the Mexican Hat we went with two boats in tow on a trailer.

I had always expected my initiation to rough water would be rather meek and as a passenger in a boat piloted by an expert, and also in a boat that had a better chance of floating than sinking. Imagine my surprise when I was told that I was to pilot one of the boats, and was handed a pair of oars, a bailing bucket, and Bob King, and told to shove off. I have had considerable experience rowing so handling oars did not worry me, but what to do with a light boat with waves that towered over us five or six feet and in rapids that made one think the earth was going mighty fast in directions I did not fully understand. But it did not take me long to catch on.

We got home Friday evening, May 10th, in good shape. I am sure that I have confirmed two more people in the belief that nowhere in the world lie the beauties that are within the boundaries of Arizona, and in the process of converting them, I only strengthened my own belief.

Journal Entry (April 4, 1941)

Goldwater's movie made him well known throughout the state when a decade later he ran for the Senate.

It is said that the time for reflection is the present. Now if someone asks who said this I'll confess that I did, for good reason too. Often as I drive along having nothing to do but watch the road and the damned fools who drive over them I think of a million and one things I would like to remember. Many times I forget them in an instant, but later I realize what I have forgotten might have proved valuable, and I wish that something about the thought had been recorded. I could wait for a year to pass and then write about what I am now addressing but then I might forget some of the things that in later years would make it interesting to me. So with all this warming up I will go into the results of three months of showing pictures and lecturing or "I wish you were dead you rascal you," referring of course to the pictures of the Colorado river trip and my drivel that accompanies them.*

April Fools Day has just passed and with it passed three months and a few days of seeming constant talking and showing about the trip. I never dreamed as I was taking that trip last summer that the pictures I was talking about would be in such demand. . . . I began to see myself doing this same thing night after night indefinitely, and this is exactly what has happened but what fun I have had doing this and how much I have learned from the delightful people I have met all over the state. Also, I have been able to see a lot of Arizona this winter and spring that I wouldn't have been allowed to without the excuse of showing the river film and pictures.

So far I have had out of town dates in the state at Prescott, Tempe, Tucson, Yuma, Wickenberg, Litchfield, Window Rock, and Kingman. In the future I go to Casa Grande, Clarkdale, Prescott again, Mesa, Globe, and Parker. What better way is there to see Arizona than by travelling around to towns like these? The long quiet desert between Phoenix and Yuma, the green fields on the way to Tucson, the rolling

---

* *Goldwater later typed out a full transcript of his talk, which one day soon may be posted on the Arizona Historical Foundation's website with accompanying pictures.*

hills to Wickenburg, and the mountains on the way to Prescott and Window Rock—all of these things have been the rewards for the work it has taken to give this show.

Rewards? At first I didn't allow anyone to charge for it but after seeing the crowds that came every time groups started to charge for this and that charity. If they didn't have a charity, I have been suggesting the underprivileged camp fund. Let's see, to date about $1,000 [approximately $14,000 in today's dollars] have been raised with this show for various purposes. I think the camp fund has received nearly six hundred dollars itself [$8,400 today]. Later I may add to this entry but these are the things that someday I will want to know about. To sum them all up, the following statistics are offered:

People who have seen shows: 20,000

Number of shows: 52

Length of actual time in giving it: 88 hours

Distance film has traveled through projector: 19 miles

Words spoken in lecture: 686,400

Miles travelled to give shows: 4,330 miles

Money raised for charity: $1,000

Headaches: 1,000,000,000

Journal Entry (April 4, 1941)

It's been a hell of a long time since I have written anything to my sons but there have been a hell of a lot of things going on in this world and keeping up with them has been almost impossible. I started to report my reactions to the war as it affected our business and I intend to keep to that and not wander off into a history of the war. Remember I advised you not to speculate on merchandise just because every indication showed a chance of a rise in prices. Remember too that a year after the war was on I told you I was right. Well, nearly two years of the war has passed and the advice still goes. We are just now beginning to feel definite pinches that might mean merchandise shortages in the future but I still intend to wait and buy as the things are needed. However, I will make an exception for blankets. Wool will be scarce and hard to get and I don't mind making future commitments now at

To develop business for the department store, Barry, Sr. showed a 16mm movie he made of his trip down the Colorado River in 1940.

low and guaranteed prices. On everything else, though, we will do as we have done in the past and wait till we actually need merchandise before buying it. In other words conduct your business as usual even though the world is not conducting itself as usual. You will have to keep your weather-eye peeled in times like these but with the peeling keep a normal sensible-eye on the way you run your business. Now as never before comes the time when the welfare of your employees is paramount. The guaranteeing to them of steady employment will come in the form of the hard work necessary to guarantee gross and net profits from the business.

The cost of business is going up as is the cost of living and you and your employees are vitally interested in the latter. I don't believe that times like these are good times to make general or substantial raises because there will inevitably come the time when business will be just as bad as the war is making it good and then the let down is too much in decreased wages that comes with decreased profits. The war has made very good business all over the country and even Phoenix has felt it. The good business here though is more from the good feeling prevailing among the farmers since the dams have nearly filled. Old Roosevelt dam was dry last summer and now it stands a good chance to overflow for the second time in my memory. No matter what you may hear or what you might believe momentarily the soil and the farmer are the important things here. As soon as our farmers get back to the old fashioned way of farming and away from this highly specialized business they have been engaged in, business will boom, boom, boom. Those farmers are the backbone of our community and I have a strong feeling that they will still be in your day and in your children's day. Anything you can do to help them will always pay you dividends.

Last year I wrote you that I took my trip down the Colorado. You have all my [notes and pictures of that river trip] so I will not say a word more of it here except that it was a wonderful experience and I hope sincerely that someday you and I can sneak off and do the same thing.* I am writing down my lecture, right now, so if you ever want to give that thing you can with my pictures.

My secretary is about to have a baby. She has faithfully stuck with me all through the months of her pregnancy and now, tonight, she is going to give up work until the baby comes. She is a tremendous help to me and I am going to miss her greatly. Before she goes I want to

---

* *Goldwater and his children and grandchildren would do just that. In 1951 through 1955, Goldwater organized trips on the Colorado River from Hite's Landing, Utah, to Lee's Ferry, Arizona, for about twenty YMCA boys. He arranged for the navy to donate life rafts for the cause. His children, nieces, and nephews all went on the 1951 trip. In 1965, after losing his presidential bid and while out of office, he made a sixteen-day Colorado River trip from Lee's Ferry to Pearce Ferry. During that trip, Goldwater tried to give his children a sense of his much longer trip in 1940 to see the Grand Canyon from the bottom up using the same boats he had used twenty-five years earlier. Two of the boats were borrowed from museums, and all bottoms received a coating of clear fiberglass to prevent leaking, which it didn't. Joining Goldwater on this trip were all four of his children, in addition to two sons-in-law, plus several family friends. Family friend Leonard Kilgore surprisingly flew in on the sixth day of the trip in a helicopter to deliver steaks and newspapers, unbeknownst to Goldwater, who had just taken apart his wet camera and laid the parts on a rock to dry and then watched them receive a fine coating of dirt and sand as the helicopter landed at the campsite. Goldwater also carried a small ham radio and generator. The last trip was another family outing in 1993 in which both children and grandchildren made the voyage.*

show her some pictures that we took last week in Yosemite in California. Guess this is all for this time. Mike has had a hell of a time getting started what with sore ears and all that but now he is going great guns. Barry has been a horse from the start and should grow into a big moose but, if you do, never take advantage of your size and strength. Remember your greatest strength is your ability to make the lives of others easy.

CHAPTER 4

MILITARY LIFE

G oldwater's military career spanned thirty-seven years, from 1930 to 1967, in which he rose from a second lieutenant to major general. His work in the Senate, culminating as chairman of the Senate Armed Service Committee, represents a second military-related career.

Recollection (January 19, 1984)*

I received my Certificate of Eligibility to be commissioned as a Second Lieutenant in the Army Infantry Reserve in 1927 when I graduated from the Staunton Military Academy, but I had to wait until I was twenty-one years old before I could accept the commission. That came in 1930, so I signed up in that capacity as soon as the first of the year got by, and that same year I started doing my annual active duty at Camp Stephen P. Little, and continued on with the two weeks of reserve duty each summer, followed usually by four weeks of instructing in the Citizens Military Training Corps. Also, just as a sideline, I instructed Mexicans in the Mexican Army on the subject of rifle marksmanship.** That was a real experience. They didn't give a damn whether they hit the target or not, they just liked to hear the gun go off; however, slowly, but surely, some of them turned into darn good rifle shots.

---

* *Letter to Dean Smith, Director of the Arizona Historical Foundation.*
** *As a child, before going to a public school where English was spoken, Goldwater first attended a school for Mexican children in Arizona where he learned to converse easily in Spanish.*

Barry Goldwater at the Staunton Military Academy, 1928.

Well, a funny thing happened down there in Nogales. After drill, in the late afternoons, some of us would go over to the Old Cave Restaurant in Mexico. They had gambling then, and I didn't realize it, but the blackjack dealer was playing me for a longtime chump, which I turned out to be. I would go down in the afternoons, drink a little beer, play a little blackjack, not for much, maybe dimes or quarters, and I would generally win a little bit. Then, one summer, when my service was over and I got my paycheck, which was rather sizeable for me then, I thought, "Well I'm going to really skin that fellow's cat down at the gambling table." So I proceeded to go in, and he proceeded to beat me out of every dime that I had, knowing full well I had just got paid, and I was going to go home. That was one of the early lessons I received that taught me not to gamble.

After service of one year, I think it must have been about 1932 or 1933, I remember A. J. Bayless, Paul Morris, a girl, and I, drove down to Nogales just to have a little fun. Well, the morning after the first night we had been there we decided to get up early, like seven-thirty, and go down and eat some real, honest-to-goodness Mexican food, which was served—I'll never forget it—in an old shed off the main drag of Nogales, Sonora. We were sitting there, eating Mexican food and drinking beer out of one-pound coffee cans, which were the standard vessels of containment for Mexican beer at that time, and for some reason or the other, Paul Morris threw a whole can of beer at me, missed me, but hit a policeman who happened to have been standing behind me. He immediately corralled us all, got us in my car, and I drove down to the police station. Now the police station had a curb out in front of it about three feet high off the dirt street, and after he had allowed the girl to drive my car back to the United States, he proceeded to attempt to put us in jail. Well, Paul Morris and A. J. Bayless, neither one of whom was known as a great pugilist, managed to knock the policeman down, and he fell into the gutter, and these two friends of mine ran all the way to the border; and then, knowing they couldn't make it through Immigration, they ran through the storm drain tunnel that drained most of Nogales, Arizona, and Nogales, Mexico.

All day long I sat in that jail. I couldn't run with the others because I had my leg in a cast. That was the first of many broken bones and pulled tendons in my knees; so there I sat in that jail cell all day, finally shooting craps with a Mexican in the cell with me, and he won everything I had except my shorts, and I wouldn't gamble for those. I had called the army at Camp Little and soon a dribble of my fellow officers showed up, looked at me and said, "Nope, never saw him before," smirked and walked away.

Finally, late in the evening, I asked to see the head police chief and I said, "Look, all I did was duck so one of your officers got hit with a beer. Now, how much is it going to cost to get me out of here because I don't want to spend the night?" He said, "$25" [in today's dollars, approximately $285]. Well, I said, "This Mexican cellmate of mine has won everything I have, including my money, will you take a check?" He said, "Yes." So, I sat down and wrote a check for $25, and signed A. J. Bayless's name to it. It's the only time I ever was involved in anything crooked like that, but I figured A. J. had it coming to him because of the way he left me in jail. Later, we had a big laugh over it, and A. J. had that check framed and hung on his wall. I saw it the last time I was in his office before he died.

LETTERS TO THE CHILDREN

Letter (June 21 and 27, 1943)

Captain Goldwater sent these letters to his son Barry, Jr., then approaching his fifth birthday, and his daughter Joanne, a few years older. They were sent while he was based at New Castle Army Air Base in Wilmington, Delaware.*

Dear Barry,

I received your letter about the rattlesnakes today and I am glad you told me about them. Now, the other day, I wrote you about the pretty things that God puts on this earth and how you must always protect them. Well, God also put some bad things on this earth but he put them there for a reason. Snakes are some of the bad things but not all snakes are bad. Some of them, for instance, kill gophers who cut up our gardens and others kill other pests. You see, God has it all figured out that sooner or later all the evil will be driven out of our lives either by the evil itself or by the good. Even though some few snakes are good snakes you must treat them all as bad snakes until you are older and know them apart. You must never play with them or go near them and when you walk in the weeds be sure and watch where you put your feet. Snakes like to be cool and comfortable so you will find them in the shade of bushes and rocks. They don't like the hot sun as it will kill them very quickly. Whenever you see a snake you tell Mommy. You must see that Mike and Sister read this letter too and then see that they obey what it says. You are the big man of the family now that Daddy is away for awhile and you must take care of your brother and sister and your Mommy, just like Daddy does when he is home.

---

* *These are the first letters to his children and the start of what became a lifetime practice of writing them to share his fatherly advice when he was away. Other samples of this advice have been included throughout the pages and chapters that follow.*

Now another thing. I heard you saying Heil Hitler when I was home. He is one of the bad snakes God put on earth and Daddy and millions of other Daddies are out to kill him. You must never speak of him as anything but a bad mistake God made once. He doesn't make many but when he does they are lulus.

* * *

Dearest Joanne,

Remember when I left last time I asked you what you wanted and you said a new nightgown. Well, Daddy was in New York a few days ago and he bought a new nightie for you. It's very pretty and cute and has your name on it. Now the last nightie I gave you, Mommy wouldn't let you wear but I want you to wear this one a lot. Daddy doesn't give you things to put away in drawers; he gives them to you because he loves you and wants you to be happy all the time.

Joanne, getting presents from people isn't the only happiness in the world. In fact, it is about the least way I know to stay happy. Happiness comes from a lot of simple things that don't cost us a penny. Being nice to people is one. Not just party nice but nice always. There will be people in your life you won't be able to stand but be nice to them and you'll be happy in the thought that they aren't as good as you or you would like them better. Then being nice to older people and people who aren't as fortunate as you—if you always do it without thinking about it—gives you the darndest warmest happy feeling you've ever had. People will begin to say of Joanne, my but she is a nice lady, and they won't know a thing about you except that you always are nice to people and have a smile for them. Now keeping busy is keeping happy too. Don't ever say—oh my, there is nothing to do. There is always something to do: make your bed, clean your room, mend your clothes, help your Mommy, help your brothers, read a book, practice your music. The unhappiest people in the world are people who "just have nothing to do." Keep your hands and your mind busy and you will go around with your head in the clouds and a song in your heart. You just grow up like your mother doing unto others as you would have them do unto you—even if they don't.

Crossing the Atlantic in Single-Engine Fighters

Journal Entries (July and August 1943)

Thursday, July 15, 1943

Captain "Hop" Craswell, commanding officer of the 27th Ferry-ing Squadron which makes him my C.O. casually turned to me and informed me that I was one of ten pilots to be the first to ferry P-47s across the North Atlantic. I wasn't a whole lot surprised because pur-suit ships are what I fly and those kinds of pilots are sort of scarce around here. Well if I wasn't surprised I surely felt highly flattered, for this trip is going to be the first time in history that a single engine military plane is going to be ferried across anybody's ocean and here I am going along. All that was over a month ago and since that time I have of course been on pins waiting the word to go but until the last few days there have been no indications. First to poke its head up was a booklet on how to fly the ship with belly tanks attached. Then a bunch of us went to the Republic factory at Farmingdale Long Island to shuttle P-47s to Newark. You see this ship is flown there then pre-pared for a long ocean voyage via boat to Europe.

The idea behind this flight is to eliminate that boat ride. Let's step aside and suppose for a moment. Suppose one of those boats would hold fifty airplanes; now suppose a submarine sank one—that's fifty airplanes on the bottom of the drink and they don't fly worth a damn with seaweed flopping behind them and a shark for a pilot. Now sup-pose we start off and fly fifty across; then suppose the law of accidents gets real out of line and we lose say five which is 10 percent which is far greater than the ATC loss expectancy. That's a hell of a lot better than losing the fifty and those forty-five will kill a lot more Germans than the fifty Old Davy Jones has on his field. All that is my idea of why to fly a fighter across. Any similarities to the facts are purely accidental.

The shuttle was number two to poke up and then today we were ordered back to Newcastle after shuttling a plane to Newark. Well, while circling Newark what should go right over my head but P-47s with belly (wing) tanks on them. So I got to thinking maybe this is it and after landing at Newcastle in the Boeing which brought us here from Newark and seeing the bulletin board, I knew this was it. Chalked on the alert room board was "Capt. Goldwater have life raft and arctic pack put on parachute." That has been done, the chute has been fitted, my various shots checked, my instrument card checked, and now tomorrow at 0900 we meet at foreign operations to discuss this little deal.

Friday, July 16, 1943

This radio compass is a wonderful thing. When, for instance, one gets lost. He tunes to 1200 (and hears dashes of the code sounds) and a needle on the dashboard will point the proper direction to turn so the ship is turned until the needle centers. Hold that reading and the first thing you know you are home—hence homing. Then power settings were discussed, emergency procedures, life rafts, special clothing, etc. Everything was very completely thrashed out for more than two hours

Captain Barry Goldwater was part of the first squadron to deliver P-47s to the English from New York, 1943.

and then we were through with instructions to fly this afternoon for two hours with full wing tanks. These wing tanks double the gas load of this ship and allow for ten hours of cruising at 185 indicated air speed. It also adds 1,800 pounds to the ship which will then total over 15,000 pounds. All this weight and its distribution present problems in take offs and landings and trim in actual flight.

We were supposed to fly them today, as I said, and everyone did but me. I went down and met my ship and she's a honey. I started her up and bingo: no manifold pressure gauge activity. As this is one of my favorite instruments, I cut her off and the crew chief started repairs which will end late tonight. I am naming my ship Peggy-G after you know who. She (Peggy) has led me through the best part of my life so I figured I might as well follow her across the Atlantic. Her name goes on tonight.

Saturday, July 17, 1943

We met again this morning at 0800 and went carefully over all instructions we had received yesterday plus a discussion of ship performance. Experience has decided that we use full boost (turbo supercharger) for take off. This baby weighs over fifteen thousand loaded and the runway goes by in a hell of a rush so full power will help. Oxygen equipment and use was discussed as was emergency procedure in the event of battery or generator failure or both. About everything has been hashed out now and we are getting eager. Capt. Turner (Pappy) is the leader. He is very good and extremely careful and I feel secure in his decisions and plans. If there's a man who can do it, he can. Well Old Peggy is still laid up so I didn't take her up today but tomorrow I shall.

Sunday, July 18, 1943

Well the old gal finally got her instrument fixed and she and I had an all day session in the blue. This morning I put in four hours non-stop in her going from here to Baltimore to Harrisburg to Philly and back here. Testing all radio equipment and getting accustomed to the Bendix radio compass. That darned thing is a honey, point right to where you should go and by God the first thing you know you are there. Two more hours this afternoon put six on her for the day and the sorest rear-end on me as any man every had. My parachute weighs seventy-five pounds and has in its back such diverse things as a knife, food rations, a frying pan, a fishing line, medicine, etc. The seat of the ship is a rubber boat all folded up with a bottle of carbon dioxide to blow it up. That boat is kind of hard and this thing at the end of my spine is kind of soft so tonight the tail end of me is sore, like riding a horse for the first time. Only Peggy G is no horse rather she is the sweetest, smoothest running airplane man ever made and she and I will get along as famously as her namesake. Things are popping now. There's a mass flight for one thousand miles non-stop tomorrow that will take five hours then probably to Farmingdale the next day.

Monday, July 19, 1943

Tonight I am very certain the eight of us jointly hold the record for the world's "sitters downers." This morning at seven we met at foreign operations and a non-stop cross country was agreed on as a fuel consumption test to Bangor, Maine and return. At 8:30 we started taking off: #1 went first, then #2, then #3 Peggy G and she rose into the air without a murmur after a run of about 3500 feet coaxed on by 2000 horse power. Then followed two turns around the field to assemble the flight which was like the picture below and which will be used in route across the Atlantic:

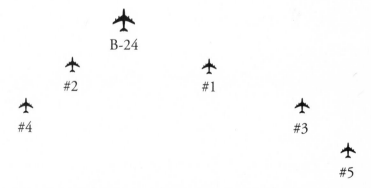

This is followed by B-24 #2 and P-47s 6-7-8-9-10 in formation with odd on right, even on left. Following the entire flight formation is a C-87 carrying mechanics, etc. and our personal baggage. Well, after three hours my rear end was a mass of dead beef and I squirmed first one way, then another. One doesn't squirm far in a pursuit ship but I found that pure oxygen helped every hour so I breathed that and it's now on my list. Frankly, a virgin horse ride offers far more comfort. After six hours plus we landed back at our base, wiser but sure as hell sorer for the trip. Old Peggy went like a top all the way with lowest manifold pressure, lowest fuel consumption and coolest engine of the lot. She's a honey and I mean from the word "clear" to "switches off." Flying over the New England states today was a beautiful thrill. Past Boston, Providence, Augusta, Bangor and many names I've heard but never seen. The day was especially clear for the east and the green splendor of its country side and the wide sweep of its blue rock lined shores made New England a place on my list to see again. Funny, I have always promised myself a trip through that country with Peggy and today we went, but at five thousand feet. Tomorrow I guess we shove off to Farmingdale.

Friday, July 23, 1943

In between the last entry and now we have left Newcastle and stayed one day at Farmingdale where the ships were carefully gone over. This afternoon we have all been waiting around to get started. At 4:45 PM we took off from Farmingdale and headed north and east. The lead ships circle at five thousand feet and the P-47s take off one after the other and like baby birds climb to be close to mother. When each flight compliment is assembled off we went: Across Long Island Sound to the coast of New England then over New Haven and the Yale Bowl, Harvard and Boston, then along the rocky coast of Maine. As the coast line swings to the east away from us we flew over the green beauty of Maine. Over small cities and pretty farms all laid-out with the neatness that is New England. Then come mountains and thousands of little lakes. It was a beautiful clear day and one could see for miles and everywhere one looked there were green forests and silvery lakes. For three pretty hours we flew north and just a few miles south of the Canadian border. This nice landing field showed up and we landed. One ship didn't leave the factory today but will come up tomorrow. It is cold here and the air smells clean and woodsy. Peggy ran like a million with her two thousand horses just purring along un-grumbling hour after hour while drinking up her seventy gallons of gas each sixty minutes. This landing field is Presque Isle. It is the jump off place for North Atlantic crossings. Here we are examined for medical clearance and briefed as to the procedures to be used in crossing. It is a large field and, well, I can't say how busy it is—that is classified. My ground speed today was an 185 mph average at an altitude of three thousand feet; weather clear and air smooth.

Saturday, July 24, 1943

This morning we were issued North Atlantic Manuals, with charts and marked maps. Then we were briefed for two and a half hours on the terrain and geologic features we would encounter from here all the way across. All emergency procedures were gone over and homing and range frequencies discussed. When one realizes the large numbers of

A later-seasoned pilot Goldwater after a jet flight.

airplanes that have left here and successfully arrived on the other side and the very few who have failed one appreciates how important these briefings are. After the briefing, the three navigators—Lead 1, Lead 2, and Follow 1—went over each chart with us and instructed us in their use. Handling these large maps while trying to fly a pursuit ship made very sloppy by wing tanks is something else and the help these navigators have given us all along is very greatly appreciated. We won't have one for another day for classified reasons I cannot tell.

Monday, July 26, 1943

This morning, after rendezvousing at five thousand feet over Presque Isle field we departed in the directions of Goose Bay. For only a few miles we stayed over the United States and then crossed into the province of New Brunswick, Canada. The carpet under us was the same lake-studded one like Maine and it remained so until we entered Quebec at the head of the Baie de Chaleur. . . . Now below us were nothing but smooth hard looking rocks, trees, and ten lakes for every square mile, and this scenery stayed unchanged right up into Labrador and Goose Bay Air Base. Distance today was 576 miles, flying time 3:30, ground speed 185, altitude five thousand feet, weather was thunder showers with rough air.

Wednesday, July 28, 1943

It looks like we will be here for a long time. Our orders are to make each leg of this flight according to CFR (Contact Flight Rules) and that means at least a 1500 foot ceiling clear across. Weather here tells us there has been only one such day all year, so only God knows when we will leave. It is a swell place though to be cooped up in. The governments of Canada and the United States have spent millions of dollars developing this wild country into a perfect airport. . . . Today is a stinker with wind and rain and cold. The sun hasn't been out all day and from the looks of things it won't be either. The sun doesn't set up here till after nine in the evening and then it stays light till after eleven o'clock. The Northern Lights put on a nearly nightly show and it is a really pretty sight.

Friday, August 1, 1943

Ye Gods another month gone by and soon it will be another year. We have been here just a day short of a week and still no weather for us to clear. This whole trip has started to have a sort of an odor to it. It seems that General Arnold is the only one who wants it done as the Fighter Command doesn't want it and the Ferry Command doesn't want it and the Republic doesn't either. Letters have been sent to Washington to clear the whole thing up so either we go on with lessened weather minimums or we return to the states and call it off. I hope it isn't the latter but I'm beginning to think that is what will happen.

A few days ago several of us walked over to the Hamilton River. This is a very wide and rather swift running river coming down to the sea from thousands of lakes south of here. Along the banks grow lots of birch and from one of these trees I cut some bark and I will write a letter to the kids on it. We ran into an Indian camp and the squaw is making some slippers for me to send Joanne, Barry and Mike. I got some good pictures of some huskies (dogs that pull the sleds in the winter); they are very friendly animals, plus very big and strong. Two of them are going back to the states with the B-24s. There are many, many combat crews in here on their way across. They too are held by the weather but should be getting out soon.

Wednesday and Thursday, August 6–7, 1943

Well so darned much happened yesterday and today that I know dog-goned well I won't be able to adequately tell about everything. First of all Pappy Turner had wired Presque Isle about the impossibility of our ever leaving Goose under our first orders which called for CRF only. In answer to his wire General Giles flew up and told us that by God it didn't make any difference where an engine quit and that as far as he was concerned if it had to quit he wanted lots of air between him and the drink and for us to get the hell on our way. That was like setting off dynamite cause all of us had been waiting too long to hear it. There was a lot to do: top off the tanks, check the oxygen, check the oil, add de-icer fluid, check radios, put air in tires, fill thermos bottles, etc. Then imagine the pilots of over fifty airplanes all doing the same thing and you have bedlam (there were additional ships waiting besides our flight of thirteen). Weather briefing told us we would find ice at 5000 feet so we decided to fly at 7500, above all the clouds and moisture. Finally at 14:45 EST the following ships took the air: Lead #1 and then P-47s 1-2-3-4-5, which was followed by the second flight. I used my turbo and drew about 48 inches on takeoff holding the ship with brakes until I reached 40 inches then with a slow thrust forward old Peggy G started down the smoothest runway I've ever seen. Soon she was airborne at 4000 feet and 120 miles per hour. Lead #1 and P 47 1 & 2 were in the distance and by indicating 225 mph I caught them and settled into my position on the right wing. We climbed to 7500 topping a thick layer of stratus and took our heading toward Greenland. For 140 miles we were above the clouds which told us we were still over land. Ahead the clouds suddenly stopped and beyond was the deep rich blue of the Danish [Denmark] Straits of the North Atlantic. As we approached Cape Harrison which would be our last land for over 600 miles I got a might squeamish. This was my first solo flight over an ocean and with only one engine. Well I said the Lord's Prayer and asked Him to do right by all of us. Then touched my Flight Saint Christopher that Peggy gave me, then looked at all my instruments, and felt my already tired bottom settle down to my job. Miles before Cape Harrison we could see gigantic icebergs floating in the sea. Even from 7500 feet they were massive and cold looking as they floated lazily in the current that had carried them from Greenland up that island's west coast then down the east coast of Labrador. This is known as the Labrador Current and accounts for a lot of foul weather in these parts. For maybe 50 miles out to sea we could see these bergs then nothing but the deep color of a cold ocean. One hour, two hours, three hours then land ahead but way, way ahead but land and believe me, land looks darned good to a man who is used to seeing it every place he looks.

So clear was the atmosphere we could see this land even though it was 150 miles away from us. We were flying above a solid stratus and these clouds ran right up to this rugged coast line we could see. The mountains of Greenland were a pale blue flecked with white snow and more brilliantly white than many glaciers. The Ice Cap covers nearly this entire island and rises to nearly 9000 feet in places. So brilliant is this cap that it blends with the sky or the clouds if there are any and this fact makes flying over the cap a dangerous undertaking. As we passed a line roughly lying between Cape Desolation on the North and Cape Egede on the South, the clouds suddenly stopped and there below us lay a sight that if I live a hundred years I will never forget: A rich blue quiet sea flanked by a very rough rocky coast line and jutting into this coast line for miles many deep cut fjords. These fjords usually ended at the foot of a glacier and these fjords would be literally covered with thousands of large and small icebergs that had broken from the glacier. They looked like salt on a dark cloth. Then the fjords with no glaciers would be a deep blue with no white specks floating on them. The glaciers run like long rivers of lather to the ice cap which is topped by block granite peaks sticking through this icy topping like candles on a cake. It was a magnificent sight of which I am unable to properly write.

Losing altitude for our approach as we entered Tunugdliarfick Fjord, we passed the little village of Narsak. Up this fjord for 50 miles then a turn to the left and there lay the steel mesh landing strip of BW1 (Blueie West 1). A quick adjustment of the altimeter to the proper pressure, a peel off over the field-wheels down, revving the RPM up to 2500, and a long circle over the 3 mile wide of the ice covered fjord, then flaps down and at 110 mph Peggy G's wheels touched down with a roar on the steel mat of the landing strip. The strip slowly rises 100 feet in its 6000 feet length so slowing down was no problem. It was very cold when I opened the hatch and I was thankful for my long woolen underwear. Only one mishap when Lt. Armacast's right landing gear pin sheared on landing causing it to collapse. Sufficient damage was done to force us to leave his ship here. Distance flown 766 miles, time 4 hours 15 minutes, ground speed 181 mph, weather good and air smooth, fuel used 295 gallons.

We were all up early this morning for an eight o'clock briefing about the route. There are many B-26, C-47 and others in so the briefing room was crowded. After that I went hiking towards the dead glacier at the head of this valley. This field is very unusual and the engineers certainly deserve a hand for its construction. It is located in the mouth of an old glacial valley about 2 miles wide and 7 miles long. Mountains severely hem it in on two sides. The landing strip runs across the gravel bottom of the valley from sea level to 100 feet above sea level. It is of steel mesh and when a plane rolls on it roars like a strong wind. The camp itself is strung out on the south side of the runway for a great distance. Walking up to the glacier I crossed a low hill. It was covered with soft tundra and this was gaily spotted with blue bells and a purple sort of stock. Over these hills grows underbrush very much like Arizona's Manzanita and just about as tough. The valley narrows down and looks for all the world like Yosemite with its polished granite walls and perpetual springs cascading their waters down the slick canyon sides. Finally the glacier showed its white face and frankly it was a disappointment. It is a dead glacier and is slowing melting away. I waded into the river to get closer to the ice and I know that the only reason that water isn't frozen is that it won't stand still long enough. This evening three of us went down to the navy dock to fish and watch the ice which was slowly filling the fjord from a south wind. We left after the sun went down and the water was beginning to freeze.

Friday, August 8, 1943

Up early today and after a quick breakfast and a short weather briefing we went to our ships for takeoff. Peggy ran like a million and took off on the first try in spite of freezing weather the night before. Her wheels left the runway at 11:30 AM after an easy but rough run over the steel mat. Lead #1 and P-47s 1 & 2 were as usual ahead of me and I followed them in a climb down Tunugdliarfick around its first bend then over a narrow lake studded pass into Brede Fjord. Continuing to climb we went into formation and turned back into Tunugdliarfick Fjord at Narsak. By the time we went back over BW1 we were at 7000 feet and still climbing. We went to 11,500 feet and leveled off above Greenland's Ice Cap. Now nothing I can say about this will give you any idea of the way it hits you. You will have to imagine an area over 400 miles long and some 200 miles wide as white as or whiter than the most brilliant snow you have ever seen. Only in a few places does black snow thatched peaks stick through. This is solid ice reaching measured thickness of over 8000 feet. This cap sort of leaks down into the fjords to where they start and all along them are tremendous crevices or cracks many hundreds of feet deep. These glaciers run to the water and there they are slowly breaking off into icebergs. After 45 minutes of this we descended and passed over Cape Adelaer where we left land again.

Here was the blue North Atlantic, and once again I settled down to a long flight broken only by gas tank switches and checks of the engine instruments now and then. We flew intermittently over low hanging stratus and then over a solid bank of clouds many thousand feet below our 7000. Outside air temperature was right at freezing all the way and occasionally I could see the right outboard engine of Lead 1 clearing its carburetor of ice. On this leg my thermos was filled with ice water and I had some field rations so after 2 hours I had a small lunch. The Reykjavik beam growing louder told us land would soon be in sight and at the end of 3 hours and twenty minutes the snow capped volcanic mountains of Iceland came into view. We went into Echelon which is ten minutes out from Meeks Field and after four hours and twenty minutes Peggy's wheels went down on another strip of foreign soil.

Meeks is located on a peninsula jutting into the sea south of the city of Reykjavik. It is wonderfully camouflaged and when one sees the buildings, one can understand it. They are merely half domes of corrugated iron and blend in with the terrifically rough, rocky volcanic soil perfectly. We are but 2 degrees or 120 miles south of the Arctic Circle and the temperature doesn't let us forget that fact. I remember how Annie Johnson [my mother-in-law] raved about this island after her trip here and I agree with her so someday the real Peggy and I will have to visit here in the peace that is to come. Today's distance 746 miles, altitude 7000, the weather was good and ground speed 191 mph.

Sunday, August 10, 1943

Yesterday can safely be put down as the most pleasant one of this trip and one of the best I've ever known. Not being able to fly to Scotland, we were instead turned loose so six of us dressed and then hiked into Reykjavik, which is some 35 miles away. It is the capital of Iceland and about 40,000 people live there. It is an immaculate town and I was impressed. The women dress both in American dresses and in their own long dark dresses with their blonde heads topped by a small black hat from which dangles a long tassel held with a band of golden colored metal. Both men and women are blond and the little babies in their carriages (they are everywhere) are cute little blondes with light blue eyes. These people drive new American cars which people in America cannot buy. American products are everywhere and for these as well as local products one pays top prices. They say that at first the local people resented the Americans but that they have slowly been won over. I could easily detect coldness towards us but every now and then it would be broken down. Many, many people speak English and the hundreds of American uniforms of all branches insure a complete winning over. We went shopping for various items which we wanted and after that went to dinner at the Hotel Barg. As Iceland is dry we contented ourselves with one-percent beer with our meal. After dinner the ballroom was opened and with a juke box for an orchestra a dance got underway. Into this room came pretty little Icelandic girls who but an hour before couldn't even be smiled at on the street but here they would dance with anyone who asked them. The whole floor looked like it was covered with dancing Mary Goldwaters [my brother Bob's wife], so blonde and fair are those girls. I danced with one whose name was Rana and she danced like a million but like the rest had no sense of humor and right there any semblance to an American girl ended. I ran into Major (Marshall) Carey with whom I had served at Luke Field and had last seen at Yuma. We had a long talk and at eleven said good-bye and started home. The six of us rented a taxi and returned singing to our corrugated iron cottage. It was two in the morning when we went to bed but the sun was still up and it was bright like a sunset on the desert. It was a wonderful day.

Monday, August 11, 1943

At 0930 this morning the orderly awakened us and announced our schedule which called for a 1045 weather briefing and a 1300 take-off. Our weather briefing and charts showed a 2000 foot ceiling with showers with tops at 12,000 feet so we decided on the top. This called for oxygen so we were doubly careful to check and see that our full 450 pounds were there. Engines were started at 1130 but due to one shop having trouble we did not take off until 1230. Peggy G as usual checked in perfectly. I have not had even an indication of anything but perfection thus far. I love to take her off with all her 2000 horses running so smoothly and the big turbo behind me roaring and its boost to power. She seems to float off in spite of her 15,000 pound weight. I went on oxygen at once and stayed on it until cruising altitude of 12500 was reached when I found that a defect in the system was drawing the oxygen at too fast a rate for our estimated 4 plus hours so I cut it off and used it only when I felt in need of it. It was bitter cold at that altitude with the thermometer going to 10 degrees below 0 degrees centigrade. However, the cockpits of these ships are always warm so I didn't mind. We were flying above the clouds . . . up there in the beauty that holds a man to flying. Soft fleecy clouds underneath surrounded by tall cumulus reaching thousands of feet above us. This beauty is the reward for a hard day's work.

I have not mentioned the accuracy of our navigators but all the way across their estimated times and their navigation have been uncanny in its accuracy. Today, they estimated Starnaway at 2 hours and 50 minutes, and on the dot I looked through a hole in the clouds and there on the shimmering Atlantic was the northern shores of Scotland. In just a short hour and a few minutes we were over the field at Prestwick after passing near Ben Lomond and Lock Lomond. Peggy's wheels touched down just 4 hours and twenty minutes after takeoff having covered 904 miles in that time. I hate to say good-bye to her as she is a wonder but I have admonished whoever gets her by an entry in the log to "Fly her like an angel and fight her like a devil." The mission was completed August 11, 1943; miles flown were 3740; flying time 19 hours and 40 minutes; average speed was 190 mph.

Letter (June 6, 1977)

This letter was written to Goldwater's former campaign manger, speechwriter, coauthor, and friend Stephen Shadegg about his military activities.

Dear Steve:

I have felt very self-conscious about the fact that I did not participate in actual combat during World War II, although I have to tell you some things that can't be put on paper—some of the things I did I would rather have been shot at, but those are not to be mentioned.

I mentioned the fact that I tried to get combat training when I went into Luke [Air Force Base], but was turned down because of age and eyesight, and then I further tried to go overseas with Lieutenant Colonel Ennis Whitehead as his aide and I flipped a nickel with another Lieutenant and lost, staying in the country. I wrote Whitehead on several occasions asking for assignment in a combat position in the South Pacific, but he was never able to satisfy my desire.

I wrote to my old instructor of military science and tactics, General Alexander Patch [at Staunton Military Academy], and offered to be his personal pilot, and he told me if I ever got in the Theatre to let him know and he'd call me in, but when I got into his Theatre it was away over in Burma and India and that was useless. Later on in the war I tried to get into B-29s, B-17s and you name it, but I was always too old, although I must say that today that age would be looked on as young, as a friend of mine flew combat in Vietnam when he was over fifty.

I participated in developing the system of gunnery training known as the Curve of Pursuit, and we did this mainly on the theory of a young Captain Clark whom we had assigned at Luke, who figured out on some forty pieces of paper (something that a computer could do today in seconds), that, theoretically, bullets fired at an enemy aircraft, starting at 90 degrees and following through to 0 degrees, would all hit the target. Before that the air force taught a 90 degrees pass which, theoretically, would find it impossible for a bullet properly aimed to even hit the target.

We brought over from the Royal Air Force a young Group Captain, Teddy Donaldson, who was an ace and who had been shot down five times, to teach us how the British did this, so we slowly incorporated these teachings into our particular way of teaching at Yuma Air Base, and our first class that we graduated averaged about 94 percent as being qualified for aerial gunnery, while the top record before that was around 6 percent, as I remember it.

The navy was already using the Curve of Pursuit, which accounted for the phenomenal victories in the South Pacific before ours began, but the air force, after coming down to see whether we were cheating (and I had actually flown a Colonel, after proper classroom instruction, and shown him that he could hit the target), adopted it as the standard practice and it went on to become the fighter training gunnery course that is still used today.

Your comment that I was exposed to as much danger as any combat pilot just won't hold water with a man who has been in combat. It's true, any time you take an airplane up, whether you are going to fly it over land or an ocean, the ice cap, the African desert, the jungles of Burma, India, or China, you are taking chances, but when you've got some fellow up there in an enemy fighter shooting at you, it makes a whole different story and, frankly, one of the disappointments of my life was not to have been able to participate in aerial combat. I did fly transport aircraft where enemy aircraft were to be expected, but I never saw one, thank God, so on the whole, I did not have what you would call a heroic military career. I did my best to do my job well wherever I was and to do whatever I was asked to do, and I have to say some of those things I would rather not have done, but they got done and things went along, so maybe you shouldn't make too much about this. Just say I tried, but "old man age" had already gotten me. You know, Steve, that's almost the story of my life. I'm always there but I'm always a little too old, and that's been somewhat the way in politics too, but not entirely so. As I look back on it all now, there has never been a disappointment in the load.

CHAPTER 5

POLITICAL BEGINNINGS

G oldwater's interest in politics is not surprising, for his family had been involved in Arizona government since its prestatehood days. So when a friend suggested he follow the family tradition, only he seemed surprised that voters kept promoting him. In 1948 the Phoenix Charter Commission recommended the appointment of a city manager, immune from politics and replacing the city's commission with a city council, who along with the mayor would be selected in nonpartisan elections. The changes were adopted, but nothing happened. Over a bottle of Old Crow, Barry Goldwater and his friend since childhood, Harry Rosenzweig, decided to run as reformers along with five other Phoenicians. In a letter to his brother Bob, Goldwater wrote, "You . . . probably think me seven kinds of a dirty bastard when you hear that I have decided to run for councilman with Harry. . . . I couldn't criticize the government of this city if I myself refused to help." He observed, "There have always been one, and sometimes two, Goldwaters damned fools enough to get into politics, and they always did it with service in their minds. . . . Don't cuss me too much. It ain't for life, and it may be fun." He made the following journal entries after this first run for office and later entries when he successfully managed the campaign of Howard Pyle, who was the first Republican to win the governorship in many decades.

Journal Entry (Late September 1949)

This should very rightfully carry the above title—"Politics"—because if my intentions don't go the way of all intentions, I will keep a record of my political life which may be very short, limited to this campaign on which I, along with six others, have embarked. Or it may go on for two years if we are elected. It all began I guess years ago like all my doings. Things don't just happen to me, they germinate, so to speak. I get these desires and the bug has to grow and grow, either to give me courage or confidence in myself, or both, and then—boom—before I think I am ready, my mouth is open and I am in them. But I would lie if I professed to be the drafted-type of politician. No one had to beg me. They just sort of suggested it, and now I find myself embroiled, along with this hot September sun, in politics.

Now I must put down, first of all, my philosophy that politics can be clean. I want to put that down now because maybe I will have to change my mind. I think, however, that politics can be governed by the same set of laws or rules that govern our actions towards each other. I believe that things can be done outright and not on the sly cloak and dagger treatment politics have always carried. I think that people who work under [city] politicians, the clerks, the police, the engineers and all the others, they will work for men and women that they admire and trust much better than for those they fear and distrust. Well that's down, now we will see what will happen.

Harry and I have gone into this along with the others but it's very flattering to me that Harry would go along. He is my best friend and with him along to keep my mouth semi closed we can go a long ways. I am honored that the others would associate themselves with me. In Harry and me they are taking on a big burden that will have to take a lot of lifting. We are both Jews and we are both supposed to be richer than God knows what and while that isn't so, people think it's so and we are stuck with it. I have never been actively involved in a campaign before. My politics have been limited to raising money for unsuccessful candidates. Our desires in this case have been activated by the realization that if this city of ours is to go on to the heights that it can go it must be taken from under the ignorant eyes of bad management and antiquated methods of doing business. That is what we are pledged to and if elected that is what we will accomplish. Well, now I am in it and we will see what goes.

Journal Entry (Undated, 1949)

The campaign has started. It is much milder than I thought it would be. If I were our opposition I think I could hang Harry and me but they so far have kept their mouths shut. We are being criticized for not going out and raising hell with them, but we are waiting our time, confining our talks to interested friends. If you can't get your friends to vote for you then who in hell can you get. We are concentrating on a big registration and hoping for a big vote. If we don't get at least fifteen thousand out, then we are whipped. Our boys are afraid of the south side, but I firmly believe that Harry's and my long years of association with the colored and the Mexican people will pay off in spite of the apparent hold the opposition has there.

Journal Entry (November 9, 1949)

I wound up my last entry with the question: "will they vote?" I now have the answer. Yes they will vote. They did to the tune of some twenty-two thousand and, where we were hoping to get in maybe four of the bunch, the whole damned ticket went in by whopping majorities. It pleases me to have been the high man, but that is due, I think, to my name being better known and probably easier to remember than some of the others. It was a wonderful experience, that campaigning. I met more people than I ever dreamed I could get to know. I found out some of my friends weren't such good friends after all, and that some of my new ones really are friends. I started with the idea that one could be in politics and remain clean, and I still hold to that with one campaign behind me. Of course, the only issue was the manager, but there could have crept into it some personal things that could have been nasty, but thank God they didn't. I know this last one was not a good test because of the issues, and I will now have to wait till another campaign, if there be another, so I can see if the idea [of clean campaigning] will work.

Journal Entry (Undated, 1950)

From his position as a member of the Phoenix City Council, operating under the charter he had helped revise and had at this time served for a

Barry Goldwater's first political adventure was his election to the Phoenix City Council.

year, Goldwater collected background data on the city's development and added his reflections. He felt good about the new government for the city.

Dark clouds of war hung over the world as we came into 1949 but in spite of the gloom of the world the bright light of prosperity was on Phoenix. We had become a city of some sixty-five thousand souls, most of who were gainfully employed and living comfortably under our warm sun. This year can be said to be another turning point in Phoenix life. . . . Now, after one year of our new manager-type government, the city shows promise of a real political future unblemished by the usual pranks of office holders.

Journal Entry (November 1950)

These are notes Goldwater made for a troop-rallying talk while he was the campaign manager for Howard Pyle's bid for governor; the talk was given on the eve of the election.

Your spontaneous response tonight should be rich reward to the men and women of this party who have stood by it through its dark years. It is a rich reward to me as Howard Pyle's campaign manager and as an Arizonan, an American, and a Republican—and I'm proud of being all three. In this spontaneous action of the Republican Party of Arizona we may well be witnessing the start of a movement that will sweep America: A movement that will return morality to politics. A movement that will return honor and stature to the service of one's state and country. The government of this nation and of this state was formed on the concept that honor was a holy thing. Our founders pledged their lives, their fortunes but most important of all they pledged their sacred honor. Today, because of the almost total ignoring of those basic concepts, we find our nation treading on the threshold of socialism. Our government's being run by people who think one way and act another. Whose fault is this? It is yours and mine—the people of this state and nation. Plato once said, "The penalty that people pay for not being interested in politics is to be governed by people worse than themselves." Now, hasn't that come true?

From your expressions I gather you are tired of this condition of government and like thousands of Americans every place, you want a change. Now is the time . . . NOW is the time. It is your job and, believe me, it will be a hard job. We have with Howard Pyle an Arizonan, and an American in the fullest sense of the words who will be our next governor. We have good Republican men and women all over this state who will serve you in the halls of government. But the mere wishing for that will not make it so. You must do what Republicans up to this year have forgotten how to do. You must work at precinct levels like you have never worked before. There are door bells to be pushed and people to be talked to. The Democrats have not stayed in power through the excellence of their candidates but through the excellence of their organization. Quit being ashamed of being a Republican. Quit hiding behind the cloak of fear. This is your job and my job—the victory will be yours and yours alone and with this victory will go the assurances of honor in politics and the start of a return all over this country to the American way of life. NOW IS THE TIME.

Note: After Pyle won by a narrow margin, Goldwater was itching for higher office for himself. He easily won reelection in 1951 to the Phoenix City Council and performed exceptionally well in the post; he then began eyeing the Senate seat of a Democratic giant, Majority Leader of the U.S. Senate Ernest McFarland, who was up for election in 1952. Goldwater's thoughts about making the run jelled when Illinois Republican Senator Everett Dirksen visited Phoenix in 1951, as he later explained to Jack Casserly: "Peggy and I attended a cocktail party for [Dirksen] on the terrace of the old Adams Hotel in downtown Phoenix. . . . Midway through the reception, Dirksen called us off to a corner and quietly urged me to run against McFarland. . . . I felt overwhelmed. Here was a veteran national politician coming to my home town, and he not only knew my name but suggested I run to help him in the Senate. . . . I would be at least a fifteen-to-one shot, and that's a lot in a two-horse race. Yet I wasn't scared." He began researching McFarland. More important, he began sifting through the results of Governor Pyle's narrow victory, preparing the realistic prospects of electing a Republican senator from Arizona. Based on his research, he thought he had a fifty-fifty chance of beating McFarland.

PART II

THE SENATE YEARS: 1952–1965

CHAPTER 6

THE FIRST SENATE CAMPAIGN

N o one was very surprised when the forty-three-year-old president of Goldwaters Department Store formally announced his bid for the U.S. Senate in the spring of 1952, for he had been running for months. It was an aggressive and well-run campaign, challenging the well-entrenched Democratic majority leader of the Senate, Ernest McFarland. During ten months of campaigning, Goldwater would fly over fifty thousand air miles as he moved about the state to deliver over six hundred speeches. Initially, he thought he could do it all himself and on a shoestring. But in June he recruited a campaign manager, Stephen Shadegg, who had earlier worked for Arizona's senior U.S. senator, Carl Hayden, a Democrat. The Republican Senate Campaign Committee in Washington, as well as the Republican National Committee in Washington, sensed a possible upset winner with Goldwater, so they willingly helped out with research material and finances. As the campaign progressed, Goldwater found additional financial support from wealthy out-of-state conservatives like H. L. Hunt, Sid Richardson, and Joseph Pew. It was a tight race to the end, but Goldwater benefited greatly from Dwight Eisenhower's coattails—particularly after the general stopped in Tucson in mid-October to ask Arizonans to send Goldwater to Washington. Goldwater always believed, too, that the support of the then highly popular junior senator from Wisconsin, Joseph McCarthy, had given him the edge with his slim victory.

Letter (January 9, 1952)

In preparation for his Senate race, Goldwater initially went to family and friends to raise money for his campaign. This letter was written to Abbott

Barry and Peggy at the GOP convention, 1964.

Johnson, Peggy Goldwater's grandfather. Goldwater would underestimate the funds needed and ultimately raised forty-five thousand dollars for his race and outspent his opponent by a two-to-one ratio.

Dear Abbott,

The reason that a Republican victory in Arizona senator-wise would be important this year is that the Republicans are going to have a very difficult time gaining control of the Senate and Arizona is one of the states in which we feel that we have about a fifty-fifty chance. The effort here is not going to entail a lot of money—in fact, we ran the Governor's campaign last year for twenty-five thousand dollars and we will not have to spend that much to re-elect him and certainly not more than that in our senatorial effort.

I know these sums sound small to you to conduct a campaign but you must remember that I have a very wide acquaintance [i.e., name recognition] in this state in every county and the groundwork for this venture has been well laid over the past twenty-two years with almost constant contact with every facet of our population.

The Republican organization in this state, thanks to strong emigration of Midwestern people, has improved tremendously until today in our two big counties, accounting for about 80 percent of our total vote; we find the Republicans having a slight edge over the long entrenched Democrats.

My personal feeling, after checking with friends over the state in the last two weeks and after the incumbent Senator McFarland completed his swing around the state, is that I have a fifty-fifty chance at the present time and I feel that these chances will prevail and possibly improve.

I am not in the least optimistic about this venture but I do know that if it takes hard work, a thorough knowledge of the people and an ability to speak both Spanish and English to meet all types of people, then I have those requirements and I say that without a feeling of gagging. To be perfectly frank and blunt, Arizona will re-elect a Republican Governor next year, has an excellent chance of electing two congressmen of the Republican Party and I feel that I have a chance to upset the Democratic majority leader.

Anything that you can get me in the way of money will be appreciated, although we don't anticipate an overly difficult time of raising twenty-five to forty thousand to conduct the Governor's race and the senatorial race. If any of your friends are interested in contributing to this effort, the checks can be mailed to me, made out to either me personally or to any other person that they might know in Arizona.

The important thing this year is to get those socialists out of Washington and that is the sole purpose of my being willing to give up a damn good business, a wonderful family and a good bit of my health to go into this thing.

Letter (January 10, 1952)

This letter was written to Goldwater's brother-in-law Ray Johnson.

Dear Ray,

Anne told me of your interest in my coming campaign and the questions you asked about it. First, I want to tell you how grateful I am that you would concern yourself with the candidacy of a person in Arizona and I thank you for it.

I have decided to run for senator against the present Senator McFarland, who is majority leader, but this has not been released locally. I feel that my campaign will take about twenty-five thousand dollars and while it in all probability can be raised locally, help from the outside would greatly expedite matters here. Contributions can be made directly to me or to you and you in turn can send them to me and a strict accounting will be given all participants. You know my personal background as well as I do so there is no need of going into that.

I do not have a cinch by any means but I feel that I have an honest fifty-fifty chance which is all any man can ask. Arizona has an extremely good chance of going Republican for the first time in its history this year, especially if Eisenhower should be the candidate but whoever is the candidate our chances are bright.

We have no laws in Arizona about amounts which can be spent by individuals and my estimate of twenty-five thousand dollars is a very modest sum compared to what others will spend. However, you must remember that I have been preparing for this year all of my life and my life has been one constant contact with the people of this state, which will now result in a saving of money.

P.S. If you would like to see the movies of our trip down the river this summer, let me know and I will send them to you.

Statement (April 24, 1952)

When formally announcing his candidacy for the U.S. Senate, Goldwater made the following statements, as reported by the Arizona Republic, *and these would become the themes of his campaign.*

Goldwater stated, "I am an Arizonan who doesn't like the spectacle of our junior senator, [Ernest McFarland], who instead of paying attention to the needs and wants of the people of Arizona, is busy being the personal representative and spokesman of Harry Truman. . . ." Goldwater called Roosevelt's New Deal and Truman's Fair Deal "a devilish plan to eventually socialize this country." Goldwater offered six reasons why he had decided to make the Senate race:

1. "I believe that a life-long familiarity with the State of Arizona and its people and intensive study of the problems and needs of this region as a businessman and citizen qualifies me to represent efficiently our state in Washington."
2. He wanted to "bend every effort" to combat the growth of federal power at the expense of states' rights and local responsibility in government.
3. "My business has succeeded because I believe in giving a dollar's value for each dollar received. . . . I believe that our government must adopt these principles if it is to survive."
4. "I believe it to be the duty of a U.S. senator to combat the intentions of the New Deal and Fair Deal."
5. "A senator should be of independent mind . . . and never a mere rubber stamp for any administration. He should be the agent of his state, alert to further its peculiar interests."
6. He opposed the "present tragic trend toward the destruction of individual freedom."

Letter (May 26, 1952)

This letter to Clarence Buddington Kelland (who helped guide GOP campaigns for the Republican National Committee in Washington) shows that Goldwater, notwithstanding the skill with which he had run Governor Pyle's campaign, was beginning to realize he needed help.

Dear Bud:

I don't know what the hell I would do without you. As I was flying home from Prescott Saturday afternoon, I thought to myself—I'd give anything to sit down and talk to Bud about the million and one things that are popping around in my mind and then this morning I get a letter from you.

I had a very busy schedule last week and I found myself beginning to get tired—my brain got to feeling like scrambled eggs must feel when they get cold. In spite of that, problems came to my mind which I want to discuss with you.

Tucson is in a dreadful haggle over the Taft-Ike fight. I don't believe those people down there realize the damage that is being done to the Republican Party by their constant bickering. A small group is now trying to undermine the county organization there and while I don't think it has any chance of success, it is still an element we shouldn't have. I am very hopeful that they will see the light and that strong leadership can bring them around before a lot of damage is done. The thing that is hurting is that the Democrats are beginning to benefit by the Republicans fighting, particularly so since [presidential hopeful Democratic Senator Estes] Kefauver was here and they see some hope in him or others who might run. . . .

Here is the main thing I wanted to discuss with you and I think if you will sit down with Ab [Herman, the campaign and research director at the RNC], you can come up with some suggestions. You will recall that I have been against outside help in this effort. Well, I am beginning to wonder if I am smart or not. What kind of help could a man from the Washington office give me? What would be the nature of his work?

Would he be a man who could do press work for me, help prepare speeches, do research, et cetera, or would he be the manager type? Frankly, what I need more than anything is a man who can organize my speeches and do research. I am attempting to get Stephen Shadegg but don't know what luck I will have. Please talk this over with Ab and please let me know your honest convictions on it. Should I have a man from Washington or should I continue doing as I am? The thing looks almost beyond my personal ability to handle without considerable help and I don't know whether local help is better than outside help. In fact, all I know at the present time is that Harry Truman is an s.o.b. . . .

Now, here are still some more things. Please let me have your thinking on the foreign policy as soon as you can. And ask Ab to send me the answers they are using to questions that are asked at rallies like this: What do you Republicans propose to do about our domestic situation? I have quite a few answers but I want to see what their thinking is so I can add it to mine. I don't mean what they are going to do about dishonesty or socialism but how are we going to get the country back on its economic feet. . . .

Now, for a peek into the future to answer your last question. Eisenhower has weakened himself with Arizona Democrats and Arizona Republicans to some extent by his statement, "I am not seeking anything." He still remains the man that Democrats will vote for and Democrats have to vote for us this year or we don't get in. As for Taft, there is universal admiration but there is a fear that he represents the old, too conservative Republican Party and I feel reasonably certain that Taft would find it very difficult to carry Arizona. I still think he can be elected but in his being elected a lot of Democrats are going to return to Congress. If Ike continues with his Dewey-like campaign, he's liable to find himself a cooked goose but what I am afraid of is that without Eisenhower or even with a weak Eisenhower, the Democrats are going to win this election. Quite frankly my opinion is the same as it was in January—that is Eisenhower could probably get 60 percent of the popular vote in Arizona and this includes Democrats and Republicans.

I hope and pray that the stupidity that has marked this entire Taft-Eisenhower fight will cease and the Party will unite for its coming effort. If I were a Democratic strategist I would enjoy nothing more than the spectacle the Republican Party is now presenting in being unable to agree, not willing to agree, of desecrating two good men and preventing candidates from doing effective jobs in their campaign.

I am sorry that this is much a longer letter but I had a lot to tell you and ask you and I hope you don't mind my doing it. There are many times when I feel completely alone in what I am trying to do and there are many times I feel like getting back in the rag business but those are only occasional as my constant desire is to win. Take care of yourself, try to get some sense pounded into those knot heads who are causing all this trouble.*

Letter (May 26, 1952)

This letter and resulting effort would prove prescient in Goldwater's first campaign, for this action would help make the difference in his narrow victory. All told, the Senate Campaign Committee would send Goldwater seven thousand dollars to assist in his efforts. Goldwater also accurately predicted the likely total votes cast in Arizona in 1952.

Dear Senator Dirksen:

About a year ago Margaret Rockwell discussed with your committee the advisability of putting some money in the Arizona effort to get votes from some of the Indian reservations, chiefly the Navajos and Hopis. I wasn't too hot for the idea at the time but since making an analysis earlier this spring, I agree with the proponents of this plan as we can pick up three to four thousand votes in that area.

This is the strategy. The part of Northern Arizona, which comprises three counties, is occupied by the Navajo and Hopi Indians. All that is required to vote in this state is to be able to read and sign one's name. There are sufficient numbers on both reservations who can qualify to warrant our going into this field.

We have already gotten the supervisors of those counties to create thirty new precincts whose precinct committeemen will be Indian Traders who are basically, if not violently, anti–New Deal. They will through the coming months register these Indians but it will take some money as these Indians are semi-nomadic in their living and one has to gather them in by the use of sings or barbeques as you and I would call them. Trucks and gasoline have been contributed for this effort

---

* *Unlike the division between Robert Taft and Dwight Eisenhower supporters in many states, a split that resulted in candidates on both sides suffering, Goldwater helped engineer a resolution for the problem in Arizona. Although Goldwater was an ardent supporter and admirer of Senator Robert Taft, he was willing to compromise so that the Eisenhower faction had solid representation at the state's convention, and in the process Goldwater won the respect of all factions. Thus, he had only token opposition during his primary.*

but money is needed and I would recommend to your committee that you consider $1500 for this effort.

I feel that this might well be the margin of victory in this state. We are hopeful for a 260,000 total vote which is 30 percent above 1950 and will include a slight margin in the favor of the Republicans. Every additional vote we can get is needed and that is why I recommend this to you for your consideration.

Letter (July 10, 1952)

Goldwater recruited his friend Stephen Shadegg to be his campaign manager in late June 1952, and it would begin a professional relationship that lasted a lifetime for both men. In this letter, Goldwater gives his new campaign manager a rundown on his positions on various issues that were important at the time.

Dear Steve:

So that you may know where I stand on these matters, here goes:

1. *Spending.* The budget must be cut to stop the dangers of inflation and to stop the attendant dangers of deficit spending. It can be cut too.

2. *Foreign Aid.* I don't know how much foreign aid can be cut out but I don't like the idea of sending any amount of money that is asked for out of this country without sound, logical reasons for its use. I don't feel that Congress or the people have been told enough about the use of this money. I feel strongly that foreign countries should work for this money and if they refuse to then we should refuse to send the money to them.

3. *Labor.* I believe in the Taft-Hartley Law. [Goldwater noted that he had previously sent Shadegg his statement on labor and his support for right-to-work laws.]

4. *Military Spending.* The military is the greatest waster of money and manpower we have. They must be made to conduct their affairs in a businesslike manner.

5. *Korea.* We should do one of three things in Korea: get out, stay there, or win the war. I say win any war this country ever enters.

6. *Corruption in Government.* One of the biggest things I have against McFarland is the fact that he has condoned the corruption at all levels in the federal government. Man must conduct himself in office on even a higher plane than he would conduct his own personal affairs.

7. *Social Security, Old Age Pensions and Welfare.* I believe in these programs but I believe in proper and honest administration of them.

8. *Bureaucratic State.* I believe the government should be returned to the people and that the federal government should get out of the states and municipalities as fast as they can.

9. *Indian Affairs.* The Indians have made no progress under the Indian Bureau in a hundred years. I believe that the states can better conduct the affairs of the Indians but above all I believe the Indians can conduct their own affairs better under a state government. The Indian is still not a full citizen and we must make him one.

10. *Foreign Policy.* We have no foreign policy and as a result the United States has been reduced to an impotent force in world affairs. I believe in a strong foreign policy that will enforce the desires of this country and protect its citizens.

Letter (November 10, 1952)

Goldwater biographer and University of Utah historian Robert Alan Goldberg reports the election results: "Eisenhower and Governor Howard Pyle, in winning Arizona by a two-to-one margin, gave Goldwater the edge that lifted him to a slim 6,725-vote victory over McFarland out of almost 260 thousand ballots cast" to become the first Arizona Republican senator since 1920. Among those Goldwater wanted to thank was Joe McCarthy in the brief letter that follows.

Dear Joe:

You would pick this time to come to Phoenix when I'm off in the hills taking a rest. The rush of the campaign prevented my thanking you for the great favor you did me by coming to Tucson. Both Peggy and I appreciate it more than we can tell you and we both look forward to pleasant associations in Washington with you.

Journal Entry (Late December, 1952)

Once again, in the space of twelve years, I must say goodbye to my business, for how long I don't know. The relationship between the feelings a man has in his heart and the words he has available to express them are, at the best for me anyway, inadequate. No one knows that better than I as I sit here this Christmas season to say goodbye to my friends and employees at the store. The words I need would have to tell of the pride and joy I have in the years we have been friends and have worked together. They would have to tell of the troubles, of the triumphs we have had together in building this business. They would have to tell of a heart that is heavy at the thought of leaving all of the people and the places and the things I have grown up with and loved. But a heart that is, at the same time, filled with considerable pride of the honor bestowed on me and the challenge it presents. This new challenge then becomes a means by which I can express to you what is in my heart.

It is a double challenge: To our friendship and to the bettering of America. By my actions in my new job and by your actions as an American at home, let's both do our darndest to meet it. Let's keep on building as we have always built, with strength and faith, with love and compassion, with the goal constantly in mind: "What is good for all is good for us." If we promise to do that this Christmas, then this won't be a goodbye, for the things we have built our friendship on will endure wherever we are. Those things will keep us together.

So ends one chapter in my life and the beginning of another. What is this new chapter to bring? Twice in my life now I have torn myself away from my family and from the place where my roots grew deep. The first time was to go to war. Now, this time, it is to go to war again. Well, not war, maybe, but certainly to go and fight for the principles of the Republic I believe in, and the principles that built our country, that built our state, and that are the foundations upon which we have grown great.

The election victory was not entirely a surprise, because we knew that McFarland, carrying the weight of Truman's mistakes around his neck, would have a difficult time winning, particularly in view of the fact that I had spent nearly all of my life campaigning for this job, whether I realized it or not. My activities in the field of lecturing, photography, exploring, in the work of human relations, civic concern for children and the community, in my business, and my constant travels over the state, had without realizing it been building up a following of supporters who have now selected me to represent them. And when we add the mistakes of the Truman administration to the advantages that I had, maybe it was to be expected that I had a good chance to beat Mac. We predicted that we would win by six thousand votes. I believe the final count came to a little over sixty-five hundred, so we weren't far off.

CHAPTER 7

LEARNING HOW
WASHINGTON
WORKED

W*hen Barry Goldwater arrived in the U.S. Senate it was still
one of the world's most exclusive clubs with hidebound rules,
traditions, and customs. He was something of a rule breaker,
for rather than being seen and not heard during his freshman year, Goldwater entered the fray. As Goldwater later said, he was baffled and intimidated
by it all when he arrived and as he tried to figure out how the game was
played. Remaining totally silent was not for him. Yet he was intrigued by
what he could learn from listening and observing. He quickly noticed the
conservative and liberal divisions within each of the national parties and
noted their long-term implications. His journal for his first year in the Senate was irregular and became even more so with the passage of time, yet it
was sufficient to provide insights into his efforts both to learn the job and
observe the way that Washington worked and to share his observations.*

Journal Entry (January 1953)

After the election, I was tired and anxious to get away from the excitement, so Peggy and I went to our home in La Jolla, California for
several days and then to Los Angeles and then back home to be with
our children before we headed off to a vacation in New York. From
New York we traveled to Washington and then to Mexico City where
we attended the inauguration of President Adolfo Ruiz Cortines as the
guests of the Mexican government. While there, I was invited to attend
a joint session of the Mexican Congress, which I did. And during the

Barry and Peggy at home.

several days we were there, Peggy and I attended receptions and met many interesting people.

We were back home for a New Year's Eve party at my sister's and then the next day, my birthday, the forty-fourth, Peggy and Mun [my mother] and I flew east to Washington and a new life. We reached Washington about 11:30 PM and were met by my old friend, Congressman Porky Patton and his wife, Mary, from Tucson. Our rooms were ready for us at the Sheraton Hotel so we moved in.

The next day I went over to the Senate Office Building to meet Jim Dalrymple, my clerk, and to attend my first meeting with other Republican senators. It's the first time since 1948 and the second time in twenty years that the Republicans have had a majority in the Senate, and with that, we only have a majority of one. This was a very enlightening meeting during which I met all of my new colleagues and had an opportunity to hear great men of the Senate, and of the country, discuss the problems which would be coming up.

The next morning, January 3, 1953, at twelve o'clock, the Senate convened in the Senate chambers of the nation's Capitol Building, and there I was sworn in as a U.S. senator from Arizona. I had the very distinct honor of being escorted to the president's chair by the senior senator from Arizona, Carl Hayden.* I said to Carl: "I bet you

---

* *Goldwater had known Carl Hayden for years, as the senior senator was a family friend. Hayden had been in the Senate since 1927, and Goldwater's father and Uncle Morris had been early Hayden supporters.*

never thought you would escort a Republican down this aisle." He said, "Well, I never thought I'd live long enough." I was sworn in by Vice-President Alban Barkley. Following the ceremonies there was a very brief business session, and then we adjourned until Tuesday of the next week.

Journal Entry (February 1953)

I must truthfully say that these first weeks in my new post constituted a period of considerable physical and mental stress, as much as I can recall that I have ever gone through in my entire life time. It is exceedingly difficult for me to describe my sudden realization of the great responsibilities that rest on the shoulders of a senator. It was difficult for me to believe that this young man from Arizona had suddenly been placed with ninety-five other men in the position of making decisions that will mean peace or war, prosperity or depression, and decisions that will affect the lives of countless people, not only in this country but throughout the entire world. To say that I felt wholly inadequate to the task would be to understate my thoughts. I felt (and feel) like a person standing at the foot of a massive mountain, wanting to reach the summit but looking at the long, hard climb ahead with considerable trepidation and with the awareness that much more knowledge must be obtained before my steps will become sure or easy.

I have experienced great comfort in embarking on this voyage because Peggy has been with me and that I have met so many men in the Senate who, after all, are just regular fellows, not unlike the men I have grown up with who believe primarily in the future of America, who want peace and freedom, men who have assumed their high responsibilities without airs, and who in private are just regular guys. These men, with their friendly attitude and helpful suggestions, have paved the way with kindliness and friendship, and have made these few days between the swearing in ceremony and the real beginning of work a more pleasurable few days than they would have been had I been cast here alone and without the solace of their help and the comfort of the love of my wife.

I do hope I can keep making these recordings, so they can be transcribed for my children to read but I am afraid that, like all my efforts in the past the entries will peter out, the voice will run out, the desire might even fade after a while, but we'll start it and we'll see what happens. For it will be interesting to look back, read, and see how my mind changes and my concept of things changes during the coming six years.

For instance, we will be confronted in the session tomorrow with an attempt by Senator Anderson of New Mexico and others to change the rules of the Senate. Some senators want to do away with Rule 22, which allows the filibuster. Now I am, basically, against the filibuster, and I so stated in my campaign. I said that if the opportunity arose where I could vote against the filibuster, I would do so. Now I find that on the opening day, this bill, which was drawn up by the CIO, a labor organization I believe to be a little bit left of center, proposes not only to change this particular part of Rule 22, but in effect, throw all the rules open to entire changes, to changes which can be introduced by anybody, and I have the feeling tonight that while I am against the filibuster, that I am also against any organization other than the Senate telling the Senate how to conduct itself. I feel that the filibuster should be changed through the normal channels, by the introduction by some member of the Senate of a rule change, and that change is submitted to the rules committee, and the entire action of the rules committee voted on by the senators.

The filibuster strikes me as an undesirable thing in this modern age.* It is undesirable because, actually, the minority can rule the majority. But I find myself torn between two questions: Is it better to change this rule or modify this rule through normal standards which have been used for years and years and years, since the inception of the Senate in 1789, or should we take the suggestions made by Mr.

---

* In time, Goldwater would change his mind about the filibuster. He would later tell Steve Shadegg, "Experience has changed my opinion. The filibuster does waste time, but the basic concept of our Constitution is to protect minority rights, to make all citizens equal before the law. The filibuster is the court of last resort for a minority . . . it prevents the momentary majority from steamrolling over men of good conscience who hold an opposite view" (Barry M. Goldwater, With No Apologies [New York: William Morrow, 1979], 57).

Reuther of the CIO and other left-wing organizations and allow their word to become the ruling word of the Senate? I don't know.

In addition, there is my promise to the people of Arizona to vote against the filibuster, which is certainly prevailing on my conscience and my allegiance to the way things should be done bears also. I wonder how I will vote. I have sought advice from several men. I sought advice from God in church yesterday. I wasn't sure what I would do. But when this question was put to a vote, I voted to table the Anderson motion because as the debate developed, it was obvious that this was a constitutional question involving the continuity of the Senate. Or, in other words, the question is whether the Senate is a continuing body or not? After listening to the debate and studying the constitution, I became convinced that it is a continuing body.

I have received my committee assignments and they are certainly far from what I thought and hoped they would be. Being from Arizona and having spent my life in matters pertaining to irrigation and reclamation, land, forests, Indians and everything concerned with the Department of the Interior, I had asked for assignment on the Committee on Insular Affairs. Because I spent twenty-three years of my life in the Air Force Reserve and National Guard, as well as in the regular service, I had put as a second choice for the Armed Services Committee. A little matter of seniority popped up and since I don't have any I didn't get on either of those committees. Instead I find myself on the committee on Banking and Currency and on the committee on Labor and Public Welfare. Well, both committees have lots to do with the lives of everybody in Arizona, so we'll just see what happens. Actually, I am very happy with the committee selections and look forward to the work that will be coming before them.

Journal Entry (March 6, 1953)

This is March the 6th, some time since I made my last few notes. I resume them today because the day before yesterday two rather auspicious events took place in my life as a senator, and before I get too far away from them, I would like to make a record as I remember them. However, before we get to that, in the time which has intervened between the last recording and this one, I have learned something I think will be important here: to become more patient. A person like me, who has always hoped that things would be done the next day, suddenly finds himself in the position of realizing that here in Washington it does not work that way. They go through long processes of discussion and debate, argument, long process of delay, long process of red tape, if you please. Government does not operate as is done in business, nor do they work here even as they do in local or state governments. Much more is involved. There are more people we must listen to. There are laws, customs, and procedures to be adhered to. There are precedents. But most of all there is the political future of the persons involved on the committees or chairmen of committee.

While I am trying to learn to be patient, I find it exasperating. It is difficult to get used to the time that is wasted here, for it is a fact that much time is wasted. Nonetheless, this may be just fine. For I subscribe to what I heard someone say the other day: It isn't the laws that are passed here that help the country; it's the legislation that doesn't pass that really does the country more good.

On Lincoln's Birthday, the traditional Republican celebration where we extol the virtues of Abraham, and the virtues of our party bearing the long trunk, I was given a number of speaking assignments: Seattle and Alhambra, California. So I left here at five o'clock one evening and flew to Seattle over night. Peggy met me up there at five o'clock in the morning, and that evening I delivered a Lincoln Day address to Seattle Republicans in the Armory to a crowd of about a thousand people I would say. It was received about like all Lincoln Day speeches are, which was politely. Then we flew down to Los Angeles and I did the speaking engagement the next night in Alhambra. While it wasn't as large a crowd by any means, it was certainly a more enthusiastic crowd, and I felt better in the delivery of my speech as well as in the substance of it. Next day, we headed back to Phoenix and there we had a delightful Sunday with Doc Running, his kids and our kids all up on Canyon Lake. On Monday, I spent the day talking to constituents in Arizona, and this is the most refreshing thing I have done since coming to the Senate. So I renewed my vows to get back to my native state at least once every sixty days to do nothing but talk to people.

In Washington, you get stifled quickly, all bound up in customs. In Washington, we get the views of people who have fears. But you get out home in Arizona, out in the West where people see their government in a clear, cold light, and they can really tell you what is the matter with it, and what they want done about it. Believe me, their views are sound. I only wish that it were mandatory for Congress to adjourn every sixty days for a matter of a week so that all members might return to their homes.

After only a day in Arizona I returned to Washington, back to the salt mines. Committee work had started on Banking and Currency, and surprisingly, I am finding the work to be delightful. My business background and training is proving to be most valuable. . . . We haven't started work on the labor committee yet, but that comes up probably in two weeks. . . .

To get to the day before yesterday, which was my most auspicious day up to this time. Over a month ago, along with some twelve or thirteen other senators, I had lunch with President Eisenhower, but I had never met the president in the privacy of his office alone. But the day before yesterday, I had a meeting with President Eisenhower in the Oval Office at nine o'clock in the morning to deliver two of brother Bob's golf seats to him.* Bob had them made up for the president and his wife; on one seat was stamped "Ike" and on the other his wife's name "Mamie." He was very gracious and received them with great enthusiasm and said that he would use them. We passed a few small words of conversation, mostly about the cattle price situation, on which I assured him that the cattlemen of Arizona stood solidly behind Benson and his plan.

Later that morning in the Senate I thought, well, the time has come when I must make a speech. I have long felt that I would not feel at home on the floor of the Senate nor lose the embarrassed feeling that I have sitting there until I got up nerve enough to stand and expound on the floor of that Senate. Consequently, during the course of the day, I stood up and asked for the floor, got it, and gave my first speech. I have never in my life been hesitant about speaking before

---

* *Eisenhower, an avid but not very good golfer, would use these pole-like seats as a spectator.*

gatherings of any size on almost any subject with which I had any acquaintanceship, but in this place it is a lot different. Your words must be carefully chosen, your subject must be carefully chosen, the facts that you have must be carefully chosen and very thoroughly documented because there are ninety-six people sitting there who, among them, constitute experts on any subject which you care to mention. If you talk loosely or use facts that are not backed, you very quickly get called on them.

To say that my knees were rattling when I stood up would be to put it mildly. But I was confident that my words would float around in the eaves of the chamber, get briefly mixed up with the historic words of the great men who had spoken there before me, and be very quickly lost and forgotten. But they will not be forgotten by me, because that will be, as they say here, my maiden attempt, and now that it is over, I have a lot of the confidence in my ability to express myself in the future. Still, I plan to proceed from here very slowly, being careful to select the subjects I know something about, and waiting until I have a year or so under my belt before attempting any further major addresses with my floor appearances, other than helping in the general debate of subjects which are germane to my committees.

Journal Entry (March 12, 1953)

I am in my office. It is just about sundown. It's been a hot, muggy spring day, and as I look out to the northwest I can see the Washington Monument, and the low hanging clouds, and I am thinking about events that have transpired since I arrived here and what, if anything, I can begin to conclude from these experiences.

One thing giving me concern is an obvious lack of unity within the Republican Party. By this I don't mean lack of purpose rather a lack of unity along the lines that the Democratic Party displays so well in the Senate. They have discipline; we don't. We seem to lack aggressive, strong leadership willing to develop issues which are so clearly with us, and then bring them out on the floor. There is a lack of interest on the floor from the Republicans; there are very few members of our party on the floor during debate or during discussion. I don't know what it is. Perhaps it is the fact that we haven't been in power for twenty years and have forgotten the organization that is needed to get things done, and it's most important we get organized for next year, 1954. I am not concerned to the point where I am going to give up hope for this unity, because there is evidence that it is going to come, and I think that as the newness of our reacquired power wears off, we will get down to business.

The big thing that has happened here in a legislative way since the last time I talked into this dictating device was the Tidelands debate, which developed into a record breaking filibuster lasting some four and a half weeks. Because Peggy and the children are not with me this year, I am, therefore, one of the few unattached men, at least for the time being, so I volunteered my services for the night-time sessions of this debate. I was glad that I did because I got to hear a lot of it and I got to develop an idea in my own mind as to what this thing really was all about. In fact, I was there the night that Senator Wayne Morris of Oregon talked for twenty-two hours and some minutes. I remember that I went home at six in the morning and after taking a bath and changing my clothes, I returned to hear the finish of what is the longest speech in the history of the Senate, if it means anything. I personally would rather see a man spend more time thinking about what he is going to say than getting up and saying it for that length of time and accomplishing nothing.

Now there is a group of people in both parties that we like to refer to as New Dealers or Fair Dealers. They are neither regular Democrats nor regular Republicans, and we've got them in both parties. These are people who, by long association with the New Deal and the Fair Deal, have become inculcated with their ideas and principles to the point that they feel the federal government should have the power over everything, that the federal government should dominate the states, it should dominate business, it should control the economy and the unions and control the life of this country. I suspect that if I told any one of these men that, they would probably challenge me, but nevertheless, their actions speak louder than their thinking and in their expression. Now on the other side, you have members of both parties, particularly among the Southern Democrats, who believe in states rights and who believe that the federal government should be out of the state and local government picture entirely, and out of the affairs of business as well.

I sense here a realignment of Southern conservative Democrats with Democrats and Republicans of the West and Middle West. The New Deal and Fair Deal folks are coming from the eastern seaboard, and it is alarming to me to see how far they have gone. They are controlled by the dictates of the labor unions, the dictates of the stronger minority groups are felt in almost every decision they make, in almost every debate they enter. This thinking is a far cry from that of the Western senator and the Southern senator who believe in the free enterprise system, who believe in the freedom of the individual and the freedoms of the states. After only four months, I am beginning to see a cleavage that is new, but nevertheless, I think it is going to develop as one of the major issues in the future and that will be the federal government against the states and individuals, and it should be an interesting one to pursue.

Since my last report, I have been to Springfield, Illinois to speak to the Federation of Retailers; up in Maine to speak to the young Republicans; and I gave talks here to the Tubercular Society, the Furniture Dealers Association meeting and the National Women's Republican Clubs meeting. On March 23rd I will stop in Minneapolis for a speech on my way home to Arizona. This spring I will give the graduation address at my old school, Staunton Military Academy, and a few days later I will give the graduation speech at a luncheon for the School of Retailing at New York University. So I have been kept fairly busy on the speaking circuit, so to speak.

Journal Entry (Late December 1953)

Goldwater at this time purchased a small 185-horsepower Beechcraft Bonanza aircraft to fly back and forth between Arizona and Washington. Soon he would find that the air force made their jets available to senators, which cut his travel time even more.

My how time flies. It is now nearly the end of December, just a little under a week until Christmas, and the family has gathered here today in Washington prior to departing to Phoenix the day after tomorrow for the Christmas holidays. We'll all return on January 4th so the children can re-enter school and I can attend the opening of the second session of this 83rd Congress. It's been a long time since my last dictation about the happenings of this year, but I think I can remember vividly enough the important things to get them down in their order of importance to me. . . .

During the last two months of this first session, I engaged in several debates, most notable of which was the five-billion-dollar budget cut to the air force, and I know that the air force took a rather dim view of a former air force officer standing up to argue against them. At one point on the floor, I was openly challenged by Senator Stuart Symington of Missouri, who used to be the civilian head of the air forces at the Pentagon, who found it odd that an air force officer would want to cut the air force's appropriation. I reminded him that my first duty was to my country and my people and certainly not to the air force. I went on to support this cut, which went through. Now, I am pleased to say, after inspecting and watching the air force, that I feel we have a better and stronger air force than we did before, and the cut, instead of hurting them, made them work harder and as a result of that, we have something to show for it.

Just prior to the Fourth of July, during the appropriation hearings on foreign aid, I introduced an amendment on the portion of foreign aid which would give four hundred million dollars to France for their war in Indo-China. My amendment said that this money would be forthcoming only when France set a target date for the framing of a constitution and the establishment of independence for those states.* It seemed rather inconsistent to me, inconsistent certainly with the principles of this Republic, that we, who have fought so hard for freedom against Britain, would now be supporting openly a country like France with colonizing ambitions. My amendment caused quite a

---

* *Goldwater's amendment stated, "That no such expenditure shall be made until the Government of France gives satisfactory assurance to the President of the United States that an immediate declaration will be made to the people of the Associated states [of Cambodia, Laos, and Vietnam] setting a target date for the adoption of a constitution for such States, and for the establishment of their complete independence."*

commotion on the floor. The debate stretched on hour after hour, and all the time I knew, of course, that it didn't have a chance of passing, but as I say, it was a matter of principle and I wanted to introduce it, which I did. I did accept an amendment from Senator John Kennedy of Massachusetts, which, in effect, toned it down to practically no effect, and that was defeated; we only picked up seventeen votes.

I am not conceited enough, or should I say, I don't like to sound like I am conceited enough, to think that this action had anything to do with France's subsequent announcement that these states would be granted their freedom. But that has come about and now it only remains to be seen if France will keep her word. . . .

We received the tragic and dreadful news of the passing of Senator Bob Taft. I don't recall a time in history when a man like this was needed as badly as he was needed and is still needed today. While I did not support him in his candidacy for the presidency of the United States, nevertheless, I have always recognized his brilliance and leadership. And while we expected his death, the news of it came with a sobering shock and we realized that our work was made doubly difficult by his passing. He was the one man in the Senate who was able to control Eisenhower's wishes stemming from the president's lack of experience in politics, and prompted by the men who advise him, too many of whom have left wing tendencies. Bob would see to it that requests did not reach the Senate or the Congress when he knew they would be defeated, and he quietly guided the president's decisions wisely in all political matters. . . .

One thing developed during the first session, and it has become more evident in the months since, and that is the fact that the Republican Party does not have leadership at the top. The president has been very reluctant to assume such a leadership role. I am very hopeful that in the coming session he will do that, but through the past several months it has become more and more evident that he does not want to bother himself or indulge himself in the leadership that is necessary for this party.

In addition, the advice that he has been getting from his little circle of advisors seems to me to continue to be of the New Deal type. In fact, the question as the year ends is: What will the president's message indicate? Another New Deal type of program or a return to the principles of the Republic? And of course, I hope it is the latter. If we had wanted more of the New Deal, we would have been much wiser to have kept the old administration in because they were quite adept at ignoring the concept of the Constitution and giving away the people's money and taking away their rights and privileges. I don't know who these advisors can be. I don't have too much faith in Tom Dewey or in Sherman Adams, and no faith whatsoever in some of the men who were taken directly out of the New Deal gang and have been retained in high places in this government. These holdovers are effecting too many decisions and I am hopeful that they will go. A lot depends upon what message the president delivers to us next January, and I will refrain from making any more remarks until after that time so we can judge the course that he chooses down which the Republican Party will be asked to go.

At the present time, the forty-seven Republicans seem to be going in forty-seven directions. But, happily the forty-seven Democrats are doing pretty much the same thing, and they also lack leadership, with the exception of former President Truman and Adlai Stevenson, both of whom are heaping discredit upon the Democratic Party, so as a Republican, I hope they continue to be that party's leaders. But for the sake of America, I am hoping that the Democratic Party finds new, vigorous leadership and will allow it to develop.

Much has been said the last few months about the influence of Senator Joe McCarthy on the Republican Party, and here in Washington it has bordered on hysteria. As I have traveled out over the country, I find that the people are pretty much in accord with what Joe has been trying to do. Some don't agree with his methods, but almost as a whole, they want to get rid of communists in government and they recognize that the job will not be easy and that it might take the methods employed by McCarthy and his committee. Unfortunately, this whole matter of McCarthy was allowed to develop into a fight between the president and his Secretary of State John Foster Dulles and McCarthy. This was certainly encouraged by the New Deal press and the left wing columnists who kept saying: "Let's you and him fight." And that finally came about. I think that Joe realizes the danger of any further utterances and I am hopeful that his present quietness indicates a wise decision on his part to wait until January until we see what the program is going to be.

This whole thing of McCarthy is a stupid example of how American minds can be influenced by the press, by the left wing writings and by the New Deal chantings of the columnists and news commentators who hate McCarthy, in fact, who hate any Republican or conservative Democrats. I have learned some things in this year. I have learned that our fears in the West about people in this country wanting to circumvent the Constitution are certainly true. And I am just as fearful tonight as I was a year ago when I was heading to Washington that this could and might happen to this country. People here don't recognize rights of the states. Rather they laugh at them. The concept of government here is one of federal domination. It's one of federal operations doing everything. Now what remains to be seen is whether or not the Republican Party along with the conservative Democrats are going to go against this notion of the federal government doing everything. Members of Congress are so engrossed over international affairs, communism, the atom, and so forth, that they have lost sight of this basic fundamental concept of government that the power of the federal government stems from the states and the people, and not in the other direction. This is going to cause divisions in the party just as sure as I am talking, because those people on the eastern seaboard look beseechingly to the government for everything, while we in the West and the South want the government to look to us and stay away from us except in the fields that the Constitution says they should be of assistance to us.

I have learned too that you can't run government like you run a business. I believe you can put a lot of good business practices into the operation of committees and offices, but I don't think that the government as a whole, being the gigantic thing that it is, can be run along strict business concepts. Still, we can do a lot better than we have been doing. We don't have to spend the money that we have been spending. I think that we can balance the budget, but I think it is going to take a lot of hard work and a lot of guts to do it.

. . . My work on the Labor Committee has been most interesting, particularly working on the Taft-Hartley Act. I think every radical in the Democratic Party is on the committee—not to mention we have a sprinkling of such left wingers from our own party on it too—but they all appear to have a very fair attitude about the law, and look both at management's side and labor's side, but most importantly, the public's side. . . . There has been a big clamor about agriculture for the past six months, as the prices received by farmers have dropped about eight and a half to nine points since this administration took office. But that doesn't compare with the nearly eighteen points that they dropped prior to our coming in. The farmer wants everything. The farmer wants to be supported. He wants a guaranteed profit, which is against the free enterprise system. . . . I have been very proud of the cattle people of Arizona during this whole clamor for price supports on beef. They have, almost to a man, opposed it, wanting the government to stay out, wanting to operate their own businesses with the laws of supply and demand governing their actions and prices. It is refreshing to find Arizona cattlemen, and I'll say this of Arizona farmers as well, acting like real, solid American business people. It is refreshing because here in the east, the eastern senators and representatives think only of what can be given to people that might gain them votes, not what can be given to people that will insure the continuance of our American system of government and our American system of free enterprise.

I have been on several television shows, have been in sixteen states and in general have done my little bit towards furthering the Republican cause, but chiefly trying to explain what we have done, what's been accomplished, because we have made definite inroads into the problems which existed when we came here. . . . My pride in this job grows with the passing of every day, and the realization of its problems increases daily, and my desire to do a good job continues to grow. I recognize the limitations that I have, but I'll do what I can to overcome them and I think in the years to come, I will have the privilege of living through an interesting development of American history, that God willing and the American people helping, we'll find this country once again solidly on the paths that the Republic was founded on.

Congress adjourned a few days after Bob Taft's death and we all went our separate ways into the country to mend our fences and talk to the folks at home. I flew the Bonanza back out to Phoenix and made the return trip in one day, but it meant fifteen hours of flying in one day and I hereby solemnly state that I will never do that again. I'm not as young as I used to be.

CHAPTER 8

PLAYING ON THE NATIONAL STAGE: 1959–1963

G oldwater's first year in the Senate was devoted to learning the ways of Washington, but, as he reported, he increasingly found himself being invited to speak at events throughout the nation. His commonsense conservatism struck a responsive chord with his audiences, and his invitations to address other groups throughout the nation grew. The news media soon discovered the outspoken senator from Arizona whose blunt words and handsome image (often found climbing out of a jet fighter plane cockpit) made great copy. Goldwater's concerns about the lack of Republican Party leadership proved quite accurate, and in the 1954 midterm election the Republicans lost control of both the House and the Senate to the Democrats. In 1955 Senate Republican leaders selected their young and outspoken colleague—who had on a number of occasions even taken on President Eisenhower's positions—to head the Senate Republican Campaign Committee. As one Goldwater biographer noted, "The importance of this assignment to Goldwater's rise cannot be overemphasized."* This post gave him new stature and even greater press attention, and his prodigious fundraising for Senate GOP candidates gave him growing influence within the party. In 1958 Goldwater was reelected to the Senate in a rematch with Ernest McFarland, who had been elected Governor of Arizona since losing to Goldwater in 1952; Goldwater swamped McFarland, defeating him the second time with a plurality five times greater than his first. By 1959 leading

---

* See Robert Alan Goldberg, Barry Goldwater (New Haven, CT: Yale University Press, 1979), 109. Goldberg notes that Goldwater served "three two-year terms as campaign chair [of this committee], 1955–56, 1959–60, and 1961–62. During his tenure he traveled more than two hundred thousand miles, gave two thousand speeches, and visited nearly every state in the union" (110).

Senator Goldwater and President Eisenhower, at Eisenhower's Gettysburg farm, 1964.

conservatives within the Republican Party were seriously promoting Gold-water as presidential timber. They had a plan to get him nominated and elected. The principal mover behind this effort was the former dean of Notre Dame School of Law in South Bend, Indiana, Clarence Manion.

In the spring of 1959 Manion had visited with Senator Goldwater in Washington at which time he told him he planned to "carefully and cau-tiously" assemble a "National Committee of One Hundred" to draft the senator as the GOP's presidential nominee in 1960. Manion explained that this effort would be underwritten by a suggested autobiography of the sena-tor, which he was confident would raise hundreds of thousands of dollars. Goldwater was flattered but thought the idea absurd; he told Manion he wanted no part of it. Goldwater said he could not stop them from doing what they wished, but he did not want to encourage them. Goldwater was mildly interested, however, in the idea of doing a book.

By July of 1959 Manion's efforts were becoming well known among con-servatives within the Republican Party. One old friend of Goldwater, Clar-ence Budington Kelland, who was being solicited by Manion to assist in the effort warned his friend not to let Manion and his cohorts make him their "cat's paw." Kelland explained in a July 9, 1959, letter, "I am not astute enough quite to fathom what is behind this movement or the motives that inspire it; but I am old enough in politics and astute enough in party affairs to know that it can only result in failure and in some discredit or disadvantage to you." Kelland, who greatly admired Goldwater and thought one day he could be president, advised, "Do not let yourself be drawn into this scheme by these men who are my very dear but misguided friends."

Letter (July 13, 1959)

Goldwater's response to Bud Kelland.

Dear Bud:

I tried to get you back on the telephone but getting you by that medium is almost an impossibility as I have found after many years of effort. It seemed that nobody in New York had ever heard of the Nassau exchange, and I finally gave up in frustration, after half an hour trying.

To make what could be a long letter short, let me say I am in complete agreement with you and I have expressed this opinion not just to you but to everyone who has approached me on the subject, and I have publicly stated, time and time again, that I have no interest in the Presidency nor the Vice Presidency, and I am not seeking either of them. Manion . . . came to see me in my office and told me they wanted to form a group that would be ready, if the opportunity presented itself, to submit my name and I told them I was not the least bit interested in it, but I recognized that I could not stop them if they want to proceed. I am very hopeful that friends such as you and Gene Pulliam and others will be able to point up to Clarence that any action at this time, or at any time that would be of an open nature, would raise hell with my effectiveness, whatever there is of it, and I would much rather proceed as I have been doing—a Republican senator trying to put the Party back together.

I don't think he is getting very far with this movement, as I have had too many inquirers on it who agree with you and with me. Let me assure you, Bud, that under circumstances as they stand today, I feel that I not only could not get the nomination but that if I happened to get it, I could never be elected. I think the country might accept a Catholic, but I don't think they are ready to take a person who is Jewish, or half Jewish, and I wish you would keep that latter statement under your hat, but I am convinced of that.

Notes (July 29, 1959)

Before turning to the first notes that Goldwater would make regarding the book that would become The Conscience of a Conservative, *the book itself needs to be placed in context, because it would become a political classic and there remains considerable confusion as to who did what and how. One commentator, for example, later wrote, "The truth is that Goldwater had almost nothing to do with the book that made him famous and launched his national political career."* This is not correct.*

When flying west, Goldwater had jotted down his first thoughts for a book, which he though he might do with L. Brent Bozell, Jr., a young conservative writer who had written speeches for him in the past. Bozell had been William Buckley, Jr.'s debate partner at Yale, had married Buckley's sister Patricia, and had worked with Buckley on his new publication the National Review. *On this date, Goldwater dictated his first thoughts over the telephone to his secretary in Washington to give to Brent to start him thinking about the book project, which the senator would discuss with Bozell when he returned. These raw notes indicate that Goldwater had no clear vision of where he wanted the book to go, other than that it should somehow capture the emotions he felt about his country as he traveled it and about the everyday people who are the country and that the book should be as basic as our founding documents and speak to all Americans.*

How many times have I flown across our county? I cannot even estimate but I am always eager for the thrill, for with it goes many emotions, among them that physical one of being up there among the clouds or alone in the blue of Heaven, and the mental one being my problem

---

* *See John B. Judis, "The Man who Knew Too Little,"* Washington Post, *September 24, 1995, http://www.washingtonpost.com/wp-srv/style/longterm/books/reviews/ goldwater.htm.*

to get to the point I started for. I have always thought the spiritual feeling of seeing my America unrolled below me to be the strongest; the greenness of the valleys of California, the better known and loved beauties and canyons of Arizona; the Rockies, the flat Middle West, the streams and farms of the East, the hills that keep the East from the West. But in this emotion is the even stronger one wrapped up in the people who live in our country—the aircraft worker of California, the cowboy of my state, the miner in the Rockies, the farmer in Indiana, the businessman of the towns and cities, the doctor, lawyer, the automobile worker in Detroit, and the tobacco man of the South, the banker of New York and the professor in Princeton—what does he think of our country? This is what occurs to me as America unrolls as a gorgeous carpet beneath my flight. What is [the feeling of the American citizen as] he contemplates his responsibility to our country? Is it apathy or devotion, distrust or respect? Does he know that this freedom can only be kept by himself; that the answer of Franklin to the lady in Philadelphia, when asked what they had given our people, was "A Republic, if you can keep it," remains as important today as then? Does he know that Thomas Jefferson warned in the Declaration of Independence that "We are endowed by our Creator with certain inalienable rights" which is the great source of all we hold dear, of freedom, and that those words are the basis of man's search for sources of freedom through the ages? Does he know, as he sits in his comfortable home, the lights flickering across the now covered years, signaling his happiness to me above, that government cannot be the provider without being the master? Is he aware of the assessment of his freedom, his happiness—his own and his children's future—by those who, through intent or ignorance, are successfully hacking away at those vitals of freedom?

What, then, would I say to those who live in this land we love? Is there a difference between what I would say to the aircraft worker, the cowboy, the miner, the farmer, the businessman, the lawyer, the automobile worker, the tobacco man, the banker, the professor, or any man living in this land of ours? I don't think so. The words of our forefathers apply to all men, as do the words of this humble person whose love of country was born of a devoted mother, devoted to the

everlasting truths of faith in God's country and himself. This is what
I believe.

Letter (August 12, 1959)

*On August 12, 1959, Goldwater met with L. Brent Bozell, Jr., to discuss
the book project, and Goldwater memorialized their meeting in a letter later
that day. The book project did not get under way, however, until a publishing contract was signed several weeks later.*

Dear Brent:

As I recall this is the approximate discussion we had today relative
to the project:

We would open up with something along the lines that I suggested in the brief memorandum I wrote on the plane. Then, having recognized that the nefarious efforts of those opposed to our way
of life have been rather successful in cataloguing and pigeon-holing
[conservative] people in the last thirty years, we would start a series of
discussions with the people under various groups as people. We might
start with the aircraft worker, then go to the farmer, the businessman,
the professional man, the old, the young, and those who precede their
title of American with a hyphen, such as Spanish-American, etc.

Throughout this portion of the discussion we would treat gener-
ously the thought that the one hope and desire of all the people of
this country is freedom. We could point up in the summation of this
portion of the book the thought that all people today want this, and
wanting it they should, therefore, think primarily of the powers that
might threaten that freedom before they think of the material things
they can gain from it.

We would follow this section by a discussion of the powers that are
operating against freedom today, and in this we can take centralized
government, big labor, big business, high taxation, the agricultural
programs, etc., etc., and foreign policy.

I think the windup should be in the form of a recognition of the
lessons of history that have shown us that all of the above powers, operating either singly or together at one time, have lowered the morals
of the peoples of other countries to the point that internal collapse

resulted. The lesson to be learned is that we are in more danger of destroying ourselves from within than we are of being destroyed from without.

It was a pleasure having lunch with you. Let's repeat it often.

Letter (August 15, 1959)

In the following letter to Eugene Pulliam, Goldwater's friend who was the owner and publisher of the Arizona Republic *and* Arizona Gazette *(among other newspaper holdings), Goldwater describes why he has not totally killed the efforts of Manion to assemble a draft-Goldwater committee.*

Dear Gene:

Relative to your letter to Pat Manion of August 11th, I would like very much to discuss this with you when we can get together this Fall. I think that after our last meeting Pat understands fully my position in this, which coincides exactly with yours, namely, that any serious outward effort at this time to place my name in nomination would result in destroying whatever little usefulness I have to my country and to our party. The whole thing to me, if it is going to be, should be a matter of being prepared should a hole appear in the wall and through it we might run. I would violently oppose, for instance, the nomination of Rockefeller, as I believe that nomination would destroy good Republican senators and congressmen. I prefer Nixon and I am for him, but in the event something occurs that prevents his getting it and Rockefeller is suggested, then we must be ready to fight.

Letter (September 7, 1959)

The other person that Goldwater wanted to speak with was Stephen Shadegg, who had most recently served again as Goldwater's campaign manager in the 1958 reelection campaign. This letter to Shadegg needs a bit of context to explain what followed. During his vacation in December 1959, Goldwater met with the editorial board of the Los Angeles Times, *who had been so impressed with the senator that they asked that he write a regular column. Goldwater explained to the* Times *that he was not a writer, not to mention that the demands on his time in the senate commanded his full attention. But it was agreed that Senator Goldwater would select a writer and the topics and begin the column in January 1960. Shadegg would do the writing (and as the correspondence shows, Goldwater suggested topics and reviewed the columns before publication). But before the column had begun, Goldwater wanted Shadegg's reaction to the book project.*

Dear Steve:

I have been offered a contract by a publisher (a reputable one) to write a book of some twenty thousand words that would express my feelings toward our country. Of course, my complete incapacity to be an author is well known to everybody, so before I even attempt a thing like this, I would like to have your suggestions.

The other day flying to California I jotted down the words that are contained with this attachment—(see notes of July 29, 1959)—with the thought that this might be a way to get at the whole matter. In discussing this with another friend, I suggested this approach.

What do you think of this whole thing? Does it make sense? Could I keep the subject interesting for twenty-thousand words, pointing out that there is no difference between the aircraft worker, the cowboy, the businessman, etc., etc., insofar as human nature is concerned and insofar as his loyalty and his feelings are concerned.

If you have any ideas, let me know about them.

Shadegg would have some ideas. Indeed, had he not taken on the weekly column with the senator for the Los Angeles Times *and other newspapers, he would no doubt have been far more involved in the book project. As Shadegg later reported, when he and Goldwater spoke about the book, the senator said, "We are not writing a platform for the Republican Party, but what I hope we can do is awaken the American people to a realization of how far we have moved from the old constitutional concepts toward the welfare state." Shadegg later wrote that Goldwater sent him a copy of the manuscript "as rapidly as the chapters were completed," and he suggested a few minor changes only. Shadegg added that commentators have claimed—both praised and criticized—Shadegg as the book's author. Shadegg explained that "Goldwater was kind enough to say that some of the speeches I had* *written formed a basis for the book. The truth is, Goldwater and Bozell deserve full credit for the writing."**

Letter (January 20, 1960)

In late January 1960, Goldwater began working with Shadegg on their column (which from time to time Goldwater openly acknowledged it was a collaborative effort, notwithstanding the Goldwater byline). Shadegg would draft a number of columns and send them to Washington for the senator's approval. The letter to Shadegg that follows is typical of their working relationship, which was sometimes handled by mail and other times by telephone. In the remainder of this chapter we have included a few additional letters to Shadegg of a similar nature about the column because the senator was far more involved with the column's content than he would later be credited.

Dear Steve:

Monday I appeared at the Columbia University School of Journalism in New York and for some two hours answered questions. This experience, added to the others that I have had during my time [in the Senate], with colleges and high schools, convinces me that as we put our thoughts on paper we should constantly resort to a definition of conservatism and an exposition of the neo-liberalism of today.

In going back through the original columns, while it is abundantly clear to those of us who understand it, I think we must repeat it and repeat it, keeping in mind that our objective is to take the onus from the word "Conservative" and to make it acceptable to people who shy away from it today. We can do this in a philosophical way, then we can attach the definitions and expositions to the concrete subjects of legislation. We should constantly bring out in this respect that the liberals of today, using the approach of belly-politics and social welfare, are in effect doing precisely those things that our Constitution and our free enterprise system was designed to prevent.

---

* *See Stephen Shadegg,* What Happened to Goldwater? The Inside Story of the 1964 Republican Campaign *(New York: Holt, Rinehart and Winston, 1965), 28.* The Conscience of a Conservative *was published in March 1960, and it would become a best seller.*

I have been reading John Locke again and I think in getting back to these basic sources for inspiration and finding it there can also be a vehicle to be used with the readers of the column by reiterating time and again the basic beliefs and principles of our founding fathers. I cannot stress this too much, because in my contacts with people I am always amazed to find that a careful study and a decent explanation of my conservative position melts away any rabid opposition that would be there were I merely to attack liberalism without explaining conservatism. On the other hand, I find that when I describe the phony liberalism of today as it really is and what its net results will be, many liberals, while not openly saying so, express with their eyes and their subsequent statements and questions a sudden concern for a position that they thought was a proper one.

To this end, I am having a book sent to you, *Conservatives and Radicals*, by Dr. McGovern of Northwestern University. I am also sending you a set of five books, entitled, *Essays on Liberty*. I think if you will read the McGovern book, which is short, that you could bolster your arguments relative to the phony liberal of today. These books have been ordered but it will be about two weeks before you receive them.

Very shortly we will get into the arguments on Federal Aid to Education, and I think all of those points that we used in the debate with [Arizona Democratic Congressman Morris] Udall should be reiterated in the column. Here, for instance, is something I came across of John Stuart Mill, who is a self-defined philosophical radical, who instigated many reforms in England including women suffrage. He is quoted as saying in his "Essay on Liberty" that:

> The objections which are urged with reason against state education do not apply to the enforcement of education but to the state's taking upon itself to direct that education, which is a totally different thing. That the whole or any large part of the education of the people should be in state hands, I go as far as anyone in deprecating. All that has been said of the importance of individuality or character, and diversity in opinions and modes of conduct, involves diversity of education. A general state education is a mere contrivance for molding people to be exactly like

one another, and as the mold in which it casts them is that which pleases the predominant power in the government, whether this be a monarch, a priesthood, an aristocracy, or the majority of the existing generation, in proportion as it is efficient and successful, it establishes a despotism over the mind, leading by natural tendency to one over the body. An education established and controlled by the state should only exist, if it exists at all, as one among many competing experiments, carried on for the purpose of example and stimulus, to keep the others up to a certain standard of excellence.

That type of expression from radicals can be extremely valuable to our purpose if we can just find them and I will increase my reading in the effort to trace down words that can, in effect, be tossed back in their faces.

In closing then, reiterate time and again the modern liberal's purpose of denying freedom versus the conservative's purpose of preserving freedom with both philosophical and legislative examples.

Letter (May 13, 1960)

Clarence Manion's—known as either Dean Manion or Pat—efforts continued based on the hope that New York Governor Nelson Rockefeller would cause a split within the Republican Party that might prevent Richard Nixon from obtaining the 1960 GOP nomination. From time to time Goldwater encountered others who thought that he should be vice president, which had no appeal to Goldwater at this stage of his career, as he explained to retired Brigadier General Bonner Fellers in the following letter. Fellers would join the Manion effort and become treasurer of "Americans for Goldwater."

Dear Bonner:

It was good to see you on the street the other morning. . . . One of the most effective ways to silence a man is to make him vice president, and I honestly feel that I can be of better service as a senator than as a vice president, or for that matter as president. Therefore, I have not been encouraging movements for the vice presidency, but I know they are in process and I can't tell free people what they have to do.

Letter (June 13, 1960)

Notwithstanding his unhappiness with Richard Nixon as the Republican Party's candidate, Goldwater explained to Manion that the split that they might take advantage of was becoming increasingly unlikely.*

Dear Pat:

The Rockefeller blow-up last week has solidified people behind Nixon that I never thought could have been counted on, but I have just returned from a rather extended trip through the South and the West, and I am firmly of that conviction. I am also convinced that any action now to change the picture would be futile and that the original presumption is still as solid as when it was made, namely, that Rockefeller would have to provide the split.

Frankly, unless some magic enters into this, it cannot occur. His own state, as of today, will not back him, and he has absolutely no strength within the Republican Party out across America. If he had six months to overcome this weakness, I might say it could be done, but I sincerely doubt that anything could be done in that direction as of now, what with Nixon's overwhelming support from state delegations.

I think, therefore, that any action on your part or on the part of any group in my behalf, or anyone else's behalf, would be doomed to failure and could contribute more harm than good to the Conservative cause which needs more articulation—not less.

If Rockefeller can create this interest to the point that something must be done about it, then the original plans would still hold good, but to try to force them without his causing it would not work. I think we should meet very shortly and discuss this and some questions relative to the book and how it is going.

Goldwater was correct, and Nixon would win the nomination but lose the election to Senator John F. Kennedy of Massachusetts, a longtime friend of Goldwater. Because Goldwater knew Kennedy well, his strengths and weaknesses, his victory caused Goldwater to begin thinking seriously of himself as the man who could defeat Kennedy in 1964. Just as he had

---

* *See Part IV: Nixon and Watergate.*

started running for the Senate long before he formally campaigned, Gold-
water began running for the presidency, traveling the country on behalf of
Republican causes and candidates.

Journal Entry (January 20, 1961)

Today marked the end of the Eisenhower administration and the
advent of what Jack Kennedy calls the New Frontier. It may well be
the end of the last chance to save our Republic, for it is apparent that
under Dwight Eisenhower we did not erase the errors of the preceding
years of drifting from the path of the Republic. I think back to 1953
and the inauguration of that year. A bright day with a new leader
under whose leadership Americans looked forward to a renewal of the
eternal truths of our Republic. I sit tonight eight years later and wonder
what happened to that glorious opportunity and challenge. It cannot be
said that we failed completely, but we did not succeed in answering either

Photograph taken by Barry at the White House, with JFK's written note: "For
Barry Goldwater—Whom I urge to follow the career for which he has shown such
talent—photography!—from his friend—John Kennedy."

to more than a small degree. Eisenhower did understand the fundamentals and he believed in them. He spoke of them with conviction but his legislative proposals did not, with few exceptions, convince Americans that those fundamentals are our best course.

Eisenhower spoke of challenge and sacrifice as Jack Kennedy did today when he said, "Do not ask what our country can do for you, but rather what can you do for your country." How often I had heard Eisenhower say this during the past eight years, and then how often, just as Jack Kennedy will, he has sent down legislation asking that the country do something for the people they could well do for themselves. This has been a strange period. We have never had a more personally popular president. I doubt that there has been, or that there ever will be, a man who had such a great chance for leadership yet who did so little about it. When he used his appeal, as in the case of the Landrum-Griffin bill [which deals with the internal affairs of unions], he got what was good for the people, in spite of a Congress that was nearly two-to-one against his Party, not forgetting that the members of his own Party in the Congress were divided on this issue. In the main, though, he refused to do what would have been best for the country. This does not mean that he was not good for us; he was. He showed dignity and kindness; he was respected. The country stayed at peace, but in the staying, a lot of respect for us fell away. We had a good economy, but toward the end some of the bad chickens that were hatched during the Roosevelt and Truman days began to come home to roost. The power of the unions, inflation, the plight of gold, the louder voices of diminishing minorities—these chickens should have been destroyed before reaching the roost, and it was our failure to do this that will haunt the memory of these past eight years. The test will come to be recognized as "what we did for our country" and we will discover that we spent too much time seeking the answer in material approaches to "what can the country do for me."

Journal Entry (March 26, 1961)

Last Saturday I spent a delightful hour with ex-president Herbert Hoover. These rare occasions when I find him in New York are among the most stimulating experiences of my life, for here is a mind that grows younger and if not keener as the years wear their grooves on the vault that contains it. To find him engaged in writing another book is not startling, as he is now, but it is thrilling to learn that his newest will probe the mysteries of who was responsible for the cold war. That Hoover places the blame on FDR and his childlike faith in Stalin who was backed up by the ever conniving British is not surprising nor is it for the moment for my purposes important.

What is important on this March day is that we are in a cold war and our foreign policy, while noticing this fact has only sporadically met its challenge head on. There have been a few times—Berlin, Lebanon, Suez, and perhaps Guatemala and the Formosan Straits—where we have met it, and in every case where we have done so we have been the victor. But too often we have been indifferent and even cowardly at times as we have yielded, submitted and simply lost. Now at this late date in World War IV—we lost World War III when we sold out at Teheran and Yalta and Korea—our new president, John Kennedy, has thankfully made a direct and strong statement regarding our position on Laos, and revived hope that this country has recognized its responsibility as a world leader. I pray that Kennedy's strong words will be followed by strong action.

If we as a nation continue to maintain the policy of containment, if we live with the status quo which means to vacillate or compromise or retreat on the far-flung battlefields of the cold war, we will make it impossible for communism not to succeed. For us to stand in fear of Russia and Red China will guarantee the eventual loss of our Republic. Today is a day of hope, then, that a new president, a young one, has the guts to do what has not been done with sufficient consistency, which is to stand up to the enemy wherever he is. Free men do not seek war, but neither are they afraid of that eventuality if that be the price of freedom.

Recollection (April 15, 1961)

Goldwater would soon find that he was disappointed with Kennedy's actions on the world stage. Goldwater prepared an extensive journal entry on his visit to the Kennedy White House shortly after the disastrous Bay of Pigs invasion, but it is no longer in his papers. Nonetheless, he recalled and recounted the incident on March 18, 1977, in a much shorter dictation for Steve Shadegg.

I had an unusual experience with President Kennedy that happened on the day of the Bay of Pigs invasion, April 15, 1961. I was strapping myself in an F-86 fighter at Andrews Air Force Base to fly to Phoenix when an air force sergeant climbed up on the wing of my plane and told me I was wanted at the White House. That is identical with a command, so I got out of the airplane, took off my flight suit, put on my civilian clothes, drove into town, went to the White House, and was immediately ushered into the Oval Office, where I was asked to sit down and offered Kennedy's rocking chair, which had been prescribed by our same doctor. In a brief moment Kennedy came into the Oval Office smoking a short Cheroot, and I'll never forget how he stood there in front of me with the little cigar hanging from his lips, and me rocking back and forth in his chair, and we just looked at each other for a moment until he said, "So you want this fucking job?"

We laughed about it, and then got down to business when he explained what happened at the Bay of Pigs and, believe me, that mess was entirely his fault.* It was not the fault of the CIA, the army, the air force, the Joint Chiefs of Staff or anyone else. President Kennedy had it within his power while we were sitting in that room to call in the navy fighters from carriers to take care of the situation, but he didn't do it, and that I think established beyond any question his rather gutless character as it applied to making decisions that amounted to something in protecting the national security of our own country.

---

* *The Bay of Pigs invasion had been initially planned by the Eisenhower Administration, which had commenced training Cubans living in the United States to invade Cuba and overpower the regime of Fidel Castro. The planned invasion was to follow a bombing attack on Castro's air force, and it went forward on the assumption that Cubans would be sympathetic to the invaders and assist in overthrowing Castro. The site of the ground invasion changed several times, and once the invasion of the Bay of Pigs was under way and conspicuously failing, the Kennedy White House refused to provide air cover for the invaders, who were slaughtered by Castro's troops. The entire undertaking was a colossal failure, making the United States appear not only an aggressor but a pathetically weak one.*

Later with the so-called Cuban missile crisis, about which I was completely briefed and here was another case of the Kennedy administration lying. While we were being briefed in supposedly absolute and complete secrecy, Kennedy's Secretary of Defense, Mr. Robert McNamara, who did more to destroy American military strength than any man we've had in our history, was telling the same story in public and on television. The truth of the matter is that there were not as many missiles in Cuba as they suggested. There were enough to have done some damage to some of our communities but not enough to warrant the big fate-of-our-nation crisis that was made of it. Kennedy called up reserve after reserve, in fact, I went on two weeks active duty for that period, and if we had put another plane on Florida the whole damn peninsula would have sunk. It was another indication that Kennedy overreacted, and was not thinking soundly.

Journal Entry (Undated)

As I sit here reminiscing, it occurs to me that I have not put down a most interesting occurrence during the time of the debate on censure of Joe McCarthy in the U.S. Senate. The Senate was very reluctant to go through with this resolution of censure because they feared, as I did, the establishment of a dangerous precedent. One day I was approached by a member of the Democratic Party, whose name I will not reveal, with the suggestion that if I could get McCarthy to sign one or both letters of apology—one to Senator Hendrickson of New Jersey and the other to Senator Watkins of Utah—that he could assure me that the Democratic side would lose complete interest in censure and that the censure attempt would die. Joe McCarthy, however, was in the hospital at this time as a result of falling on a glass table in Milwaukee the week before and infecting his arm. He was on the thirteenth floor, as I recall, at the Bethesda Naval Hospital, and his lawyer, Eddy Williams and I attempted to get the letters signed by him in that place. It was at night and no one was supposed to go in Joe's room. However, we did and at one point Joe actually had the pen in his hand to sign one of the letters. For reasons I'll never know, he suddenly threw down the pen and very emphatically told us that he would never apologize. He became quite upset and rang for his nurse who came and on seeing us there, called for the Commandant of the Hospital. He came immediately and was threatening to have us placed under arrest when I told him who I was, introduced the attorney, and related to him in a rather vague way our mission. He told us to go and not to bother Joe anymore so we left. This was how close we came to being successful in having the censure proceedings stopped, and had Joe cooperated, this would have come about, and he could have continued his useful service to the U.S. Senate.*

Journal Entry (May 27, 1961)

It is now our national goal to place a man on the moon at the end of this decade. We must spend and spend more and more at home and around the globe as a matter of sacrifice. . . . These are the words from our president. Words, words, words punctuated by dollars, dollars and more dollars. What has happened to the threat of communism? Has the groveling before the blackmail demands of Castro been swept under the rug? Not one concrete statement from the president on what we propose to do to stop the communists' daily advance and

---

* After he left the Senate, Goldwater explained to Jack Casserly why he had voted against Joe McCarthy's censure by the Senate. He knew how ill McCarthy was, so he had quietly tried to help by getting New York's Francis Cardinal Spellman to talk to McCarthy, which he did, but it didn't help. "Knowing his illness—and many senators did—I wanted to offer McCarthy mercy," Goldwater said. "Some disagreed with that. But I said you pray for people who need the prayers—good or bad. If the Lord is willing to give him a hand, let us give him a hand. Other senators said he deserved the same as he'd given others, I didn't blame them for that view. However, I believe a man can be put out of action without a public lynching. The mood among Senate liberals was to lynch McCarthy. I was probably wrong in defending him, but I didn't want any part of it, especially in the respectful setting of the Senate. It was ruthless behavior in both cases. After the censure, Joe drank himself to death." Goldwater added, "I've never spoken this candidly about McCarthy before because it's not part of my character to harpoon people. However, McCarthy was a very important part of our generation, good and bad. And that's just how I felt about him—very mixed feelings. He recognized the communist menace, as many of us did, and conservatives recognize him for that. But McCarthy went overboard in his investigations because of his inability to handle power and alcohol. Joe became enamored of power. That's what really made him sick and changed him into such a drinker. He was off in an unreal world of self-importance and self-indulgence. Joe re-taught us a very old lesson: Power corrupts" (Barry M. Goldwater with Jack Casserly, Goldwater [New York: Doubleday, 1988], 130).

make them the defender and not the attacker. Are we to find [the answer in] disarmament pacts with an enemy whose philosophy has never known honor? Will the striped pants in Geneva slow the day of the enemy's success? I don't think so. It never has. What must be done now is to attempt a new estimate of the situation and in clear language state what we, as conservatives, see what is wrong and what we would propose as a workable solution.*

Letter (September 5, 1961)

To Stephen Shadegg.

Dear Steve:

. . . I don't believe there's any coincidence at all that the growing interest in conservatism has come at a time when Americans are waking up to the fact that the enemy is not only at our gate but has moved in among us. The fact that this enemy has accomplished these things has caused the American mind to seek out the truisms of communism, and this has extended his thinking into the outer world.

Here is where we move into the second effort that is becoming increasingly evident here and is reflected in the column of Ralph de Toledano, which I enclose in the book. This column is self-explaining of the thought that I have advanced as this second effort as you will readily see when you read it. Also, the column from the *Wall Street Journal* goes a bit further and deeper into this than does Ralph, but I think that we can take these two efforts and expound them into a series of columns and I suggest that this would be a proper time to do it what with the public's attention focused on the apparent fact that communism has made greater gains than any American dared realize and that at the same time the Administration appears to be making every effort to hush this fact up.

The long years of failure of American socialism are being recognized by the American people, and I suggest that you will find this

---

* *Goldwater would do exactly what he suggested in this entry, and in 1962 he published his second book,* Why Not Victory? A Fresh Look at American Foreign Policy.

reflected in the refusal of the House of Representatives to go along with federal aid to education or the "back-door" spending scheme of the president for foreign aid or even for the total amounts that he asked for in this measure. Ever since the Fourth of July recess, there has been a decided change in the House of Representatives occasioned without a doubt by their visit home where they had a chance to learn firsthand the feeling of their constituencies. I think this could be woven into a series of columns that I am suggesting because it will give backup to the courage of those men, who in a sizeable majority, have begun to say "no" to the wild-eyed schemes of Kennedy. These schemes, of course, are but a perpetuation of the New Deal philosophies first expounded by Roosevelt and now that Americans see their failure, they are demanding their end and the House is reacting; however, the Senate has not yet felt the heat and they continue in their careless way to vote for his proposals.

Journal Entry (September 9, 1961)

The session has now dragged into the ninth month with not much prospect of its ending before another two or three weeks. It has been a lack luster session with the cards stacked perfectly against conservative government and fiscal responsibility. Majority Leader Mike Mansfield of Montana has proven to be a good and sensible leader—a mild mannered gentleman easy to get along with—it is a shame he is a Democrat.

The Senate's work so far has been oriented further to the left than any Senate in our history and if it had not been for the Fourth of July recess taken by the House, the country would now be encumbered with additional dangerous legislation and more irresponsible spending. The visit home by the House members brought them face to face with the distrust of the New Frontier held by the people. When they returned it was with a new attitude that they approached the bills before them. Their actions have stopped federal aid to education, back door spending and unlimited appropriations for foreign aid, plus other accomplishments indicating their understanding of the mood of the American people. This is encouraging for when the members of the Senate get some exposure during recess, I have a feeling that this mad rush to socialism will slow down beginning with the new session next January.

Earlier this week, on Tuesday (the 5th), I drove to Gettysburg to visit Ike at his farm. He had invited me in a nice letter written in reply to my invitation to him to address the Arizona Bar next year. I have never seen him looking as well as he did or seem to enjoy his life as much as he appears to be doing. Retirement has done well by him but it has not dulled his ability to be caustic—and he had plenty to say about the failures on the part of JFK. Eisenhower is deeply worried over the ineptness, or as he said, "the dangerous ineptness" of Kennedy's foreign policy. Eisenhower was particularly critical at JFK's abandonment of the full plan [Eisenhower's administration had developed] on Cuba, his cowardly failure to provide air cover and sea back up. Of course, Ike's intimate knowledge of Berlin gave his criticism of Kennedy's action in this area a special ring of authority when he said that we are in real trouble there—a point he emphasized again and again.

As the conversation moved into the domestic fields, it centered on Kennedy's fiscal irresponsibility. Eisenhower feels that Kennedy does not understand our economy even though its needs have been made crystal clear. Ike said he expects that Kennedy's manipulative attempt to control inflation by having all apparent increases in income swell the tax coffers, with the hope this move could bring down the deadly deficit we face, was an unrealistic approach. I told General Eisenhower that in a paralleling move, I expect JFK to seek full emergency powers to regulate the economy by Christmas; that many signs point to this, and the stage has been set by threats against the steel companies made by Democrat members of the Senate and by the president himself. This jaw-boning is not the answer.

Of course, our conversation eventually got around to politics and when we entered that avenue, I was pleasantly surprised. Ever since our Republican Party in Arizona adopted a Statement of Principles and abandoned the outmoded policy platform, we have been gaining strength. I tried, without success at the 1960 Convention, to interest the Platform Committee to do the same for the National Party, but could not convince them. So I was most pleased to learn from Eisenhower himself that he felt this was a wise approach. In fact, he said he had presented such an idea in a recent issue of the *Saturday Evening Post* which, somehow, I missed. I told him of my feelings and now with the power of his authority and prestige in agreement maybe we could prevail upon our Party to state its principles. I told him that it is my plan to discuss this theme from now on in Republican speeches across the country and to stress it from time to time in my syndicated column.

Journal Entry (September 11, 1961)

At the moment I am in a Boeing 707 over the central part of Kansas, heading toward home and Peggy. With me are the memories of the past few days: A wonderful meeting in Springfield on Tuesday, another big one in Canton, Ohio the next night followed by a very successful "sales meeting" in Chicago by Paul Fannin, which can only redound to the good of Arizona. That was followed by a good Republican meeting in Kankakee and the next day another real good one in Pontiac. Last night at the Dirksen Dinner in Chicago, Eisenhower spoke and by all standards a fine success. Ike was at his best, which he always is when he is speaking his mind and not parroting from others. He tore into JFK on foreign policy and domestic matters making it abundantly clear that he thinks the country is in trouble both here and abroad and from my travels I have the distinct impression that Americans agree with his assessment.

Journal Entry (September 21, 1961)

In the air again and this time heading back to Washington for the wind up of an excessively long session that was devoid of constructive legislation. I have just completed two productive days in the Los Angeles area where I found people deeply troubled by the indecision of JFK regarding communism. Unfortunately, Richard Nixon is sitting around peeking at his cards in his game of solitaire.

1962

Letter (June 27, 1962)

Goldwater was loyal to a fault with his friends, and he expected the same loyalty in return. As he would explain more fully in a journal entry, he was surprised when Shadegg used the friendship to the point of abuse. In this letter, Goldwater confronts Shadegg about the unexpected announcement of Shadegg's Senate campaign, of which Goldwater, the top elected Republican in Arizona, was not advised.

Dear Steve:

No matter what happens in this campaign, it will have no effect on the friendship I have always felt for you.

Let's review the whole situation, and I think from it you can have a better understanding of your own position. You and I discussed on several occasions the advisability of not opposing [Arizona's senior Democratic senator Carl] Hayden for a variety of reasons I will not list here, and when we went into the County Chairmen's meeting, I believe in February, held at the Westward Ho, we were in fairly close agreement that we would not encourage opposition. This was discussed by the County Chairmen, after the point was raised by me and, you will recall, they were unanimous in their disapproval of my suggestion. You then discussed the problem of money and made the decision as state chairman that there would be no money available for a senatorial race. At that time [Arizona Congressman] Sam Steiger told us that Evan Mecham was considering running and that he, Sam, was encouraging this. No formal decision was reached at that meeting for, as I recall it, no votes were taken on any matter, except a poll prepared by you, the results of which, I believe were announced at a later date.

Subsequent to that meeting Ev Mecham came to my house one Sunday morning to advise me that he was going to run for the Senate, and we had a long and thorough discussion of the problems involved. I am sure I told you of this meeting in complete detail.

Now, let's jump up to the fund-raising dinners held in Phoenix and Tucson. During that three-day period you, Harry [Rosenzweig], Bob

[Goldwater], Paul [Fannin], John [Rhodes] and myself were together a good deal of the time and engaged in intimate discussions about Party problems. I remember distinctly discussing the senatorial race at least three different times, but at no time during these discussions did you make any reference to any desire or thought on your part of entering the primary. I do recall that you threatened to resign as state chairman, but knowing the strain you were under, we laughed you out of it. In a telephone conversation with you held the day I returned to Washington from these meetings the matter of the primary came up and I mentioned to you John Haugh's and Dick Kleindienst's interest in it. Later you phoned me to tell me that you were going to enter the race. Frankly, I was quite surprised, because one does not take such an important step as this without thorough consultation with close political advisors and friends. There are many things that should have been talked about such as the effect on the Party in this crucial year of your leaving the chairmanship, the job of replacing you, the effect of your earlier decision not to spend money on this race and the impact your entry would have on the Party structure.

I recite this rather lengthy history to you to point out that there are grounds for people in the Party to be concerned about your actions, but I believe you can defend yourself against those by reminding them that it was your own decision and it was a decision that you have, as anyone else, every right to make.

If you are accused again of not inviting some individual to the strategy meetings, you can just remind the individual that these meetings were started in 1950 during the first Pyle campaign and have been held at indefinite intervals ever since.

If I were to boil down this whole question, I would say that the surprise element is the root of any unfavorable reactions you might be receiving and I think you would have to agree that would be expected, particularly when there was ample opportunity to talk this whole matter over with people very close to you, personally and politically, just a few days prior to your decision.

In closing let me reiterate my opening remarks. I have found nothing more valuable in this world than friendship and my friendship for you can certainly survive the rigors of politics.

Letter (July 5, 1962)

This letter to Congressman William E. Miller of New York, chairman of the Republican National Committee and later Goldwater's vice presidential running mate in 1964, is typical of Goldwater's constant concern about the well-being of the Republican Party.

Dear Bill:

On Saturday General Eisenhower was host to a gathering of Republicans at his farm. During the course of his remarks, according to the press accounts, he cited the need for unity in our Party. With this I am in complete accord and for years I have been urging this action whenever I have spoken with Republican groups.

Imagine, then, my dismay on reading the Sunday *New York Herald Tribune* to learn that the Saturday meeting was a prelude to setting up an organization in Washington to duplicate what the National Committee is doing.

Most of those named as leaders of this new group contributed to the divisive tactics of the 1960 campaign when long-time and experienced Republican Party leaders were shunted aside, ignored and embarrassed. In this list also will be found those who were responsible, in large part, for policies of the Eisenhower Administration which ran counter to the traditional principles of the Republican Party and the counsel of regular Party leaders.

In other words, these are the same people who caused most of our present Party troubles. It is unthinkable that they should be given another opportunity to lead us down the path to political destruction.

We already have a National Committee. Where is there unity in two groups working the same field? How can unity exist when this outside organization competes with the functions of the National Committee? This can lead to the same kind of confusion and distrust which cost us the presidency in 1960, and it should be resisted by you and all Republican leaders.

This Party needs workers in the main tent, not in the side show, so let the people who will work for unity be welcomed into the framework of the Republican Party. There are millions of disenfranchised Democrats who will vote for Republicans, but they are not going to be influenced by an organization whose purpose, as I see it, is to shun the regular Republican channels for purposes that are not clear at this moment but which can contribute to weakening a major Party. Let's be done with these splinter groups. Let's all join hands and work through and with the Party to insure sanity in government and progress in our country and the world.

Journal Entry (Early September 1962)

These entries are included, for they are typical of the grind of being on the road constantly and show how at times this began to get to Goldwater. Nonetheless, he continued to do it for many years to come, finding a few hours of relaxation in the travel itself. Goldwater is clearly working to win friends, as he is also taking the pulse of the nation for his own possible bid for the presidency.

Maybe it's old age but it is the first time in a rather long career of "hiking the hustings" that I feel tired, like the nose cone of a rocket after reentry worn-down from the heat and a lot of the protective paint peeled off. I must appraise this past weekend—which was a long one—for it may mark the last one of these "county fair" type events that I'll do.

Last Thursday, the 30th of August, I drove to Pikesville, Maryland, for a dinner for Fife Symington, Jr.—it was, in my opinion, a success for some 1,300 people showed up to pay him their respects. It was well planned and well carried out and if the launching can be any basis of judgment, Fife will be elected to the House.* There arrived the usual period of handshaking and autographing which was cut short by Fife's invitation to visit his home for a drink. What was promised as a ten minute drive stretched into twenty so after two drinks in his attractive home it was a wild drive to the airport to catch the flight to Alaska, where I was headed to assist the election effort of the Republicans.

The first day in Alaska was spent mostly on a helicopter visit to the oil fields. This is important to Alaska as she badly needs new sources of income. It is a state that in many ways reminds me of Arizona in

---

* *Fife, III, Fife, Jr.'s son, later became the governor of Arizona.*

my youth. Wide open, with a great variety of geography and challenge on every turn. Wages are fantastically high as is the cost of living. To grow, capital must come to this new state, not to mention guts and imagination—the same factors which have built Arizona. Late in the evening I met with some of the more substantial businessmen to ask for money for the party and the results were not too encouraging. Later, in a meeting with the candidates, I got a good indication of what I suspected: there are a number of dedicated, hard working and serious candidates but no party organization or political savvy. This, of course, can be corrected and when I return to Washington I intend to locate a "pro" to send to them to help them out. In Alaska, as I have found in many other states at this time, there is no evidence of Democratic organizations, just the slick professionals from the labor unions, who are keeping the Democrats together. After meeting with the candidates, I went to a well attended reception at a local club where I must have shaken six hundred hands. This was encouraging.

On Saturday, a chartered F-27 took forty of us to Fairbanks, where a chilly 35 degrees greeted us along with an enthusiastic crowd; some three hundred people gathered in the high school gym for a political discussion followed by lunch in the jam-packed Elks Club. The interest here was inspiring and I dare say if it can be maintained until Election Day we will do well in that area. Then back to Anchorage and a fund raising dinner at the same club I visited the night before, but this time the crowd was at least seven hundred people. This was because of the efforts of young Republicans who are battling the odds of apathy and Democratic strength.

On Sunday evening, the Senate candidate, Ted Stevens, and I departed for Juneau. Along the way the pilot deviated from course so we could see the majesty of British Columbia's mountains and glaciers. This was truly beautiful and awesome; it whetted my desire to return some day for a closer and longer look. Juneau is a unique little town tucked snugly into the bottom of a canyon. It is also the state's capital and therefore a bastion of Democrats. In spite of this fact, and not to mention that it was Sunday, an encouraging turnout of some 150 people greeted our arrival. In Juneau we had a good session, but I departed Alaska knowing that the battle will be hard and the need for better organizations very obvious. But I also left with the recognition that there is a good group of dedicated young people who can with their zeal do a lot to overcome the odds they face.*

Sunday night was spent in Seattle and I departed for Portland on Monday. This was my second visit to this city this year and the enthusiasm continues to mount. A press conference was followed by a refreshing luncheon at Bishop Jim Carmen's house. Jim is now the Bishop of Oregon and one of the finest men I have ever known. We discussed Steve Shadegg at some length and I was not surprised to discover that our estimation of him is the same. Now that I have mentioned Shadegg's name I might as well record the difficult time he has caused me this summer. In June, without any consultation and with no warning whatsoever, Steve announced he was running for the Senate in the Republican primary. Evan Mecham was already in the race, after a long discussion with me for I had no knowledge of Steve's intentions.

With Steve's being the state chairman and my campaign manager twice people naturally believe I have approved his candidacy, given our long and close personal and professional friendship. However, given my earlier conversation with Mecham, I felt I must make a declaration of neutrality, which was sincerely and honestly done. But Steve has continued to "use me" and I fear that it may cause a split in the Party which may reflect on the efforts of other Republican candidates. Steve has done his best, working through our mutual friends, that regardless of my announced hands off policy, he has been trying to get my unqualified support, which has been a disappointing experience. It is disappointing because I have never before had a friend use me as Steve has. I like winners and I play to win at all times but never have I known anyone quite like Steve, who will use anything or anybody to advance his cause regardless of what that use may do to his friends and in this case, his Party. As I said, the experience has been disappointing but illuminating for I do not intend to be twice fooled.

The meeting Monday afternoon at Lewis & Clark stadium was attended by about five thousand who were most vocal in their response to candidates, particularly [Sigfrid Benson] Unander who

---

* *Republican candidate Ted Stevens would not be elected to the U.S. Senate until 1966; he has won reelection every six years since serving in the 90th through the 110th Congresses.*

now, I believe, has a better than good chance of unseating Wayne Morse.* Being left to my own desires after the rally I visited Tuttle in the hospital; he is very ill but is reported to be on the mend. He has been exceedingly helpful to me ever since my joining the Senate and his advice and help is missed.**

Tuesday morning I was picked up and flown to Pascoe, Washington, in a Cessna 220 where we had a lunch followed by a rally in the high school gym. I continue to be amazed and encouraged by the growing percentage of young people in the audiences. This I must add is being commented on by all Republican speakers wherever they appear. It indicates an awareness of the dangers of the New Frontier and uneasiness over JFK's very apparent inability to lead. I am further encouraged by the way these young people are moving into key slots in the Party machinery across the country. It can only rebound in a revitalized Party and a strong rebirth of conservatism in our country. It comes as other great changes have come, at a time when the country is in real and serious need—God has never forsaken us and I know He never will.

In the South this resurgence of the young is so great that I feel we may well win in South Carolina and there is an outside chance in Alabama. In fact, at the candidates' school held in Washington early this summer I met some 155 candidates for the House and Senate only five of whom appeared to be over fifty. I am of the definite opinion that we will take the House in November and make good gains, say four or five seats, in the Senate. The concern in the country over the proposals of the New Frontier, the fuzzy headed group who surround the president and the president's lack of leadership plus the historic gains of the "out" party in off years all bear heavily but decisively on this opinion.

Journal Entry (September 23, 1962)

It is Sunday night the 23rd of September and again I am on an airplane bound for Washington. My convictions are more certain than

---

* *Sig Unander failed to unseat Wayne Morse.*
** *This is a reference to Holmes Tuttle, a wealthy Southern California businessman who could be counted on to support Republican candidates and causes.*

ever that this mood I find myself now cannot be kept up. Not just because of physical reasons, which I must admit would be the least defensible one for my health is good, but I feel I am getting too "edgy" with people—too short—and I cannot allow that to continue. Also Barry's leaving home this coming week to accept a job in Los Angeles brings home suddenly that Be-Nun-I-Kin [our home] is now for the first time without children and Peggy will be alone and I know she will not enjoy this. It must come to every home sometime, the emptying, but it does not come easily, for the empty rooms are the same as empty hearts.

After going through his brutal schedule, he noted, "Well, I am not physically tired but there must be another way and I am looking for it."

Journal Entry (October 27, 1962)

In this entry, Goldwater states that just as he predicted earlier, President Kennedy would have to do something about Cuba because of the problems his failed Bay of Pigs invasion had caused. Goldwater believes that what became the Cuban Missile Crisis was provoked by the Kennedy White House for political reasons shortly before the midterm elections in 1962, where the Democrats were about to take a beating.

Some time in early September I made a notation that President Kennedy would start to campaign around the country and in short order discover that his Democratic colleagues were in trouble, and in trouble because of his indecision on Cuba. I said further in my comments that he would, sometime around October 15th, move into Cuba. He has not done that, but he has pulled what I think is a very cute political maneuver, in that he has made all of the noises of rattling the saber about Cuba in an effort to convince the American people that he is firm. I think that it is a political gesture and that only.

What effect it will have on the elections in another week is very difficult to say, but I do think in some of the close elections, involving chairmen of committees, like Senator Hayden in Arizona, the argument of not changing horses in a crisis might bear some fruit. On the other hand, he has made the position of many of his Democratic colleagues untenable, those who have spoken out against strong action in Cuba, going so far as to call those who want such action war-mongers and wanting to bring on nuclear war.

This could be very decisive in states like Colorado, Pennsylvania, Oregon, Utah and others where the Democrats really have now had the limbs sawed out from under them. That this has been a political move by Kennedy there is no question in my mind, because for the past two years, my air reserve squadron has been briefed weekly on the military build-up in Cuba, and I am sure this same information must be available to the president and the Security Council, and we have often openly wondered why something wasn't being done about it.

It is my contention that as the president ventured forth from Washington, he immediately began to get reaction from his Democratic candidates that Cuba was raising hell for them and, coupled with this, were the boos and general expressions of disrespect and discontent with the president's actions that he found in Connecticut and Chicago. His coming back to Washington was not because of a cold; it was because of the fact that he knew that Cuba had to be stopped as an issue and he took the steps he has taken.

I have, for the past several days, been attempting to get Chairman Miller to agree to a joint statement between Congressman Wilson of the House Republican Campaign Committee, himself, and me [as chairman of the Senate Republican Campaign Committee] calling for the immediate dismissal of [United Nations Ambassador] Stevenson, [Ambassador at Large Chester] Bowles, and the others, who have been advocating the soft policy toward Cuba and Russia. Up until now, I have not had much success because it is quite evident to me that as soon as some suggestion is made in this direction, Miller gets in touch with Eisenhower, and Eisenhower, being the rather indecisive fellow that he is, has advocated against this. But I am hopeful that Miller will be able to stand up from other pressures in the coming week and we can come up with some kind of forceful statement.

There is something as phony as a three-dollar bill about this whole Cuban Missile Crisis thing as President Kennedy has now presented it. For example, two Russian ships have sailed into Havana harbor loaded with oil. Now, oil is as valuable to a military operation as blood is to a person's living, and I think this should be questioned. Kennedy now has enough military personnel stationed on Florida to damn near sink that state, and I have a hunch that before the election, he will either invade Cuba, or there will be strategic bombing missions on the missile sites. This is a thought that I will not make publicly, but which I want to record, and that is, that there is a deal already working between Kennedy and Khrushchev along the lines of "let me get tough; then you get tough; and between the toughness we can work out a deal on Berlin and Cuba." If this is attempted, I don't think the American people will buy it, and I don't have much faith, frankly, in the president's ability to stand up under crisis. Possibly he can do it by himself, but not as long as he is listening to the people that surround him.

Journal Entry (October 30, 1962)

This is Tuesday, October 30th, and just one week from about this time the polls will begin to close in the Eastern part of the nation and as the sun progresses towards the other side of the Pacific they will close all over this country. It is too early to say what will happen. It is too early to say what President Kennedy's now obvious political gesture regarding Cuba will have on these elections. . . .

Kennedy has now promised to never invade Cuba and in my opinion this is giving the communists one of their greatest victories in their race for world power that they have enjoyed to date. I issued the following statement on this, warning about making Castro's communism a permanent fixture in the Western Hemisphere: "It should not be forgotten in our belief that tensions have been eased through a Soviet promise to dismantle Cuban missile bases, that such action would merely return us to the status quo that existed before the build up began," I said in my public statement. "But if we give a firm pledge never to invade Cuba in return for such Soviet action, the Communists will have won an important victory." I also called for Kennedy to get rid of the soft on communism advisers. . . .

With the political situation in Arizona, I must say that this has been an unusual experience; because I am sort of in the position of "I am damned if it happens and damned if it doesn't." Mecham now seems to have a chance against Hayden but his followers curse me hourly because I am not nursing him at every minute in the campaign. If he loses, I am certain to lose the backing of those people who hold that feeling. On the other hand, if Hayden loses, I am bound to lose the backing of those people who would feel that my backing of

Mecham has been instrumental in beating Hayden. . . . But be that as it may we just have to see what will happen and take things in stride.

Hayden won reelection. The Democrats retained control of the House and Senate, and Goldwater would spend 1963 preparing to run for the presidency against Jack Kennedy. Robert F. Kennedy, Jr., the president's nephew, later recalled his uncle's respect for Goldwater. JFK was looking forward to a run against his friend Goldwater for president in 1964. "At the time of his death, Uncle Jack had told his family that he wanted to engage in a series of forums with Goldwater in every region of the country modeled on the Lincoln-Douglas debates," Robert Kennedy, Jr., explained. "The contest would be a clash of ideas, without the meanness and personal attacks that mar so many political disputes." Goldwater was interested in this race until November 22, 1963, the day Kennedy was assassinated in Dallas. Not only was Kennedy killed that day, but so was the prospect of Goldwater becoming president. Before that time, national polls and national magazines saw a viable contest between Goldwater and Kennedy. When the nation recovered from the shock, it did not require sophisticated political analysis to know that the country was not going to be interested in three presidents in four years. Long after Kennedy's passing, Goldwater shared his assessment of the Kennedy presidency.

Notes (March 18, 1977)

In my humble opinion, Jack Kennedy would have been a good but not a great president if he had lived and finished his term. He would have been a popular president because he was admired and liked by a lot of the younger people, probably a lot of the older people too. I say this because he was a man that I liked and I liked him very much. He was a friend. But he was not the caliber of man to be a great president of this country. When we met during the Bay of Pigs, and on other occasions, I had looked forward to running against him with all the enthusiasm that I could muster. In fact, he and I had talked about it. We talked about the possibility of staging an old-fashioned cross-country, Lincoln-Douglas type debate on the issues of the day without any Madison Avenue, without any makeup or phoniness, just the two of us traveling around in the same airplane, stopping and debating,

Senator Goldwater with President Johnson.

and going on to the next stop and doing it again on another issue. But when Jack Kennedy was assassinated it ended that dream. In fact, it ended my dream and desire of running for president and I announced that I would not run. I was compelled to change my mind by the young people of America, particularly the Young Republicans who professed to be conservatives and who were, and so I finally agreed at my home in Arizona a few days before Christmas 1963 with my right foot in a plaster cast to take on Lyndon Johnson, even though I knew at that time there was no way he could be beaten. Of course, Johnson was elected, not so much that I was his opposition but because the country was not ready for three presidents in two and a half years. Lyndon Johnson was not a good president. He never could have been a good president; he was not honest enough to be a good president, although some very good legislation passed under his administration that probably should have been passed long before. Don't get me started on that s.o.b. and his weaknesses, his dangerousness, and his exploitation of others.

When Goldwater ran for president he did not run for reelection to his Senate seat, which by state law he could have done; he felt it was not right to do so, unlike LBJ who ran for the vice presidency and the Senate four years before. His term in the Senate ended in early January 1965, and he was out of office.

PART III

AFTER THE 1964 PRESIDENTIAL RACE

CHAPTER 9

SETTING THE RECORD STRAIGHT

G oldwater wrote letters to those assisting him during the 1964 race, but he was so busy during the campaign that he made no effort to record his thoughts. As will be shown, he considered a book based on notes he made after the campaign, but those have been lost, and his advisers counseled him against such a book.* Clearly, Goldwater had not been prepared for the viciousness of the campaign Lyndon Johnson waged against him nor the false and ugly portrait the national media would create of him. His feeling about the campaign—as it was proceeding—was reflected in a passing letter to his daughter Joanne after he won the California primary.

REACTIONS TO THE NEWS MEDIA AND LBJ'S TACTICS

Letter (June 4, 1964)

Dear Joanne:

The California campaign is over and we now face some fifteen state conventions to determine where we are going in the National Convention in San Francisco in July. I could comment at great length on what I think you learned from that campaign in California, but I will resist the temptation and only comment to this extent that if you

---

* The 1964 campaign and election has been recounted in a number of works by both insiders and those with access to insiders, including Stephen Shadegg's What Happened to Goldwater? The Inside Story of the 1964 Republican Campaign (1965), Theodore H. White's The Making of the President—1964 (1965), and J. William Middendorf II's A Glorious Disaster: Barry Goldwater's Presidential Campaign and the Origins of the Conservative Movement (2006).

some time feel the urge to get into politics, and I don't say no to this urge, that you will reflect upon the dishonesty experienced in that campaign, to guide you away from any such activity.

One is elected by one's positions, and if he tries to be something other than what he is, in the long run, disaster befalls him. People are not elected to office because of a pretty face, or curly hair, or a youthful appearance. The deep and the real thing is what do you stand for—and having taken a stand, will you stay with it.

Goldwater easily won the GOP nomination at the 1964 Republican National Convention in San Francisco. The win was engineered through hard work and the genius of F. Clifton White, a political scientist who strategized for years how to accomplish a quiet coup in which the conservatives within the Republican Party might take control. Many, including Goldwater himself, were unhappy when conservatives attending the convention booed Governor Nelson Rockefeller when they did not want to hear what he had to say. Rockefeller, however, baited them knowing it would make the right wing of the party look bad, which was fine with him. As the moderates and liberals in the Republican Party lost control, they attacked Goldwater and his supporters, declaring them radical extremists and in doing so providing Lyndon Johnson all he needed to make the same claims against his opponent.

The most memorable moment of the 1964 convention came at its end during Goldwater's acceptance speech at the Cow Palace Convention Center. The campaign against Goldwater was evident from the moment one approached the convention hall. As former National Review *editor Jeffery Hart explained, "A billboard in lights across for the Cow Palace set the tone. Goldwater's slogan had been, 'In your heart, you know he's right.' In lights against the sky the billboard read: IN YOUR GUTS, YOU KNOW HE'S NUTS." Hart continued, "Then there were Goldwater's never-to-be-forgotten words. . . . They represented his fury at being smeared as an 'extremist'—that is a Bircher, or worse. He roared, 'I would remind you that extremism in defense of liberty is not vice! And let me remind you also that moderation in pursuit of justice is no virtue.'"**

---

* *Jeffery Hart,* The Making of the American Conservative Mind: National Review and Its Times *(Wilmington, DL: ISI Books, 2007), 158.*

Goldwater lost to President Lyndon Johnson by a vote of 43,126,506 to 25,176,799, which translated to Johnson winning 61 percent of the total vote versus Goldwater's 39 percent. Goldwater had carried Arizona plus five Southern states: Alabama, Georgia, Louisiana, Mississippi, and South Carolina. Goldwater had never believed he could win in 1964, even when Kennedy was still alive, but he believed that he could further the cause of conservatism if he could come within 5 percent of Kennedy—and he might position himself to be a nominee who could win. The gentlemanly contest he had once envisioned with Jack Kennedy was not possible with Lyndon Johnson who played to win by any means fair or foul. When Johnson ran his now famous television commercial of the little girl picking petals from a daisy, counting down to a suggested nuclear holocaust that Goldwater might cause if elected, the senator called Johnson and demanded he withdraw it along with the tactics that were implemented by Johnson's young White House aide Bill Moyers. Goldwater later told Jack Casserly, not in bitterness but rather in disgust, his feelings about Moyers, which we mention here because Moyers's refusal to talk to Goldwater about his actions years after the fact are inexplicable. Goldwater, who was not a man to hold a grudge, did develop one of his few political grudges largely because Moyers refused to discuss these matters with him.

Over the years, I've watched Moyers appear on CBS News and the Public Broadcasting Service. He has lectured us on truth, a fairer and finer America. He portrays himself as an honorable, decent American. Every time I see him, I get sick to my stomach and want to throw up. . . . I tried to speak with Moyers. . . . He declined to return about a half dozen calls.*

George Reedy, Moyers's successor as White House press secretary and a working reporter who had been covering the Senate for years, later told Goldwater that he had no tolerance for Moyers's dirty tricks operation and confirmed to Goldwater that Johnson and Moyers had a spy within the Goldwater campaign operation who kept the White House informed of every planned move. Reedy said, "I felt this espionage operation was silliness

---

* *See Barry Goldwater with Jack Casserly,* Goldwater *(New York: Doubleday, 1988), 200.*

because we had the race won. However, some around the White House rev-
eled in dirty tricks. I was out of step with them. That was one of the major
reasons why LBJ and I drifted apart. I really like Barry Goldwater. He has
always been a decent, honorable man." Goldwater refused to go to the gutter
to respond to Johnson's attacks on his character. (In fact, Goldwater refused
to employ dirty politics in any of his campaigns.) As he later told Casserly,
he had a number of opportunities to play in kind during the 1964 race, like
when LBJ's chief of staff was arrested in the men's room of the YMCA a few
blocks from the White House for disorderly conduct (engaging in homosexual
activity). Goldwater explained,

We knew about the arrest within two days. LBJ also was told of the
arrest but remained silent, so I said nothing. The *Chicago Tribune* and
Cincinnati Enquirer learned of the story but decided not to publish
it. The *Washington Star* called the White House about the incident
on Tuesday; and Jenkins immediately left his office. Abe Fortas and
Clark Clifford, two intimates of Johnson, immediately called at the
Star and asked the editors to kill the story. Reports of the affair were
now all over Washington as Fortas and Clifford made the rounds of
news offices to suppress the damaging disclosure. Finally, seven full
days after the incident occurred, the story broke.

My staff saw the incident as a political windfall. Jenkins had been
arrested previously on a similar charge, yet he had continued to work
as Johnson's top White House confidant [raising national security
issues, since he was subject to blackmail]. . . . Reporters pestered me
for a reaction to the Jenkins story. I said nothing, nor was I going
to make an issue of the incident. We would separate Barry Goldwater from Lyndon Johnson on this matter. I told no one what I was
thinking except [my campaign manager, Dennis] Kitchel. He was to
pass the word to everyone on our staff to say nothing—no comment
whatsoever. . . . Meantime, the White House anxiously awaited what
we were going to say about the matter. It drove them crazy when I
refused comment. Here was the guy they were painting as a cowboy
who shot from the hip, the Scrooge who would put the penniless on
the street with no Social Security, the maniac who would blow us and
our little children into the next kingdom in a nuclear Armageddon. If

he would kill a million men and women, why wouldn't he destroy one individual? Why was the extremist pursuing moderation? . . . It was a sad time for Jenkins' wife and children, and I was not about to add to their private sorrow.*

Statement (November 1964)

In a press conference following the concession of his defeat by President Johnson, Goldwater was asked if he thought the press had treated him unfairly during the campaign. His response only hints at his feelings, but unlike Richard Nixon who had thrown a tantrum at the podium two years earlier when losing his bid to become governor of California, Goldwater was rather matter-of-fact about it.

I'd never seen or heard in my life, such vitriolic—un-based attacks on one man as had been directed to me. Sometimes, they didn't spell it out. But "coward—uneducated—ungentlemanly—bigot" and all those things. I've never in my life seen such inflammatory language as has been used by some men who know better. . . . I think these people should, frankly, hang their heads in shame. Because I think they've made the fourth estate a rather sad, sorry mess.**

Notwithstanding his statement immediately following the race, Goldwater was not bitter about his experience in the 1964 campaign and soon was telling reporters how much he enjoyed the forced retirement and being with his wife again. As they sat on the hillside in the shade of their Arizona home, he told Washington Post *reporter David Broder that he and Peggy would sit "watching the sunset, and occasionally humming to ourselves, 'Hail to the Chief.'" He declared he was "too old to go back to work and too young to get out of politics." He quietly told his friends that he was thinking about running for the Senate in 1968 when he was sure the aging Carl Hayden would (and did) resign. Meanwhile, he had unfinished business. He opened an office in the basement of the Goldwaters's store with his Washington secretary Judy Rooney (who later married Eisenhower's nephew Earl yet remained Goldwater's private secretary, as Earl did his aide, until*

---

* *See Goldwater with Jack Casserly,* Goldwater, *203–4.*
** *See "Mr. Conservative: Goldwater On Goldwater," HBO (2007).*

he retired). Mail poured into his office, particularly speaking engagement requests. Rooney reported it was as if he had not left the Senate. He was every bit as busy and in demand, and the speaking circuit gave him a chance to earn money far in excess of his Senate salary while continuing his missionary work for conservatism.

But there was one matter that had occurred during the 1964 campaign that Goldwater was not prepared to walk away from. No incident in the 1964 race had troubled Goldwater more than the vicious attack by Ralph Ginzburg in his publication FACT magazine. In the September–October 1964 issue of FACT, described as a "special issue on the mind of Barry Goldwater," the headline cover screamed "1,189 Psychiatrists Say Goldwater is Psychologically Unfit to be President." The magazine claimed that it had undertaken a "national poll" of psychiatrists and that 1,189 of those polled had said that Goldwater was not psychologically fit to be president; only 657 thought that he was. In addition to the poll, based on nothing more than newspaper and television knowledge of Goldwater, was an article written by Ginzburg entitled "Goldwater: The Man and the Menace."

Ginzburg set out to smear Goldwater as a lunatic and did not let a lack of evidence preclude him from doing so. Aside from taking issue with Goldwater's political positions (which he distorted), the article accompanying the purported poll made one false claim after another, such as asserting that Goldwater was "uneasy about his masculinity" and that he suffered from "intense anxiety about his manhood, anxiety that was aggravated by his work in a ladies' department store. It concluded that he was "sadistic" based on such practical jokes as his purportedly having shipped live mice through the store's pneumatic tube system to the secretarial pool. It asserted he was "anti-Semitic" and denied his Jewish heritage, that he was "a man who obviously identified with a masculine mother rather than an effeminate father," and that he was hostile toward his son Barry, Jr.

To support the claim that Goldwater was paranoid, Ginzburg stated that Goldwater had suffered from "two nervous breakdowns," and on that fact alone, "Big Business . . . would refuse to appoint him to a high corporate post, and the Military . . . would deny him access to top-security material." Ginzburg claimed that "many people around Goldwater think he needs a psychiatrist—probably not because they realize how sick he is—but because of the daily symptoms of hostility he manifests." Ginzburg reported that only "during the convention in San Francisco . . . did his aides begin to realize how paranoid he was." To further bolster his claim, Ginzburg quoted—or appeared to quote—from a number of books, magazines, and news articles about Senator Goldwater.

Another section of the special issue of the magazine purported to quote from psychiatrists who had responded to the questionnaire accompanying the poll question: "Do you believe Barry Goldwater is psychologically fit to serve as president of the United States?" FACT claimed that (mostly unnamed) psychiatrists had responded to the poll questions with statements like those set forth below:

> *"In allowing you to quote me, which I do, I rely on the protection of Goldwater's defeat at the polls in November; for if Goldwater wins the Presidency, both you and I will be among the first into the concentration camps."*
>
> *"Basically, I feel he has a narcissistic character disorder with not too latent paranoid elements."*
>
> *"I believe Goldwater has the same pathological make-up as Hitler, Castro, Stalin, and other known schizophrenic leaders."*
>
> *"[Goldwater is] mentally unbalanced. He is totally unfit for public office and a menace to society."*
>
> *"Mr. Goldwater could not get life insurance without a rider for mental illness."*
>
> *"[Goldwater is] a man of low character, a coward, weak, insecure, confused . . . sick, down deep into his structure."*
>
> *"[Goldwater is] grossly psychotic . . . a mass-murderer at heart and a suicide. He is amoral and immoral. A dangerous lunatic!"*

GOLDWATER VS. GINZBURG

Goldwater hired the Washington lawyer—later a federal judge—Roger Robb to take legal action against Ginzburg. Robb, a seasoned political observer, after studying the FACT magazine reported to Goldwater, "It is probably the most outrageous libel that I have ever seen." Robb advised Goldwater that given the fact that he was a public official it would not be an easy case to win, for under the control law of New York Times v. Sullivan they would have to prove that Ginzburg published with "actual malice"—meaning he knew the defamatory statements were false or he acted with total disregard to whether they were true or false. Ginzburg, of course, would claim he believed the statements to be all true.

Robb also provided Goldwater information about the man who had defamed him. Ginzburg had recently been convicted of violating the federal obscenity law for sending obscene publications through the mail, namely Eros *magazine, "The Housewife's Handbook on Selective Promiscuity," and a newsletter called* Liaison. *Robb further warned Goldwater about the high cost of such a lawsuit. At minimum he estimated it would cost twenty-five thousand dollars. (In fact, it would cost three times that amount, which, adjusted for inflation, would today cost about a half-million dollars.) Notwithstanding the negatives (cost and opening himself up to questioning about his entire life), Goldwater filed his lawsuit in September 1966. The case went to trial in May 1968. Set forth in the pages that follow are excerpts of testimony that are not only "Pure Goldwater"—they are under oath. The case was tried in the U.S. District Court for the Southern District of New York before Judge Harold Tyler. Goldwater was on the witness stand for three days. (In fact, his testimony runs over 731 pages of trial transcript and exceeds 150,000 words; we have selected small portions that we believe to be informative.)*

Testimony (May 6, 1968)

BARRY MORRIS GOLDWATER, the plaintiff, called as a witness on his own behalf, being first duly sworn, testified as follows:

DIRECT EXAMINATION BY MR. ROBB:

Q: You are the plaintiff in this case, just for the record?

A: I am.

Q: Where do you live, Senator?

A: My home is in Scottsdale, Arizona.

Q: How long have you lived there?

A: All of my life, fifty-nine years.

Q: You were born in 1909?

A: That is right.

Q: How long has your family lived in Arizona?

A: My grandfather came in 1860.

Q: How did your grandfather happen to come there? Do you know?

A: Well, my grandfather was a Polish Jew and when the Russians ran the Jews out of Poland his family was sent out. There were twenty-two of them in that family. They went all over the world. He went to England. There he married my grandmother and moved to California in about 1850 and stayed in California for about ten years, and then moved to Arizona in 1860.

Q: What did he do in Arizona?

A: Well, he started out hauling merchandise in a wagon, he and his brother, and they would sell the merchandise to the gold miners, and then he later ran a store and a pool-hall and a liquor store. My grandmother was a dressmaker.

Q: Finally did he establish a store called Goldwaters?

A: Yes, it had the name Goldwater in it. It was established in 1860 and has had the name ever since.

Q: Is it still there?

A: It is there, but we no longer operate it.

Q: Senator, tell us, if you would, about your education.

A: Well, I was educated in the public schools of Phoenix. I went one year to the Phoenix High School, four years to the Staunton Military Academy in Virginia, and one year to the University of Arizona.

Q: That brings us up to when?

A: Education-wise?

Q: Yes, sir. What date?

A: That was 1929. I left school at the end of my freshman year.

Q: What else happened in 1929 that had some bearing on that?

A: Well, my father died in March of 1929 and I just didn't go back to school when the term ended.

Q: What was your father doing at that time?

A: My father was running the store and I argued with my mother, that I felt I could better learn the business starting at the bottom working up than I could in school, and she finally agreed with me. I stayed home.

Goldwater explained his start at the store, first helping the janitor and then working his way up to chairman of the board before going on active military duty. He ran the store for some fourteen years and described it for the New York jurors as "a small Saks Fifth Avenue or Bergdorf-Goodman . . . a high-priced specialty store serving both women and men." He described his thirty-seven years of active and reserve military service from second lieutenant to major general and his creation of the Arizona Air National Guard.

Q: In the course of your work with the Air National Guard, will you tell us whether or not you had anything to do with the question of segregation or desegregation?

A: Yes. One day two Negroes came in who had been fighter pilots.

Q: Came in where?

A: Into my office. They had been fighter pilots in World War II, and they questioned the policy of a segregated guard and, frankly, I hadn't even realized it. So I went to the adjutant general, and he in effect told me while he would not approve of it, to go ahead and do what I wanted. So I consulted with other officers, and the air guard was desegregated.

Goldwater testified that as a member of the Phoenix City Council he desegregated the restrooms at the airport and donated personal money for a

Goldwater after a successful landing.

lawsuit to desegregate the high school. He explained that before running for president in 1964 he had served twelve years in the U.S. Senate.

Q: Let us get right down to brass tacks here, Senator. . . . Did you ever have any psychiatric difficulty in your life?

A: No, never.

Q: Did you ever have any occasion to consult a psychiatrist?

A: I never talked to a psychiatrist in my life.

Q: Were you ever treated by one?

A: No.

Q: Did you ever have a nervous breakdown in the sense that this meant some mental difficulty?

A: No, I never have. . . .

Q: Can you recall . . . an occasion [when others have described you as overworked]? . . . Would you go ahead in your own words and tell the jury what happened?

A: We have always been very proud of our connection with Prescott, which was the first capitol of the Territory of Arizona, and my uncle served [as mayor for] twenty-six years, and my grandfather served a term as mayor. We had to close the store down in 1929. I think it was about then sales just fell off so much that we could not handle it. We always wanted to reopen the store, so in 1937, I think it was, we leased a small storeroom up there and ordered fixtures and so forth, and it turned out I had only one carpenter; they all left to do another job.

So I just pitched in and helped the carpenter and the plumber and the electrician. I think it was about five days and nights that I did not leave the place. I would sneak a little sleep at night. I got pretty tired. It was just tired like people get. I have always worked hard and I am used to getting tired.

Q: What happened after that?

A: We went over and had a little celebration for the opening of the store, and the next night I remember my brother and his wife and Peggy and I drove out to a ranch near Phoenix for dinner, and my brother has always driven rather fast, and I got a little mad at him for driving fast, and I told him what I thought about it. He said, "This doesn't sound like you. I think you are too tired." And Peggy said the same thing. I agreed with them. Either the next day or the day after we went to Hawaii.

Q: Who is "we"?

A: Peggy and myself. We went over there, and by the time I got there I felt all ready to go again. We spent a few days riding surf boards and swimming, and came back home.

Q: How long were you gone in all?

A: It could not have been over ten days. We went over by boat. I think it was a four-day trip. We spent two or three days, and came back on the boat.

Q: Was that the whole episode?

A: That is it.

Q: Did you consult a doctor on that occasion?

A: No, I didn't think it was necessary. I just was tired.

Q: Was there ever any other occasion where you had a similar attack of tiredness or exhaustion?

A: I have never been that tired before or since.

Goldwater testified that he had given the defendants all his medical records from the air force and his personal doctor. In the air force he had taken a complete physical every year, which was necessary for him to retain his rating as a command pilot. He testified that he had top-secret security clearance in the air force, which he had held since 1943 or 1944, and Roger Robb entered a copy of it into evidence. Goldwater testified that he had life insurance, without a rider for mental illness, continuously since 1929. Robb then proceeded to take Goldwater through a series of questions relating to statements in FACT *magazine.*

Q: Now, on page 11 of this magazine, the left-hand column, the top: "It's anybody's guess what caused Goldwater's two nervous breakdowns, but perhaps his work in the department store had something to do with it." And then further down in the same paragraph at the end: "Is it possible that Goldwater's nervous breakdowns were provoked by his intense anxiety about his manhood, anxiety that was aggravated by his work in a ladies' department store?" I believe elsewhere in the article there is a reference to anxiety about your masculinity. Did you have any anxiety about your manhood?

A: I never had any doubts about it.

Q: Did you ever have any feeling of unease or shame or anything of that sort about working in a store that sold goods to ladies?

A: No, I was very, very proud of it. I enjoyed the work very much and I participated in everything from sweeping up the floors to buying merchandise, planning advertising promotions, and just running the store, and I enjoyed it and it took me quite a bit of time to make up my mind to get out of that work and get into politics.

Goldwater denied Ginzburg's claim that "in recent years Goldwater had some rather unusual ailment." Rather they all emanated from "a rather vigorous boyhood" catching up to an older man. Robb closed his first day of questioning by reading the commendation that was awarded Captain Goldwater for his flying P-47s over the Atlantic.

Testimony (May 8, 1968)

During the second day of direct testimony, Goldwater's attorney continued to take the senator through the false statements in the magazine, as well as his reactions to them.

BARRY MORRIS GOLDWATER,

Resumed:

DIRECT EXAMINATION CONTINUED BY MR. ROBB: . . .

Q: Now let us get back to the magazine again. . . . Turn to page 9, left-hand column, the first full paragraph, about a third of the way down the pages: "Weepy, timid, and frail, Peggy Goldwater is one of the shyest and most withdrawn wives in American politics. . . . Do you consider Mrs. Goldwater weepy, timid and frail?

A: No, I don't.

Q: Do you think that is a true statement in this magazine?

A: No.

Q: What is the fact?

A: That is completely false. I would say that my wife, like most women that I have known, will cry at the proper occasion; women are usually emotional. She is the least timid of any woman I have ever known. While she is not outgoing, she can approach any problem and do it with force and determination. She raised our four children almost alone, because I was away in war and I was engaged in politics, and a timid woman could never have raised those four wonderful children the way she did. I have never known her to back away from anything. She started the Planned Parenthood Clinic in Arizona when that was not a popular thing to do, and she has carried through on it until today, and it is popular and it is accepted by all of our society, including the Catholic Church, who opposed it at the outset. She as a woman did something rather commendable, I believe, when she, along with another woman, started the Blood Bank in Arizona, and I believe it is now one of the biggest in the country. She approaches any problem with great firmness, although she never seeks publicity; she wants to be in the background.

And "frail"? Well, I think if you look at her you can tell she is not frail. When I read that word "frail," I think of the first year we were married and I took her on a hunting trip up in the Kaibab Forest on the north rim of the Grand Canyon, and then we rode about eleven hours through a sleet storm, and if you have ever ridden a Western saddle in a sleet storm and get those little pieces of sleet in there every time you leave the saddle, you've got to be pretty tough to take it.

I remember one trip she went with me down the middle fork of the Salmon River in Idaho, and we had to pack in riding about twenty-three out of twenty-four hours on horseback through a light snowstorm, and then we were held in for three days in a miner's cabin with a blizzard, and I fished with her in that blizzard twenty feet apart, we couldn't see each other, and she was catching fish. I consider her to be one of the best deep water fisherwomen I have ever seen. We fished —we both like to fish—and we fished the waters of Mexico and Peru, and most all the good fishing waters. I saw her one day fight a marlin for four and a half hours.

Q: A marlin swordfish?

A: A marlin has a sword, but it is not a swordfish. He got away, and she didn't say anything, didn't get mad, and just went on fishing. Oh, she is anything but frail. In fact, "weepy, timid and frail" paints the wrong picture of my wife. She is not a tough woman, but she is a very simple woman, and she knows what she wants, and she goes after it. Now, the second part of that "is one of the shyest and most withdrawn wives in American politics," all I can say is thank God that she is.

Q: What do you mean by that, Senator?

A: I am very glad that she takes the attitude her first duty is to her home, and not necessarily to the business of politics.

Q: That leads me to direct your attention to a statement on page 29 of this magazine, in the right-right hand column: "From TV appearances it is apparent that Goldwater hates and fears his wife." What about that, Senator?

A: That is just as far from the truth as you can get. I have loved my wife and still do and always will. I don't know how you can hate someone that you love. I have no fear of her, but I have great respect for her. As I mentioned earlier, she is a rather determined woman when she gets her mind made up, and I respect that determination. I think we are both sort of that way, but it has never caused any trouble. To me hate is the worst word in our vocabulary, and I wouldn't use that against my worst enemy, let alone my wife. I don't know who this man [one of the psychiatrists quoted] is because he did not sign the letter, and I cannot comment any more than that, because I don't know the background which he called on to make such a statement.

Q: When you read that statement in the magazine, Senator, what effect did it have on you?

A: The effect that the whole magazine had on me, that if you take these individual statements out of other magazines and newspapers and individual statements, it is one thing, it's sort of like dropping a grain of sand, you can carry a grain of sand, two grains of sand, you might carry a pound, but when you come up with something like [this *FACT* magazine] that that weighs several tons, the effect is rather depressing. I was extremely upset by this because I had never seen this attempted before in American politics.

I talked with you about this prior to determining that we would file a suit, and I think I told you at the time, and I still have the same feeling, that after having read this, and after having been defeated, which did not bother me a bit, when I walked down the street even in New York, people naturally recognized me and they smile. I don't know whether they are smiling out of respect for me or friendliness or whether they are thinking there goes that queer or there goes that homosexual, or there goes that man who is afraid of masculinity.

Q: Or hates and fears his wife?

A: Yes, and all the other things that have been put in here. Frankly, things that have nothing to do with the printed word taken out of text or context— look at pages 3 and 4. You ask how I felt about it. I still feel the same way. I think this kind of thing should never be permitted in American journalism, particularly as it applies to politics.

Q: Why?

A: Because if this can be done, you are not going to find decent people willing to stick their necks out in politics, to have this kind of scurrilous material heaped on his neck and the neck of his family. As I told you at the time, one of my intentions or interest in filing this suit was to destroy this precedent, if it can be destroyed, so good men and women in this country will not be subjected to this kind of treatment when they are only trying to serve. I don't say I am perfect. I know I have imperfections. I think most of us would admit to those things. But I do not hold for one minute that anything in this [magazine], in its total conclusion in any way reflects upon my character or person. . . .

Q: Senator, let me direct your attention to paragraph 4 of the magazine—page 4 of the magazine . . . : "From his sadistic childhood pranks to his cruel practical jokes today, from his nervous breakdowns under pressure in his twenties to his present-day withdrawals and escapes in time of crisis, from his obsessive preoccupation with firearms in his youth to his present fantasies about brandishing nuclear weapons to scare his enemies, from his conviction that he is surrounded by deadly enemies at home—whether [union chief Walter] Reuther, [moderate Republican Governor Nelson] Rockefeller, the American Press, or Someone Who is Out to Kill Him—to his belief that every Russian ballerina is a spy, he shows unmistakable symptoms of paranoia." Now, the particular part of the sentence that I would like to direct your attention to is the one about "brandishing nuclear weapons." Do you see that?

A: Yes.

Q: Then over in the next column is this sentence: "And one need not know the name of Freud in order to wonder whether a man who constantly and compulsively must prove his daring and masculinity is a man fit to lead America and the world in this day of the Bomb." Then, on page 63 of the magazine, the left-hand column, the letter starts outs "I believe Goldwater is grossly psychotic." Do you see that?

A: Yes.

Q: The last part of it says: "But in addition, he consciously wants to destroy the world with atomic bombs. He is a mass-murderer at heart and a suicide." I suppose those references might be phrased colloquially by saying the suggestion is you are trigger-happy for the atomic bomb. Let me ask you if that is true?

A: No, it is not true. In fact, I have repeatedly in public statements advised against the use of atomic or nuclear weapons in Vietnam, and I have never at any time suggested that the weapons that these words refer to, the large megatonnage weapons be used. In fact, I may be naive, but I don't think we are going to use those large weapons. But to get to your question, if I may be excused a comment in answering the question, I would say that that sentence is typical of the really objectionable part of this magazine in that there is nothing there in quotes; these are merely the surmises of the writer. . . .

Q: Have you ever advocated [atomic or nuclear weapons] being used?

A: No. I said we better get along in the planning of them, because if we don't other countries will, and if we do not get on with it, we won't have an arsenal in 1970. . . .

Q: So you would say, I take it, that the statement that you unconsciously want to destroy the world with atomic bombs is inaccurate?

A: Totally inaccurate. I don't consider Reuther, Rockefeller or the American press as my deadly enemies. A political enemy is one thing, but to use the word "deadly," I can picture somebody out to kill me. I know this isn't true.

Q: What about the statement that you wanted to brandish nuclear weapons to scare people?

A: This is the figment of the imagination of the writer, because he cannot quote me or anything to prove that I have ever suggested brandishing nuclear weapons. . . .

Q: Let us go down that column, page 4, the right-hand column: "But his father, who obviously affected the course of his life much more, is almost ignored by all the biographers, and by Barry Goldwater himself. Perhaps the fact that the senator's father, Baron Goldwater, was effeminate, tyrannical, and hostile toward his children has something to do with this oversight." Was your father effeminate, tyrannical and hostile toward his children?

A: No, he was not.

Q: What can you tell us about your father?

A: My father was not a large man. He was about five foot five. He was anything but effeminate. He is the one who started my brother and me learning how to box. He used to take us to the fights. He taught us how to play pool. He used to play baseball with us. We did not see a lot of our father because he traveled a lot. He was in New York a good part of each year buying for the store. But when he was home, he was everything you would want in a father. I have often said I wish I had had a chance to know him better. I went away to school when I was fourteen. I was away four years and he died the year after I came back from school. He was never tyrannical. In fact, he was the opposite. I don't think I ever saw him lose his temper. I knew he had a temper, but I don't think a man is worth much if he hasn't a temper, frankly. He was never hostile towards any of us. He was a disciplinarian. If you misbehaved, he disciplined you, but never by force. His favorite form of discipline was denying you something or making you sit in the hall and watch the clock for two or three hours. Many times we asked him to spank us instead of doing that. He never laid a hand on me, but he was a very firm disciplinarian. He was anything but what is said here. I resent very much the term "effeminate." . . .

Q: The next paragraph [from the magazine] is one I want to read to you [with internal citation omitted] and ask you to comment on at some length: "Contributing to the estrangement between the Goldwaters, father and son, may have been their religions. Baron Goldwater was Jewish, had attended a synagogue in San Francisco, and although Phoenix had no synagogue and he married an Episcopalian, he 'never renounced his faith.' He even closed the Goldwater stores on Jewish holidays. His son was baptized, raised as an Episcopalian, probably was never circumcised, and reports, 'I was told I was an Episcopalian before I was told I was a Jew.' In this context, two things will be pointed out. First, ' . . . it should be noted that many Arizona resorts traditionally have barred Jewish members of guests—and there is no record of the senator raising any fuss over this open discrimination'; second, the December, 1963, issue of *Pageant* magazine quotes Senator Goldwater as having said, on a Washington radio station, that 'It is very difficult for me to understand the Jew. The greatest enemy of the Jew in the world has been the Democratic Party and their stupid treaties they've made with other countries. That's why I can't understand Jewish friends of mine, in the big cities, going all out for the Democrats.' Obviously, the senator does not identify with the Jewish part of his heritage, but exclusively with his mother's. (As George Jessel has said, 'There is only one thing I have in common with Barry Goldwater. We are both ashamed of the fact that he is Jewish.')" I might as well start with the end, Senator. Are you and have you ever been ashamed of your Jewish heritage?

A: No, I am very proud of it and I have said so time and time and time again, and I will always say it. . . .

Barry, Jr., Michael, and Barry, Sr., at the Colorado River, 1965.

Q: Did the fact that your father had gone to a synagogue in San Francisco have any bearing on your relationship whatever?

A: I never knew that he went to a synagogue in San Francisco. He never told me that he did. He used to take me to Sunday school and later to church.

Q: Do you know whether he did close the store on Jewish holidays?

A: Not to my memory.

Q: What about the statement here: "It should be noted that many Arizona resorts traditionally have barred Jewish members or guests and there was no senator raising any fuss over this open discrimination." Is that true?

A: Well, it is true if you say "any fuss," because I don't think you solve these problems of discrimination by trying to be the front runner or champion. I think you get far more done if you go behind the fence and do it, and I think we have accomplished that in Arizona. I remember one resort that probably practiced this more flagrantly than the others, and I went to the owner and told him he was wrong, that he would have to change this. He eventually did. But he told me at that time, he said, "I am not opposed to Jewish guests. I only want to have the right to select. Now, if you ever have any friends who want to come to my inn, all you have to do is call me and they will be allowed in." And I have had many Jewish friends ask me to call this particular inn, and they have been accepted. I think today, while—well, I can't say that we have completely stamped this out. I think generally a Jew would have no difficulty getting into most hotels or inns in Arizona.

Q: What you are saying is you have not raised Cain or [started] picketing, but you have worked privately to change the situation?

A: Yes, the same way I have worked in the fields of integration of the Negroes. I think you do far more by reasoning than by raising a fuss.

Q: Now we come to the statement . . . : "Recently Goldwater said on a local Washington radio station that 'It is very difficult for me to understand the Jew,'" and so forth. Will you comment on that?

A: Well, again, I think this is something that should be read in its total. I used, of course, to argue politics with my relatives who lived in New York at that time. They are all dead now. They were Orthodox Jews and they were Democrats. I argued, of course, that I couldn't understand their being so faithful to that party in view of the tie-ups that the Democratic Party has seemingly historically made with countries that haven't been friendly to the Jews. That was the gist of it, although I think you would have to read the whole thing to understand it. . . .

Q: Senator, let us go back for a moment to page 3 of the magazine, in the left-hand column: "In Goldwater's candidacy on a major party ticket, she"—meaning this country—"faces the possibility of electing a president whose grasp of international affairs matches Harding's, whose personality traits are reminiscent of Forrestal's and McCarthy's, and who is backed by a well-organized blindly ruthless, totalitarian, secretive, and powerful movement."* I direct your attention to the last part of that sentence, referring to "a well

---

* *President Warren G. Harding has been considered by many historians to be incompetent and corrupt, but the charges are baseless. See John W. Dean,* Warren G. Harding *(American President Series), ed. Arthur M. Schlesinger, Jr. (New York: Times Books, 2004). Secretary of the Navy and later Secretary of Defense James Forrestal committed suicide, and Senator Joseph McCarthy falsely accused people of links to communism.*

organized, blindly ruthless, totalitarian, secretive, and powerful movement." Have you any comment to make on that?

A: Yes, I have. Again, the writer is merely writing what is a figment of his imagination. I see no attempt to back that statement up. I don't know who he could be referring to. It might be the Republican Party; it might be the 27 million people who voted for the Republican ticket of which I was a member. This is an example of my biggest complaint about this kind of journalism, if we can call it that. You take the sentence at the top of the page "That the senator is divorced from reality is unfortunate, that he may soon be able to divorce all of us from reality is terrifying," this is merely the writer's opinion.

Q: I take it you have no intention of divorcing anybody from reality?

A: No. Reality is with us every day; you cannot do that. . . .

Q: Over on page 14, the left-hand column, at the bottom: "The child who startled girls in the bathroom and shot at churchgoers, the young man who scared sales girls with mice in pneumatic tubes still delights in mean practical jokes and exhibitionistic acts of hostility." Let's take that sentence. I think you have already mentioned about startling girls in bathrooms. Is that true?

A: I don't think I ever startled any girl in a bathroom. . . . There is another statement in there that I don't know where they got it, that I shot at churchgoers.

Q: That is what I was going to ask you about. Did you ever shoot at churchgoers?

A: No, I didn't. But I did own a ten-gauge cannon, and I remember that it became impossible to get ten-gauge blanks, so I had ten-gauge live ammunition from which I would remove the shot when we wanted to use it for parades or rodeos, or anything like that, and one evening during a golf tournament in Phoenix some friends of my mother's came over to the house and took the cannon, took it out on the front porch, upstairs.

Not knowing about the shells [that they weren't all blanks], they loaded it with a live one, and this fellow pulled the trigger just about the time church was getting out across the street, and, of course, a ten-gauge cannon with about a nine or ten-inch barrel does not have a very effective range, and from the porch across to the church I would say it was, oh, a hundred feet, and the pellets did fall on the grass of the church. But I had nothing to do with it. In fact, I was in the basement when I heard the thing go off and ran up, knowing probably what had happened. But I wasn't in that at all.

Q: What about this mouse episode?

A: Well, way back in those years when our business was a relatively small one, having between sixty and seventy employees, we became rather a close organization. And I can remember this one girl who used to delight in playing jokes on me, such as putting a dead scorpion in my desk.

Q: What is a scorpion?

A: A dead scorpion. That is something that looks like a lobster. Personally, they give me the willies. You find them in your shoes and clothes and beds. So she put one in my drawer one day, and I got a handful of dead scorpions. I nearly jumped out of my skin. So the next chance I got, I found a dead mouse in the basement and I put it in one of the pneumatic tubes that go up with the money, and she was sitting there scooping the money out and she scooped out a dead mouse and she chased me all over the place and finally threw it at me. But she always managed to get even. . . .

Q: Senator, again on page 14, towards the bottom of the page, right-hand column, there is a reference to your reading habits [internal citations omitted]: "His reading habits have not improved much, either. . . . Goldwater reads and rereads Karl Von Clausewitz *On War*, with its exposition of total destruction of the enemy by any available means. . . . But, mostly, 'I read these little two-bit Westerns you buy,' he said. 'In fact, I usually have a brief case with Mickey Spillane and all of those things.' And when he is not reading *On War* or Mickey Spillane, Goldwater watches shoot 'em ups on TV, for he 'is an addict of TV Westerns and watches six or seven a week.'" What can you tell us about your reading habits?

A: I think they are fairly normal for a man who travels much of the time. I have read and I have reread Von Clausewitz *On War*. But [the author's] deduction that his total exposition is one of total destruction is not quite true. For Clausewitz, I might say, up until some of the modern Chinese writings, *On War* had been the standard primer of warfare, and having been through the Air War College and taken quite a few of its correspondence courses and having written quite a bit in this field, I referred to him occasionally.

Q: How many of the courses have you taken?

A: I forget, maybe six. I have taken the senior officer's course, which is tantamount or comparable to a Master's degree at the Air War College. . . . I am reading right now two books that I find very interesting, one is the *History of War of the United States*, very well written, and another is David Shoenbrun's treatise on Vietnam, *How We Got In And How To Get Out*. I read all I can, but I don't get a lot of time. I do like shoot 'em ups on the TV, but I am sort of ruled out there, because my wife likes Johnny Carson, and every night when I get to bed I watch Johnny Carson. . . .

Q: Turning over to page 16, right-hand column: "In his twelve years in Congress, he has not had one important bill passed, but 'He wears his lost causes, his "no" votes in the Senate against overwhelming majorities—like merit badges.'" . . . Have you any comment to make on that?

A: I think I sponsored or was a co-sponsor of sixty-odd bills in my twelve years. While nothing I sponsored might have been earth shaking, I did make some things possible. I made it possible for Indians to lease land on their reservation which gives them a source of income they never had before. . . .

But I want to remind you of one thing, that in the twelve years I have been in the Senate, the Republicans only controlled the Senate two years. When a party controls the Senate, that party's members get their bills out and get their names on the bills. It is very rare that a member of the opposition party can be successful in getting a major bill through. That does not bother me too much anyway. I did say [when I went to the Senate that] it is my aim not to pass laws but to repeal them. I don't think we necessarily solve the problems of our country by constantly passing legislation. . . . However, in my twelve years I did not repeal any law. . . .

Q: Now let's get down to this: "In short—the courage of a cow-ardly juvenile delinquent. One of the examples of such courage was Goldwater's declaration to a Republican breakfast meeting in Mississippi that '[Chief Justice] Earl Warren is a Socialist.'" What can you tell us about that?

A: Well, this is completely wrong, because I never made that state-ment at a public gathering. I recall having lunch with President Eisenhower and [House Minority Leader] Charlie Halleck, of Indiana, on the day that Mr. Earl Warren was appointed chief justice. In fact, we had not heard of it until we sat down to lunch, and the president asked, "What do you think of it?"

And I said, "Well, Mr. President," or words to this effect, because it has been some time ago, "I have known [California] Governor Warren for a long time. In fact, I have been his aide, his military aide on two different Guard encampments. I like him very much, and like his family, but," I said, "I think he has been leaning towards Socialistic ideas for some time."

And at that point the president's neck started to get a little red, and that is the time you stop talking.* So that is when I said it. I never released it for publication. I don't know to this day how it ever got out of the confines of President Eisenhower, Charlie Hal-leck, or myself. I was asked about this at a meeting, I think it was in Jackson, Mississippi, if I had ever said it, and I said, "Not publicly." There were no press men in the room; it was not on television. So, again, this is an error, although I did say what I have been reported saying here. But I never publicly made that accusation. . . .

Q: Now, this paragraph says: "John F. Kennedy also came in for a good deal of Goldwater's bile. 'I sincerely fear for my country,' said he 'if Jack Kennedy should be elected president. The fellow

---

* After leaving the presidency, Eisenhower would state that his worst mistake as president had been his selection of Earl Warren to be chief justice of the United States.

has absolutely no guts or principles.' What about that [statement Mr. Ginzburg quotes from the *Indianapolis Star*]?

A: I would have to see that statement. I don't remember making it.* I recall having no reason eight years ago to have made a statement like that, and I happen to have some faith in the *Indianapolis Star*. I would have to see who wrote it, where it came from, because I don't remember making it.

Q: What was your relationship with Mr. Kennedy?

A: Well, very cordial. He was the ranking—he was second in rank on the Democratic side of the Public Works and Welfare Committee, and I was top on the Republican side. We got along very well. I would report to him after my weekend forays to help elect Republican senators, and ask how he was doing in different places. We had a lot of fun. He was a very, very fine man, and had a wonderful sense of humor. He had a mind that was like a blotter. He could come into a committee room not knowing what the bill was about, and in about five minutes he would be debating with you as if he had written the bill.

I recall many interesting little things that happened. I took a picture of him once. He asked me to stop by the White House to have a drink on the way home. So I did, and I took a picture of him; and I think he liked it, and I do, too. He inscribed it, "To My Friend, Barry Goldwater, whom I urge to follow the career for which he has shown such talent, photography. From his friend, John Kennedy."

Q: What is the date of that?

A: There is no date on that. I put that in 1960–61, I believe.

Q: After he was president, of course?

A: Oh, yes, he was in the White House.

Q: So, apparently Mr. Kennedy didn't feel you had poured bile on him?

A: No. We got along very well, considering he was a Democrat and I was a Republican. We forgot those little differences. . . .

---

* *Goldwater is not denying his feelings about JFK; rather not recalling publicly stating those feelings.*

Testimony (May 9, 1968)

Robb's direct examination on the third day was brief, making clear that Goldwater in no way—and contrary to the FACT article and poll—identified with Hitler. Robb ended his direct questions by raising the point that Ralph Ginzburg's attorney, Harris B. Steinberg, was banking on the jury going along with the idea that under the free speech clause of the First Amendment there must be open and robust debate.

Steinberg, a very able trial lawyer, had a near impossible task, and he spent his first day in of cross-examination in a tedious review of Goldwater's medical history-seeking to show that none of the medical information Goldwater had submitted had really addressed his mental health. This questioning elicited no new information about Goldwater whatsoever.

Testimony (May 10, 1968)

BARRY MORRIS GOLDWATER,

Resumed:

CROSS EXAMINATION CONTINUED BY MR. STEINBERG: . . .

Next Steinberg began taking Goldwater through virtually every statement that Ginzburg had written in the magazine, to ask if it was true or false, important or unimportant. We have not repeated this tedious questioning, except when it proved enlightening or revealing. Most interesting were Steinberg's efforts to show the jury that Goldwater was an extremist and that he was supported by extremists, but the senator made clear he was not an extremist. We pick up the cross-examination by Steinberg after he read from the New York Times the names of various extremists groups and individuals who had backed Goldwater. Steinberg was frustrated because the senator said he was unaware of their support.

Q: Well, when something is published in a newspaper like the *New York Times*, doesn't it surface to the people advising you? Doesn't it come to your attention or their attention enough to put you on notice?

A: This was never brought to my attention.

Q: Nobody in your campaign staff was troubled enough about it to bring it to you and say, "Senator, let's get these guys off our back"?

A: I think that would be a fair statement. . . .

Q: Wait a second, before we leave that. . . . How about [Christian evangelists] Billy Gene Hargis? Did it come to your attention that he was backing you?

A: I think somebody told me that he was backing me.

Q: Did it come to your attention, that Mr. Hargis said, "It behooves all of us to work to get him elected," meaning you, and he urged the Conservatives should strive to elect congressmen of their persuasion so that President Goldwater would have a teammate that would assure action? Did it come to your attention that he said that six hundred adherents from twenty-two states, many of whom were also members of the John Birch Society, were people who were supporting you, voting for you?

A: Will counsel tell me—

Q: Here, let me show you this.

A: What is it connecting Billy Jean Hargis with? He is a minister, so far as I know.

Q: All you know is, he is a minister?

A: He is a minister connected with some organization, but I don't know what it is.

Q: Do you know anything about his views or political views?

A: I would place him a bit on the extreme side.

Q: How far on the extreme side?

A: Not ever having had any definition of extremism, I just don't know where that would be.

Q: You offered yourself as an expert on extremism? You made a statement at the convention about extremism. What was that statement?

A: Extremism in the defense of Liberty is no vice, and moderation in the pursuit of Justice is no virtue.

Q: I take it, having made that statement and put it into the public field you consider yourself some expert on extremism? Isn't that so?

A: I would not take that to mean that I was an expert. Might I try to explain, if you are getting into this field?

Q: Yes.

A: I was discussing with General Eisenhower the next morning, or President Eisenhower, this very statement, and he asked me what I meant by it, and I said, "Well, just as I said," I said, "General, the most extreme thing a man can do is to destroy another man." And by this word "destruction" I meant kill.

I said, "Yet you led the largest army ever assembled across the English Channel for the purposes of defending liberty, and I don't call that an example of extremism, as you are getting into it." This seemed to satisfy the general. He said, "I had not thought of it in that [con]text before."

Q: What did you say?

A: I said I was glad I satisfied him.

Q: So you feel the most extreme thing a man can do to another fellow is kill him. But what does that have to do with definitions of positions in politics?

A: I'll get back to what I said. There has been no definition that I have seen explaining what is an extremist. Now, I will accept an extremist of the Left as being a communist and an extremist of the far Right as being a fascist.

Q: An extremist of the Left is a communist and an extremist of the Right is a fascist?

A: To the far extremes of the political spectrum would be communism and fascism.

Q: Now, where do we put Billy Jean Hargis? You said on the Right far enough to be a Fascist?

A: No, not far enough to be a Fascist. . . .

Q: Senator, you have heard of a man named Gerald L. K. Smith?*

A: Yes, I have heard of him.

Q: You consider him an extremist?

A: I would say of the worst kind.

Q: And an anti-Semite?

A: Yes.

Q: Did he support you for the presidency?

---

* *Smith was a well-known hatemonger of the 1930s and early 1940s.*

A: Not that I know of.

Q: Did this article come to your attention during the campaign?

A: No, I have never seen this before —

Q: Have you ever heard before today the substance of what is contained in that?

A: No. I just scanned over it.

Q: Well, look at it.

A: I think I see what counsel is getting at.

Q: Well, did you ever hear during the campaign that Gerald L. K. Smith was actively supporting your candidacy?

A: No, I never did.

Q: Did you ever repudiate the support of Gerald L. K. Smith?

A: Not having heard of it, it would be difficult to repudiate.

Q: And nobody in your campaign staff, none of your research workers, none of the people who were paid to write your speeches keep up with the developments in the campaign or the press coverage ever brought it to your attention, that Gerald L. K. Smith was supporting you?

A: Not to my memory.

Q: Where were you? Fishing?

A: No. I was fishing for votes, yes.

Q: What about a man named Robert Welch? Did you ever hear of him?

A: Yes.

Q: Who was he?

A: He is the founder of the John Birch Society.

Q: A friend of yours?

A: Pardon?

Q: A friend of yours?

A: His brother was a friend of mine. I think his brother has passed on. I think he used to spend the winters in Arizona, and that is where I met him.

Q: Would you call Robert Welch a friend?

A: I would not call him a friend and he would not call me a friend. I have publicly repudiated him many, many, many times.

Q: When did you first publicly repudiate him?

A: I think the first night I met him and he gave me that famous book of his to read, and I told him he better burn it, because there wasn't a word of truth in it.

Q: What book was that?

A: I think it is the *Blue Book* [of the John Birch Society] or the *Black Book*.

Q: You have no difficulty in remembering it is the *Blue Book*? You don't forget the color?

A: I saw it once that night and I took it back to him the next morning and told him he should burn it up.

Q: Do you know whether he supported you during the campaign?

A: I have no way of knowing, because, according to the Birch Society, they don't back candidates.

Q: Does the *Blue Book*, which you say you read and which you handed back and told him to burn, say as follows:

"I know Barry fairly well. He is a great American—I raised around two thousand dollars in my state and sent it to him early in 1958—Barry Goldwater has political know-how and the painstaking genius to use the know-how with regard to infinite details. He is a superb political organizer and inspires deep and lasting loyalty. He is absolutely superb in his Americanism, has the political and moral courage to stand by his Americanistic principles, and in my opinion can be trusted to stand by them until hell freezes over. I would love to see him president of the United States, and maybe one day we shall."

Wasn't that statement in the *Blue Book* which you read, which you say you turned back to him to burn?

A: I don't think that is in the *Blue Book* that I am referring to. He publishes a little pamphlet, magazine, I think it is called "World Opinion" or something like that, and I think this article appeared in that, because I can remember seeing this. But I don't think it appeared in his so-called Bible, or whatever it is. That little pamphlet is a blue pamphlet.

Q: You do remember seeing this, but you say it was a different thing?

A: Yes, I can remember this, and I can also remember in 1958 Robert Welch when announcing the formation of the Birch Society in Indianapolis was asking the question of whether he would support Goldwater or Nixon for president, and he said Nixon is too far to the left, and Goldwater is a Socialist.

MR. ROBB: A what?

THE WITNESS: A Socialist.

Q: This business of calling people Socialist is pretty rough stuff when it is not true?

A: Well, I don't think it is anything too wrong about being a Socialist. To me Socialism is an economic theory. It is not a theory of government, as I understand it, and if we continue in this government, tend to governmental control of our business, we are safe in calling that Socialism. . . .

Q: Did you ever say of Truman that he was on the way to Socialistic ideas?

A: I think I did.

Q: Did you ever call Senator McFarland a Socialist when you were running against him?

A: I think I did in an indirect way. I know it is attributed to me, but I can't recall the details of it.

Q: You do say now you see nothing wrong in Socialism? You don't equate it with extremism? Do you?

A: It would be extremism as applied against our economic system. I would look on it that way.

Q: Didn't you on *Meet the Press*, November 19, 1961, have the following exchange of conversation with Mr. Spivak:

"Mr. Spivak: In Atlanta yesterday you, too, went after the extremists, and this is what you said, 'The real extremists are the people to the left. The Socialists in the Kennedy Administration.'"

"Senator Goldwater: That is right.

"Mr. Spivak: Will you give us the names of the leading Socialists in the—

"Senator Goldwater: I don't have time to go clear through them.

"Mr. Spivak: Just give us the names of some of the important people.

"Senator Goldwater: I would say Arthur Schlesinger—there are two other members of the Americans for Democratic Action—and this is the group to whom I refer as the extremists of the left—one is Ted Sorenson—there are three in the cabinet posts."

Q: Did you say that to Mr. Spivak?

A: Yes.

Q: So you were in fact saying the real extremists were Socialists, and you thought of Socialism as a term of derision, as a term little better than Fascist or Communist, didn't you?

A: I wouldn't put it that way.

Q: How would you put it?

A: Socialism to me is an attempt to centralize the control of the government in the hands of a few, and I always felt that those gentlemen were inclined that way. I also said earlier that extremism would embrace that on the Left as it would embrace the same on the Right. . . .

Q: You made a speech, did you not, in the U.S. Senate explaining your vote against the Civil Rights Bill, and you said "This is fundamentally a matter of the heart," did you not?

A: Yes.

Q: What did you mean by that?

A: I think you can read it in the speech. I have always maintained that law can go just so far in the solution of our civil rights problems that we are only going to completely solve them when men get their hearts into the thing.

Q: Did you feel that when men get into court and take due process of law and the U.S. Supreme Court makes rulings that they should be respected and followed?

A: I do.

Q: Did you make the statement that "I don't necessarily buy the idea that what the Supreme Court says is the law of the land, because the Court's decisions are jackassian"?

A: I made that statement and I later retracted it and changed my position after consulting with lawyers as to what the role of the Supreme Court is in respect to the supreme law of the land.

Q: But you did make that statement in August of 1963, as recently as that?

A: I don't know the date, but I changed my position.

Q: You remember in your book, the *Conscience of a Conservative*, saying that "I am not impressed by the claim that the Supreme Court's decision on school integration is the law of the land?"

A: I remember that, and I changed my position on that. . . .

Q: Did you have the feeling that the press and television were biased against you or were events in a manner which was conspiratorial against you?

A: I don't know if conspiratorial would be the word, but I didn't think it was entirely fair, put it that way.

Q: You thought more than that—you not only thought it was not entirely fair, you thought it was deliberate attempts on their part to lie about you, to put you in a false light maliciously, didn't you?

A: Well, malicious is a very strong word, I am not speaking of the press in its entirety. There was friendly press; there were some press that bent over in my direction. But I would say the majority of the press was not friendly to my candidacy.

Q: Not friendly is sort of a cleaned up version of what you felt at that time, isn't it, Senator? Didn't you charge them with outright lies, utter dishonesty?

A: Yes, I think I did.

Q: And that is what you mean when you say they weren't friendly?

A: Yes.

Q: Among those newspapers and mass media which you thought were lying, out and out liars and utterly dishonest, also you say "Newspapers like the *New York Times* have to stoop to utter dishonesty in reflecting my views"?

A: I think I did.

Q: Did you say "Some of the newspapers here in San Francisco, like the *Chronicle*, are nothing but out and out liars"?

A: I think I did.

Q: Did you say the Columbia Broadcasting System network had pulled three sneakers on you that you would never forgive them for?

A: I probably said it. I can't remember what they are right now.

Q: Did you mean it when you said it or were you joking?

A: No, I wasn't joking. I don't joke when I say things like that.

Q: You don't joke, do you, because when you say something you want people to believe you, right?

A: That's correct. . . .

Q: By the way—I would just like to digress from this a minute— you have a bulldog, don't you?

A: I had a bulldog.

Q: You had one?

A: Had two of them.

Q: He had a gold tooth, didn't he?

A: He had a gold tooth, yes.

Q: Did you and a dentist friend pull out his tooth one night and put a gold tooth in?

A: No. He broke one of his big teeth off. Bulldogs have two big teeth in front. He broke the top off and it was obviously hard for him to chew, and so this dentist friend of my sister offered to pull it out and make a cap for it, and she said "Well, as long as you are going to do it, you might as well make it gold." So he had a gold cap on his tooth and he wore it until he died.

Q: Did you ever tell anybody that you and the dentist one evening after a few drinks had taken the dog's tooth out and replaced it with a gold one?

A: No, never did. . . .

Testimony (May 13, 1968)

After failing to paint Goldwater as being cruel to animals, Steinberg con-
tinued taking the senator through virtually every statement that Ginzburg
had written. Again, we have not repeated what the jury must have found

deadly boring; rather we have extracted only a few exchanges that were illuminating.

BARRY MORRIS GOLDWATER,

Resumed:

CROSS EXAMINATION CONTINUED BY MR. STEINBERG: . . .

After reading an extensive segment of Goldwater's deposition, where he and Steinberg had discussed whether Hitler was crazy and Goldwater asserted that he certainly was, Steinberg continued:

Q: Wouldn't you agree, of course, Hitler is an extreme example, but wouldn't you agree when a nation is at a critical turning point and at a time of peril that before selecting a leader in such a critical time it is helpful to have a psychological insight into that leader's fitness, and that could only be gained, unless he submits to a psychiatric examination, by reading and studying his utterances and past history and interpreting them?

A: I think it would be desirable, if there was an indication that there was a need of it. Men in public life are subjected to all kinds of examinations. For example, we have to make our total property, our assets, liabilities, etc., available when we are elected to office. There have been occasions when health records have been spread upon the record. But if there is a need in the people's mind for a psychological examination, I think, that both parties would agree to it. I don't think it is a matter of paramount importance. I do think it is a matter of paramount importance when an untrained man undertakes to write a paper on the psychological fitness of a man to be president without submitting this man to an examination or even talking with this man. I think that it is wrong. I think it is a very dangerous precedent, and that is why I am opposed to it.

Q: Senator, even before the *FACT* article came out, as you have acknowledged in your previous testimony, there were rumblings by some people, rightly or wrongly, who thought you were nuts. There were rumblings of some people who were questioning the fact that you had nervous breakdowns. It was open to you to allay those rumors by submitting yourself to a psychiatric examination and making the results public, wasn't it?

A: The thought never crossed my mind, because I had never had a nervous breakdown, and the first reports of these so-called breakdowns came in May or June. As I said, I had never been advised by my doctor, nor did I feel it myself, nor did any of my friends who watched me from day to day tell me "You are acting a little differently than you were a few weeks ago, we are worried about you, we think you better see a psychiatrist." That never happened. I was not concerned, as I told you earlier. In this business of politics, people call you nuts, just like if you told me the Mets are going to win the pennant, then I would say you are nuts. I don't question your stability by that remark. I just use it facetiously, as we have used it in America forever, I guess. . . .

Q: You are a politician, are you not?

A: I like to think of myself as one.

Q: In fact, in your air force form they asked you your occupation, and you put down as your last one "Politician," you are proud of it, are you not?

A: I was proud of it. I am unemployed now.

Q: But you would like to be reemployed?

A: I hope so.

Q: You are applying for a new job?

A: A renewal.

Q: In fact, Senator, an important reason for your bringing this lawsuit, an important reason for your suing Mr. Ginzburg and the other defendants, is that you feel it is necessary for you to bring this lawsuit and for you to air and to lay at rest this question of your nervous breakdown, because you feel that unless you do that it will hurt your chances for reelection in public life, isn't that true?

A: I feel it is necessary to bring this suit, and I did not get at it lightly; it took me well over a year to make the decision. I think we must, if we can, remove the precedent which this has established, which in connection with the Supreme Court decision in the *New York Times v. Sullivan* case, I believe it is, leaves open how much a man in public life can be libeled. If this is allowed to remain a precedent, I don't fear solely for myself, because in my own home state where people know me, they know I am not a nut, and they know

I haven't had any nervous breakdowns, but, let us say, somebody wants to run for the president and he is not known by two hundred million people, all a person would have to do who is opposed to him politically would be to put out a repetition of *FACT*. This is one of the reasons I might say for my having brought this suit I think it is a very dangerous precedent, probably the most dangerous precedent we have ever had in American politics.

Goldwater would win this lawsuit and establish new precedent in the process. He did not seek to overturn New York Times v. Sullivan *but rather to show that a public official could prevail notwithstanding the high demands that the* Times v. Sullivan *case places on the public official plaintiff.* Goldwater v. Ginzburg *created the still-valid precedent that a public official plaintiff can prove "actual malice" (knowing falsity or reckless disregard to the truth or falsity of what is being published) by showing negligence, motive, and intent. Based on Goldwater's testimony, he established that he was not paranoid, that he had not suffered nervous breakdowns, and that he was not an admirer of Adolph Hitler nor a nuclear madman. During the trial, Goldwater's lawyer brought out the fact that Ginzburg set out to defame Goldwater, knowing that psychiatrists were politically opposed to him, therefore anticipating the result from the highly unscientific poll. Ginzburg had written the article about Goldwater to dissuade people from voting for him. Thus, by winning the case Goldwater accomplished his goal. Financially, it was a wash, if not at Goldwater's expense given the legal fees. The jury awarded him one dollar in compensatory damages and seventy-five thousand dollars in punitive damages (which just covered his legal costs). Ginzburg appealed all the way to the U.S. Supreme Court, which would refuse to hear the case.* *

---

* *Goldwater was entrenched back in the Senate in 1970 when the U.S. Supreme Court denied Ginzburg's appeal. In denying the appeal, most striking was the fact that Justice William O. Douglas participated in the case (and filed a written dissent to the denial of the appeal), notwithstanding the fact he had been paid by Ralph Ginzburg to write for one of his magazines. Not surprisingly, Goldwater privately reacted to this clear conflict of interest by sending a letter to several colleagues to encourage them to go after Justice Douglas for his remarkably unethical behavior. Goldwater had little success. In his retirement years, he confided that he had encouraged House Minority Leader Gerald Ford to institute impeachment proceedings in the House against Douglas and promised if the matter ever came to a vote in the Senate, he would call in every chip he had to send Justice Douglas into early retirement.*

CHAPTER 10

SEEING THE WORLD
AND SPREADING
THE WORD

D
eparture from the Senate provided Goldwater an opportunity to
travel, which he did extensively while out of office. He traveled
through Europe, Asia, and South Africa (for a photo shoot of
big game). We have selected his report from his travels in 1967, because it
is representative of the other reports he sent back to his children to share his
experiences and to remember them as well.

REPORTING ON THE 1967 TRIP TO VIETNAM

Letter (January 11, 1967)

Dearest Children,

This is sort of a semi-formal report from Kyoto, Japan to bring
you up to date on what Mommy and I have been doing since we last
left the United States. We spent two days at Maui, a spot that all of
you must visit sometime; it is by far the most beautiful of the islands
that we have seen. New Year's Eve was spent there and, of course, it
was quite gay being my birthday and less importantly the start of the
New Year. We left there on Sunday and being the only two passengers
on the plane, the pilot flew us up the North Coast of Molokai which
is a stretch of sheer cliffs going up some three thousand feet right from
the ocean's edge. It is covered with dense jungle and highlighted by
long troughs of falling water. The flight from Honolulu to Tokyo took
close to eight hours and all they did was feed us, wine us, and then do
it all over again. We arrived in Tokyo in a rainstorm and through some

inadvertent mix-up, it turned out to be the New Year's holiday which goes on for three days. . . .

Tokyo is a very fascinating city as is the whole of Japan that we have seen. The meals and service in the hotels are as perfect as any we have ever seen. In fact, to tell the truth we have never seen anything to even approach the way people treat you in this country. We had lunch with the ambassador and his family and then one evening we had dinner with some old air force friends at the Military Hotel. The holiday provided us with some very colorful sights because the women were all out in their kimonos, and out in the literal millions and we enjoyed driving around looking at them, taking in a museum here and there and visiting a shrine.

Mommy talked me into visiting one of the famous Japanese baths, which is really a combination of a Turkish bath and a rubdown by a girl. I must say I was kind of shook up at first when this nice young thing in shorts ushered me into a dressing room and indicated that I should remove my clothes, which I did down to my shorts and when she indicated that I should also remove those, I kind of reddened in the face. The last time that happened to me there was a brass bed in the room and it cost me two dollars. Anyway, I was dunked in the steam bath then seated on a wooden stool with not a darn thing on and she washed my back, scrubbing it hard, then put me into a hot tub of water. After that came the rub-down and I've never felt such strength as those little gals have in their fingers. They have to go to school for two years to learn this and I have already enrolled your mother in for the post-graduate.

From Tokyo we came down to Kyoto yesterday on a train, the likes of which we do not have in the United States nor will we have for years to come. It's called the Bullet; it is extremely modern and streamlined and travels a little over 200 kilometers an hour, which is roughly 130 to 135 miles an hour. . . . This is a fabulous country. The people are well employed; the stores are more crowded than any store I have ever seen in the United States at any time of the year. . . . They are now the world's leading ship builders; they supply about 70 percent of the transistorized small radios sold in the United States and approximately 40 percent of all televisions sold in our country.

Letter (January 14, 1967)

Dearest Children,

Here we are now in Hong Kong and it is a rather dismal, overcast evening with the sun having almost gone down to the point of allowing night to creep over the hills.

Our stay in Taipei was so very interesting that I couldn't let another day pass without telling you about it. To begin with we drove from Kyoto to Osaka and about a half hour before the plane was to take off for Taipei we were informed that we had not received visas to the Republic of China and that we would have to return to Tokyo to get things straightened out. I got on the phone, made a few calls, one to Tokyo and one to Osaka and very shortly things got straightened out and we were on our way but had to sign a letter of indemnity to clear the lines if anything did happen. It was an uneventful flight, well above the overcast all the way to Taipei and because of smog conditions we weren't able to see much of that island as we were coming in. We were met at the airport by our old friends, General and Doris Pitts, whom we knew in Washington. He is now Commander of the 327th Air Division on Taiwan which is the home, of course, of the Republic of China. Taipei is about 150 miles from the mainland of China where the Communists are holding sway and are having right now one hell of a time. I'll talk to you when I see you because I don't believe it is safe to talk too much in this room about everything I heard.

We were taken to the Grand Hotel where later we found we were guests of the state and believe it or not, all of our time there didn't cost us a red nickel; not even for shoe shines, breakfast, lunch or extra toilet paper. That afternoon I called on Foreign Minister Wei and had an interesting and long discussion about some of the fundamentals and background of the communist picture in that part of the world. That evening Bill Pitts and his wife hosted a reception at their home for us and later a dinner at the Grand Hotel and even though Mommy wanted to stay up and raise hell all night, I clubbed her and got her to bed at a relatively early hour.

On Saturday I had two most interesting meetings in the morning; one with the Minister of Defense, who is the son of President Chiang Kai-Shek. The next meeting was with Vice President C. K. Yen and

I found him to be the most informed man I have run into on the whole subject of the development of the economy and other matters relating to the Island of Taiwan. We had lunch that day with Mr. and Mrs. Hummel, who is Charge de Affairs for the United States in the absence of the ambassador. It was a wonderful luncheon and, I found some chili that is hotter than anything Mexico ever heard of. I ate too much of it on my rice and the sweat poured down my back, thank God, instead of the front of my head.

That night proved to be one of the most interesting nights of our whole life because we attended dinner at the home of President and Madame Chiang Kai-Shek.* As you know, I have long been an admirer of his and have long agreed completely with his policies, particularly those he enunciated to me as never being able to have peace in the Far East until the communists are driven out of China. Of course, he feels very deeply that we are going to have to help him in this and I have a sneaking hunch that we will. I spoke with him for about an hour before dinner having to use a translator. I found him to be just as charming and interesting as I knew he would be. He is eighty years old but, frankly, he doesn't look a day over fifty. He wore a khaki uniform with no medals to the reception and to dinner where I sat on the right side of the madame. Chinese ambassadors to Rome, Mexico, Korea and Thailand were there also with other dignitaries of state and after dinner I had another forty-five minute discussion with him through the translators. In fact, Mommy was beating me over the back of the head because protocol called on me to leave first but I have never felt it was my place to break up the conversation of a president so I was reluctant to go but I did. Lo and behold the next morning he delivered an autographed picture to me and wait until you see it. It came in a beautiful wooden cabinet with the seal of China on the outside and the picture framed in a silver frame with his own Chinese handwriting as an inscription. Later in the day Mommy received two

---

* *Chiang Kai-Shek served as head of the government of the Republic of China from 1928 until his death in 1975. He failed in his effort to remove the Communists from China and was forced to escape to Taiwan, where he served as the president of the Republic of China.*

hand inscribed books of the madame's paintings which are beautiful things and you will love them. . . .

On Sunday, we flew down in the president's airplane to pay a visit to the 3rd Tactical Air Division of the Chinese Air Force and I was particularly anxious to do this because, as you know, I was the first instructor that the Chinese Cadets had when they came to the United States in 1942 and at the Division Headquarters I met one general and three colonels who were among the nearly one hundred cadets that I trained during their stay in the United States. . . . We engaged in a typical Chinese dinner of ten courses and Mommy has the menu which we will show you. Of course, we ate with chopsticks and I found out after having eaten too much that if you clean your plate it is the hostess's responsibility to fill it with the same thing you had just cleaned so I had about five thousand shrimp. You have possibly heard of the drinking game called Gom-bea and when a person in China proposes a toast and says Gom-bea, it's down the hatch with everything in a small wine glass. Thank God the wine was weak because after about twenty-two Gom-beas I could hardly see past the end of my nose. . . . To come back to a foreign country after twenty-five years and find young men that you taught having grown into older men with responsibility of command of an entire air force and to find them doing it in a commendable way is, I can assure you, a source of satisfaction that I probably will only experience in life again as I reflect upon the successes of my children and their spouses.

Letter (January 19, 1967)

Dearest Children,

The length of this letter will not be dictated by the fact that we are on a seemingly endless flight from Saigon to the United States by way of Hong Kong, Tokyo, Honolulu and Los Angeles, but because we have been doing so much since the last letter I wrote. Please remember that these letters are not just descriptions of our trip to you but the carbon copies will serve as reminders to your mother and me of this vacation we had in January of 1967.

It's dark outside now, we've been in the air approximately two hours out of Hong Kong, destination Tokyo and it seems to me that we have consumed a couple gallons of de-icing liquid [martinis] and because Mommy is nearly asleep beside me, I thought I'd get this off.

After writing you the last letter, we left Hong Kong and had another interesting flight, which they all are, to Bangkok, Thailand. I might say that before I get into any description of our visit there that we were the guests of the State of China and found out after being in Bangkok a few days that we were also the guests of the state there, so we saved some money and had a delightful time. . . .

The first day we were there, we had lunch with the ambassador, his wife, and others in the Tea House at the ambassador's residence which I must say was very beautiful. Thai food is as interesting as any of the food one eats in the Orient and surprisingly hot. In fact, we continue to find chili hotter than anything we have ever found in Mexico or the United States. Of course, rice is the basic food and on this they build everything but it certainly is good. I will say, however, that my stomach was not laid out to accommodate such things as one eats in the Orient and I had nothing but belly trouble all across that part of the world. It's good food to eat but it just doesn't go along with a long life built on hamburgers and steak.

In Bangkok we stayed at the Oriental Hotel which is probably the oldest one in the city and the only one facing on the river. The river is quite a wide one, extremely dirty because they throw the garbage, sewage, dirty clothes and a few dead bodies into it, and it being on a tidal plane, the ocean currents cause the river to run upstream and downstream with quite a strong current. Our room was an old room, showing French influence, the ceilings were about fourteen feet high, the plumbing was installed by Napoleon's plumber and the floors were of ancient teakwood. . . .

While here, we were taken care of by a very attractive young woman about to become a mother by the name of Puncie. She took us to the boxing matches one night and, let me tell you, Thai boxing is the roughest thing I have ever seen because they not only use their fists, but their elbows, their knees and their feet, and I actually saw one fight ended by a man kicking the other to the ground with repeated hits on the thigh. . . .

The most beautiful things to see in Bangkok are the Buddhist temples and there were three of them that we saw that were outstanding called Emerald, the Reclining Buddha and the Gold Buddha. I have pictures of all of these and I'll show them to you so I won't go into any detail except to tell you that they are fantastically wonderful in their jubilation of gold and stone.

While in Bangkok I had the pleasure of visiting with the minister of Finance whose name is Pote and, also, Mommy and I went to an evening birthday party given by Field Marshall Thanom, who is the prime minister, for his wife and the other leading man there was General Praphas, who is deputy prime minister and minister of interior and commander-in-chief of the army. This was a real party and I have often wondered since what would have happened if Mommy and I gave a party like that in Phoenix to commemorate either her birthday or mine.

Well, we are beginning to let down into Tokyo so I'll hope to end this part of the letter before we get the wheels and gear down and go in.

To continue. . . . On Sunday I left your mother at the hotel and flew down to a place which I think very shortly will become historic, the new Tactical Air Command Refueling Base at Sattahip. I have some maps of that area and when I get to it, I'll send you each one so you'll know what the general layout is. From this base the KC-135 tankers take off to refuel the reconnaissance and fighter planes that are based in Thailand and which attack the enemy in North Vietnam and without much fanfare of the enemy in Laos also. The important thing about this base that I say will become historic is that I feel that any day soon the decision will be made to move the B-52s from Guam to this base so that getting to the targets in North and South Vietnam will entail only a matter of an hour to an hour and a half instead of the fourteen hour round trip they now have to engage in from that remote island in the Pacific. I might add, although I might repeat it, that intelligence shows that the thing that the Vietcong fear the most in Vietnam are the B-52s and their bombs which they can't hear coming. This is an ideal base, beautifully laid out, completely planned and built better than any base I have ever seen in the United States.

We left Bangkok rather reluctantly because it turned out to be a great spot and we had not really anticipated visiting it but I was extremely impressed with the beauty, the cleanliness of its people and the determination of its leaders to protect the people of that country against communists.

We flew in a T-39 to Saigon taking what is called the bamboo route which is to the south of the Gulf of Siam, the Southern China Sea, then across the delta to Saigon, landing there about five o'clock in the afternoon where we were met by General Westmoreland and the assistant ambassador. More later, for the wheels are down, the flaps are down and we are about to land in Tokyo so I'll cut it off and the next episode will be Saigon.

This part, which will be the final part, is being dictated just after we left Honolulu on the way to the mainland.

Saigon is a very old and a very quaint city carrying unmistakable signs of the French occupation for many years. The hotel we stayed at was the best one in town but probably the worst hotel I've ever seen any place, short of the old days in Calcutta. There was a bar on our floor and, thank God, there was a curfew at eleven o'clock because by that time they were really getting into action. I didn't get to see much of Saigon because I was too busy being briefed here and there so I'll go into that.

Monday night I attended a stag dinner hosted by General West-moreland and attended by the members of his staff. On Tuesday morning I visited with the American Embassy and later with the head-quarters of the United States in Vietnam and then a long discussion with my old friend, General [William Wallace] Momyer, commander of the Seventh Air Force. I had lunch with his staff and a very thrill-ing little thing happened to me on the way out of the Officers Club. As I walked through the part where the pilots were having lunch they all gave me a hand. Believe me, a thrill went up and down my weak old back. Spike Momyer brought me up to date on what his tactical fighters are doing and while I can't tell you about it here when I see you, if you are interested, I'll go into it with you, but it is a fantastic job now amounting to more missions than we flew during parts of World War II.

After lunch I went to what is called MACV, which is really the head of all the military planning operations over there. I had a brief-ing on the overall situation in Vietnam and then intelligence briefing. I then flew by helicopter to visit with General Seaman, commander of the Second Corps who briefed me on this very successful operation that is now going on, Cedar Falls. This is also known as the Iron Triangle and it is the first real massive attempt that we have made to get at the Vietcong using our heavy armor and heavy equipment and the tactics they were designed for.

Leaving there I continued in the same helicopter to Bien Hoa Air Base where I visited the Third Tactical Fighter Wing. To give you some idea of what a strange war this is, the targets that these fighter pilots attack on the ground are only three or four minutes away from the end of the runway while on the same field from which they fly their missions, commercial airliners are landing to carry GIs back to the mainland and, also, helicopters are landing with the wounded. I had a nice visit with the pilots as they returned from their missions and we just had a good old shop talk. I might say that the sound of mortar fire can be heard almost anytime, any place in the whole country, even around Saigon, and Mommy even got used to the boom boom. I continued in the helicopter back to the main base at Saigon which is called Tan Son Nhut, and from there I dashed down to the hotel, picked up Mommy and went out to have dinner with General Momyer. Your mother was the only woman present, so you can imagine what a good time she had.

The next day, Wednesday, I took off at 0800 from Tan Son Nhut in a T-39 and stopped at Nah Trang where I was briefed by the commanding general of the First Corps Area. This is well up toward the demilitarized zone or lateral 17 and this is very mountainous, very rugged country in which there are quite a few minor campaigns going on at the present time.

From there, in the same airplane, I flew to Da Nang where I got into an airplane called the Cod, which means carry on deck, and I was flown out to the Kitty Hawk, an aircraft carrier, some hundred and fifty miles up the China Sea. There were flying strikes off this carrier almost constantly while I was on it and I had a very good opportunity to look at the photographs they had of the target complexes of North Vietnam and to talk with the pilots. I came away from this visit convinced that I had been right and that everybody else has been right who had been calling for it, for open bombing of North Vietnam. Photographs show the clever ways that these North Vietnamese hide oil drums, tanks, motor vehicles and ammunition, knowing that we will not strike within the thirty mile radius of Hanoi unless the targets have been struck before. This will not be an easy job even with the complete go-ahead because they have probably as much equipment stored up there as we have available to us. . . .

That night Mommy and I went to Ambassador [Henry Cabot] Lodge's house for dinner and it was the kind of dinner you would expect, but it was interesting. Afterwards the men retired to one room and the women to another which is an old custom. What do you think the topic of conversation was between the ambassador to South Vietnam, his assistants at the post and an ex-senator from Arizona? It revolved around the fascinating, interesting and highly secret subject of the hottest item in the black market in Saigon, and it turned out that this item was the foam rubber falsies that the Vietnam girls wear. It is discussions like this that will win the war.

An emergency developed that evening because Premier Ky was out of the country and visiting Australia and the rumor was that a coup was going to be attempted. As soon as I learned of this, I realized the ambassador's problems, so Mommy and I said goodnight and returned to the hotel. . . .

I forgot to tell you that on the last morning we were in Saigon, I flew an airplane down to the delta which is the Fourth Corps Area and which is the place that the most deadly, serious and tough fighting will take place. There are about eleven thousand square miles of just delta land down there where they grow a lot of rice. There are about four thousand hamlets and about a third of the nation of Vietnam lives there. I walked through a village that had been taken from the Vietcong and which is being rehabilitated by Vietnamese people, aided and guided by Americans. This is a very interesting program that I'll tell you about when I have time.

Mommy is curled up on the seat beside me, sound asleep. I'm having my first martini, lunch is about to be served and in just about three hours we will be back in Los Angeles and then on to Phoenix tonight. Tomorrow morning I am flying to Washington in the T-39 and then on to New York, back to Michigan, then to Phoenix, then back to Dayton, off to Fort Myers, Florida, and then back to Arizona for a few days rest. It's been a wonderful trip, a trip that I hope all of you can take some day, but I hope when you take it, there is peace in the world.

Column Correspondence with Karl Hess in 1967

When out of office, Goldwater resumed writing a three-times-a-week column for the Los Angeles Times *from 1965 to early 1968. Because of the demands on his schedule, traveling the world and speaking all over the country, he did as he had done before and found a collaborator, Karl Hess. Samples of Goldwater's letters to Hess from the last year of the column are instructive about the reason for the column and Goldwater's thinking, and there is overlap with his trip to South Vietnam. Goldwater ended the column to avoid conflict with his efforts to get reelected to the Senate in 1968. His view of his speechwriter Karl Hess is revealed in a letter of inquiry about Hess years after the column had ended and Hess had departed from his conservative beliefs and was claiming credit for the key phase of Goldwater's 1964 nomination acceptance speech.*

Dear Mr. Keller:*

Karl Hess worked for me in 1963 and in 1964, including my campaign. I retained him after the campaign but found out shortly after that that he had begun to change his stripes from what I had always known to be extremely conservative to a rather radical position on the left. We parted company in a friendly way, and since that time he has been speaking around the country and I have heard nothing from him.

Karl is a very unusual man. His formal education did not include finishing high school yet he holds one of the highest IQ's ever recorded in this country. He is a great expert with the English language and rapidly attaches himself to the particular style that is being used. Karl is confused and this is his trouble. He calls himself a libertarian and tries to equate that with conservatism unsuccessfully. I agree with you about his views and your report of his actions I must say is typical. At one time he was assistant editor of *Newsweek*. As to the phrase regarding extremism [in my 1964 acceptance speech], Karl had nothing to do with that. It actually was first used by Aristotle and then later

---

* *Letter to the Honorable Millette F. Keller, December 8, 1971.*

by Cicero and it crept into my acceptance speech by a very learned scholar on Lincoln.

Letter (February 1, 1967)

Dear Karl:

Thoughts for another column on Vietnam: There are actually two wars going on in Vietnam. One is a military war which I think we are winning and probably winning at a faster rate than many people believe.

I believe that we have solved or almost solved, I should say, the problems of guerilla warfare. Our men are becoming acclimated to these problems, our supplies seem to be catching up with themselves and, I might add, that had not supplies been so low in the opening days of our efforts there, we would be much further along. I mentioned earlier the high competence of our commanders and the unified way in which they are attacking the military problem.

The other war is one that we are just beginning to become engaged in and is probably going to be the tougher of the two. This we might call a political war within South Vietnam because it is an effort to establish a government in the hamlets and districts, something they have never really enjoyed before. In the nearly twenty-five years of war since the French left the country the government, at its best, has been very unstable and, to a large extent, didn't even exist in the districts and hamlets. Our approach to the solution to this problem is called rehabilitation. This involves several phases, the first being to drive the Vietcong out of the hamlet, then to secure the hamlet with our own troops and troops of the South Vietnamese Army and following this is the intensive campaign of education done entirely with Vietnamese people, supervised and helped by our own civilians and troops.

Naturally, when one tries to throw State Department personnel with military personnel for the first time, there are conflicts but from my observance in South Vietnam and my talks with civilian and military leaders, there is great confidence that these natural conflicts are being overcome. As the education of the villages proceeds there comes a natural desire to have leadership, so this leadership is elected by the democratic process practiced for the first time by the people. . . .

Can this war be won? I believe it can, but it is not going to be won quickly or easily. In closing, I think that the new constitution being drafted can help in this effort, particularly if we have rehabilitated a large number of hamlets, impressing the people as we go along that there can be democratic processes whereby their rights and complaints can be listened to and solved. That's all for right now.

Reports from South Africa

Letter (December 8, 1967)

Dear Children,

A report is proper at this time on our [unfolding] visit to South Africa, so while waiting in our room for your mother to get home from the daily hairdo, I'll take advantage of the time to sort of bring you up to date as to what we have been doing.

The flight from San Francisco to Frankfurt, via Montreal, was a long succession of martinis and caviar with practically no sleep. Frankfurt was dismal, as it always is, and with too little sleep, we made the mistake of getting up and trying to see the city. That

Goldwater captured this elephant on film at the Mala Mala game reserve, South Africa.

Barry and Peggy with a rickshaw driver in Cape Town, South Africa.

night we took off for a long flight to South Africa with one stop at Acorn about the middle of the Gold Coast of Africa and then arrived here about noon. . . .

We went to a very delightful luncheon that second day in Johannesburg at which we met Mr. and Mrs. Barlow and Mr. Harry Oppenheimer who between them it seems own not only South Africa, but Central Africa, parts of Egypt and Belgium, and quite a chunk of the United States. That night we had dinner at the head of the broadcasting company's house, but unbeknown to us, our plans were being changed. Mr. Barlow had us picked up early the next morning and flown down to a game reserve called Mala Mala. This sheer luxury is a real foxhole on the war on poverty. The accommodations for twenty people, air conditioned rooms and meals are better than you could ever find in the United States.

Thank God for wild animals and for those of us who like to see them. More and more of Africa is being placed under Game Reserves and while most of these, and the largest of them, are governmental, there are many private ones as this one, Mala Mala, turned out to be. It covers about twenty-two thousand acres and we were driven over this in the afternoon by Mr. Basil Kennedy, a delightful South African, who has spent thirty years in this locality and I think he knew every lion by the size and color of his dung. We traveled in Land Rovers and we saw every animal I'd ever heard of and, of course, I took pictures of them including the giraffe, the rhinoceros, the warthog, the impala, baboons, zebras, water bucks, lions, reed bucks, kudus, and wildebeest, if my pictures didn't turn out, I'll throw the camera right down Don Dornan's neck.

We returned to the lodge, as I would call it, about five o'clock in the afternoon and then at five thirty we motored two and a half miles to a tree that must have been over a thousand years old, and some seventy feet up in the tree was a platform complete with an icebox, gin and tonic, for me, and vodka for your mother. Below us hung the carcass of an impala, and a few feet away on the ground was another carcass. We waited three hours and finally the dim light of the one-hundred-watt bulb hanging over the bait showed a lioness approaching with three cubs. The lioness immediately jumped up and grabbed the bait and began chewing on it, hanging with her paws to the meat. The young ones, which were about seven months old, were a sight to see alternately biting the tail end of their mother and chewing on each other's tails. This went on for over an hour at the end of which the lions crept off and went to sleep, so we climbed down, got in our car and went back to the lodge, had a wonderful dinner around the campfire and went to bed. . . .

Tomorrow, we journey to Pretoria, which is the capitol of South Africa where we will have lunch with the Foreign Minister and then come back to Johannesburg for an evening press conference and a departure to Cape Town. We both wish you could be with us and we hope . . . you will include South Africa on your travel list. They are delightful people, just like Western Americans and Johannesburg is a great thriving city looking far bigger than San Francisco.

Letter (December 19, 1967)

Dearest Children,

We have finally concluded our short vacation to South Africa and Rhodesia and we're now en route home over the Atlantic Ocean. At the outset I will say it is strange to me to be sitting here in an airplane traveling nearly six hundred miles an hour going over the same waters that, twenty-five years ago, I thought I was doing a great job in crossing in eighteen hours. I wrote in a diary that I kept of one of those trips that some day man would be crossing this ocean in a matter of a few hours but I never dreamed it would come about so quickly. Here I sit in perfect comfort, a martini in one hand and the microphone in the other and what a contrast this is to what it used to be sitting up front in a vibrating old crate with more wind coming through the cockpit than on the outside.

Our visit in Rhodesia was very interesting, very pleasant but I must say, quite hectic. What started out to be a trip completely divorced from politics, press conferences, television, etc., turned into the same old routine I go through every day, every week, every month at home.

Rhodesia is not being hurt by the sanctions but our country is being hurt by our attitude toward South Africa and Rhodesia. . . . In Rhodesia we were the house guests for two days and two nights of Lord and Lady Angus Graham and we enjoyed this immensely because it was on a farm, very quiet except they have four children, two dogs, about ten cats and the whole menagerie sits down at the table for breakfast, lunch and dinner with a dog carefully resting his head on the table right by your plate so that if you aren't careful, your food is digested doggy-wise and not by your own stomach. We traveled extensively through the farming areas of Rhodesia, the mining areas, the cattle areas; in fact, we saw the whole damn thing and it was spectacularly interesting. . . .

I had two very good meetings with the Prime Minister of Rhodesia, Ian Smith, and we talked about airplanes and the economy. I won't try to take up your time in this letter trying to explain the apartheid or separate development theory that they are following in both Rhodesia or South Africa, but I would like to try to explain it to you when I see you next. As I said earlier, I think the United States is wrong in their attitude toward both of these countries because we cannot compare the Negro problem of America with the Negro problem of South Africa or Rhodesia.

All in all, it's been a wonderful trip, although I must say we have missed the United States and, of course, we have missed seeing you, but probably before you get this letter we will see you at home on Christmas. I often wish that all of you could have been with us, particularly to see the animals of South Africa. They are beautiful and graceful, they are dangerous, they are numerous but, thank God, some effort is being made to save them from the ravages of the hunter.

I can look down thirty-three thousand feet below and now see the whitecaps of the North Atlantic, and I remember the first briefing I had when I flew an airplane across this expanse of water when we were told that if you are forced down into the water you can expect to live about twenty minutes, so I sort of privately laughed my head off when the stewardess stood up to explain how to put the life jacket on in case we were forced down. I'll stop it here, it's been a long, rambling letter, but I did want you to know what happened on the last few days of the trip and the pictures and I hope I have them by Christmas and will show you better than my words what we saw. Mommy joins me in sending our love to you.

In addition to the lawsuit in 1968 and his travels, Goldwater focused on getting reelected to the Senate. When Senator Carl Hayden resigned, his aide Roy Elson ran against Goldwater for the seat and was overwhelmed with Goldwater winning 57.2 percent of the votes versus 42.8 percent for Elson. Goldwater all but ignored Elson during the campaign, turning his attention to national and international issues. As will be noted in Part V, Goldwater returned to the Senate a seasoned political professional who

Senator Goldwater with Vice President Nixon.

was as concerned about what was occurring throughout the free world as he was in Arizona. Goldwater returned to the Senate as Richard Nixon entered the White House. Publicly, Goldwater had long supported Nixon politically and did so to the bitter end—and even beyond. Privately, he had great reservations about Nixon's politics and then his honesty. Ultimately, Goldwater would become exhausted with Nixon's utter disregard for anyone other than Nixon.

PART IV

NIXON AND WATERGATE

CHAPTER 11

RECALLING NIXON

G oldwater returned to the Senate in 1969 as the Nixon administration began. Goldwater's relationship with Nixon, however, dated back to his first term in the Senate when Nixon was vice president. It was a complicated relationship. The fact that Nixon was the most prevalent subject in his private journal, not to mention the actual entries, suggests that Richard Nixon was something of a puzzle to Goldwater, which he continued to work on until he gave up in disgust.

Recollections (July 18, 1977)

Goldwater prepared this material for his co-author Steve Shadegg when developing material for a book. But this "pure Goldwater" material is far more revealing than anything that made its way into any of his autobiographical books. It provides a good overview of his thinking on Nixon.

This is just a general summation regarding Dick Nixon. To begin with I didn't know him before 1952 [when he became vice president–elect] and I didn't see him at the Republican Convention earlier that year so it wasn't until I came to the United States Senate that I recall the first occasion we met.* I do know that after I went to Washington we soon began to see each other more than occasionally and I formed an

---

 * *Goldwater also recalled a passing meeting with Nixon, however, at an earlier time when Nixon first ran for Congress, but as he told Shadegg (May 10, 1978): "I may have met him someplace in California but where I don't know. At [the time of Nixon's 1948 congressional race] I was Commander of the Arizona Air National Guard and our unit was assigned to a Wing stationed at Burbank, California, so it is possible that on one of my journeys to California I met him because of the mutual interest in politics."*

immediate liking for him. He was a very hard working man dedicated to the Republican Party and had a delightful family.

When I became chairman of the Republican Senatorial Campaign Committee in 1954 I began to see even more of him and we began to work together on matters of concern to the Party, namely and mostly, the selection of, and helping to elect, people for the United States Senate. During both of Eisenhower's terms my meetings with Nixon were more or less confined to politics; he would invite me to his Senate office [which the Senate provides for the vice president] where we would discuss the Party, where we thought it was going, etc. I particularly remember his great concern after we lost thirteen Republican Senators in 1958 and we talked at length about what I thought the problem was, what he thought the problem was, but nothing much ever came of that in a constructive way. It really wasn't until the Republican Convention of 1960 that I began to know this man and it was at that time that I should have learned the kind of man he was, but I didn't.

In 1960 I remember talking with him about issues that he should avoid during the convention in Chicago, and I remember specifically his promising me, one morning here in Washington, that right-to-work would not be one of the issues that he would raise or insist on being in the Party Platform. I had returned from Chicago to Washington the night before to take care of some work in my office, and when I finished my conversation with Dick on the telephone, I went out to the airport and flew back to Chicago, getting back there in the afternoon. I was scheduled to address the Republican Finance Committee the next morning, around 8:30 or 9:00 AM at a breakfast, and I no sooner mounted the rostrum to speak when a high-level messenger came and said that Leonard Hall, [chairman of the Republican National Committee], needed to see me immediately. I said, I can't see Len, I'm beginning to speak. The messenger said he didn't care what I was beginning to do because Len was about to blow his top and I had better get over there. Well, I made my excuses and went to Len's room and, sure enough, he was livid. His face was as red as a tomato and he was using the kind of language that Len seldom used but did with great adroitness when he felt it was necessary. When he calmed down he told me the trouble. Nixon, the day before, had gone to see

Rockefeller in New York and made promises to Rockefeller, including putting the right-to-work measure in the Platform, along with other items, and that he, Len Hall, was going to quit. Len Hall called Nixon a liar not once but several times.

Finally, I got Len to the point that he gave up the idea of quitting but that sort of started things off that year. You will recall that Nixon's dealings with Rockefeller caused a great furor at the convention. In fact, South Carolina entered my name as their presidential nominee because of that and it took all kinds of juggling and skipping and flying around to get out of it. The point is that I should have learned at that time what a two-fisted, four-square liar the man was long before I did.

Well, Nixon got the nomination, he ran for president, and I worked my tail off for him in 1960 and he lost by a small amount mostly because of the bad voting in Chicago. I remember in that instance that [Illinois Republican Senator] Everett Dirksen called me and asked if I would implore Bill Rogers [who was then Eisenhower's attorney general] to send United States Marshals in to supervise the precincts but Bill said no, it would take a word from Eisenhower, so I called the president and told him what I thought was going on in Chicago but by the time he got around to doing anything about it, the votes had all been counted and Nixon had lost the election.

During the ensuing four years Nixon continued to work for the Republican Party and, of course, he ran for Governor of California and lost and then blew his top. When it came to 1964, he didn't work for the nomination; he didn't seem to want it; in fact, he knew what I knew, that no Republican could win that election, particularly after Jack Kennedy was killed. I was nominated, of course, and I will say this, that Nixon did work hard for me and after I lost the election he really began to work and worked at it methodically, systematically up and down and across the country, raising money for the Republican Party, making speeches for candidates, etc. All of this was the lead up to the 1968 election.

But I might say relative to the start of Watergate that I should have smelled a rat in the summer and fall of the 1972 election. For years, I had been asking the Republican National Committee to purchase a jet aircraft so that we could use it for campaigning, and in a non-campaign period, lease it out. Well, finally, I was called by Maurice Stans, [Nixon's former secretary of commerce and top campaign fundraiser], and was told to buy a jet if I could find one. I was told to use it to campaign with, transport as many people as I could around the country, etc. We found a North American Sabreliner and purchased it for $750,000 and right then is where I should have smelled a rat because the Republican Party never had that much money laying around at any time in my memory. We kept the jet about two months, sold it to North American Aviation for about a million dollars and they in turn sold it for probably a million and a quarter. Again, I should have begun to ask questions because they paid the gasoline bills, repair bills and I was allowed to use the chief test pilot for Sabreliner for North America, who acted as chief pilot with me doing most of the flying. We flew about 180 hours during the 1972 campaign. As I say, I should have started to ask questions. It wasn't until about two-thirds of the way through the campaign that I began to hear these stories emanating from Washington about Watergate, and I just attributed these stories to the *Washington Post*, for which I didn't have a great deal of regard at that time. When I returned to Washington before New Year's of that year [1972], I asked a friend of mine at the *Washington Post*, [managing editor Ben Bradlee], if there was anything to the stories, and he said, you better believe there is, and then provided me with background that caused me to get into it myself and that is how I came to make the statement I made to the *Christian Science Monitor*.*

Even at that late date I still had faith in Dick Nixon, and I kept defending him throughout that year, even though I advised him on two other occasions to come clean, lay the whole thing on the table, tell everything about it that he had not told the people and everything would be all right. I even remember one time when visiting Bolling Green, Kentucky, to make a speech and while there I was presented with a bottle of "Watergate Whiskey." The next evening I was invited to the White House along with other Senators to discuss this whole Watergate thing, so I carefully wrapped it in tissue paper, gave it to him with a shot glass, but I knew it didn't please him one little bit. At

---

* *See Chapter 14: Watergate.*

that meeting every one of us told him exactly what we thought about the situation, that he had to come clean, he had to clear the whole matter up, he had to either burn the tapes or make them available to the people. Well, things got worse and worse and worse and worse. Now I think this is enough just to give you some background and I have to go vote.

✦ ✦

EARLY DOUBTS—1960S

Goldwater was in his second term in the Senate as the jockeying for the 1960 presidential race began. By this time Goldwater had great influence over the conservative wing of the Republican Party, and he was never sure that Nixon was a conservative. Indeed, Goldwater worried that he was part of the liberal wing of the party. The subtext of Goldwater's thinking is that Nixon is just a bit too slippery in his positions.

Journal Entry (March 24, 1960)

I just can't reach back through all of the campaigning and select the place or appearance where it first came up, but at sometime during those nearly two hundred speeches leading into the 1960 campaign, with their questions and answers sessions, arose my deep concern about Nixon. It would have served history much better had I kept an account of the birth of this concern, and the way it grew in my mind from the questions of my audiences. But as has been the case in other such attempts during my public life, this effort to record events would die wanting for attention. This, then, is but a brief recap of this development which has troubled me, for it can well mean our losing the presidency and the Congress in 1960. It might be called, "The Strange Detour of Richard Nixon."

I probably should have sensed the possibility of this change in Nixon's adherence to conservative principles with the event in September 1959 just prior to my departing on a vacation. When speaking before a group in Chicago I related a conversation I'd had with Dick a few weeks earlier. It was just after he returned from his visit to Moscow. We were meeting informally in his Capitol office when I broached the subject of Khrushchev's coming to our country. He told me that he had learned of the invitation by radio when returning to the United States. As I recall, he indicated that [Secretary of State John Foster] Dulles had always been against such a visit and that he, Dick, was surprised and (either shocked or disappointed—I cannot vouch for which) at the decision.

The morning after I made that speech, a member of Nixon's staff reached me at [my brother-in-law] Ray Johnson's apartment and I was asked what I had said. I repeated my words, and I was told that I should not have related that conversation with Dick. My vacation was only two hours away, so I told the staffer to tell Nixon to get off whatever hook he felt himself to be on the best way he could; I was going fishing. Well, I further recall that I soon had more long distance calls from Nixon, for he tracked me all over Mexico City when I refused to accept his calls. He was clearly unhappy I had reported what he had told me.

Now that I look back on that incident, it marks the first time that I ever had a question in my own mind as to Nixon's adherence to principle. In fact, it raised a question as to his very honesty. But as I said, I was tired and wanted that vacation, so it has only been lately that memory of that small incident has suggested that his strange detour had begun. Since then, with increasing tempo, and I might add, with gusto, people all over the country have been asking me where Nixon stands: Is he conservative? Or another "me-tooer"? Is he another Republican to whom the principles of our Party are not valid or is he one who is willing to risk defeat by standing for the principles we espouse?

During the period of my Lincoln Day recess of the Senate, when I have been giving speeches, which included visits to Kalamazoo, Vancouver, Portland, Spokane, Los Angeles and Midland, Texas, that I began to hear the question more and more, "Where Stands Nixon?" Before that the inquiries were directed in the broadest way regarding his general philosophy, they were not aimed at any one area. People just wanted to be reassured of his support of conservative principles, and since I believed him to be so, I told others of my belief. During the Lincoln Day period, however, the questions began to narrow down into specific fields like agriculture, education, fiscal affairs, foreign policy, etc. Not knowing of any specific stands in these fields, I could do no more than assume that his philosophy in them was oriented to the right and I answered the question accordingly.

The first sign that Nixon might not be a true conservative came when he publicly aligned himself with President Eisenhower, the attorney general and the secretary of state in approving the removal of the Connally Amendment to the law that made us a participant in the world court.* His position was difficult for me to understand for as a lawyer he should have known that in the absence of any international common law such a court could not function other than as a kangaroo court. If Nixon was a conservative, then that philosophy would have dictated against such a stand. Speaking to many groups has convinced me that Republicans generally did not agree with the president, the attorney general, or the secretary of state and, particularly, the vice president, and their position on the Connally Amendment.

In addition, Nixon has been fuzzy about his positions relating to federal aid to education. He is, at the moment, reported to favor federal aid in the medical fields. He has been associated with Democrats, as his advisors on this issue, and on the whole his statements and actions have been such that the question, "Where Stands Nixon?" comes at me in a steady barrage. On this last trip, which included Palm Beach, Dallas, Los Angeles and San Francisco—a total of nine appearances before audiences ranging from 25 to 2,000, from college students to retired people—"Where stands Nixon?" has been the leading and most frequent question. The purpose of this last trip was to raise money for the special election being held for the Senate seat in North Dakota.

On Tuesday of this week I met with the top editorial staff of the *Los Angeles Times* for a general discussion. The first question asked, and the one that held the floor the longest, was about Nixon. It was

---

* *The Connally Amendment, offered by Texas Democratic Chairman of the Senate Foreign Relations Committee Senator Thomas Connally, was a reservation on the jurisdictional reach of the International Court of Justice (World Court) created with the United Nations to resolve disputes between nations. President Eisenhower sought to remove these restrictions and repeal the reservation to the treaty. Conservatives opposed repeal of the Connally Amendment.*

during this discussion that I received the first real confirmation of my suspicion as to the reason for Nixon's detour. Mr. Bassett, who has been a leading figure in Nixon's past elections, remarked to the effect that Republicans have no place to go but with Dick Nixon, and this being the case, he was correct in trying to attract the liberal or left-wing votes. From this and other discussions I have concluded that this is indeed the thought that motivates Nixon as he detours around conservative principle. If that is so, and as of now we must assume it to be the case, he is in dire danger of losing the 1960 election. Republicans, beginning in 1940, have had nothing but "me-tooism" on the part of our candidates. For Nixon to believe that the working people of the Republican Party will push for his election when he enunciates the philosophy of the New and Fair Deals is naiveté that I find almost impossible to associate with a man who is known for his political sagacity.

Los Angeles Times publisher Harrison Chandler and his wife attended the Tuesday evening forum in Pasadena where I discussed the various conservative positions before an audience of some 2,000 people. Following my speech I had a general question period. The moderator went through eleven written questions before he came to one not involving Nixon. But most all the questions during the hour involved Nixon's apparent move to the left. When the session ended I reminded Harrison of the discussions that afternoon in the *Times* office and he said that he was amazed at the widespread uncertainty and concern about Dick's positions.

As I write on March 24th, it is not early in the campaign. Rather the campaign is an on-going affair with the Democrats having a five-way contest that dominates the pages of the press and the scripts of radio and TV. Dick has chosen to remain a silent contender, at least for the time being. It is time, I believe, for us to know where Nixon stands and what his true intentions are. It is also a time that he be made fully aware of the danger that accompanies the position he seems to have assumed. To that end I have, on three occasions, told him about my concern. However, on the first two occasions, I did advise him that the undertones of discontent were of such a nature that he should wait and see if they developed into a major threat; and on the third occasion, where I also met Nixon key advisers [Congressman] Rogers

Morton, [Congressman] Bill Miller, [Newspaper Editor] Herb Kline, [Congressman] Bob Wilson, I stated that the situation was growing to a point where I thought he should at minimum clarify his position on the Connally Amendment so that it would be crystal clear.

I further urged Nixon at this meeting—and this is an opinion shared by many pros including Vic Johnston—that he should campaign in North Dakota, where on June 28th we have what is to me a crucial Senatorial election. Nixon had been advised against it because they felt Republicans could not defeat [Eisenhower's Secretary of Agriculture, Ezra Taft] Benson's policies there, so he questioned why he should risk his prestige in such an election contest. Knowing of his intent to disavow Benson's solution to the farm mess, I argued that here would be a good place to expose his own answers to the farm policy, and, as to the risk involved, how could he expect to gain the electoral votes of North Dakota if we fail to elect a Senator. No final decision has been made on this as yet, but I doubt that Nixon will follow my advice in any of these instances. Nixon, I suspect, will reason that I am a member of the conservative wing of the party and, as such, I am unduly alarmed at what I feel to be his vacating his position to the right, but I would have to vote for him regardless, and with that valid assumption, he can scratch the liberal and left-wing fields for votes. This I can assure him can create a situation from which I doubt that he can emerge with the laurel wreath. His reward will probably be the loser's condolences. (Others are as concerned as am I. This feeling of disappointment with Dick at this early stage is not confined to merely people who are at the top of the Party in California and elsewhere, but it is related down to the worker in the field, and I have had many people this week contact me personally and by phone expressing their deep regret at their inability to work any longer for Nixon.)

To conclude this short dissertation on Dick's detour to the left, let me add that as of now I do not know who is advising him. I cannot determine who is steering the campaign so I assume that Dick himself is at the helm.

Journal Entry (March 27, 1960)

Peggy and I are returning to Washington from Charleston, South Carolina, a journey that ends a ten-day swing across the nation and back, which has confirmed my earlier conclusion: namely Dick Nixon is in trouble. Yesterday, at the state convention of Republicans in Columbia, South Carolina, there was the first concrete demonstration supporting this conclusion, showing that it is more than an observation of mine. I must however, before relating that, go back a year to a similar meeting in Mississippi.

At Jackson, Mississippi, the Republicans approached me to see if I would aid them in having a states' rights plank inserted in the 1960 GOP Platform, and I told them if they could hold the three hundred delegates from the South, that I might be able to add some more from the West for a total that might be enough for success. However, they could not budge from this position once it was launched. They assured me they could maintain that strength but I have heard nothing more from them. While that situation in itself has no direct bearing on the substance of the points I want to note, I have recorded it because it may have importance as the campaign progresses. What did astound me, however, at Jackson and subsequently in Louisiana, Tennessee, South Carolina, North Carolina, and in fact in every southern state I have visited, there was an obvious reluctance on the part of Republicans to accept Nixon. All these people are troubled by the Little Rock incident,* together with Nixon ruling from the Chair while presiding over the Senate, which greased the way for the civil rights bill of 1957. These actions have cut into his popularity to a considerable extent. Republicans knew that in all probability he would be their party's 1960 candidate, but it is clear that they were not too happy with this fact.

But to go back to Columbia on Saturday, the 26th of March, I made the keynote address and received good applause when it was finished, and returned to my room to gather a few things prior to departing for a day's rest near Charleston. Within a few minutes Gregg Shorrey and Roger Miliken, [both key players in South Carolina Republican politics at the time], came to my room and told me that the convention had by acclamation given me the votes of their thirteen delegates for president at the National Convention. To say that I was surprised would not be entirely true because I had been queried as

---

* In 1957 President Eisenhower federalized the Arkansas National Guard to assure that nine black students could attend the Little Rock Central High School.

to my reaction to this action some months earlier, but I never dreamed they would or could go through with it.

I will not try to comment on my reactions at having received my first delegation support nor would I ever be so bold as to imagine they will be anything but my first and last. Time will be the moderator of this episode in my life. The observation that should be made here, however, is that to me this was the solid evidence that what I have been attempting to relate about Nixon's weakness in the South is a fact, and that his actions at the moment are a subject of dissatisfaction with the conservatives in our party. This action by this group of southern Republicans is more of an expression of their dissatisfaction with Nixon, I am sure, than an expression of their desire for me. If this is repeated in other states, then the effect may well be to cause Nixon to alter his course to such an extent that conservatives can "buy" him and his detour would end with the resumption of the journey down the right road.

Journal Entry (April 6, 1960)

The events since my last entry are indeed interesting, not only as they relate to my present, and to some degree, my future position, but more importantly as they impose their weight on the future of our country and our party. That there is a strong and determined move by some Republicans to move Nixon's thinking toward the left cannot be doubted in light of these events although none are directly connected to the other. Rather they have occurred with matters, in some cases, not directly connected with politics per se, and in other instances intimately connected.

For example, the overwhelming majority of the columnists favor a liberal Republican candidate over a conservative one. In fact, they seem to be keenly anticipating the day when there will be no conservatives and are doing their evil best to hasten that situation. I offer as witness to these efforts men like Joe Alsop, Walter Lippmann, Roscoe Drummond, the nefarious liar Drew Pearson, Marquis Childs, flitting Doris Fleeson, and others who have spent their formative years of journalism under the influence of the socialist New and Fair Deals. Who in addition, to my knowledge, have never participated in politics, yet who pontificate on the subject as peers. The fact that they know no other philosophy than that with which they were indoctrinated and have a feeling toward conservatism ranging from mild acceptance to open revulsion, taints their writings on the subject of politics with bias and more disastrously, ignorance. It seems these columnists, who write mostly for the great urban presses, influence the average politician and, I fear, even that master one, Nixon. It is they who tell him to disregard the conservatives, and to be moderate, progressive, liberal, and, I fear, he listens to them.

Now, the direct force, the one which comes from a political source, is President Eisenhower. He has openly endorsed Dick, which, I feel, he should. While the president speaks in a conservative vein, he practices it only in a limited way. I relate here two instances that have occurred this year to back up my contention that while the president has conservative instincts, he is easily swayed by the advice of the liberals in his cabinet. During the discussions of the extension of minimum wage laws and federal aid to education, I attended the leadership meetings at the White House in my capacity as ranking minority member of the Labor and Public Welfare Committee, which would hear such legislation. I distinctly remember Eisenhower agreeing in no uncertain way with his economic advisers, and his Secretary of Commerce, that there should be no suggestion of increasing the minimum wage or extending its coverage during that year. In spite of this, Secretary of Labor Mitchell was able to persuade him to send down a milder approach than even the Democrats supported. This was done, mind you, even though he had agreed with the overwhelming majority of the Party's leadership that it should not be done.

This situation was repeated in the case of federal aid to education when Eisenhower stated emphatically at another leadership meeting that there would be no federal aid to education suggested by his administration. In spite of this, Secretary Flemming was able to persuade him that an aid bill should be offered and within a few weeks it came down to the Senate. I recall an earlier experience of a similar nature going back to probably 1954 or 1955 when I visited President Eisenhower seeking his support of an amendment that would abolish compulsory unionism from the Labor-Management Act. We got into a discussion of states' rights, and I recall him slapping the table rather resoundingly and saying, "Damn it, Barry, I believe just as much in states' rights as you do, but I must live with my Secretary of Labor."

Because I have made no mention of that episode in my rather loosely put together journal, I might go further at this point and state that it was this contradiction in Ike that caused him the political trouble that he experienced. There has never been in my mind, and there is not now, any question as to his conservative bent. But the fact that liberals in the Republican Party were able to persuade him that the only way the Party could succeed would be by becoming more liberal, or as they like to put it, middle of the road, they persuaded him. Eisenhower's complete lack of knowledge of politics and his unwillingness to step in and learn this game, caused him to rely on these people who were just as inexperienced as he in the matter of practical politics, and the fact that he constantly yielded to them greatly reduced his effectiveness as a president, and resulted in great damage to the Republican Party and, I believe, to his tenure as a president. I will comment here, also, so that I may use it at a later time, on the speeches Eisenhower has made since retiring from the White House he invariably attacks the centralizing of government and yet his own administration did nothing to halt this trend. He believes in his heart as a conservative, but unfortunately during the time that he had an opportunity to exercise such principles, he did it only to a limited degree.

Now getting back to the point from which I departed after relating Ike's endorsement of Nixon, we will continue from this endorsement and the obvious confusion between Ike's pronouncement and performance. I can understand to some measure Dick's dilemma as he tries to set a course. If he is a man who sets his course not by the stars of principle but by the winds and tides of expediency, he will never be on any definable course. He will be torn by what he knows is right but difficult, and that which is wrong and easy.

For example, today the Secretary of Health, Education and Welfare came to the Hill and explained in a very poor way a proposal of the Eisenhower administration to provide medical care for the aged. But no matter how it is explained it will come out socialized medicine. Strange days have descended upon our Party when its leaders will travel this route, and equally peculiar is the desire, at least inferred, of Vice President Nixon to grasp it to his breast. They must know of its ultimate consequences; they must realize the danger; but why espouse it? Why, I fear, it is another seizure of "me-tooism," another product of the years 1940, 1944, and 1948. To me this is a certainty. We have a president whose instincts and training tell him to be conservative, but his closest advisers, for the sake of a mirage of votes, tell him a little of the radical is okay. In short, what we have offered the people and what the Vice President apparently wants to take as his stock in trade is a dime-store new deal.

Journal Entry (June 8, 1966)

Nixon, of course, lost the 1960 election, and it appears that several years passed before Goldwater again makes him the subject of his journal. Since some of his papers have been lost, however, it is not possible to be certain.

Dick and I met in his hotel room this morning for approximately an hour, during which time we had a thorough discussion about the presidential race in 1968. First, we agreed that the candidate would be a person known today, so that would limit the field to Dick, George Romney, Ron Reagan, and Chuck Percy, if he wins the Senate seat. Rockefeller is completely out. However, it was agreed that Rockefeller is now furnishing the money and the brains (not his own, but others) to further Romney's interests.

Dick reported to me that confidential friends in New York think that Governor Rockefeller can be beaten in November 1966, which might just cause a switch with [New York Senator Jacob] Javits sliding into the gubernatorial spot and Rockefeller getting completely out of government. It was agreed that the only chance that Romney had of picking up enough delegates would be to get into the primaries and work all of them. Dick told me that if this happened, he, himself, would enter the New Hampshire primary, which is the first one, to stop Romney before he could get started.

There is no question in my mind but that Dick wants to run. However, he did say this, that the Republican Party and the people are clamoring for a new face and that neither his face nor mine would fill that bill; the same is true with Rockefeller or Bill Scranton, and because of Hatfield's unfortunate position of opposing the war in Vietnam, we ruled him out. It gets us really back to Reagan and Romney, with Percy a possible figure, if he wins, and, personally, I don't think he's going to, although I would like to see him win.*

The question then gets on to Reagan, who has told me that if he wins in California, he does not want to be pushed into a presidential race as early as 1968. However, I pointed out to Dick that I didn't want the presidential nomination either, but I didn't see how we could stop Pete O'Donnell and others, Clif White, for example, from organizing a draft movement for Reagan who, if he wins the Governorship of California, certainly will be a bright new face and one for whom the great bulk of conservatives (or if you want to call them Goldwater people) will go for. If Reagan emerges as a candidate Dick would not run, in my humble opinion because, as he stated it, while we need a fresh new face, it's just not going to be any face, but with Reagan he felt that this one would be acceptable, which gets us to Governor Romney.

There are workers in the field now trying to line up prospective delegates for the Michigan governor, but they are not working too hard nor can there be too many of them because I haven't crossed their trails in the several trips that I have made. Both Nixon and I feel that the nomination cannot go to a non-regular or to a person who did not support the ticket either in 1960 or 1964. We agreed to stay in close communication. To sum up the morning's meeting, I would say that the total of it indicates a stop Romney movement as a means of preventing the Eastern establishment from regaining control of the Republican Party, which both of us feel now rests in the West.

Letter (May 20, 1968)

Goldwater would campaign vigorously for Nixon in his 1968 bid for the presidency, and after a meeting in May, he sent Nixon a copy of a letter he had sent to Governor Ronald Reagan's advisor, and a friend of Goldwater's, Thomas C. Reed. Both letters are reproduced below.

Dear Dick:

For reasons which are very apparent, I would appreciate your keeping this copy of my correspondence completely confidential. Again, it was great seeing you; keep on doing your good job.

---

* *Charles Percy was elected to the U.S. Senate.*

Dear Tom:

When we last saw each other I told you I would write from time to time and I think at this particular point it is proper to lay out some observations to you.

I told you that I didn't think Ron could make an impressive showing in the primaries without personally campaigning and even though he got about ten percentage points more in Nebraska than I thought he would, it is still not good enough. What I am afraid of happening is that by a sort of half-hearted effort in which he continues to disclaim any interest in it, you are accomplishing for Rockefeller what he cannot accomplish for himself, namely, a standoff on the first several ballots at the National Convention. If this is the purpose of your campaign, then I would say the chances are slight to good that you will accomplish it.

In view of Ron's oft-quoted to me very strong and negative opinions relative to Rockefeller, I can't believe that this is the intent of your campaign. As I see it now, Nixon will come out of Oregon with over seventy percent of the Republican vote and, while Ron may cut into this more than I think he will, this will still be another defeat for a man who doesn't need to be identified with defeat. As I have indicated, I do not know what your purpose is and if I did, I could speak more cogently to it, but because I only have to surmise, I think I stated it correctly above.

If by chance Ron is considering running in the second spot with Rockefeller, which I find it almost impossible to believe, I think he would suffer a rather calamitous defeat because Rockefeller can't beat the Democrats.

It is still my thought that California would be very wise if the governor, sometime after the 15th of June, issued a statement that he was releasing his delegates but that he was going to be for Nixon. Nixon has more hard-core delegates now than when we talked, and with Tennessee coming out for him the other day, I think you are going to see this hard-core group grow.

I have a great interest in Ron born out of a personal friendship and admiration, and I don't want to see him come out of this thing a man like Rockefeller who wins in his own state but can't win any place else. There is no need of hurting a great man [referring to Reagan], they are kind of hard to find.

CHAPTER 12

NIXON'S PRESIDENCY: FIRST TERM

Needless to say, Goldwater was pleased to see his friend Dick Nixon in the White House, not to mention his son elected to Congress from California. Goldwater records his many thoughts and reactions to Nixon from the start of his presidency.

1969

Journal Entry (February 8, 1969)

I am sitting in my den in Scottsdale looking out at the beautiful city of Phoenix under particularly clear conditions. I was recalling the evening that I visited with President Johnson in the Oval Office, just prior to the 1969 inauguration when he gave me President-elect Nixon's telephone number, or rather the telephone number of his daughter Julie in Connecticut where Dick was that night observing his birthday. Back at the apartment Peggy and I called Dick to wish him a happy birthday and it turned into a rather lengthy conversation relative to the problems of government, etc.

I talked with President-elect Nixon again the evening of the Alfalfa Club dinner on January the 18th where we had a few moments to chat as the head table assembled. I passed on to him at that time my feeling that he was moving too slowly in organizing his government in depth. At that time, he had filled less than eighty jobs out of some three thousand, which have to be filled to insure him control of government. I pointed out that if he did not do this and do it soon he would find himself in Eisenhower's position, which was one of being president but not really having control of the bureaucracy. Frankly, in the weeks since, I have seen no change in the tempo of appointments, even though he assured me that night that in the next week there would be many announcements.

There is growing dissatisfaction among the members of Congress, not necessarily from the standpoint of the appointments he is making even though that is bothersome, but from the seeming unwillingness of his staff to tell any of us just what the situation is regarding those names that we have sent to the White House as recommendations for appointments. This is extremely reminiscent of the days of Eisenhower when the control of the Party seemed to slip from his hands and into the hands of [his White House chief of staff] Sherman Adams. While I see no indication that Dick is losing any control of the Party or the government, I am troubled by what is going on. For example, they are keeping a number of civilians in the Defense Department and State Department who have contributed most to our dilemma around the world. I am thinking of Mr. Morton Halperin about whom I have written [Secretary of Defense] Mel Laird, pointing out the dangers of his retention and asking for a meeting with Laird when I return to Washington to fully discuss keeping these people whose only interest is in the disarmament of our country.

The inauguration, of course, was a howling success and I mean howling in every true interpretation of that word. Frankly, I think it should not have been the festival that it was because we are at war, we have domestic problems, we have money problems and yet it was a regular Roman gala with money being thrown away like it grows on trees. I hope that future celebrations can be toned down unless the country happens to be in a period where celebration is called for.

It was my pleasure, together with [Arizona Senator] Paul Fannin, to introduce and recommend to the Judiciary Committee my old friend, Dick Kleindienst, to be the Deputy Attorney General. I think he is going to be outstanding in this job and I have a strong feeling that Kleindienst is going on up the ladder.

Because I am sort of the grandfather among the freshmen Senators, they have asked me to organize what we jokingly call the 91st Congress Club, and I go under the title of Professor because I have held a number of meetings for them so that they can better learn the workings of the Senate and the workings of some of the departments.

Accordingly, I held two meetings with the Senate Parliamentarian, the clerks, and other key professional staff, on the Senate floor where they explained their duties and then were asked questions. Later I had a briefing for them from the Joint Chiefs of Staff. I hope it does some good because I can remember how I felt when I was first a freshman.

My office is being besieged by letters and telegrams concerning the *Pueblo* and investigations going on regarding it at Coronado.* We are refraining from any comment at this time because I would like to wait until the navy has completed all of their actions and the Senate and House Committees have held proper hearings. Nonetheless, I think it again points up the complete inadequacy of Robert McNamara as Secretary of Defense and I hope that investigations will serve as a warning that we cannot afford the kind of thinking that he presented in the efforts of defense. . . .

Journal Entry (February 15, 1969)

It is coming up about one o'clock in the morning of the 15th of February and I'm sitting in my radio shack** waiting for a scheduled visit with KR6MH in Okinawa, so I thought I might put down a few observations of this Lincoln Day recess visit to Arizona. This Lincoln Day recess has been more or less typical of what I have been doing for many, many years, which I think helps to keep the party together in Arizona and elsewhere.

Last Friday I flew a Lear Jet out to Arizona with Judy Eisenhower and Dean Burch against 160 knot headwinds all the way, finally arriving in Phoenix but tired; in fact, too tired to go to the Early Bird program at my brother's house, but I went anyway only to find out that

---

* The *Pueblo* incident occurred on January 23, 1968, when North Korea captured the U.S. Navy spy vessel the *Pueblo*. North Korea claimed the ship was within its territorial waters, and Commander Lloyd M. Bucher, Commanding Officer of the *Pueblo*, was tortured in an effort to make him confess. In December 1968 Bucher and his crew were released, and when they returned to the United States, they appeared before a navy court of inquiry, which recommended they be subject to court martial. Secretary of the Navy John H. Chafee rejected the recommendation, stating, "They have suffered enough." Bucher continued his navy career until his retirement.

** This is where Goldwater had his ham radio equipment.

they added seventeen new members, which augurs well for the coming campaigns.*

Saturday was a day of relative ease but on Sunday I had to travel to Tucson to speak before the presentation of the award won by the 167th Fighter Group, which, of course, I helped start over twenty-three years ago.

Monday morning was spent seeing people in the office and then Monday afternoon we traveled to Nogales where I met with the representatives of the Mexican tomato business and the American tomato business over the embargo placed on Mexican tomatoes by an over-zealous Secretary of Agriculture Orville Freeman who, I am sure did this, only to embarrass President Nixon. [Freeman had served both Presidents Kennedy and Johnson.] The Mexicans have been conjecturing for sometime as to whether the Republicans would be better for them than the Democrats and, now, with the embargo in place and quite a few Mexicans out of work, the word is going across the entire country of Mexico that this is Nixon's fault when this has really been Johnson's and Freeman's fault.

I tried for three days to get an appointment set up with President Nixon to discuss this rather sensitive international problem, but I am beginning to worry that a wall has been built around Nixon, the same as was built around Eisenhower many years ago. This whole matter is going to be brought to a full discussion with [Nixon's top aide for Congressional relations] Bryce Harlow, next week, because I finally gave up in disgust at not being able to see the man who told me on repeated occasions that anything I wanted from him I only had to ask. I've asked for only two things: A decent statement from him relative to

---

* *Goldwater's long-time secretary Judy Eisenhower recently explained, "The Early Birds was a special event affair for the Republican VIPs. Early Birds was an off-shoot of Trunk 'n Tusk. You paid big bucks to join the Early Birds and you got to meet personally with whoever the big shot was speaking at the Arizona State Central Republican Committee. I assume Dean Burch was with us because he was flying home to Tucson to be with his family. He had been in Washington testifying before the Commerce Committee's Communications Subcommittee because he had been recommended by the senator, and nominated by the president, to be Chairman of the Federal Communications Commission."*

the Central Arizona Project during the campaign, which was refused and, now, a few minutes with him to discuss this Mexican problem. But I finally gave up on this and returned to Arizona.

Later that evening we had a nice Lincoln Day dinner in Nogales and I arrived back in Phoenix by airplane around 11:30 PM. The next day, Tuesday, was a typical morning, and then a trip to Flagstaff for two cocktail parties and another Lincoln Day dinner and back again to Phoenix by midnight. By Wednesday I was so tired that after a busy morning plus a visit to the hospital in the afternoon to check a condition of the nerves in my right arm, I called off the meeting of the Maricopa County Republicans that evening and stayed home with Peggy.

Thursday was another really busy day with most of it being spent in Yuma visiting with the Wellton-Mohawk people, the Mexican Chamber of Commerce over the Algadones green card problem, a stop at two television stations, a press conference, followed by an evening Lincoln Day dinner and then back home by air around midnight.

Today I traveled to the University of Arizona for a discussion on transportation problems before the Annual Seminar on Transportation and then to Prescott for the annual Lincoln Day meeting, which was most enjoyable, and then back by air arriving home a little before midnight in time to take my midnight to 6:30 AM in the morning shift, and I am sitting here now listening to a god-awful harmonic noise and wondering whether I am going to get through.

When I was briefed by the air force last week they expressed real concern over the fact that four or five young civilians who had written the dangerous strategic papers for McNamara were being kept on by the Defense Department. Upon further inquiry by young Bill Baroody revealed that these men were no longer working at the Defense Department but, unfortunately, Mr. Kissinger has picked them up and now our efforts must be to dislodge them from their new posts [at the National Security Council]. Baroody told me that my old friend and advisor from the University of Virginia was going to be placed in a high position with the Defense Department, a fact that makes it relatively clear to me that as of this time the Defense Department is cleaning house and will be operated on a sensible basis by a sensible man—Mel Laird—and I hope I am sensibly correct.

Journal Entry (February 21–24, 1969)

On Friday morning before departing from Washington for New York with Peggy, I had breakfast with Mr. Bryce Harlow, who told me that the president is anxious to meet with me at regular intervals. What he means by regular I don't know and I'm just going to wait and see if regular means: once a week, once a month or maybe once a year. I called to Harlow's attention that appointments were going too slow and if the president continued to lag in this that he would not be in control of his government.

On Saturday, February 22nd in New York, I addressed the University Club and I think this was my fourth appearance before this group, which I was told is some kind of a record. I explained my opposition to a non-proliferation treaty. That night Peggy and I attended the Air Force Association Ball and, as always, notwithstanding that I was trying as hard as I could not to, I had too much to drink, which always seems to happen when I meet old friends from the air force. I guess it will always be that way.

After we had returned to Washington Sunday, I had a call at 2:00 AM in the morning on the 24th from Barry, Jr., who told me that he had decided to run for the vacant House seat in District 27 in California. This vacancy was occasioned by Congressman Reineke being appointed lieutenant governor under Reagan. I am extremely proud of Barry and the way he has embarked on this venture. I suggested that he bring his brother, Mike, in to manage the campaign and he has done this. In fact, there are only about two weeks left until the primary election, and from what I hear he has a very smooth organization and we have been able to help with the financing and whatever else we could do in keeping with our wishes and staying inside the law.

I suggested that Barry call Governor Reagan to clear it with him, which he did and the following day I had a call from the governor in which he told me a rather strange story, which I relate here and it will remain here unless proven true or false. It seems that on Inauguration Day, when the balls were held in the different hotels around Washington, Ronnie was chosen to be the host at the reception at the Sheraton, which was where we were living at the time because our apartment was being redecorated. The plan, Reagan told me, called for the president to come to each hotel, visit the box of the host, then be escorted by the host to the microphone and introduced by the host. It seems that this procedure was ignored in Ronnie's case, however, because the president, for some unexplainable reason, came in from the opposite side from where the governor was sitting, and was ushered to the stage and introduced by Art Linkletter. I am positive Art was not in on this, because Nixon walked right by Reagan's box, and he didn't even shake hands or say hello.

Later on Reagan was introduced and received a tremendous reception. So was I, and, of course, I went through that routine of making a speech that I don't even remember other than it was well received. I mention this because the question is who caused Nixon to do a thing like this to the governor of the biggest state in the Union, a man whose popularity remains high and without whose help Nixon cannot be reelected. The question is whether it was Finch or somebody else? I'd like to ascribe it to a total mistake, but mistakes like this just don't happen in politics. So we'll have to wait and see. I informed Harlow of this situation and suggested that he might figure out a way for the president to smooth over his strained relations between himself and Governor Reagan.

Journal Entry (March 5, 1969)

On Wednesday evening, March the 5th, I went to the White House for my first formal visit with the president since his election, although we have kept reasonably well in contact by telephone. We met in the living room on the second floor of the White House and Bryce Harlow was with us.

First, I discussed the troubled situation on the Mexican border caused by the embargo placed against Mexican tomatoes and he promised to get on this immediately. He was not aware of this situation, nor was he aware of the worsening of relations between the United States and Mexico because of it.

Next we discussed Otto Otepka and he told me that he had already made a decision to offer Otto a top position on the Internal Security

Control Board.* It would be impossible, which I already knew this, for Otepka to be put back in his old position in the State Department, the post from which he was fired because of his disclosure of security risks. It was the manner in which Otepka did it that caused the trouble and makes it impossible for him to be retained. (I talked to Otepka after meeting with the president and urged him to take the position being offered but I have heard nothing from him since that time.)

We discussed the situation that exists in practically every department and agency where the bright young men of the Kennedy-Johnson years have been retained. I pointed out the dangers in this and asked him to read a paper that had been prepared on the subject for me. I mentioned, in particular, the case of Morton Halperin, who had been dismissed by Mel Laird at Defense only to be immediately picked up by Henry Kissinger. I showed the president a list of others and he seems to understand the dangers and I hope we will see some action here cleaning out others.

Louise Gore** came to see me shortly before I went to the White House to tell me that she had decided to get out of elective politics and get into appointive politics. She is interested in an assistant secretary level post at the State Department and I gave this information to the president who seemed to be elated and indicated that he would take immediate action. Time will tell on this one.

I asked the president a question, which is no doubt on the minds of many Americans: How long is he going to continue the bombing halt in North Vietnam, and continue the peace talks in Paris in view of the increasing activity by the enemy against villages and towns and our forces in South Vietnam? What he told me was reassuring but I was not particularly pleased with the time limitation that he has in mind. He said he would resume bombing within six months if negotiations were not successful, and we would have to withdraw from

---

* *Otepka, as deputy director of the Office of Security at the State Department, won the appreciation of conservatives for his exposure of suspected communists during the Eisenhower years. During the Kennedy and Johnson years he was considered too suspicious of liberals and was removed from his post at the State Department.*

** *Described by the Washington Post at the time of her death in 2005 as "the grande dame of Maryland Republican politics and twice a candidate for governor in the 1970s."*

negotiations. However, I have the strange feeling that the continuance of these attacks of the last several days by the North Vietnamese on the South may be toughening his position so that he may end the bombing halt sooner. Secretary Laird came close to saying as much on his recent trip to Vietnam and I think the American public would back the president completely and with full understanding if he would allow the air forces to take up where they left off before the election.

That was about the extent of our discussions and after an hour I left to perform my duties as the toastmaster for the Annual Goddard Space Award Dinner. The president said he wanted these visits to be regular and that they could be quickly arranged any time that I had anything I thought would be of interest to him.

Journal Entry (March 15, 1969)

Yesterday Nixon announced a change in the deployment of the Centennial anti-ballistic missile [ABM], which I rather expected. It is going to be about half the cost of the old system and I think it can best be defended as a research and development type of project, not to mention it will reduce sixteen existing bases to two. Frankly, I think I could debate both sides of this ABM issue and convince no one, including myself, on what is best for our defense. I recall during the secret hearings on the test ban treaty that I asked one of the eminent scientists if he could develop an anti-ballistic missile without atmospheric testing, and he said no. I asked the same scientist this same question just a few weeks ago and he sort of smiled, and said he knew I was going to ask that question again; he said he thought they could begin development but that was about as far as he would go with it. In truth, I don't think we can develop an effective anti-ballistic missile without atmospheric testing, although there are types of missiles that I am not privileged to discuss even in this journal, but of which I am very aware, that will not require nuclear warheads, or testing, and could be made much cheaper. There is one real sleeper coming along that could solve all the problems, so I think Dick is correct in going into this research and development type of approach. This could get into a real political fight, however. It is possible that it could be the basis for Ted Kennedy's campaign for president. As far as I am concerned, research and development must be continued in this country with the hope that someday we can develop a very effective shield against this threatening weapon.

Journal Entry (April 24, 1969)

[Former Eisenhower aide, and later head of the Atomic Energy Commission,] Admiral Lewis Strauss came to my office and we had lunch and a prolonged discussion about some of the things that concern both of us. He told me that in June of 1968 Nixon called on him for help in two specific areas: (1) He was to get General Eisenhower to endorse him for fear that the general would pass away before he might do it and Lew was able to accomplish this for which Nixon was so grateful he wrote him a longhand letter of thanks. (2) The other was a request for the admiral to seek out any wrongdoing in the Atomic Energy Commission, which he once headed, that might have taken place under President Johnson but which could be blamed on Nixon if he didn't know about the wrongdoing or if prompt action, if necessary, were not taken. The admiral went to his friends on the Commission and organized a task force group that ferreted out some extremely interesting and dangerous information, including the fact that there were serious shortages of fissionable material, not in grams or pounds, but as high as half tons.* Names and dates of these wrongdoings were obtained and given to Nixon. Yet Nixon has not spoken with Admiral Strauss since that time, and there have been no disclosures made, or as far as I know, any efforts made to ferret out and expose the guilty ones. I told Lew that this did not surprise me because, while Nixon called me almost every week during the campaign, I have seen him infrequently, even though he insisted that our meetings be regular. I also told the admiral of my continuing concern about the retention of certain Pentagon civilians either at the Pentagon or, when they were let out there, in other departments, particularly under Kissinger. Last week I renewed my interest in addressing this troubling situation by

---

* *When dictating Goldwater used the words "were shortages" to refer to missing fissionable material, which was made clear in Barry M. Goldwater with Jack Casserly, Goldwater (New York: Doubleday, 1988), 257.*

furnishing Attorney General John Mitchell with a list of these people, which he had requested at a luncheon he, Kleindienst and I had at the Justice Department last Monday.

The admiral then told me an interesting story, which I have used in an accusing way against the Kennedy-Johnson administration. I had been told that the war in South Vietnam started when Secretary McNamara and General Taylor gave the order to shoot back. The admiral gave me the full background of this situation. It occurred on September 14, 1961, at a meeting at the White House. I assume it was a meeting of the National Security Council but, whatever, McNamara recommended to the president that 16,000 troops be sent to South Vietnam. [Under Secretary of State George W.] Ball immediately spoke out against this action and warned that if this step were taken that inside of two years there would be at least 300,000 American soldiers in Vietnam. [Secretary of State Dean] Rusk spoke up and said that George Ball was speaking from a very strongly felt position on this but that he, Rusk, thought this move to be a good one. So that is how it all started.

He continued later.

I am not quite certain at this point where my last entry left off but the most interesting thing that has happened since has been Barry, Jr.'s victory in the primary in California and his almost certain victory coming up next Tuesday, the 29th of April, and if this comes about he and I will be one of the few father-son teams ever to have served in the Congress and, I believe, the first such team ever to represent two different states.

My run-in with the administration over my desire to see General Bill Quinn appointed ambassador to Greece came to a rather surprisingly unsuccessful conclusion the day before Easter, when [Nixon's aide] Peter Flannigan called me and, in no uncertain terms, told me that the man that Attorney General Mitchell had recommended last June was to be the man. It shocked me to learn that none of Nixon's aides, not Harlow, Flannigan or Fred LaRue knew anything about the promise Mitchell made to me in Chicago or, if they did, they were lying to me about their lack of knowledge. Had I known of this situation, I would have never suggested General Quinn, but having been asked to submit a name for Greece, and then having gone over three months of working for it, only to learn that the position had been promised almost a year ago, caused me to tell Flannigan that as far as I was concerned the president had reneged on the payment of an IOU and, while I would continue to support the president, even though at times I might not be in agreement with him, the White House should not bother calling me to do anything for them because coming from a family of gamblers, you welch on an IOU only once, there is no second chance.*

Recently I flew the SR-71 at Mach 3.13 and at 81,000 feet becoming the 221st person in or out of the service to achieve that speed.** Also, this morning I flew the A-6 of the navy as I am trying to get a flight in all of our tactical aircraft in connection with my work on the Air Power Subcommittee.

Journal Entry (May 17, 1969)

A lot has happened since the last few notes I made for this journal I'm supposed to be keeping, so I'll try to bring it up to date as best I can. Peggy, with sons Barry and Mike, and Mike's wife Connie, and I went to church with the Nixons at the White House a couple of Sundays ago and then Barry and Peggy and I flew to Winchester, Virginia, with the Nixons in his helicopter, while Mike and Connie drove down to Virginia in my car. There we had lunch with Harry Byrd, Jr., and his wife and children, and then all of us, including Mike and Connie, flew back to the White House with the president, the first lady, Tricia, Julie, and her husband David Eisenhower.*** All of this, of course, happened the week after Barry won his special election to represent District 27 in California in the House of Representatives in Washington, which

---

  * *General Quinn and his wife Bette were among Goldwater's closest friends in Washington. This had to be painfully embarrassing to Senator Goldwater.*
 ** *And, no doubt, one of very few persons ever to do so at sixty years of age.*
*** *Mike Goldwater recently recalled that at the luncheon on Senator Byrd's farm, he and his wife Connie happened to sit across the table from the helicopter pilot, Lt. Col. Sample, USMC, and Mike mustered the courage to ask if they could ride*

Photograph of President Nixon taken by Goldwater on the presidential helicopter returning from Senator Byrd's farm in Virginia.

was the biggest thrill in my life. I know that Peggy felt the same. His brother Mike put together the finest political campaign that I have ever seen. His organization was superb in that they had 4,000 people to fill 2,400 jobs on Election Day and it went off great with Barry winning nearly 60 percent of the vote. He is now in Washington trying to put his staff together and temporarily he is living with us in the apartment but I expect that he will, in his independent way, very shortly

---

back in the president's helicopter with the rest of the family and the Nixons—if they had room, of course. The pilot soon reported it was all set if Mike could find someone to drive his father's car back to Washington, which a young man sitting next to them volunteered to do. Mike reported, "So off we went to the local high school football field, where the helicopter was parked with a red carpet across the fifty yard line, leading up to the whirlybird's stairs. Flying back to Washington Dad took a great photo of the president looking out the window of the helicopter, which I sent to Julie and Tricia; it is one of the best I have seen of him (see photo above). When the helicopter landed at the White House, Connie stood up and started to disembark when Mom grabbed her hand, and told her that the president always gets off first. Upon hearing that, Nixon looked at Connie and said, 'That's all right sweetheart.' But, of course, he disembarked first."

find a place to live, but it will be great having him in Washington. I have checked and he and I are the first father and son team in the history of the country to represent two different states, one in the Senate and one in the House. Barry's first Saturday night in Washington, he escorted Tricia Nixon to Tricia's first formal ball at the White House and I know he was thrilled even though he doesn't like to admit it. She's a very beautiful and charming little girl with her father's nose and I told her father that on her it looked good.

For the first time in history, as far as I know, a justice of the Supreme Court was forced to resign because of actions that, at their best, were improper. Justice Abe Fortas had accepted retainer money from financier Louis Wolfson, who is currently serving time in the federal penitentiary for violations of the law. Fortas is an honest man, he is a good lawyer and quite a decent chap but when one is a member of the Supreme Court it's like being Caesar's wife, nothing can be done to bring any doubt upon the character of a justice. Of course, this gives the Nixon administration a tremendous break because Chief Justice Warren is retiring at the end of this Court's term, which will be in the coming month of June, and the president will now have two appointments. Who they are going to be the Lord only knows. While two justices will not radically change the direction of the Court, it can certainly help turn toward interpretations of the law that are more in line with the Constitution.

The Warren Court has been a disastrous time in American history because these nine men were guided, not all of them but most of them, by what they would like to see happen in the United States, what they would like to see the United States become, rather than what the Constitution says that the United States should be. Their judgments were subject to sociological influence rather than legal and Constitutional influence, and it will be like a breath of fresh air to have a Court oriented more toward law and the Constitution than we've had for the past nearly eighteen years.

I have had my first falling out over the new administration with some of my fellow Senate Republicans. It was provoked by a speech made by [New York] Senator Javits to the Commonwealth Club in San Francisco where he, in his typical non-Republican way, criticized the president for not having ended the Vietnam war in the last two and a half months since taking office. It is long past time when we find out just where people stand, since I feel, to be candid, that a few of my Republican colleagues would actually be more comfortable in the Democratic Party than in the Republican Party. But if they intend to stay members of our Party, then I would suggest that they confine their criticisms to their votes and not make public statements condemning or criticizing our leader. The alternative now seems to be another Kennedy, which is dreadful. I say this to cast no personal aspersions against Ted Kennedy. To the contrary it is just that I feel that his being president would bring on another national disaster like those that befell his brothers and this country can't stand any more such tragedies, not to mention it can't stand another four years of rule under what was once the Democratic Party.

At this writing, the heated debate on the ABM [anti-ballistic missile] treaty has not come out into the open yet. I've made several speeches in favor of it and will continue to do this because I feel it would be a terrible blow to the administration to lose, in particular to our chances to secure serious talk on disarmament. If we fail to provide this country with the defense that the ABM system would provide and, more importantly, with the ongoing research and development in this whole field, which we so desperately need, it would be unfortunate. As day passes day in the long series of hearings we've been holding in the Committee on the Armed Services it is becoming more and more obvious that the eight years under [Secretary of Defense] McNamara has come very close to destroying the military might of this nation, doing so as no enemy, or combination of enemies, could do. His so-called cost effectiveness operation has been reduced to a shamble, and his system of procurement contracts is now coming out to be the costliest mistake in the history of purchasing in the Defense Department.

I continue in my battle to separate the uniform from the civilian operations at the Pentagon because the military men are being blamed for the mistakes made by the civilians. I keep harping on my lifelong conviction that is in keeping with the Constitution, which means that the civilian should always be superior to the military. This is not to say the military can or should be ignored. But that was the way that McNamara handled it because he completely ignored the military, did things on his own, and, as a result, we have a military that is strong as far as it goes but it doesn't begin to go far enough. In fact, as I write this, the Russians are catching us in fields in which they have been behind us and they are ahead of us in other fields where parity has long existed.

Journal Entry (July 4, 1969)

At the present moment, I'm flying on Continental Airlines from Kansas City back to Los Angeles and then down to Newport Beach to join [my son-in-law and Little Peggy's husband] Ricky, Colonel Shade and his four sons for an all night cruise in the Pacific to reach someplace 150 miles south of Newport Beach, California, to try albacore fishing tomorrow.

I left Los Angeles this morning and flew to Kansas City to give an address to the DeMolay organization on the fiftieth anniversary of its founding.* I have been honored in my life by having been made a member of the Legion of Honor of the DeMolay and in that capacity, I am chaplain.

Everywhere I go these days, I am asked what I think of Nixon's performance as president so far, and my answer always begins with a statement that I don't believe that any president can be judged in a matter of a few months. In fact, only history can tell whether a president was a good president or not. For example, the longer Harry Truman lives, and the longer history goes, the better president he becomes in my mind. I disagreed with him violently when he was president, but I find that his type of leadership, whether he was right or wrong, is what we need today and I sense that we are beginning to get it with Richard Nixon. I think as time passes, the glitter that has been bestowed upon the Kennedy name will disappear in the realization that he didn't have enough time to prove whether he was a good president or a bad president; he was just a helluva nice fellow in a job that he won by a very small majority. But history will be the judge.

---

* The Order of DeMolay, a youth organization (twelve to twenty-one years of age) sponsored by the Masons, was founded in Kansas City, Kansas, by Jacques DeMolay in 1919.

I think Nixon's actions in Vietnam have been wise in that his troop withdrawal has been based upon a formula whereby the South Vietnamese divisions, as they come into proficiency and can take over, will do just that, relieving an equivalent number of American boys. Twenty-five thousand returnees, which was the first number announced in June, is based upon the readiness of two South Vietnam regiments and two South Vietnam divisions equal to about twenty-five thousand men. Another survey will be taken in August, and my expectation is that at least fifteen thousand additional men will be announced as returning at that time and possibly more. I do feel as of today, which is Independence Day, 1969, that the president must, in the very near future, take a very definitive and strong stand relative to the Paris Peace Talks by saying, in effect, "Either do it or get off the pot." In other words, if we can't begin to see some achievements in Paris, we're going to resume bombing and by resuming bombing, I would suggest a complete bombing of Haiphong and the opening of the Red River dikes, even though the navy seems to think this is not a profitable venture.

At the moment, inflation seems to be the biggest problem facing the president, and I think he has taken the proper steps to slow it down; however, we won't feel the effect of these steps until probably the beginning of the fourth quarter of this year. The continuation of the 10 percent surtax, while I disagree with it completely, nevertheless is a must, and I will vote for it when it comes to the Senate, just as my son voted for it in the House, even though he had extremely strong reservations against it.

Nixon's announcement in the last few days through Secretary [of the Treasury] Kennedy that he was meeting with the leading bankers of the country to urge restraint in lending seems to me a good step as well, for if we can get the bankers to agree to this and then get the labor unions and business in general to agree to restraint on their part, I think we can begin to see a falling off of the cost of living increase by the fourth quarter; but if this doesn't happen, I think we are in for one serious mess. I hate to make this prediction, but if we don't have inflation ironed out by this time next year, if we don't have the war ended by this time next year, the Republicans will suffer losses and the president's chances of being reelected will be diminished.

I mentioned earlier the vote on the surtax, and I want to point out here that this is one of the few times in his political life, my son, Barry, as a Congressman, has called me to ask how he should vote on a measure. I knew that he had campaigned against the surtax and knowing of his strong, unalterable belief in honesty, in which I take great pride, I told him that in this case I thought he would have to forego his campaign promise and that he could balance this off by saying that while he did not favor a reduction nor the elimination of the 7 percent investment credit, he nevertheless felt that by eliminating this, we could slow down the heavy investment in capital goods, and the resulting increase in inflation. I told him that there would be times when he would have to be a team player, even though the vote might make him feel like vomiting afterward. If there was one lesson that I learned in my previous twelve years in the Senate, it was that—and it took me a while to learn it—but I have since tried to be a team player on the Senate floor because I've always been one in active politics, although I don't know how much longer I can stomach being this with some of these liberal Republican players such as Jacob Javits, Charles Goodell, Clifford Case, and the others. There is an old English tavern saying that goes like this:

> I do not like thee, Doctor Fell;
> The reason why I cannot tell;
> But this I know and know damn well;
> I do not like thee, Doctor Fell.

While I wouldn't want my relationships with some of the so-called Republican colleagues to be reflected entirely by that statement, nevertheless, I think the time is coming, if it is not long past due, where some of these purported Republicans had better join forces with the radical left; and in turn, some of the conservatives who are Democrats should join with the conservative right. Liberal GOP Congressman John Lindsay's recent defeat in New York points this up where a Republican, supposedly running as a Republican, was defeated by another Republican, and now he decides to run as a liberal. Lindsay is backed by the likes of Javits and Goodell, and I imagine, by Case and

I would suspect eventually, by Rockefeller, but I hope this time I am wrong about Rocky.

We may be living at a time that is the beginning of a change, a shifting, and the regrouping of political philosophy and parties in this country. It was just about a hundred years ago, or a little over, that this same sort of regeneration took place, and the Republican Party was formed out of the remnants of the Whig party. Since that time, our luck has gone up and gone down, but today, when we stand a chance of really doing something for our country, it is a shame that we are impeded by the likes of these eastern gentlemen who are really philosophically, and in practicing ways, better Democrats or better left-wingers than they are Republicans.

There is a break in the cloud pattern beneath us and I am certain I can detect the Canadian River running across the Panhandle of Texas, and it forces me to recall with such pleasure hunting down there a number of years ago, and right at this moment I'd love to be down there with the birds and the deer, but with a camera rather than a gun. Please pardon a corny kind of thought right now riding up here through these clouds, getting an occasional glimpse of the earth, but I just think how great it would be to spend four or five days with my pals, a jeep, a little bottle stashed away, a little food, a couple of bedrolls, and sleep out under God's heaven, being winked at by only God's stars, and by the light of the moon, that we mortals, in a few weeks, are going to first invade.* Flying over this country as I've done for forty years of my life, on countless hundreds of thousands of miles of travelling to every state and nearly every significant town and city in many of them, has never diminished my great love of seeing it again and again, and the true thrill that is always mine as I look down on this land of the free and know that it's a little bit mine and a whole lot everybody else's. Also the thought and pride that my family, in the past hundred odd years, has worked for the good of the country, and we might have had a little bit to say in whither it goest.

---

* Goldwater would attend the Apollo 10 liftoff from the command center in Houston, Texas.

Journal Entry (September 8, 1969)

My old and very dear friend Everett Dirksen passed away yesterday after a rather lengthy illness culminated by an operation on his lung to remove cancerous growth a few days ago. I will never forget that night back in 1951, when he was standing on the roof of the Adams Hotel in Phoenix with me, and persuading me that I should run for the U.S. Senate. Ever since that night he has been a close personal friend and valued advisor. One of the really great memories of my life will always be the nominating speech that he gave for me in San Francisco at the convention in 1964.

Today marks the crucial vote in this year's fight against the military Authorization bill. This is on the C5-A Transport Aircraft and I think we will win it. There has been an amazing conglomeration fighting against the construction of this airplane and these people are also against everything military. In fact, I have for a long time accused them of essentially being isolationists along with their interest in unilateral disarmament. When Robert McNamara was Secretary of Defense they had their man in the cat-bird seat and they didn't have to worry about disarmament, because he was accomplishing this by not acquiring new equipment. Now that he is gone the task is being taken on and led on the Senate floor by men like senators Fulbright, Proxmire, Javits, Brooks and Case.

About ten days ago I had a most interesting visit with President Nixon at the Western White House in San Clemente, California. Peggy and I had been invited over for cocktails at 6:30, but he asks us to come at 5:30, so he and I could visit and Pat and Peggy could get their heads together. I again stressed to him the important need for getting every Democratic hold-over out of all the bureaus, particularly the Defense Department. I called his attention to the fact that in the current debate our opponents are being furnished top secret information almost hourly; in fact, this information finds itself in the press. I talked to him again about Louise Gore, and shortly afterward she was appointed Ambassador to the UN.

Nixon told me two very interesting facts, which I will relate here and will not release until I feel the time is proper. Ex-president Johnson had visited with him just two days earlier, and President Nixon said that during their conversation Lyndon said that he had made two mistakes while he was in office: one was taking bad advice from McNamara, and the other was his believing that he could trust the Russians. The president told me that Lyndon warned him to never trust the Russians, that he should not engage in disarmament talks with them, that he should not agree to go to any table with them because they have yet to show any honesty. Nixon was strong in making his point, ramming one fist into the other hand, when assuring me and asserting, "I will not trust them and I will not talk disarmament with them." It remains to be seen whether he will, or not, because pressures are great on the Hill to once again knuckle under, to bow down to the Russians who are winning everything they want without going to war.

Nixon talked about his problems in Vietnam, and at one point, he turned to me and asked, "What would you do?" I said, "Mr. President I don't think that you would do what I suggest, because I am probably too strong but I've always believed when we go to war we go to war to win." I suggested there are two approaches: one would be complete withdrawal, which of course we couldn't do, and the other would be to get set for a never ending war, which we couldn't do either. So I said what he should do was to put the negotiators at the Paris Peace talks on notice, and thus warn Hanoi, that come November 1st—the first anniversary of the Peace talks and the bombing halt—that unless something was truly accomplished by that date that not only would he resume bombing, but that he would attack the important targets in the North, including the Harbor of Haiphong, and the dikes of the Red River upon which they depend for food. I told him that I did not believe Hanoi would dare continue the war if she felt certain that we were going to do these things. But as I say, we'll just have to wait and see, for we are fighting a war we do not seem inclined to want to win. Somewhat tentatively, however, we did agree that we were making a little better progress in getting troops out and bringing peace. But I for one have to see much more of it before I'm going to be thoroughly convinced it is real progress.

1970

Journal Entry (March 24, 1970)

It is President Nixon's second year in office. While I dislike record-ing this, I believe what Arthur Krock told me over a year ago has come to pass.* Arthur said that if Nixon did not have control of the government by June 1970, he would never get it, and as of this date I can safely say that he only has control of the Justice Department and Defense Department and that is it. All the agencies and bureaus and departments of government are still filled with holdovers from the Johnson-Kennedy administration and they are making the president's task of governing an extremely difficult one.

It was just about a year ago this time that the president suggested that we should visit with each other at least twice a month and more often if needed, but it has been since late August of last year that we have visited, leave alone talk. In that time he has drifted more and more away from availability and whether he realizes it or not, a very effective shell has been constructed around him. For example, over a year ago he suggested that I visit with Henry Kissinger and that he would set it up. This was never done. The same suggestion was made in August and, while Kissinger was within fifty yards of us, no meeting has taken place.

I personally called Kissinger in the fall of 1969 asking for a visit, and I was granted one but he was not available when I arrived at the White House later. Yesterday, my son, Barry, who departed for Israel today, asked for a quick briefing from Kissinger on Israel, was told he could have it. But when he arrived he was told that Kissinger could not make it, so a young assistant was sent, who did not even know the population or the geographic size of Israel.

What I am writing about does not stem from just my own expe-rience with the Nixon White House but I hear it constantly by my congressional colleagues in the Senate and the House. While some

---

* *Krock, considered the "Dean" of Washington news people, was chief of the New York Times Washington Bureau.*

Cabinet members do respond to their mail from us, others completely ignore it and, frankly, I can recall with prior presidents, Democrats no less, having an easier time getting answers from them than we have today with a Republican at the other end of Pennsylvania Avenue. Because of this growing distance between this president and members of his Party, he is running into problems like his failure to get Judge Haynsworth confirmed for the Supreme Court, and now the possible failure of Judge Carswell.*

Our attitude toward foreign governments continues to be dictated to a large extent by pressure from minorities in our own county. Witness the senseless abandonment of Rhodesia. Witness at the present time also the precarious balance being practiced by the White House between the Arab and the Jew. Witness the indifference of this administration to the Republic of China's desire for modern weapons. All of these decisions appear to be dictated by whether or not a position is politically important to satisfying some part of the United States electorate rather than what it does for our position in the world, not to mention what is in the best interest of our country. I will watch these developments closely because if the situation does not change rather drastically, by late summer our congressional election efforts will fall short of the goals we think we can and should achieve.

Journal Entry (August 6, 1970)

About two days ago I received a rather difficult to understand message from [Nixon's White House aide] Harry Dent's office stating that there would be a meeting of Southern conservatives in his office at 4:30 on the afternoon of August the 6th. I called Harry, and reminded him that I was not a Southerner although I am a conservative. I told Harry I thought it would be a mistake to start dividing the Party into conservatives and liberals, especially when such a meeting would not be kept secret for very long.

He told me that it was not as I thought, for he had invited Sam Devine of Ohio, Bob Dole of Kansas, Les Ahrens of Illinois and me to

---

* Nixon would fail with Carswell too, with Republicans giving him only the mildest assistance in dealing with the Democrat-controlled Senate.

meet with him in his office as well and then to meet with the president at 5:00 to discuss what our differences might be with his administration. When I arrived at Harry's office, however, I found Southerners gathered; in fact, these are the people that were already meeting when I came in; they were arguing with Attorney General Mitchell about the enforcement of civil rights laws in the schools in the South. They included Senators John Tower of Texas, Strom Thurmond of South Carolina, Ed Gurney of Florida, Congressman Sam Devine of Ohio, Harry and Mitchell. When we eventually moved to the president's office Vice President Agnew, Congressman Les Ahrens, Senator Bob Dole, and Bryce Harlow were added to the group.

Since this was a gripe session, the president asked for comments, so the Southerners started complaining of their woes about the racial problems of the South, particularly the Internal Revenue Service decision to tax private schools, which they believed would have a dire impact on the South, not to mention how it would impact the image of the president for they explained this was being labeled "The Nixon Integration Plan." Now, I don't happen to agree that the race problem is as big in the South as these fellows say, although I do know that in the outlying districts in the South, those districts away from the larger cities where the rednecks live, in these places race is still a big issue. Most of the younger members of the Congress from the South agree that race is an isolated problem, and they only want Nixon's enforcement not be as rigid as they have been led to believe it will be.

When it came my turn to voice my particular beef I said—although it might not be exactly the words I used—that I was going to be brutally frank, because the president and I have been friends for many years, and I didn't think anybody in this room, or for that matter anyone in this country, had campaigned harder for him in both his presidential elections. I told him I thought that the Republican Party was the hope of America, but the way the Republican Party was headed now, it was going to wind up being a minority party again soon, and out of power. I minced no words in saying the administration reminded me of when Eisenhower came into power and failed to remove some thirteen thousand Truman appointees, and went on to subject himself to eight years of abuse from people in government who actually hated the Republican Party and who would never follow the policies laid down by the leadership. I reminded the president that only a few weeks after his inauguration I had advised him that if he did not get control of his government by May he would never get it, and I said, frankly, Mr. President, you don't have control now and I don't see how you are going to get it unless something drastic is done.

I told him that his policies were not being followed in the executive branch, and even the legislation that he favored, and which had been passed, was not being put into action the way it was intended but, rather, through regulations written by the agencies and the bureaus, the intent of the legislation and the president's policies were being changed by the bureaucrats—those who were there before he arrived and would be there after he left. I reported that this had been the thrust of a speech I made about two weeks ago, which has received unusually favorable comment from all across this country.

I proceeded to give him several specific examples, citing cases in several of his departments. I told him that only a few of his cabinet members understood the problem and were really doing anything about it, and these included Walter Hickel at Interior (to some extent), John Volpe at Transportation, Mel Laird at Defense and Mitchell at Justice. But the other cabinet officers are allowing the holdovers from the Democratic administrations of Kennedy and Johnson to rule the roost. I reminded him that he had been elected because Americans wanted a change in the direction of the government, and he has not been able to provide that change because he has not cleaned house in the policy-making areas of his various departments.

I was pleased that heads were nodding all around the room in agreement with me, including the vice president and Mitchell—and even the president himself. When I finished my little dissertation I noticed the president had taken copious notes. When he responded he reminded me of the difficulties of getting rid of these people and then to fill these posts. To this, I responded there was no difficulty in getting rid of anybody if he worked at it hard enough.

As we were leaving, in an aside, since I was sitting beside him, he asked why I hadn't visited him since August 28, 1969, almost a year ago. I answered, rather facetiously, that the goddamn Coast Guard wouldn't let me go within three miles of his house at San Clemente, and I only live fifteen miles away in Newport Beach on many weekends. This kind of got to him, since he could hardly forget shortly after his inauguration that he told me that we had to see each other regularly, at least twice a month. Of course, I had seen him at several formal state dinners at the White House, where nothing can be discussed, but that was not the kind of meetings we needed. So he did tell me that he hoped we could visit in California the last weekend in August. So I pulled his leg a bit, telling him that I would be glad to if I could get in touch with him, but making a telephone call from where I live in Newport in the summer and where he lived in San Clemente in the summer, all of some fifteen miles distance, required a telephone line reaching approximately five thousand miles back through Washington to reach him, and as a taxpayer, I objected to this kind of waste. He laughed about this and said that he had to pay taxes too.

I don't know what is going to come of this session. I told him it was not personal; I told him I would continue to work for him and that I thought he could be reelected president, but that if he continued to allow the government to be a replica of what it has been for so many years, we would be in real difficulty.

Journal Entry (December 16, 1970)

A few days ago, the president's office called asking that I come to the White House to visit with the president at 4:00 PM that afternoon, which was the 14th. A member of my staff drove me down there, we got there a bit early and I had to wait about half an hour for him, but I was finally ushered into the Oval Office at 4 o'clock. I had brought with me the large Arizona bronze eagle that the artist, Jack Fowler, had given me about a year earlier to present to the president. It had been thoroughly X-rayed, examined, looked at by the Secret Service. After the president accepted it he opened a small drawer in the front of his desk and gave me a golf ball, tie clip, a pencil, cuff links, and Lord knows what all else, which I, in turn, passed on to my staff when I went back to the office.

The meeting started out with just the two of us in the Oval Office, and I had a Coke and he had hot tea delivered by Manolo, his butler, and we exchanged a few greetings and words in Spanish. Not having any idea what the president had on his mind, I'll have to reconstruct it as best I can, so it may sound a bit incoherent.

He first asked me what I thought of the appointment of John Connally to be Secretary of the Treasury, and I told him if for no other reason than the fact that it made Senator Bill Fulbright mad as hell, I thought it was a good one. But I had other reasons for thinking it was good. Connally had been the secretary of the navy, and a good one; he's a true conservative, a solid businessman type, and he will be able to present forceful arguments on behalf of a responsible budget, particularly in the military fields. While Treasury Secretary David Kennedy was probably the best equipped man in the country in a technical sense, he was not a fighter, and was not politician enough to understand how to get his points across in Washington. I think, politically, Connally's selection was a ten-strike, reminiscent of the days of Franklin Roosevelt, because he has appointed a Democrat with whom the Democrats can't argue too much because of his dominant position in Texas and the value of their twenty-six delegates.

We also discussed the problems in Vietnam and Cambodia, not at any great length, but I assured him that I thought he was absolutely correct in his resuming the bombing in the north, particularly the SAM sites, which the enemy was using to shoot down our reconnaissance planes. I told him I thought his Vietnamization plan was going along about as well as could be expected, but I still had growing reservations about the South Vietnam infantry being able to come up to battle standards in any number sufficient to offset the skill and equipment of the North Vietnamese and the remaining Viet Cong when they replaced our troops.

We did talk at some length about the SST.* I was openly critical of the administration's failure to properly present this case to the Republican members of the Senate. I told the president what I had been able to do

---

* In the 1960s the British and French developed supersonic transport aircraft— ultimately the Concord—for short- and long-range passenger travel. Fearing that America was behind in this cutting-edge technology, Congress funded an American SST design effort, selecting the existing Lockheed L-2000 and Boeing 2707 designs, which were more advanced, larger, faster and longer-ranged design than the Europeans. In time, the Boeing design was selected for continued work. Meanwhile, the Soviet Union set out to produce its own design, called the TU-144. In the United States, however, because of the great expense, the uncertainty of

with the help of people from the industry, but I wished he had placed a better man on the job of selling it, because Nixon aide Jeb Magruder had not gotten off his fat butt and done much about it

Again, I returned to the subject that is a sore one to me, although I hope it will not sound like I have been grinding on him but it probably will. I said, "You know, Mr. President, we sat in this room a few days after you were inaugurated, and you told me that you had to keep in constant touch with me, at least twice a month." I reminded him that, other than group meetings and White House functions, this was the first time since August of 1969 that I had seen him alone. Facetiously, I even asked if he thought I had syphilis or something, and was keeping me away. I mentioned to him, what he well knew, that I am a former standard bearer of the Republican Party, and whether he or the Party liked it or not, he never consults with me about political matters; in fact, I told him I have been invited to my first Republican National Committee function in six years; it is an invitation to address the Finance Committee on January 14th. Nixon told me he was sorry about this, for he would like me to become more aggressive and get on more television shows. "Well, Mr. President," I responded, "I've been on more television shows than any three Republicans put together." Nixon said he didn't know that.

This hit a nerve. So I again told him that this indicated that he was living in a cocoon, and that people had built this complete shelter around him, and those of us who wanted to help him just couldn't get through that wall. He didn't believe this, so he called in three of his aides, all of whom reluctantly confirmed the fact that he was not in close enough touch with the rank and file Republicans here in Washington, and probably did not really know what is going on.

After they left, I explained to him my candid analysis and opinion that if the election were held this next week he couldn't win it. That didn't mean that he couldn't be reelected but unless something happened

---

economic viability, and environmental concerns, the SST was opposed by many. Its sonic boom as it broke the sound barrier, its noise at takeoff, and the potential that its engine exhaust might damage the ozone layer were the principal complaints that influenced members of Congress, who ultimately killed the SST program not long after this conversation.

to the economy to pick it up, and unless things do not continue to go as well in Vietnam as they seem to be, he is in trouble.

We discussed the vacancy in the chairmanship of the Republican National Committee, and I suggested Senator Bob Dole for the post. Nixon said that Minority Leader Hugh Scott was opposed to Dole, and Scott claimed that thirty-one Republicans lined up to support him opposing Dole. I informed the president this was hogwash, and not possible because I had seen a copy of the telegram that was to be delivered to the president containing thirty Republican names urging the appointment of Bob Dole. I emphasized to the president that the chairman needs to be an effective money raiser, and while I never have thought well of members of Congress occupying that seat, if we could get a dynamo to serve as the chairman's executive secretary, I could certainly go along with a continuation of the idea that started with Bill Miller, and have a member of Congress fill the post.

I told Nixon, in answer to his question about NASA, [at the time he was thinking about creating an environmental protection agency] that I would give NASA [the National Aeronautics and Space Administration] the major responsibility in providing answers to our environment or ecology problems, whichever word you want to use. He seemed to think that was an interesting idea because he took a note; in fact, he filled one sheet of paper with notes on what I said, but I've seen him do that before and not much happened.

Like a broken record, I reiterated again that he still did not have control of his government, and that until he had absolute control, policy could not be changed and would not be changed, and with the exception of Defense and the Attorney General's office, maybe Interior and Transportation, the other departments were more in the control of the Democrats now than ever before. He realizes this and pointed out some things that he was doing to make corrections.

I decided that I would not discuss with him my interest in the ambassadorship to Mexico, rather I'll wait for a more propitious time to do that. This was not the occasion. We finally broke up about 5:00 PM, and we went our merry ways. So now we'll see what happens.

1971

Journal Entry (January 27, 1971)

Looking back over the past several months I continued to be amazed at the ineptitude that President Nixon has shown in the operation of the government. This amazes me because if there is a politically astute animal in American politics, it is Dick Nixon. I believe the trouble to be that he has allowed himself to he surrounded by people who really aren't too smart in the field of politics so he does not know what is going on.

I think back to the SST, and rancor that caused in the 91st congress for it wound up being a real hassle, with the Senate really falling apart in later December 1970. Had Nixon or his staff at anytime within two weeks prior to the vote asked me, I would have told him they were going to lose and I would have given them a figure that would have been no more than one vote off. The White House continued to think they had it won up to the end and consequently there was no expertise made available to support either the Republicans or Democrats who might have supported the president.

The technique that Senators Proxmire and McGovern used in gaining a victory over the SST, or at least a temporary one, was the big lie technique. Indeed, we did an OpEd piece for the *New York Times* with that title.* Never on the floor of the Senate have I heard such outright distortion and lying as I heard during those days. It

---

* *The science regarding the impact of the SST on the atmosphere was divided, with eminent authorities on both sides of the issue. So too were the economic studies of the impact of the production of this aircraft in the United States. Nixon issued a statement from the White House saying that failure to fund the SST would "be like stopping the construction of a house when it was time to put in the doors." He observed, "The SST is an airplane that will be built and flown. This issue is simply which nation will build them." He found the Senate action "unfortunate," and urged that it be corrected. It was not, however, for much to the displeasure of the White House, after all their effort, Boeing itself walked away from the project. Many aviation experts believe had the United States built a wider and more comfortable SST they would have become the norm for long-distance travel.*

made no difference. Senators using such techniques were corrected but they would immediately stand up and repeat the original distortion. Because we had no real answers to the economic arguments, and because my answers came from actual experience rather than studies of so-called experts my thoughts were not to be heeded, and because we had no real leadership from any place in the administration, this battle was lost.

With the opening of the 92nd Congress, I really ran into a cute one with Nixon and Senator Hugh Scott. I was one of the original senators, who a year ago, convinced Howard Baker of Tennessee that he should seek Hugh Scott's job as Minority Leader; he lost last year by just five votes. This year he was determined to try again, although his determination wasn't as deep or enthusiastic as it was a year before, so his prospects weren't as good. About ten days before the Republican's caucus, where the vote would be made, I had a call from Bryce Harlow asking me to visit with Hugh Scott, because Scott was all nervous; he did not believe that he had it won. Harlow indicated that President Nixon wanted Scott as his Senate leader, so I visited with Hugh at some length; we both performed separate nose counts and we both came up with a Scott victory. Then the night before the caucus Vice President Ted Agnew called me late at night to tell me that the president definitely wanted Scott dumped: Would I do everything in my power to help Baker get votes? I explained to Agnew the rather strange situation that existed since I had already put the word out that the president wanted Scott, and now he was telling me that the president didn't want Scott. I told Agnew that I didn't think that Scott could be beaten. In fact, he wasn't, and he won this time by four votes. I was not overly concerned with the defeat of Howard Baker because I recommended to the president that Bob Dole be made National Chairman, and he was appointed, so now we have the National Committee safely tucked in our pockets there is no real threat to Nixon's re-nomination, although there already are noises coming from New York that Rockefeller may make another go at it.

Journal Entry (May 9, 1971)

These entries brought his journal up to date for later April and early May.

On April the 22nd I was invited by President Nixon to stop by the White House at 5:00 in the afternoon on my way home. I knew nothing of the nature of the visit but I thought that it might be in response to a recent letter I had written him urging a full disclosure to the American people of the state of our military vis-à-vis the state of the Soviet military—an issue that much concerns me.

When I reached the White House I knew that this was just not a friendly, personal meeting because there were at least ten other senators there, all generally favorable to the president, plus one or two of them who had left him on the SST vote. We were all seated in the Cabinet Room and, as usual, the president insisted that I sit to his immediate right. (This is an obsession of his I don't know why, maybe because I once was the Party's nominee, but I must say I enjoy it because it puts me in a place to be able to observe the rest of the table, their reactions, etc.) He stated that the general purpose of the meeting was to thank us for the support we had given him in the past and to ask that that support continue throughout the ABM authorization and the military authorization.

He then turned to me and asked if I had anything on my mind and I played a familiar tune by reiterating the contents of my recent letter urging him to disclose what we know about the Soviet's strength. I laid emphasis on the importance of this stating that without this we would be sorely handicapped in trying to debate the outright lies that would be used by the opponents of military authorization and appropriation. When I had finished he went off on a rather long discussion of foreign policy and eventually brought in Henry Kissinger who continued in this general manner, and it went on so long that I finally broke in and said, Mr. President, I don't think we are getting any place. You don't have to worry about us, we are going to back you on the ABM and we are going to back you on the military authorization, but I just want to repeat what I had said before about the urgency of the lifting of classification about the Soviets and this time I was joined by several other senators who agreed that this should be done. The meeting continued in a meaningless sort of way and, honestly, I don't think anything came out of it except a chance to say hello to an old friend and to assure him of our continued support. After about an hour and a half of this the meeting broke up and we went our separate ways.

A later entry was added on this date regarding the anti-war movement, which was turning increasingly ugly and violent.

There have been widespread rumors for months that on such and such a day there would be a massive protest in Washington by people opposed to the Vietnam War but we didn't know just who they would be, what they would represent and what specifics they would ask about. It turned out that the first wave of protestors were rather divided groups. Some of them were actually veterans with good, solid stories to tell and strong arguments to use and I enjoyed speaking with a number of these men more or less in private, if you can call street corners and curbstones conversations private. It was obvious, however, that there were a large number of these protestors who had never been in uniform, who weren't old enough to have been in uniform, and who were nothing more nor less than dirty, unkempt young college-age kids looking for entertaining action, which they figured they would find in Washington.

The second day of this protest a group of about fifty of these grubby types showed up in my outer office, the reception area, and there they enacted a war scene with some of them playing dead, some of them yelling and screaming obscenities in front of my secretaries, and one jackass throwing red paint all around the office. Thank God he missed the four extremely valuable oil paintings and two pen and ink sketches hanging on the walls of my reception area, and the only thing that was damaged of value was a reproduction of a Kachina doll made by the Hopi Indians, but I think I can clean it up.

When it happened, I didn't hear the commotion in my outer office because I was in my own office going over papers but thankfully members of my staff, Leonard Killgore and Terry Emerson, called the Capitol Police who very quickly removed these people from the office. A bit later, I met with the entire group of them, and I told them that before I would allow them to disrupt my office again, as they told me they planned to do, I would close the office the following week when they planned another demonstration. As the week ended the dirty ones went home.

As for the coming week, when we expect the full thunder of this unhappy element of the left, I sent private word to the president who is at the Western White House in San Clemente that unless some leadership was shown from the White House, and unless the DC Police were allowed to act in a manner unhampered by the Democratic leadership in Congress, which has tolerated this activity apparently in an effort to make Nixon look bad when all this is happening, that I would find it very difficult to support Nixon even for re-nomination at the 1972 convention. This is a bad situation. Demonstrations that hamper the government's operations are as troubling as anything in this city since the Civil War. It would be a display of cowardice for the federal government to allow these people to shut down Washington, as they plan to do.

The only reason I am going to close my office when they return is because all of the girls working in my office live outside Washington and to get to their job they must cross the bridges the demonstrators say they will close down. They claim, as part of their effort to close down the federal government, they will block every bridge leading into Washington by dumping old trucks and cars on them or even stretching their bodies out across the roadway. Richard Kleindienst, as Deputy Attorney General, was given the job of supervising this whole operation of dealing with these close-the-government demonstrators, and it was through Dick and John Mitchell, and DC Police Chief Wilson, that the president finally came out with a statement from San Clemente to the effect that the demonstrations would not alter his course in the war and he gave the signal that the police, the army, etc., would be handling this entire thing in an appropriate manner.

About five in the morning of Sunday, May 2nd, the DC and Park Police, backed up by guardsmen, descended upon Potomac Park, and with loudspeakers announced that the park was closed and that everyone there was to get out immediately. I'd guess that over 7,500 young people had to flee the park and they sought refuge at other places in the city, the one place being, unbeknownst to me, Georgetown Hospital and the University, where I was to appear at 8:00 AM at the hospital to begin therapeutic treatment for my old bones. This surprise attack by the police broke up the party because after that nothing really happened outside of a few sporadic demonstrations, demonstrators throwing restaurant garbage cans into the streets and throwing obscenities. But soon these hooligans were rounded up and detained at the RFK Stadium for fingerprinting, photographing, and then released on $10 bail.

About as close as I came to any excitement was after I left the hospital that morning. I smelled teargas in the air and knew it must be coming from the Georgetown University campus, so I wandered over in that general direction, cold as hell with nothing on but a light sport shirt, and during the course of my wanderings about Georgetown, and subsequently walking home, I talked to twenty-five to thirty of these young people. I guess it was the cold coupled with my discovery that these were really pitiful, ignorant young people who have no conception why they were there or no conception of what the Congress could do under its Constitutional authority about ending the war, nor even any idea of what President Nixon himself has actually done and was doing to get America out of the war, that got to me. I don't think I ever felt so downcast in my life as I slowly walked home thinking of the ignorance of these young kids, and I was even more worried about the lack of knowledge of their parents, and the reluctance of their schools to teach about the workings of the Constitution and our government. It is not encouraging for the future.

Well, the whole protest to close the government petered out without much happening; their attempts to shut down Washington and the Congress itself failed miserably and I'm sure that thousands of young people went home with the rude awakening that when the United States Government makes up its mind to act, it can act in a tough, concessive and effective manner and that any and all attempts to close it down should be forgotten. If the system is to be changed, let the system be changed within the Constitution and not by revolution, bloodshed and violence.

Letter (June 15, 1971)*

Dear Mr. President:

I have just recently returned from Europe where I had the honor to serve as your representative at the Paris Air Show. I was greatly flattered at being asked to take on this assignment and I only wish that I could bring back to you a report glowing with news that presages genuine benefits to the United States.

Frankly, what I saw and heard in Paris concerned me deeply. I am afraid my forty-two years of experience in American aviation did not prepare me for what I think is the real problem growing out of the cancellation of plans to build a U.S. supersonic transport.

I found that leaders of European industry, aviation and engineering are now convinced that America no longer looks to the future but only wants to stay where it is and become an isolated country with a minimum military force. I believe these groups have overcome their initial shock and disbelief that the United States would voluntarily give up her important lead in aviation technology. They are moving now with enormous speed to take advantage of the vacuum left by a nation that once prided itself on the ability to produce a better technological "mousetrap" than any other nation on earth. I am not exaggerating when I tell you that I believe that a wild scramble for supremacy in many areas of technological development has already begun.

Perhaps I should remind you that I am not unknown in Europe and I count many friends in industrial and commercial organizations. As your representative at Paris I had the privilege of meeting with many of these old friends and of obtaining from them the deep down honest reaction of Europe's leaders. And I must say that everywhere I went I found people who are now convinced that America no longer wants the superiority in aviation that she has held for the last thirty-five or forty years. Everyone I talked with told me of more activity aimed at taking over where America has left off. I found that while the SST held first place in the interest of those attending the Paris Air Show, the efforts to prevent Lockheed Aircraft Corporation from going bankrupt were also being discussed. Of course, the

---

* This letter to Nixon was publicly released on this date.

involvement here of the British Rolls Royce Company has emphasized European concern.

I am sure you can understand the attitude of European industrialists who learned their technology from us and absorbed, at the same time, the American spirit of competition. They view the SST decision with almost total disbelief. If the Lockheed Corporation goes down the drain for lack of Congressional concern it will merely compound Europe's impression that the United States is rapidly becoming a has-been world power.

This, Mr. President, is the important message that I received during my sojourn in Europe. It is indeed a strange experience for an official representative of an American President to be attending an international air show where the world's attention is focused on a new, progressive air transport product, which we do not possess. Perhaps it was the first time in many years that American air enthusiasts had to take a back seat to three other nations—including our Cold War adversary, the Soviet Union—on the development of a commercial aircraft demanding a high level of technological achievement.

It is worthy of note, I believe that the American exhibitors at the Paris show were visibly discouraged. Visitors at the show were flocking to see the exhibits of other nations. The United States had nothing new to offer and consequently attracted very little interest.

I found it very difficult to explain why a Senate and House made up of American officials refused to back your ongoing view of the future. The same people who found it easy to understand the reaction of the liberal doves to the war in Vietnam found their attitude on the SST, on withdrawal of troops from Europe and on the Lockheed proposal quite beyond their comprehension.

I began my assignment at Paris feeling slightly embarrassed that our nation had no entries in the newest aviation development. But this feeling quickly gave way to concern and even fright as I discovered how firmly Europe is now convinced that America is abdicating and is striving to divest itself of practically all interests that are not confined to the social engineering problems of our inter-cities and our ghettos.

I only wish that I had been able to take a majority of the American people to Paris with me, for I am convinced that they do not understand the key role that aviation, commercial and military, plays in the affairs of the world. I am sure they do not understand that if we give up our lead in aviation technology and in research and development in other areas we will within a decade become a second or a third rate power.

I hope to be able to discuss this whole problem with you personally in the near future. In the meantime I shall leave off this discussion to present a short aerodynamics analysis of propulsion, lift, accommodation, instrumentation and other factors that I observed in the SST's developed in Europe.

There really is not much that I can tell you that you do not know about the Russian 144 and the British-French Concorde. I was extremely impressed with the obvious excellence of the French workmanship in the factory at Toulouse and also with their testing techniques at the same place. We Americans like to keep our head in a sack thinking that nobody else in the world has the know-how we have and, frankly, it was surprising to see the great advancements they have made in the development and manufacturing of aeronautic components.

In my flight in the Concorde, during which we did not reach Mach 2 because the afterburners failed to light, I was extremely impressed by the quietness. Even though this ship is instrumented for test, they did have a few seats in it and I am sure that the interior was not as completely soundproofed as the production models will be. Nevertheless, I did not hear the engines start. On takeoff, climb and cruise the cabin was exceedingly quiet; in fact, it was as quiet as any of ours with the possible exception of the 747. The test instrumentation is highly sophisticated while what I saw in the Russian 144 appeared to be very old and extremely unsophisticated but, frankly, no one knows what they had hiding under the floor.

The 144 has a decibelic noise level that would be quite above what we call acceptable but because they are using fan engines, I am sure they will be able to quiet them as we have been able to quiet the proposed ones for our own SST. The major difference in the two airplanes is to be found in the propulsion system with the Concorde relying on afterburners, which have a built-in noise that can never be quieted. The Russians are using the fan jet and while still noisy, as they develop more of a by-passability these engines will quiet down. I did not hear the Concorde on takeoff so it is impossible to compare it to the 144, which is, as I said, extremely noisy.

Aerodynamically, both airplanes are rather similar and while the cabins are both smaller than I think American passengers would readily accept, nevertheless, they can be quite comfortable. By the way, a survey made by the British-French combine shows that the average air traveler in Europe would accept a 30 percent increase in fare for SST flights across the ocean. Back to the airplane: both cockpits are very small with the instrumentation in the French one much more sophisticated than that of the Russians but, again, we do not know what they might be holding in reserve for their own eyes.

To sum it all up, Mr. President, I think that one of these airplanes and probably both of them will be in Trans-Atlantic service by 1975 whether or not they make money on them. This is going to be a strain on our competitive airline situation and it is a situation that I think we must address ourselves to as soon as possible.

Journal Entry (June 17, 1971)

I have just returned from the White House where I had a forty minute visit with the president. So I want to jot down the things we talked about before they slip from my mind.

The first thing we discussed was the advantage that would accrue to the United States if Germany were to buy some fighter planes, particularly from Northrop Aviation. I had discussed this very briefly with Tom Jones [the president and chairman of the board of Northrop] at the Paris Air Show so I told the president about it and he immediately picked up the phone and called Henry Kissinger and told Kissinger to get in touch with German Chancellor Willie Brandt immediately. Willie Brandt is in this country but was not in Washington. I don't know where he is, so that mission has been accomplished.

The president then told me that he had been suggesting to Germany that they join with the United States to build the SST, which would give combined competition to England and France, and also to Russia, but he didn't seem to think there would be much of a chance of it. I discussed the report I had made to him earlier on the Paris Air Show, and reiterated that if there were five nations represented there the United States was in sixth place. I told him that I had never seen American businessmen so down in the mouth as I saw them in their little chalets around the field as they watched Russia and France walk off with all of the interesting parts of the show. The president is extremely bitter about the fact that we were not building the SST and he has asked me to go ahead with my public discussions on the subject, and he also asked me to keep up my efforts against those who are attacking the Military Industrial Complex.

The president said that those senators who are now trying to change the war powers of the president were out to destroy the United States; it is as simple as that; they were not interested at all in the military draft [which Nixon had ended] but interested only in changing the American way of life. (Personally I feel this may be a little farfetched but I can't blame him for thinking as he does because after I left his office, the Senate today went through amendment after amendment prepared by a group called the Committee of the Peace through Law to which a number of senators and congressmen belong.)

The president asked me what I sensed of the mood around the country and I told him that I felt the Vietnam War was no longer an issue, and that by this time next year it would only be a sour memory. When discussing this he condemned the *New York Times* for wrongly publishing the so-called Pentagon Papers, material that had literally been stolen from the United States and for which he said they had probably paid some money. Candidly, my feeling is that this information is good that this story [about how the Democrats deceived Americans regarding Vietnam] has come out. We both agreed that the release of these classified documents would have no bearing on the presidential race next year, unless we could develop the theme that every war we have had this century has been started by a Democratic president, and it has taken a Republican president to end it. Of course, the personal irony of this particular war, as is evident from these documents, is that there were so many misstatements and actual lies that were made about it during the 1964 campaign.

Nixon got into some other subjects as well. One was Red China and he felt that what he has done toward Red China will guarantee a better peace position in the future because, as we both know, Russia and Red China are mortal enemies, and Red China is fearful of Russia and the better position we can place ourselves vis-à-vis Red China, without actually recognizing her, will be helpful.* I am inclined, in a way, to agree with him that we must take further steps with Red China. But he told me that the United Nations would not yet accept Red China. He reiterated his strong admiration and affection for the Chinese living on Taiwan and told me that he would never do anything to double cross those people who have been our friends for so long.

He told me, that frankly, he didn't think much would come out of the present negotiations with Paris on Vietnam even though occasionally there were rays of light but he said that we would continue as we have been and that he was not going to be pushed into getting out of the war in Vietnam until we had the prisoner of war situation straightened out, and he felt that Vietnamization was still proceeding at a proper level.

The president told me that some interesting things would be forthcoming relative to Berlin so I think that he feels that we are reaching an accord with them that we haven't enjoyed for sometime. He discussed Japan and recognizing what I've long known that she was going to be a great economic power, possibly the greatest in the world by the year 2000. However, she was also beginning to make noises like the Japan of old, namely, showing interest in building up arms and armament. Still the president feels that it will be fifteen to twenty years before the world will have to begin worrying again about Japanese military interests and conquests.

He feels that the domestic economy is beginning to improve; that unemployment will improve more slowly but consumers are beginning to buy again and that profits are beginning to go up so that by this time next year the economy will be in better shape, although it may not be a lot better. He feels that it will be sufficiently improved by that time to remove it as a political threat to his reelection. I shared my reading with him, that since the war was becoming a non-issue, that if the economy was getting straightened out, or even a start was made on it, that we would be able to brush aside these issues in 1972, and unless the Democrats come up with a nominee they don't have at

---

* In late April 1971 Nixon formally announced his plans to travel to China.

this time, I thought that he will be reelected, although I advised him that if the election were held today it would be an extremely close one. He agreed on this.

CHAPTER 13

NIXON'S PRESIDENCY: SECOND TERM

G oldwater actively campaigned for Nixon's reelection, which
started in the fall of 1971. As he later recounted, the fact that
they supplied him with a jet, while pleasant and enjoyable to fly,
it also raised suspicions about the money being raised for what was not
a close race. Watergate, however, was not a factor until after Nixon was
overwhelmingly reelected.

Journal Entry (November 22, 1971)

I arrived at the White House early this morning, about 8:30 AM, for
a meeting with Henry Kissinger, knowing that I might have to wait. I
had to wait about a half an hour because Dr. Kissinger was in with the
president. He finally came and we went into his office where we had
a light breakfast and touched briefly on many points that don't need
mentioning but one or two should be noted. Kissinger is concerned
and I later found that the president is too, about the lack of conservative support for the president's foreign policy on the floor of the Senate. They both feel, and rightly so, that inasmuch as the Democrats
attack the president daily, that we should be attacking the Democrats
and defending the Nixon successes. I reported to him that I felt Mr.
Nixon had gained strength in the last month and that if the psychological effect of his newly displayed leadership continues, he was going to be
nearly unbeatable by this time next year. In fact, I even went so far as to
prophesize a landslide if things keep on moving as they have been.

Kissinger told me that they had detected nearly four thousand trucks stationed near Hanoi and that if the Congress went in recess the president was to destroy these trucks to convince North Vietnam that even though we are withdrawing our troops, we are not abandoning our will to win. This, of course, is extremely sensitive and must never be told to anyone, and he will act during the recess so Congress can't howl, and that all the spending bills will have been passed before the Democrats can add any anti-war measures to these bills. I'm anxious to see what will happen.

Our conversation explored the fact that the accumulating evidence shows that liberalism per se in this country is a thing of the past and that today they are devoid of issues, devoid of men of principle and stature to express them, and we both are wondering what will emerge out of the void. As I was leaving Kissinger's office he told me the president would like me to drop by so we went into the Oval Office and sat there with Bob Haldeman, Kissinger, the president and myself discussing pretty much what we had talked about in the Kissinger's office although the president spent more time emphasizing the need for conservative backup in the Congress. I assured him I would do my best to see if we couldn't provide it. However, I suggested that he should stay in closer touch with the Senate and not come running up at the last minute and expect just anybody to answer accusations made by the enemies of the White House.

I again reiterated my hope that the president would disclose the major Soviet threat to our country, but I didn't get any place as usual. I told him as I had Kissinger that the major criticism I am hearing today about the president is that he has allowed our military to reach a second place in the world position. I pointed out to the president that while this was a false charge it is easily believed, and is being overused effectively by the zealots on the Democratic side. (I mentioned this as well to Secretary Laird before suggesting that he provide an outline that would be given to each Republican so that they can refute these charges against the president.)

Journal Entry (December 18, 1971)

I met with Vice President Spiro Agnew in his Executive Office in the Old State Building at 12:15 where we stayed and talked for a while, and then went across to the White House and had lunch in the Executive Dining Room. Agnew told me some rather amazing things: First, that he didn't know the president any better today than he did when the president first asked him to run in Miami. This rather surprised me and I asked him in view of this did he feel he could move in and take charge the next day if he had to if the president happened to pass away. He said that he could but he would have to rely in the domestic field on people for advice that he did not trust, namely, Elliot Richardson and others. He felt that Dr. Kissinger could give him good advice in the field of foreign policy and said that Kissinger did try to keep him posted on what was going on, although he did not know about the China trip until it was actually underway. He said the president never telephones him but relies on getting messages to him through third parties, which does not make Agnew very happy. He recited the instance of the Gridiron Club last year when he refused an invitation to their dinner because he doesn't like the press, and then he was told by a subordinate at the White House that the president wanted him to go and the vice president said if he wants me to go, let him tell me. This went on back and forth, clear out to Hawaii and back, and one day the vice president received a call from the president from Camp David. They talked for about a half an hour, Agnew said, and never once did the president mention the Gridiron dinner and then the next day he had another request from a subordinate to go to the dinner and he gave him the standard answer. At a very late date, I think the morning of the dinner, he received a handwritten note from the president asking him to go. I mention this only to indicate the type of trouble Agnew is having.

It all seems to hinge on John Ehrlichman of the White House staff, and the vice president told me, and this is a very top secret, that he would not run again if Mr. Ehrlichman was going to stay in the White House. These are the most salient points of the meeting that we had. He wants to run and will run but he has decided not to if Ehrlichman is retained in employment in the White House.

Journal Entry (December 8, 1971)

Goldwater regularly paused to question the wisdom of remaining in the Senate. This entry is typical of the debate he conducted and resolved by running for two more terms.

Here it is December, 1971, and I'm about to complete the first three years of my third term in the United States Senate and I think it might be wise at this point to put down some of my reflections and observations for possible use in the coming three years should I decide not to seek reelection.

At the outset, I ask myself the question, knowing what I know now, would I have sought to return to the Senate after a four-year absence and my feelings are rather torn. Even though seniority was waived so that I could return to the Armed Services Committee, I still sit as a junior member of that body with more military experience than anyone on it; I'm not a participant in conferences and I must carefully wait my turn to ask questions until about eight others have had their time. All of this is livable, but I have become more and more convinced, having had four years to look at it from the outside, and now three years to live through it again, that the whole archaic system under which the Senate operates, namely, seniority, is wrong but I can't for the life of me think of a better way to do it. This system does not make available immediately the best talents of the Senate and in some cases an exceptionally talented senator must wait many years before he can serve on a committee to which he could make outstanding contributions.

I am beginning to wonder, also, as to the wisdom of allowing people to serve more than three terms; not that I fundamentally feel that a man when he passes seventy automatically becomes a moron, but I am beginning to appreciate the fact that youthful leadership, if not always, usually is the best, particularly in times such as we find ourselves in now. The problem of inflation, for example. There seems to be no sense of realization that government spending has created more problems that it solves, including furthering inflation. Likewise, there seems to be no sense of historic value among men of the Senate who should know and appreciate our history. We are following the same paths that were followed by the ancient government of Rome and by the government of Austria when it brought on the depression of the late 1920s and 1930s. We are becoming a military power of second rate stature at a time when the world only understands strength and needs more of it, not less of it.

We find the American people with a decreasing sense of trust of the Congress and its leaders, a feeling that we are really not doing the job and that a better one could be done. I have returned to a Senate where open distortions and falsehoods are mouthed by members of the body too often. While I would be the first to admit that it cannot be said that the floor of the Senate has never been exposed to this before, I have never seen it so flagrantly practiced as I've seen particularly recently. I am thinking of the case of the SST and now during the confirmation proceedings for William Rehnquist, my nominee for the Supreme Court.

I think of the number of years that I've spent in public service, and while I realize that there are many men who have spent more time, I still feel a responsibility to Peggy and now to the grandchildren and, of course, to Arizona. I don't know what the latter two obligations will consist of but I do feel that in view of the fact that Peggy thoroughly dislikes Washington and has fallen in love with Arizona that I'm coming more and more to the mind that at the end of this term I won't seek reelection. There are other papers that I have written to document this in case somebody at some time should raise the cry that Goldwater's afraid of being defeated, that's why he is not going to run. As I've told my close friends, I feel that it's time that the older members of the Party got out and let the younger members have their day and that's going to have a big bearing on my decision.

I'm deeply concerned at this point in our history and my life, as to whether or not this country is going to remain a free Republic or whether we have gone so far down the road to socialism, particularly now that we have controls over the economy here in Washington, that we will find it impossible to return. No country in the history of the world has ever made an exploration into government control and then found it possible to completely extricate themselves from that situation. Also, I see the power of organized labor being a great force in America and the corporate structure and businessmen have become nothing but weak-kneed sops who are afraid to even voice their own opinions. This doesn't apply across the board, but American industry and American business and American genius no longer speak out with the authority that they did when they were making this country the greatest one in the world, in a material sense.

It is a terrible time in our history, a very peculiar one, but not unusual in the sense that we might think no other country or people have ever faced it; in fact, they all have. The sad and terrible thought is that none of them has had the guts to come back after facing the failure of the loss of freedom. The only thing I believe now that could change my mind about seeking another term would be a genuine belief that I could do some good in restoring American principles by remaining in the Senate but, again, I am not the only one imbued with love of country and certainly there are those who are younger with far better intellects and far better methods of expressing them, so I'm going to end this little dissertation now and, of course, I will add to it from time to time and then when it becomes necessary.

Barry, Jr., has been doing an outstanding job in the Congress. Everyone speaks highly of him and I know that he is deeply respected by his constituents in his district. I have a feeling that if the old man weren't around he might do even better because he would not be, so to speak, working in the shadow of his father and because he's young and talented and because it has been true in our family that each generation has produced someone who has reached a degree of prominence in politics, I might be wise to leave the ball in his hands and go home and play with my memories.

1972

Journal Entry (January 26, 1972)

On Wednesday morning, January 26, 1972, I attended a leadership meeting at the White House at 8:00 AM. I could not stay through the entire meeting because Senator Hayden [of Arizona] had passed away the night before and I had to make the announcement to the Senate

Barry, Jr., and Barry, Sr., the day after Jr.'s election to Congress.

but I was able to stay during the entire presentation of the background reasoning leading up to the president's speech the night before. That speech dealt with overtures that had been made to the North Vietnamese in an attempt to end the war and I will try to relate as much as I can about what I heard. The impressive thing to me was that Henry Kissinger had made thirteen secret visits to the Paris negotiations and remarkably not a word of it had been leaked out to the press.

What the entire presentation boiled down to was the realization on the president's part that the North Vietnamese were and are using our positions against us. In other words, when we would make a presentation they would counter, turning our own words on us. But now the initiative has switched to our hands and the enemy is completely on its back and the world knows this. This can be documented by the complete transcripts that were kept of each conversation that Kissinger had in Paris. In addition, the communists have been trying to turn our people against our government, and in this, as a result of my questioning Kissinger, it develops that every time a Fulbright or a Church or a Kennedy stands up to speak against our position in South Vietnam it serves to strengthen the hands of the enemy, and the North Vietnamese are convinced—because they are listening to what transpires in our Congress—that our own people will overthrow us if they just hold out. In other words, Dien Ben Phu was not lost in Asia; it was lost in Paris.

A date certain for withdrawal of American troops in South Vietnam was turned down by the president because of the military impossibility of such a proposition, for the South Vietnamese are not ready. What the North Vietnamese want, and mind you they want this and only this and they will not talk about anything without our agreeing to it, would be for the United States to abandon the government of South Vietnam and turn it over to the Communists. The president stated emphatically that this surrender will not be done, even though he knows that the peaceniks in the Congress will continue their hue and cry to get out of there at any cost. He feels, as I have often said, that if we do this it will be the end of the United States as a world power for it would destroy the confidence of the world in our willingness to see through our obligations.

It is amazing that highly intelligent men like Senators Fulbright, Church, Cooper, Javits et al., cannot comprehend this, but then I suppose the men who were in their positions in 1917 and again in 1939 could not comprehend their views either and we wound up in wars.

During the meeting, I raised the fact that I did not believe the leadership on either side truly understood the threat that the war powers legislation presented and I pointed out that only Secretary Rogers and myself had testified for the retention of the presidential powers as the Constitution intended it.

In closing, one of the most disturbing parts of this whole meeting to me was the very obvious fact that the vice president had not been clued in and knew nothing about the speech, the contents of it or the background. I have written Kissinger expressing my dismay at this seeming oversight. This is being written a week after the speech and I believe I can say at this time that world opinion and national opinion have solidified behind the president and that this move plus his others have completely removed Vietnam as an issue for this year.

Journal Entry (July 14, 1972)

The president called me today from the Western White House about 3:15 PM, while I was taking a nap. I had an unusually long conversation with him. He wanted to know my feelings about the Democratic opposition now that McGovern and Eagleton have been chosen presidential and vice presidential nominees. I told him that I did not think that the personalities of these two men were really the issue. Rather the issue would be built on and around the platform they adopted in Miami by the New Democratic Party. I inject the word "new" because there is no resemblance to the old Democratic Party that I have known all my life with the one that emerged in Miami. I told the president that I do not think the country is ready, nor will it ever be ready in my opinion, for a platform calling for a government so radically changed as the one the Democrats have come up with at their convention. I told him that already the feeling in the country was beginning to jell against this platform and as of now the particular plank that most people object to is busing school children to accomplish integration.

The president [said he] realized this and that the Republican Platform would contain a strong simple plank against busing and I hope he is telling the truth. I told him that it was imperative that [former Congressman and White House aide] Clark McGregor, who has replaced John Mitchell as the head of the Committee to Reelect the President, be urged to immediately clean house at his reelection committee.* The president assured me this would happen.

I have not told the president nor will I that I am not planning on going to Miami to attend the 1972 GOP Convention, unless he, the president, personally, requests that I make a speech—and not just a seconding speech, or a quick walk by a television camera. I don't want to become just another "has been" for I have seen too many of them pathetically wandering around our convention halls when they are no longer needed, and no longer wanted, and no longer thought of seriously. Rather I plan to spend that time in the West with my family and

---

* *Men with ties to the Committee to Reelect the President (CRP) were arrested by Washington, DC, police in the Watergate offices of the Democratic National Committee on June 17, 1972. Former Attorney General John Mitchell, the president's campaign manager and the head of CRP, resigned on July 1, 1972, for the ostensible reason of problems with his wife Martha. Former congressman and Nixon legislative liaison man, Clark McGregor, would take Mitchell's post. But the campaign had been, and would continue to be, run from the White House, and from his private law practice Mitchell remained very involved. Other than the Washington Post, and an occasional CBS Nightly News report based on these stories, the Watergate break-in and arrests were a non-story throughout the 1972 campaign.*

I hope on my new boat. My speaking plans for the coming campaign have not been coming together fast enough to satisfy me so I think that if nothing happens by the end of July I will disassociate myself from Nixon's Reelection Committee. And as far as assignments go I'll speak where I want for what and who I want and confine my activities to Arizona and the five states I have been assigned in the Senatorial contests.

It is kind of hard but I must realize that the end of the road of my political career is in sight and that the Party I have worked so long for and so hard for no longer needs my kind of leadership or help. I know that this realization comes to everyone who has chosen political life as his or her bed. So I will accept it with graciousness, in fact, I accept it with a rather comfortable and satisfied feeling.

Journal Entry (August 28, 1972)

This entry would probably not have been made had not Walter Cronkite made his comments after my appearance before the Republican Convention, and my appearance on the program so much later than planned. With that in mind, however, let's go back to early February when I wrote a letter to Bob Dole, chairman of the Republican National Committee, stating that unless I were personally invited by the White House to address the convention, I was not planning on attending. As the months went by it became increasingly evident that I was not wanted at this convention and, frankly, I was very happy and was making my plans to spend the available time in California with my family. I instructed my staff that I did not want this discussed with anyone because I honestly would have preferred not to have been in Florida at the convention.

However, just about one week before the convention I was called by the reelection committee and was told that a speech would be in good order, and they suggested that it might be a tribute to those who had passed on since the last convention. Remarkably, when I received the list it contained more Democrats than it did Republicans, and numbered around forty people in all, so I immediately shot down that idea. Within twenty-four hours after calling me the committee called requesting a copy of my speech, and I told them in no uncertain language that it wasn't ready and they would get it when it was ready, possibly the morning of the date I was to speak, which was a Monday evening. My staff worked on the draft and I took it home to Arizona and reworked it a bit on Friday. I then flew over to Nellis Air Force Base in Nevada, where I spent the night, and the next day I jumped a ride to Edwards Air Force in California, and then down to Palm Springs for the Hump Pilots Association gathering [of old friends from World War II], after which I flew all night back to Washington to work again on the speech so that it would be ready on Monday. It was in good shape, or as good as we could all get it, and so Monday afternoon I gathered a few friends and we flew down to Miami.

Some rather strange things happened in Florida. First I was told I would speak at 8:30 PM, prime time on Monday evening. But then I was called by [Nixon aide] Bill Timmons who said they wanted to put off my speech until Tuesday night at 8:30. But I said no, I would speak Monday night or not at all. Timmons left it hanging as to when I would speak. Late Sunday, I had been called by [Nixon speech writer] Pat Buchanan who asked if I would change two words in my speech, which certainly were all right with me but still no indication that I was even going on. Anyway, come Monday evening, I proceeded as originally planned. We had two rooms in the Hotel Algiers so we went up there and had my hair done for television and lo and behold if they didn't send the former State Chairman of Mississippi, Fred LaRue, up to try and talk me into making two major changes in the speech and we discussed this, of all places, in the bathroom. I said I would not take out the reference to the young American men who had deserted their country, nor would I take out the references to former Attorney General Ramsey Clark, and if they insisted I do so that I was going back to Washington that moment, so those items stayed in and they proved to be the best part of the speech as far as the delegates were concerned.

Thankfully, we had the good sense to make our own press releases, but we didn't make enough of them, because when I left the hotel to go to the convention hall no press releases had been prepared by either the National Committee or the Nixon Reelection Committee, but at the last moment I understand a few releases did get out to a few people of the press. Well, I soon discovered that during my speech to the convention the president's plane arrived in Miami and the president made an impromptu speech to a large crowd of young people that his advance people had gathered, which preempted everything at the convention, including me. Of course, that was exactly what they had in mind for me. Now I don't know who is to blame for all of this but it got so evident that it began to be funny, and we were soon laughing at the whole damn thing. For example, at no time was my name mentioned in any printed schedules, not in any of the newspapers that I saw, and trying as hard as I could to find when I was supposed to speak.

And so went my experiences with the Republican National Convention of 1972 and, as I said, it will probably be my last hurrah because it is obvious, extremely obvious, that some key people don't want me to be around the Republican Party. Because I am rather tired of being used whenever they need me, and I have a little bit of feeling of honor left; this will not happen again.

Journal Entry (November 22, 1972)

On November 7, 1972, Nixon won a landslide reelection victory, and headed for Camp David to totally reorganize the Executive Branch of government for his second term.

This morning I flew from Orlando, Florida, to Andrews Air Force Base in Maryland and then was picked up in one of the president's helicopters and flown to Camp David where it was snowing and cold. After a rather short stay in one of the numerous cabins, and this one had a pool table in it that I didn't use, I was driven in an enclosed golf cart to the president's lodge, which is a small nicely furnished cabin where a blazing fire was going. His man, Manolo, greeted me in Spanish, and he took me in to see the president. We sat in two chairs separated by a small table, and then my old friend, [the White House photographer] Ollie Atkins, came in and took a picture of us and then took a picture of the two of us with my camera.

I had no idea why the president had wanted me to come to Camp David, but I went. We were scheduled to have a half hour meeting but we spent an hour together, just the two of us all alone looking at each other, eyeball to eyeball, across the little coffee table, and using the kind of language that comes to us naturally, lots of four letter words interspersed with rather long ones, but mainly it was real straight-talk language that most people would plainly understand.

The president started out the discussion by telling me that Nelson Rockefeller had come to see him. He didn't want the impression to get out around the country that he was only listening to the liberal side of the Party, so he had asked me up there and did I mind him handling the publicity on my visit; I said that was no problem because my public relations man was not available and if he wanted to put out anything, put it out for I didn't care what he said.

I told him at the outset of our conversation that I thought he had the best opportunity and challenge of any president in the history of this country to turn the country around and turning it around may sound different than I meant it. I didn't mean to turn it 180 degrees backward, but I meant to get it on the Constitutional path that the office of president was intended to follow. I reminded him that four years ago I told him that if he didn't get control of his government by May he would never get control of it, and he admitted to me today, as he did then, that I was right. Of course, when I say I was correct I'm only one of many, many people who feel that way.

After the election I had telephoned the president and reminded him of his promise to me; in fact, not a promise, but a statement to me about two and a half years earlier that he has made two mistakes. One, he had not bombed North Vietnam soon enough, but that point was behind us now, and the second was that he had not cleaned out the State Department. Before we got into any details on that, I reminded him that cleaning out the State Department didn't mean getting rid of subversives and all of that, it was just getting it into line so that his policies could be followed.

We had a discussion about George McGovern and what I thought about his 1972 campaign, and I told Nixon that I had written a piece for *Playboy Magazine* where I said that basically McGovern was an intelligent but shallow man, not really able to think through the major problems that face us and too willing to follow the advice of the last person who talked with him. The president expressed his disappointment and displeasure at the whole campaign because it had gotten so nasty, and I told him that I had expressed on a number of occasions, particularly toward the end of the campaign, my surprise that the son of a Methodist minister could be so dirty. Nixon liked this comment so he made the crack, "You always knew how to stick it in them, Barry." Well, I guess the truth can be pointed at times.

When we discussed the organization of the State Department, I suggested that he get rid of the GS-16s and above [the top ranking non-political Civil Service posts in government] even though that would actually take an act of Congress. He said he didn't think the Democrats would go along with it and I argued with him to the effect that he should call [former President] Lyndon Johnson and [former Senate Majority Leader] Mike Mansfield and other Democratic leaders to get their support to get rid of the policy-making levels who are now covered by Civil Service. These are employees frozen in place by a law Eisenhower approved, a law that Harry Truman criticized Eisenhower for embracing because Truman thought that these top levels in the departments positions should be appointed by the president and subject to the president's will. Nixon made a note of this while saying he did not think it would be possible but he was going to explore it.

Nixon is going to keep Secretary [of State] Rogers for a while noting that Rogers did not have the—he didn't use the term "guts" but I will—to get rid of people. He's thinking of putting a man named Bill Casey over in the State Department who is a great getter-out-of and then the president said he thought there were ways to remove the bureaucrats without congressional action. He mentioned a number of examples of ways of doing this that have never been tried, or even thought of, before and he recited them to me. Based on his remarks I now feel certain that the State Department will be reorganized. If Bill Casey becomes the Under Secretary and can do that job it is fine by me.*

I brought up the name of John Connally at this point. Actually, I sensed Nixon wanted me to raise Connally's name, so I did and he was tremendously enthusiastic and spoke very highly of Connally and wanted to know my thoughts on him. I said I believed that Connally

---

* *Bill Casey, who would become director of the CIA under President Reagan and crossed swords with Goldwater when he chaired the Senate Intelligence Committee, was not appointed to the State Department post by Nixon; rather he was made chairman of the Securities and Exchange Commission.*

was one of the outstanding men in the country, a man who could be appointed Secretary of State without any trouble regardless of party affiliation.* The president said he thought that within a matter of months Connally would make the switch, and become a Republican. I responded that he should have made the switch during the campaign but Nixon pointed out that to have done so might have alienated some of the Democrats with whom he had great influence, so they stuck with Connally and with Nixon. I had to agree to some extent with his point but, nevertheless, I feel that Connally is a man we have to watch because I'm convinced that the president thinks that Connally can be the next president. I am not so sure. The president asked me to talk to [Kissinger's assistant] General Al Haig when I can about this whole subject of the State Department and what Haig feels about it, where changes can be made and changes that must be made and will be made.

Now let's get to the other subject we talked about, the Defense Department. Mel Laird is leaving Defense and we both agreed that the Secretary of Defense is not the most important person at the Pentagon. Equally important are those people down below the Secretary who either do or do not follow the policies of the president. Nixon is putting a Texan named Bill Clements in as deputy secretary, a man he says who will have the respect of the other subcabinet officers, and the military, and who can undertake an effort to improve procurement.** I dwelled at some length on this subject pointing out the problems of the Pentagon in the future. It is difficult to justify 90 billion dollars for defense by justifying the individual cost of weapons. The waste and duplication is terrible. I cited the fact that we now have four tactical air forces and I reminded the president, who was in the navy and I was in the air force, that I was not raising this situation because of air force partisanship, rather the fact of the matter is that we only need one tactical air force, not four. I made clear that I didn't give a damn whether

---

* *During the 1972 campaign, former Texas Governor John Connally had headed the "Democrats for Nixon" organization.*
** *William P. Clements served as deputy U.S. secretary of defense in the Nixon and Ford administrations; he later became the first Republican governor of Texas since Reconstruction.*

the navy or the army, the marines or the air force were in charge of that tactical fighting operation, my only point being that we do not need four, or three, or two of them—just one that can really do the job.

Nonetheless, I did remind the president that as a matter of law the air force has been given this responsibility, but that the army has been making inroads. The president didn't know that, in fact, the army now has more pilots and aircraft than all the other services combined. But that's still beside the point. The point is that we have four different military forces doing the job that one could do and I don't care who does it.

I also pointed out something that Admiral Rickover told me. I once said to Rickover, who in my estimation is the greatest scientific engineering brain to ever walk the halls of the Pentagon, anyway, I said, "Admiral suppose you wake up at four or five in the morning with a really bright idea for a new or improved weapon system. The next day you write it all up, and you give it to your staff and direct them to implement as quickly as possible. How many years would it take to get that improvement or that new weapon into the inventory?" Rickover answered, "Seven years, if at all." That, of course, is shameful, so I explained to the president that we are procuring military equipment under the old system much like the Russians once used, while the Russians are procuring their equipment under the capitalist system that we invented, and had once perfected. Today, the Russians do it in three years; it takes us seven years, if at all. I wanted the president to understand that we are wasting massive amounts of money in spending for individual weapons, and I gave him a number of examples. I won't go into the detail that I went into with him because, and suffice it to say I'm inclined toward defense like I once was toward my mother's breast.

When discussing duplication in government operations, Nixon brought up intelligence. He noted that we have three intelligence services and he said he knew that the British had such a system, and it works beautifully for the British government, but he said he questioned whether we needed such duplication of effort. He reported that Dick Helms was retiring as Director of the CIA, since he is coming up on sixty years of age. Helms is going to be offered an ambassadorial post, probably in Iran.

I lean toward the British system of the three independent gathering agencies, which I suspect may account for the fact that the Brits do have the greatest intelligence system in the world. I asked the president who he was thinking about for the CIA post, and he said a fellow by the name of Schlessinger. When I said the historian, and author, who I knew was a Kennedy man, he said, "No, not him." Rather James Schlessinger who has been doing a lot of behind-the-scenes work for Nixon, a fellow who has been wrapped up in atomic and nuclear research.

From his comments, I gather that what the president wants is just one intelligence gathering agency. So I said to him, well, Mr. President, if you are talking about eliminating three intelligence groups, we also have three communications groups in the military. There was a time when the navy operated on its own frequencies and the army and air force had theirs and they were incompatible, there may be some reason for it, but I personally as a radio communicator see no reason why we should have three communications systems or organizations. Nixon made a note of that too, and said he had not thought about it.

Then we got into procurement, as I mentioned, and I told him that in my opinion Dave Packard could probably iron out that mess at the Defense Department faster than any man I knew of in the country. Nixon agreed but said Dave will not come back into the government; he has had his stomach full. Clearly, the president is fully aware of the problems of procurements, duplications, and the jumping across of military lines.

We discussed his reorganization of government. I reminded him, the old tune I have played him on many occasions, that his policies cannot be implemented by the government when the individuals who oppose him in these bureaus are running the place, and I cited as an example, one with which I am painfully familiar, regarding Indian affairs, and the ineffectiveness of Rogers Morton, or for that matter anybody else who is secretary of the interior, can't get anything done because they don't have control of that department. Notwithstanding the fact the president gave an excellent statement on Indian affairs during his first term, not one sentence of the president's message has ever been implemented. You can go right through all of the departments and find the same situation everywhere. That is why I suggested to him, and he got out his pencil and took notes, that he call in leaders of the Democratic Party for a private conference.

Now, let's see, there are a couple of things left. The president asked me who should be chairman of the Republican National Committee, and I said, Mr. President, don't take another congressman. You need a pro. As we talked he mentioned George Bush, and wanted to know what I thought about him. I said I think that would be a hell of a good choice. The president said he was very unhappy with the caliber of the great majority of Republican candidates he saw around this country during the 1972 campaign, and I can understand that. Nixon wanted to know if I had anybody to recommend for the National Committee, and I said well, the only man I can recommend is Dean Burch, but he was doing a hell of a job for the president as chairman of the Federal Communications Commission. Nixon agreed and he said he was not going to bother him. I said I thought Bob Dole had done a good job as chairman but Dole primarily is a senator, and although he wants the chairmanship again, I reminded the president that we have a rule that prohibits Dole from seeking the National Committee post.

The president was very complimentary to me about my years as chairman of the Senatorial Campaign Committee, and he said we needed to find a real nut cutter for that post too. What did I think about Tennessee Senator Bill Brock? I said I thought he would be great, but he should only take the job if he is willing to say to his constituents I'm not going to be much of a senator to you for two years because I'm going to be out getting senators elected. Bill Brock organized the Youth for the President organization and did a great job. There are no ifs, ands, or buts about it that he's an attractive guy, and so I told the president I'd back Bush and I'd back Brock as well. I agreed to see Hugh Scott tomorrow, whom he wants me to announce my support for his reelection. I told the president that I would tell Scott that I would support him only if he supported Brock, otherwise, to hell with him. And that was a decision we made.

We did not talk about Vietnam because I know exactly what is going on, since I have been advised that a cease fire is imminent, and the White House wants me to make a statement when that happens, which I will do. But I don't know exactly when because they don't know themselves.

During the conversation I told the president that I was not inclined toward running for the Senate again in 1974, because I would be seventy-two when my term ended. He found my thought ironic for he said he had been thinking about making a speech to the effect that nobody should run for reelection to the House if they are over sixty-eight, and no one should run for reelection to the Senate if they are over fifty-five, and no person, including judges, should serve past seventy years of age. I assured the president that I would be replaced by a man equally as loyal to him and equally as conservative and equally as strong a party man, should I not run.

The question came up about Agnew and 1976. Nixon wanted to know if I thought Agnew would seek the presidency. On two occasions Ted Agnew had told me he didn't want to run again for the vice presidency in the last election because of his difficulties in dealing with John Ehrlichman [the president's top aide for domestic policy], and the other reason was because he needed to make some money. He says he is a poor Greek and he was going to be a poorer Greek when it's all over, but now that he is vice president again, I told the president we would have to consider him. The president asked me not to commit myself to Agnew, and he said he would not commit himself.

It is my reading of this situation that Nixon strongly favors John Connally. I did not tell him because he surely knows that to get the GOP nomination for Connally would take some doing because Connally is certainly not his heir apparent. While I don't agree with Nixon completely on this, he seems inclined toward a man like Connally for president because he has the strength that is needed to get things done. He gets along with people, he understands business, and he understands organizations. Still, I think Ted Agnew has a tremendous appeal to the American people.

Nixon asked me what I wanted if I didn't run in 1974, and I said I didn't want anything. He said, "Oh, come now, what would you like?" I said, "Well, I've always thought I would make a good ambassador to Mexico," so he made a note of it, and said "It's yours" if I wanted it for the last two years of his presidency. So we have something to look forward to that could take care of several of us for sometime.

Letter (December 1, 1972)

Dear Mr. President:

My meeting with you at Camp David last week was, I believe, one of the most enjoyable, productive, and profitable meetings we've ever held. I wish we could do this more often, although I'm not urging it because I know you're loaded with thousands of people who want to see you, but we think alike on the problems that face you, and maybe once in a while I might be able to give you a hand. You face the opportunity of being the greatest president we have ever had because you realize fully what you have to do to reorganize this uncontrolled bureaucracy that we're faced with today, and I wish you Godspeed as you take on this Herculean task, which must be done if we are to preserve this form of government. Frankly, I am more fearful of what's going on in the power laden offices around this town than I am of internal or external Communism. Take whatever steps you have to, but get this government back under the control of the president and the Congress.

I have written your new Secretary of Defense [James Schlessinger], outlining some of the basic problems that I've seen over there, and I want to help all I can. He should feel free to call on me at any time because the way that the Pentagon's been operated has bugged me for a long, long time.

I would certainly appreciate it if you could keep to yourself the matter that we discussed just at the end of our meeting, which applies again to something we agree on, the age a man should think of retiring from the responsibilities of government work. I would appreciate the request I made of you being kept just between us two. I can't think of a better way to wind up my public career than in serving my country in the country to the South that I love and know so well. We can discuss this at any time and certainly I want to talk over with you when the proper time comes the techniques that must be involved in doing what we discussed.

CHAPTER 14

WATERGATE

Watergate and its aftermath were a particularly difficult period for Senator Goldwater. Not until the spring of 1973 did he appreciate the seriousness of the matter, and at that time he began to follow it closely. Goldwater worked behind the scenes to try to get Nixon to do the right thing, but when Nixon failed to do so, as the senator described it, the situation grew "worse and worse and worse." In 1973 Goldwater also found himself drawn into the problems facing Vice President Spiro Agnew, who by that time had won the senator's friendship as a true conservative. Even as Watergate grew into a serious national crisis, Goldwater resolved his conflicted feelings about Nixon by giving Nixon the chance to do what was right. It was not until after Nixon left office that Goldwater's feelings of disgust and pity toward Nixon were finally resolved—and he wanted nothing more to do with him.

1973

Interview (April 11, 1973)

Goldwater later described this interview with Godfrey Sperling, Jr., the national political correspondent of The Christian Science Monitor, *as his "blowing the whistle" on Nixon. It was prompted by his off-the-record conversation with Ben Bradlee, who had told Goldwater that Nixon was in serious trouble. This interview was given shortly before the Senate Watergate Committee commenced its public hearings and is the first of Goldwater's many efforts to get Nixon to do the right thing. The following are excerpts from that interview.*

The Watergate. The Watergate. It's beginning to be like Teapot Dome. I mean, there's a smell to it. Let's get rid of the smell. . . . I have called

Goldwater, Jr., and Sr., spellbound by speaker.

on the president to do this. . . . He has to. The president has to give assurances. I think the people will believe him. I don't want to see this man end his term with something hanging over him that will keep the Republicans from electing another president on the mere idea that, "well, we couldn't trust that Nixon. And how could we trust Connally, or Agnew, or John Doe or whomever?" . . . Now Nixon in my book is doing a helluva good job as president. I think the American people are very satisfied with his foreign policy. I think they agree with him very unanimously in his domestic positions. But all this is going to mean nothing. And what worries me is that unless the president comes out with something—"We did it. Or we didn't. This is the reason. We're involved. Or we are not involved." Unless he does this in the relatively near future . . . the Democrats can make real hay out of whether they are true or not.

Now John Dean [Nixon's White House counsel, then much in the news] happens to be an old roommate of my son's. And I've talked to him. I've never pumped him. But I asked him, "Is there any truth to this." And he said, "Not at all." And I believe this kid.* But I do

---

* *Goldwater is referring to a social event during the summer of 1972 during a visit to his son's home when he asked John Dean if anyone in the White House was involved in the Watergate break-in, to which Dean responded then—as he would today—that to his knowledge no one at the White House had advance knowledge about the break-in and bugging of the Democratic National Committee headquarters.*

believe the president has to say something. . . . The situation is salvageable. If the president was not involved.

Letter (May 10, 1973)

To a close friend.

Dear Bert,

I am so fed up with Watergate and all the lies that it takes something like our friendship to have me even write about it.

I have been speaking as loud as I can to the press lately about the cover-up on the Kennedys, Johnsons, and Democrats and only the Republicans seem to be the ones who receive this treatment. We get absolutely nothing from this and must assume that the conservative element and the president only get the dirt thrown at them.

When they give the Pulitzer Prize to Jack Anderson, the *New York Times* and the *Washington Post*, I think it is time to call it the Benedict Arnold Award.

Public Statement (May 16, 1973)

On April 30, 1973, because of the unfolding discovery of the cover-up related to Watergate, the president's chief of staff, Bob Haldeman, his top domestic adviser, John Ehrlichman, his attorney general, Richard Kleindienst, and his White House counsel, John Dean, all resigned because of Watergate. Senator Goldwater's office—with whom all of these men had varying degrees of association—issued the following statement, which was a clear shot across Nixon's bow.

It is not easy for me to say this about my country or my president, but I think the time has come when someone must say to both of them, let's get going. We are witnessing the loss of confidence in America's ability to govern; we are watching the price of gold go to disastrous heights having an equally bad effect upon our stock market.

A visit to the Pentagon, which is the seat of our ability and responsibility to maintain peace in this world, leaves one with the impression that the services are suffering, suffering from a lack of civilian direction because of the vacancies not yet filled at the secretariat levels. A reorganization of bureaus is a decided must for the continuance of our form of government.

I realize that the Watergate is a blot upon the political record of the United States, and I join all Americans who want this cleared up until no doubt remains as to what happened, why it happened, and who caused it to happen. At the same time, though, we have a far greater responsibility to our children and I might say to ourselves than to allow the sordid Watergate to wash out all other concepts of responsibility. I mean responsibility to the world, to our own people, and particularly that responsibility which is ours as a world leader to continue to lead, and it is to this end that I urge my president to start making moves in the direction of leadership, which has suffered from lack of attention because of an understandable concern about Watergate.

Journal Entry (May 17, 1973)

This morning while attending the mark-up session of the Space Committee I was called to the phone by General Al Haig at the White House. He told me that the president was concerned and interested about my press release of yesterday [above]. He said he didn't know how the president could act more vigorously because of the Watergate affair, and I told him I felt that the majority of Americans did not associate Mr. Nixon in a guilty way with this sordid mess and that he should be out in front leading the people.

I particularly pointed out to General Haig the vacancies that exist in secretariat jobs across this government. He admitted this and said they were beginning to work on it. I also reminded him of the great slow down in the reorganization programs. He admitted this too and felt that the president would be acting on it immediately. I told him that I said what I did only after attending the weekly Republican luncheon at which I distinctly gathered the opinion that everyone there felt as I did and I didn't issue the statement until I had conferred with Senator Scott, the Minority Leader. I think the general got the message loud and clear. I didn't back down one inch and I hope to see some action.

Letter (June 20, 1973)

On May 22, 1973, Nixon issued a detailed and lengthy statement setting forth his defense and explanation of the many charges against him. As history has shown, his statement was riddled with falsehoods, particularly his core defense that he had not known of the cover-up of Watergate until told by White House counsel Dean on March 21, 1973. After being advised in the broadest terms that Nixon was lying, Goldwater wrote the following extraordinary private letter to Nixon, which he typed himself, in an effort to push Nixon into behaving like a president.

Dear Mr. President:

Frankly, I think this letter should start out as Dear Dick because I am writing it myself as you will quickly detect. I am writing it on my little portable typewriter because I don't want anyone but you to read what I have to tell you. I am doing this, in my opinion, in the best interests of yourself, the office of the presidency and I think, most importantly, the country and to quite an extent, the Republican Party.

I have made several suggestions to you through television and the press and I have heard no direct comments from you, but I have heard on one occasion from General Haig who asked for a clarification, which I gave him. I want you to understand that what I am saying to you comes right from the heart, comes from years of friendship and comes from a very deep devotion to everything you and I have believed in. You may be angry with me for saying these things, but I have never been one to hold back when I think words are needed, and I think they are needed at this particular point.

I am going to make several points: Number one is that you have not started to get acquainted with the Congress. Having a few up for leadership meetings, having a few for state dinners is not getting down to the little fellow who has to go out in his district or his state to keep the Republican Party going, to keep the radicals out of office and to support you. Someone said in the press this morning that they had seen more of [Russian Premier] Brezhnev than they had seen of their own president and, frankly, I think that is a hell of a crack that you should take very seriously. You know having been in the Congress what a great asset it is to be able to say to people at home, "Now last night when I was talking with the president I said ___." When you have visited with that member of Congress he becomes your friend, he will understand you better. He becomes easier to talk to and you probably have enlisted forever the support of a member of your Party and even the support of other members of the other party. I know that Mel [Laird] has been brought in to do this but I have the strong feeling that Mel is not going to be able to do it because you are not going to let him.

Somehow, and I don't know how this is going to be done, you have to stop living alone. You have to tear down that wall that you have built around you. You have to emerge from the cocoon that you have been in all the years I have known you. I know you to be a very warm person because I've seen you that way on one or two occasions, but did you ever think that one or two occasions out of twenty-five years of friendship is a mighty small time to pass judgment. You must, and I repeat, you must begin to have members of Congress into the White House to visit with you and you must visit with them so they can let their hair down and you can gripe when you have gripes to exercise. No one who I know feels close to you. ~~Even as a~~ I will make one possible exception, I feel close to you and I have never had any trouble visiting with you, and I have avoided bothering you because of the great pressures on you, but you've got to become the warmhearted Nixon and not Nixon the cold, which you are now.

As I travel across this country I find our Party in much better shape than the opposition would like to believe it is in. The Watergate is something they are beginning to shrug off, although it is bound to have some minor effect in the next election. What you must be doing more and more of is getting closer to the Party. I have talked to George Bush about this, and he has told me of his plans of a fall get-together in Washington. I think it is great, but I think you should go further than just visiting with a selected group of leaders of the Party; I think possibly a National Committee meeting sometime in the fall would be wise. It would give you a forum with the leadership of the Party where you could express yourself, if you will only do it, so they can go home and report that all is well. If this isn't done, the Party is going to continue in a leaderless fashion dependent upon only senators and congressmen and governors who are more and more assuming the leadership of the Party that seems to be vacated by you. Whether you like it or not, you are the leader of the Party, and you have to act like it even though it does take time.

As I said on one news release, you have to start being the leader of the country, and I think in the international fields you have done a superb job that is recognized even by your strongest opponents, but in the domestic fields, it is the other way. We have a fuel shortage, no leadership from the White House. It is rather dismal. I know you might say that you are working on it, but nobody on the outside would know it. Whatever happened to the reorganization of the State Department that you promised me on three separate occasions? It hasn't started and I can tell you that they are your worst friends in town, and they have become so arrogant that whenever anybody, even a senator, criticizes them, the senator is questioned and an apology is demanded, and I think if you don't start the reorganization of that bunch, you are going to regret it even more than you have in the past. An act like this is an act of leadership, and the people will respond to it.

You still have problems in the White House and one of them is a man named Len Garment who is working exactly 180 degrees from the direction that you would like to see his assignments take. You must get rid of everyone who is not 100 percent for you, the country and the Party, and it is going to take a little more doing if you let Mel and General Haig have a hand. I think you can clean house and replace them with people who are more closely attuned to your ideology and philosophy.

Last fall I was exposed to the reorganization plans of the Interior Department. Today only one small step has been taken. Why not go all the way? This would be another indication of leadership. I am telling you these things, Mr. President, because I want to see you go down in history as one of our best presidents, and if you confine your activities to the international field, you will be looked upon that way, but when they start subtracting what you haven't done in the domestic fields, it can come out a flat zero, which is not to your credit, nor the country's, nor the Party's.

I am terribly sorry that I felt it necessary to write in this vein, but I think I would be derelict in my friendship for you and my feeling of obligation to my country and my Party if I didn't tell you what is on my mind. These things will have absolutely no bearing on my support for you. I will continue to support you, back you, and as I have often told you, do anything you want me to.

Journal Entry (July 24, 1973)

This morning I had breakfast with [Senators] Jack Javits and Bob Anderson and we discussed ways that, in view of the leaderless party we now have, both conservatives and liberals might be able to formulate policy through the National Committee that would in turn begin to draw up guidelines for 1976. I have discussed this with George Bush who feels there is merit to it and we will meet either Thursday or Friday morning for breakfast to further discuss it. I said that I thought this was necessary for those men interested in seeking the office to begin to make a little more candidate noise and I was referring to Rockefeller, Reagan, Agnew, Baker and Percy as of now.

Following my speech before the Aero Club, I was driven to the White House where shortly after 2:00 PM I entered the West Wing and was then escorted to the office of Mr. Bryce Harlow. Bryce had called yesterday to arrange this meeting saying the president wanted to see me.

Bryce started the conversation by asking me what I would suggest the president be doing. So I told him I wanted to come right to the point and not beat around the bush. But after I answered his question, I explained, the president may not want to see me. I told Bryce that after long thought and discussion with other leaders of the Party that I had come to the conclusion that the only way Richard Nixon was going to be saved would be for him to appear before the Ervin [Watergate] Committee. I said that if this wasn't done soon, and by soon I meant before the August recess, the president's reputation may not be redeemable. I told Harlow that I did not think the president was guilty but that clearly and for good reason the public was growing suspicious as to his veracity. I told Harlow that I thought his actions on releasing select transcripts of the his taped conversations was stupid and had only served to even more firmly confirm in the people's mind that this president can't be trusted. I further explained that the growing conscience of the Party leaders was that unless the president did something to redeem himself, he will finish his term but he will have lost all power in the Party, even the ability to select his successor, and it might even go to the point he will not be invited to the next convention. Finally, I told Bryce that I would be pleased to see the president and to tell him exactly what I had told him. He did not suggest I do so. Now we just have to wait and see what happens.

This has been another strange day coincident. Following a statement I released saying that the whole Watergate thing smelled, the president issued a statement within hours, making it appear as if he had listened to me. This has happened before. So news commentators have intimated that the president is taking his guidance from me and while I would not agree with this, nevertheless, what has happened certainly seems more than a coincidence.

Journal Entry (September 9, 1973)

Today, Sunday, the 9th of September, 1973, I have just returned from a visit with Vice President Agnew at his home in Kenwood. He called me on my way out of town on Friday evening and asked me to visit so on the way back from the Quinns' farm, the Quinns left me off there and I went in to visit with Agnew.

He wanted my advice, which I gladly gave him, and it is wrapped up, of course, with his current problems. I must start off by saying that I am absolutely convinced that this man is not guilty of anything and I'll add by saying that the attorney general, Elliott Richardson, has been acting in a very, very strange way in the whole matter. Richardson has refused to disclose to the vice president the nature of the charges against him, and neither the vice president (or his lawyers) know what they possibly can be. It seems that only the vice president can wait for a grand jury to act, or he can also wait for a decision from the attorney general as to whether a president or a vice president can be removed from office by an impeachment action of the Congress when he is under indictment and without having been proved guilty by the courts.

It turns out that there is a precedent that the vice president wanted advice on, namely, when Calhoun was running for reelection as vice president he was charged with having received payoffs or bribes. Vice President Calhoun in his case immediately went to the House of Representatives and requested that the House act to undertake an impeachment investigation to determine if the charges were true and if they were true, then impeachment proceedings would follow. The House found Calhoun completely innocent and that was that.

Vice President Agnew wanted my reaction as to whether I thought it wise for him to proceed with such course. To make it short, I advised him to do it and to do it very quickly, not later than Tuesday or Wednesday of the coming week, and not to let the president or any of his staff know what he was going to do. Now why did I make that last suggestion? Well, this is where the matter gets extremely ticklish. Let me offer some background on my thinking.

If someone were to ask me if I could suggest someone to write a scenario for a Watergate type of operation, I would turn to one man and he happens to be the president of the United States, Richard Nixon. It has his hands all over it, hands that I have known for a long time. Well, it has occurred to me on several occasions lately that the vice president's troubles might well stem from the same kind of mind and planning. Let's face it, Nixon cannot run for reelection, and he is not in good standing with his Party; it may well turn out that he will be *persona non gratis* at the next convention. I don't believe, nor have I believed for some time, that Richard Nixon would stand still for Ted Agnew to be the Party's nominee. What better way, then, to solve this potential than by dishonoring the vice president, causing him to resign.

Now let's look into some other factors. Last May, I believe it was, the vice president told me that he knew about his activities while the governor of Maryland was being investigated by the United States attorney in Maryland, and he expected trouble. This trouble broke about the 1st of August. The president knew about this investigation at least a week before the vice president was informed by letter. The truth of the matter is, Ted did not receive the information, rather it was sent to his lawyer who gave him the information. The president didn't say anything about it during that week. The vice president, two days after being informed, asked to see the president, but was told that the president was at Camp David, and maybe, just maybe he could go up that night to see the president. But soon General Haig called Ted to tell him that the president could not see him rather that he, General Haig, would visit with him in the vice president's office at 8:00 PM. It wasn't until 9:00 PM, however, that the general showed up and here it gets a little hazy to me but he may have been accompanied by

Mr. Harlow or someone else. Whatever is the case, they told Ted that in their opinion, it would be best for him to resign to avoid embarrassment and to avoid embarrassment to the office of the president. Ted told these gentlemen that by no means, and under no circumstances, would he resign, that he was going to fight this thing through.

When Agnew finally met with the president he took a more conciliatory attitude, and told the vice president that maybe there were ways to work this out that the immediate action was not as imperative as Haig and Harlow thought it to be. The president said he asked Mr. Henry Petersen of the Justice Department to investigate the whole thing. But it strikes me that Mr. Petersen's investigation has been anything but directed toward helping the vice president. In fact, some of the things the vice president told me I don't even want to put down on paper because they are difficult to believe.

Many of us in Washington have felt for some time that someone was out to get the vice president. It never really dawned on me who that someone might be until I sat there talking with Ted and my telling him I was going to speak right off the top of my head and that I would never mention it again. That someone could well be the president of the United States wanting to get rid of Agnew so he could replace him with either Connally or Rockefeller, and I'm not sure of the latter, as the person to succeed him. Clearly, this is a strong accusation to make against the president, a deeply troubling, terrible feeling to even think about it, but having watched the developments in Watergate, having watched the mentality that certainly is behind it, having been able to almost foretell to the moment what was going to be done, I now sit here this Sunday evening with the dreadful feeling that maybe Mr. Nixon has more power than is good for him and he is using it in a way that is not good for any of us.

It became obvious to me in talking with Ted that at least three former close friends of his have either been forced by threat to falsely testify or they have been threatened, and they have so testified without any knowledge on the part of the vice president as to what allegations they made. There is to be a meeting tomorrow morning at 8:00 AM when General Haig, and I imagine Mr. Harlow, and possibly Attorney General Richardson will meet with Ted to outline to him some suggested new approach they had cooked up in his behalf supposedly. This whole series of revelations has caused me to suggest to Agnew that he go to Carl Albert, the speaker of the House, and request that at least one or two other top-ranking Democrats be there as well, and Ted should be accompanied by Jerry Ford and Les Arends, and he should formally lay a letter of request for an impeachment investigation before the leadership of the House so that it would not become embroiled immediately in politics. I hope that the vice president will do this because it is going to be most interesting to see the reaction of the president.

I know from personal experiences that the president does not like anyone receiving more attention than he receives. I went through this in two conventions where I received what to his mind was an undue acclaim and, as we all know, everything in the world was done to delay, if not even prevent, my appearing at the last convention (and I have outlined that last incident for this journal). There is no question today that the vice president is far more popular than the president and the president is not enjoying popularity with the Republican Party and, in fact, may have lost complete control of the Party, which, I hope of course is not the case. But if there is any validity in what I am relating regarding Nixon's being involved in this Agnew matter, then it would be for the best of the country and the best of the Party if Agnew takes this matter to the House for them to investigate. I can think of nothing else now that relates to this.

Journal Entry (September 14, 1973)

We are traveling to Phoenix on American Airlines Flight 111. This morning I went to the vice president's office and was there over an hour. We had a continuation of the discussion I held with him Sunday evening and he told me what had happened since then. He reported that he has been asked by the president to resign and the president has made it impossible for him to go to the House of Representatives as he wanted to do.* He was given the president's decision by Al Haig and Bryce Harlow. The president has only talked with him twice during this whole period. In fact, Ted told me that in the five years they have been associated he has seen the president fewer than the times he can

---

* Goldwater later explained to Jack Casserly, "I learned much later that Agnew had not told me the truth. He had, indeed, gone to the House and met with Speaker Albert and others. The Democratic leadership was not anxious to become part of a Republican dispute which was already in the court."

count on two hands. This utterly amazed me because the president could with his power keep the attorney general off the back of the vice president, and let the Constitution function as designed. In fact, the president could encourage an impeachment proceeding by the House of Representatives but the president obviously is going to do nothing to help someone who has stood up for him, and helped him during his long Watergate travail.* This more and more makes me think, as I had written previously, that this is an effort to get rid of the vice president. In fact, I have seen a paper stating that there are three witnesses to the fact that the attorney general has said that he will get the vice president. At some propitious time this will undoubtedly be used by the television station that turned up with it.

The vice president again asked for my advice. Should he resign? My immediate reaction was, no, fight it out but I told him I'd like to think about it this weekend. However, there is one thing to fight, but when you are fighting the president of the United States, that is another thing. But I don't think the president or his staff has any idea of what is going to be turned loose if the vice president is forced to resign. What they don't seem to realize at the White House is that the vice president is more popular now within the Republican Party than the president. In fact, the president is a mighty unpopular man and in spite of what he may think, and in spite of what we may wish, the black cloud of Watergate hangs over him and it will hang over him, I'm afraid, forever.

Already two intelligent and honest newspaper people have approached me on the theory that this whole effort on Agnew is the brainchild of the White House, either to remove Agnew as a successor to Nixon or deflect attention from Watergate. More and more I have to accept this as having great potential truth and it being a possibility. When I returned from meeting with Agnew, I called Bryce Harlow at the White House and told him that I thought he should think very carefully through the possibilities that could occur should the vice president be forced to resign and, believe me, if the vice president

---

* *Agnew took the position that the vice president, like the president, could only be removed from office by impeachment. The Justice Department produced a legal opinion to the contrary, but there is solid legal and practical precedent supporting Agnew's position.*

doesn't say that he was forced to resign, others will. I told Harlow that I didn't know just exactly what position this would place many of us who have been defensive for the president, not that I knew if Agnew was guilty or innocent, but I didn't like the way it was all being handled.

What I do know is that if this is an effort to get either John Connally or Nelson Rockefeller into the vice presidency at the expense of Ted Agnew, that action will split the Republican Party wide open and very likely make it possible to elect a Democrat. If normal procedures are followed, I believe the Republicans can elect another president and I wouldn't oppose either Connally or Rockefeller if Agnew is politically dead, which I suspect is the case. The vice president, in fact, pleaded with me to seek the presidency again and asked me not to close my mind to it and I agreed that I wouldn't; in fact, no one can do that.

Anyway, I told Bryce Harlow and I had told the vice president there is a meeting this October of a group of people who want to put my candidacy together. The meeting will be in Washington and the reason it is being called is because of the utter lack of leadership of the Party exhibited by the president. The way he handles Agnew will come into it. I am hopeful that Harlow will tell the president what I said because I don't want to see this Party torn apart for the result will be disastrous.

The vice president told me that he has the feeling that if he goes through with a fight, and does it as vigorously as he would like, that it could tear the country apart, and bring more investigations into the office of the president, and on Nixon himself, adding even more general havoc. If he feels this way, then resignation is the only thing. However, if he resigns and then is forced to stand trial and found guilty of things that I am convinced are only innuendo and hearsay, then that becomes an entirely different story.

Apparently what the Justice Department is doing is finding a few people in high income brackets in Maryland who have had troubles with the Internal Revenue Service, and the Justice Department is giving them immunity if they will say something bad about Agnew or their relations with Agnew. Of course, to prove these statements untrue is very difficult just as it would be very difficult to prove them true, but the proof has to rest more on Agnew's side this time than on the others. He has a heavy burden.

I am writing this down as I did in the past. Judy will keep only one copy, which will go in our usual well-locked place; another copy will go to Peggy for her reading and her burning. In case anything happens to me, I want a complete record of what I have been thinking about in this whole shameful, rather disastrous period in American history. I hope we have not become witness to a Gestapo takeover of the way Americans have always lived, respected justice and upheld it. The procedures we are seeing are an unconscionable and totally disgusting thing to me.

He continued in a later entry.

It is now 4:30 MST; I'm in my house in Arizona. The first thing I learned when stepping off the plane was that Bryce Harlow and an associate would land at 6:15 in Phoenix so they could confer with me. I must have touched a nerve this morning when I called Harlow. It's going to be interesting to see who the friend is. I have just finished calling the vice president at his home in Washington and reported this development to him and he believes that the friend may be Fred Buzhardt, the president's counsel. He thinks that they may be coming out here to give me a snow job on the seriousness of the charges against him.

I have to take Peggy down to the Phoenix Art Museum for a 6:00 ding dong [apparently a reference to a fundraiser] but I'll come back to the house and we'll see what happens. I'm to call the vice president around 11:00 his time, which will be 8:00 this time and if I am through that's exactly what I'll do, but this begins to look a lot more interesting than I thought September the 14th might be. I'm now awaiting for the arrival of my friends from the land of Oz.

He wrote the following in an even later entry.

It's 8:30 here. About 15 minutes ago Mr. Harlow and Mr. Buzhardt left. They didn't say much. And I'll think about what they said tonight and I'll elaborate on it a little bit tomorrow. But the long and short of it is that I think the vice president is probably going to have to resign. They seem to have literally cooked up a pretty good idea for him to do it on, an income tax problem, which he could say he didn't want to take through the courts involving his office. I told Bryce that my concern was not specifically Agnew, although I let him know that bears heavily on it, but what it's going to do to the thinking of people in the Party and out of the Party who sense a plot to get rid of Agnew so that the president can appoint in his a place the man he would like to see as the nominee in 1976. I know that Harlow understands this. I think that is the reason he came out, but we'll have to think about it, brood a bit about it, and we'll see what comes.

Journal Entry (September 15, 1973)

Well, it's the 15th of September. I'm sitting up here at my house look-ing out at the white cumulus clouds above the Estrella and South Mountains and, frankly, wondering why in the hell a man would leave this place for that nightmare we are in, in Washington. I have noth-ing to add to what I said last night after talking with Ted except what have we come to in this country when an attorney general or a United States attorney or any of their helpers, most of whom have never prac-ticed law, can bring the pressure to bear on a man with Internal Rev-enue Service troubles to the point that he is offered clemency if he is willing to squeal on a friend. It goes something like this. I've had many people in the course of my political career call on me wanting to give me money for my campaigns and they have either given it to me individually or given it to my manager in my presence. Now let's say that these people get into trouble with the Internal Revenue Ser-vice and, believe me, whoever is president can easily arrange that, and then the attorneys, knowing that the chances were good that this man had given money to me, pushed the penalty of the Internal Revenue Service violation so hard that a man when offered clemency would say yes, I gave Goldwater cash or a check in return for a political favor. Even if this were not true and even if it were proven to be not true, my name would be tarnished forever politically and I'm afraid there is a possibility that this might be the case for the vice president.

One thing I must add is that I did call the vice president and did have a chat with him, telling him that I had not learned anything par-ticularly new except that Harlow and Buzhardt both denied vehemently that any leniency had been offered in exchange for damning statements about Mr. Agnew. Ted told me he thought he would go to Ocean City for the weekend with his family, think it over, and then come to some decision early next week. The timetable seems to be next week with a formal disclosure within ten days, but we'll see how it goes along.

Letter (September 20, 1973)

Dearest Peggy:

In the event that I will have to return to the Senate Friday night missing our anniversary, I would like to bring you up to date on some of the things that have happened and will happen. . . . I talked with you earlier today telling of the visit to the White House and the Air Force Wives Club at Bolling, and now I am awaiting tomorrow to be with you . . . prayerfully for our anniversary.

As you know, the military authorization bill is the most important thing I have to take care of and once that is out of the way I really don't have much in the way of committee assignments, except for two relatively important amendments for which I have to be here Saturday when they will be called up.

Now, to bring you up on the Agnew thing, and please keep this under your hat. On Monday I had a call from [*Washington Post* reporter and daughter of my dear friends] Sally Quinn stating that her fiancé, Ben Bradlee, had told her that the *New York Times* was going to break with an exclusive the next morning that Agnew would resign. She asked me what I knew about it and I told her nothing for it was the truth. Something in the back of my feeble mind began to click and I thought if somebody could halfway leak this without being caught, it might stir Ted up to the point of fighting instead of quitting. Consequently, I told Sally that for her information only, which I knew would get to Ben and with no attribution to me, that it was 99.5 percent certain that Agnew would resign. I got the desired reaction. Agnew's camp is fighting mad; the White House is really in a stew, and while I am still of the opinion he will resign, I think the finger of suspicion is being leveled at the White House, which I have a strong conviction is deserving of it as well.

I saw Ted today with no conclusions reached and I also saw the president, during which time he ribbed me in a laughing way. This whole affair has me terribly worried because if they have used the devices employed to cause Agnew to resign, those same devices can be used on any person in public or private life. The action is simple: find someone who is a friend of the target and find something wrong with his tax returns or cook up something and then go to the man and say, if you will level some charges against the target, we will grant you immunity. Once these charges have been made, whether they are right or wrong, usually it will suffice to destroy the person in question. This is the Gestapo-type activity that I have some suspicion may be blossoming. You can appreciate the necessity for secrecy.

Looking ahead, I will be in Phoenix on the weekend of October the 25th and probably will be with you the weekend preceding that; I am not certain yet but fairly so. . . .

I love you.

On October 10, 1973, Vice President Agnew resigned, after negotiating a no prison, three years probation, and a $10,000 fine plea deal with federal prosecutors, which was later described as "the greatest deal since the Lord spared Isaac on the mountaintop." Later, the State of Maryland forced Agnew to repay the state $268,482—the amount he had taken in bribes as governor, payments that he had demanded continue when he became vice president. Agnew went to his grave (September 19, 1996, at seventy-seven years of age) claiming he had been framed. Nixon appointed his old friend—a well-liked, long-time Republican leader of the House—Gerald R. Ford to be vice president (and Ford was easily confirmed by both the House and Senate).

Public Statement (November 6, 1973)

On October 20, 1973, President Nixon fired Watergate Special Prosecutor Archibald Cox. Attorney General Elliott Richardson and Deputy Attorney General William Ruckelhaus refused to fire Cox and both resigned. Solicitor General Robert Bork, the third ranking person in the Justice Department, carried out the firing. Within forty-eight hours several dozen bills of impeachment were introduced in the House of Representatives. The House Judiciary Committee, which had been exploring an impeachment inquiry, got very serious about it and very quickly. Almost daily new headlines kept those inside the beltway on the edge of their seats, and the entire federal government appeared to be spinning out of control. Deeply troubled by the mood in the capital city, Goldwater and his staff drafted a statement for the senator to steady Arizonans. The talk was not "pure" Goldwater, but it was pretty close, and it is relevant because few saw the potential gravity of the problems better than Goldwater, who was demanding that attention be paid to the processes of government.

Good evening.

I am taking this opportunity to address a short message to my fellow Americans. It is a message of the gravest importance to every one of you, every man, woman and child. For as a nation we stand at the brink of a national disaster. Nothing less than the future of our country is at stake.

Because for many months we have seen the constant enlargement of this crisis. From small beginnings a violent tempest sweeps across the land—a hurricane of vicious attacks, intemperate exchanges, ugly rumors, brazen breaches of confidence, wild accusations, evasive responses, tricks and counter-tricks—a holocaust that engulfs us all.

Startling revelations explode almost every hour of the day. Sensation crowds on sensation until we begin to wonder how much more our overwrought nerves can stand. Truly, these are times that try men's souls. I speak for no one but Barry Goldwater. Certainly not for Richard Nixon. Certainly not for his critics. Not as a senator, nor as a Republican. For this crisis has long since transcended party lines and factions. It has gone even beyond personal loyalties.

I am not attacking or defending anyone or any institution. I am not asking anybody to change their opinions. I am talking, not about beliefs but about methods. Neither am I asking anyone to ignore or forget what has happened and is happening. For there has been much done that should not have been done, and much left undone that should have been done. The road to Watergate and beyond is strewn with sins, crimes, misdemeanors, indiscretions and folly.

I am simply asking everybody who by word or deed can influence anyone else—the members of Congress, the White House, the lawyers and the would-be lawyers, the press, the electronic media, the preachers, the professors and the pundits every one of them—to check their wild stampede, to pause a moment in their tumult and trumpeting, and in some degree of calm to give a moment of thought to what the consequences of this hysteria can be if it goes uncurbed.

I am asking for a moment of restraint, of reflection and of quiet looking ahead. For what we are witnessing may reach much deeper than the fate of an elected president. It may affect the present and the future of every American.

The loud voice of history and the inner voice of common sense tell us that nothing is more terrible than the torrential passions of human beings in the mass. It is like a forest fire. It surges on with ever-increasing intensity far beyond the underbrush that is its first victim—on until it consumes the monarchs of the forest and the humble habitations of man. On and on until everything lies stricken in a desert of charred remains. Such a storm of human emotion, if those who fuel the fire continue at their frenzied pace, can go far beyond the ruin of individuals. It can destroy vital institutions. This is overkill with a vengeance.

FOR HYSTERIA LEADS TO PANIC.

PANIC LEADS TO CHAOS.

AND CHAOS MEANS NATIONAL DISASTER.

The past great scourges that have swept nations and civilizations before them have recognized no distinctions. Nor will this one. Disaster will fall not only upon the president and the people who defend him. It will fall upon those who attack as well as those who defend. Ultimately it will hit the innocent as well as the guilty. It will sweep us all in its great vortex of tragedy. This chaos will touch our lives on every side. It will affect what we own and what we receive as income. It will affect all our personal and business relationships. It will spew hatreds that will divide and devitalize our community life.

Equally dangerous in its impact, it will sweep our lawmakers into blind, unconsidered action. For in the confusion of these mad days every street corner becomes a forum for public debate. And every street corner loafer becomes a constitutional lawyer. Hot in the pursuit of votes we see representatives of the people in Congress propose in the name of reform or investigation preposterous innovations that will disrupt the balance of government power that has served us so well and will tear at the fabric of the Constitution.

Two centuries of history are looking down on this scene. And the ghosts of the great men who shaped our institutions must stare in amazement and consternation at this panic of self-destruction. Forty years ago, in the great banking crisis, President Roosevelt told the American people that they had nothing to fear but fear itself. That reassurance was a wonderful tranquilizer but it happened to be far from the truth. For there was plenty for people to fear at that time. I am not telling you that there is nothing to fear but fear. For there is much room for fear. And there is much that is wrong that must be corrected. There are plenty of rascals that need punishment. I am offering no cheap tranquilizer, but I am asking for a moment of tranquility. I am asking in the name of reason, in the name of sanity, of justice and enlightenment, in the name of the great God above, for a moment of quiet thought and reflection.

If we can have such a moment to quiet the hysteria that grips us we may be able to proceed to the task ahead, to put in order our house of government, to eliminate the incompetent, punish the guilty and to make sure that what has happened may not happen again. But all this, in an orderly, deliberate fashion.

To the Congress, to the White House, to the administration, to the press and the news media, to the pulpits and the universities, to each and every one of us, I plead for restraint in this crisis. For to stay on this road of unreason means stark tragedy. In the words of the street: In God's name, cool it. Give us time to think and look at the road ahead. Good night.

1974

Letter (May 7, 1974)

To a close friend.

Dear Bert,

Your letter of April 26 is one of the nicest and warmest that I've ever received in my life, and it's going to be retained forever in a file I call "Alpha." These are the only letters I ever want to read when I get older and through with this business.

Frankly, I had told Peggy a year ago in writing that I would not run for reelection. However when the Watergate thing broke and when it became more and more obvious that Nixon either didn't have the ability to clear himself, or the willingness to do it, and in the case of either or both no real interest in the survival of the Republican Party, I figured that if we're to have a viable two-party system in this country, some of us older bastards better hang around to help the young ones.

That's my whole purpose in doing what I'm doing. Believe me, I would much rather be basking in the warmth of my desert home or out on my boat with friends like you having nothing to do but figure out what the proper direction of travel might be at the time.

Things are in a real mess in this country, Bert. I am very, very apprehensive about what will happen within the next several years. I once wrote that we would either be free or slaves by 1980, and I used to laugh at myself about it, but now I'm beginning to think there's more truth than poetry to it. The make-up of this Senate is absolutely disgusting. They either are purposely driving us down the road to socialism, or they are so ignorant of what they're doing, we're getting there in spite of it.

I'll do my damndest. I don't expect to ever be more than a senator that people can come to for advice, but I will continue to sound off if I think sounding off should be done. At least I can sleep at night.

Journal Entry (August 7, 1974)

Almost a year had passed since Goldwater picked up his small portable dictating device and again set out his thoughts for his journal. On July 24, 1974, the U.S. Supreme Court ruled 8-0 in U.S. v. Nixon *that the president must turn over copies of his secretly taped conversations with his staff regarding Watergate to the federal grand jury investigating these matters under the new Special Prosecutor Leon Jarwoski. As Goldwater was about to learn, the tapes show that Nixon lied, and in fact he initiated the cover-up of Watergate by ordering the CIA to block the FBI's investigation—which only slowed the FBI down for a few days, yet it was still a criminal obstruction of justice.*

This is the morning of August the 7th, 1974, and I'm sitting in my apartment in Washington purposely not going to work because I have a luncheon date with Dean Burch and General Alexander Haig at Dean's house at 12:30 to talk over the question of my asking the president of the United States to resign.

Now what has led up to all of this? Other things that I have written have told of the development of Watergate and, of course, that history is known. To bring it into more immediate focus, about ten days ago the Judiciary Committee of the House of Representatives voted to impeach the president on three articles containing fifteen different points. The vote was twenty-seven to eleven. [Not all of the Republicans joined the vote; mostly the conservatives rejected impeachment.] The House then set a date for their debate starting on August the 19th with the vote on August the 29th. On Monday of this week, August the 5th, I was called by [Nixon aide] Dean Burch from the White House and he asked to see me at 4:00. A little before 4:00 he came to my office and gave me a draft of the statement that the president was going to release precisely at that time. In effect, what the statement said was that the president had lied to the American people, had lied to his friends in the Congress, including me, about his knowledge of the cover-up involving the whole Watergate matter. That was the final straw. I had taken his dishonesty down through the years thinking that they were just mere lapses, or short detours, but now that I look back on it and remember the important points of the dishonesty that has marked this man's political life, I am appalled that I put up with it as long as I did. I guess it was more respect for the office than for the man and the grave feeling on my part that the office should not be injured, but I was wrong in protecting him as long as I did. I am attaching a list, and it is a short list, of the dishonest things that I have known this man to do down through the past fourteen or fifteen years.

Monday night I stayed up most of the night wondering what to do, or what to say, because I knew it would be put to me. I drove to the Senate early Tuesday morning and no sooner had I sat down at my desk when George Bush, the Republican National Committee chairman, called. He told me that he was going to the White House to attend an emergency Cabinet meeting, which was the first one called in a year and a half, and he felt, and I had reason to believe too, that the president would resign. George asked me my opinion and I told him, frankly, I didn't think the president could get fifteen votes in the Senate. And as far as I was concerned, I was through with him; I was not going to protect him any more, although I reserve my right to make up my mind on impeachment should he insist on standing for that.

The Cabinet meeting was to start at 11:00 and at about 11:15 I was handed a note while seated in the Space Committee hearing room conducting a hearing. The urgent note said that General Haig and

Dean Burch at the White House wanted me to call. It shocked me so that I did the discourteous act of getting up and leaving, although I had just asked a witness a question, and I must apologize to this witness. I couldn't get the general on the phone because he, of course, is an important fellow, and he was in the Cabinet meeting and, so was Dean. However, Dean came to the phone and I told him what I had told George Bush and that I thought one or the two of them should pass it on to General Haig so that the president would have no misapprehensions about what was taking place on the Senate side.

Later I attended the Republican Policy luncheon and during the course of the luncheon Vice President Ford came in and told us what had happened at the meeting at the White House. But mentioned nothing about the president resigning, saying that the president has indicated that he would stand firm and demand an impeachment trial. At that point I could contain myself no longer, so I stood up and told my colleagues what I had told George Bush and what we all by then knew about the president.

Almost immediately thereafter I had a telephone call while still in the Senate dining room from General Haig, and the operator inadvertently said that the general was in the Oval Office, which is the president's office, and from the slight delay in the general's picking up the phone, I am convinced that the president was listening on another line. The general asked for my gut feeling about the Senate, and I told him that I thought the president would be lucky if he got twelve votes and that those would be the constitutionalists from the South who would insist on going through the full constitutional impeachment process. I told him I was through with the president, that I would not defend him any longer, but maintained my right to judge on impeachment if he insisted going that way. I told him the president had lied to me for the last time and that that was the attitude of most of my colleagues, particularly the conservatives on whom he was banking. I am almost certain the president heard that conversation.

Now we have to go back a few months when some liberal columnist, I don't remember who it was, suggested that I was the only person who could walk into the White House and demand that the president resign and he would listen to me. I laughed that off as an effort on the part of the liberals to get me to expose myself in such an effort and I never once thought of doing it, even though I will say that many, many members of the House and Senate and Republicans across this country have begged me to do that. Truthfully, until now I didn't think the president should resign. I thought he should stand for impeachment and take his chances but, as I said earlier, when he dropped that last shoe (with the Supreme Court releasing the tapes that put the lie to his entire defense), that was it as far as I was concerned. He should go for the good of the country because I don't think this country is going to survive in a good way a trial that [Nixon's impeachment] lawyer James St. Clair tells us could last for six months, which could mean seven months more or nearly eight more months of this Watergate mess being plastered across the papers and across the television sets of America.

Well, at the luncheon meeting my colleagues began getting up and suggesting what group or who might call on the president to ask him to resign or to at least express the sentiment of the Senate. I left the meeting early before any decision was made, but later the Minority Leader, Hugh Scott, asked me to come to his office, which I did at 4:00 PM, and we talked the whole matter over and decided that the president should be made aware of the feelings of the Senate. Later Senators Norris Cotton, Wallace Bennett, Bill Brock, John Tower, Jack Javits and Bob Griffin came in the room and we sat there until about 5:45 at which time it was decided that I would go to the White House, tell the president the situation and suggest that he resign.

I stopped by on my way back to the office to see my dear friend, Senator John Stennis, and asked him if he would go with me. He said he would go if I insisted because he felt the president should go, but he leaned more toward the constitutional process of impeachment. I believe if I pushed a little bit he would have gone. I wanted him to go because I know the president has great respect for him.

I called Dean [Burch] and told him what happened and asked if it would be possible to see the president, and my luncheon with Dean and Al Haig in a few hours is the result of that call. Then I will know whether or not I am going to the White House and probably destroy myself politically because this isn't going to be popular in Arizona but I don't care. I think the president has to go and the sooner the better for he has no chance in an impeachment trial and the country cannot put up with the disgrace he has brought to the office of the president. I had even considered, before telling the president that it was time for him to leave, announcing to my Arizona constituents that I would withdraw from the Senate race and allow some other Republican to take my place. I talked that over with Peggy; she told me it would be wrong, that I would be running away from things and I suppose she is right. I later talked the whole thing over with my son, Barry, but he was too busy voting on the House floor and too busy trying to make up his own mind to add anything to what I had heard from Peggy.

This is the worst period I have ever spent in my life in an emotional way. I don't think I've had a good night's sleep in months; it's hard for me to even eat; it's hard for me to concentrate and think because I'm brokenhearted over the fact that a man that I worked so hard for, in fact, gave a great portion of my life for, risked my own neck in a presidential campaign knowing I would lose just so I could keep the Party together for him, it kills me to think that such a man who I call my friend could do such a thing, not just to me, but to the whole country. Well, I will know a little bit more in a while.

Journal Entry (August 8, 1974)

Again, in the quiet of the apartment, it is a dismal day outside, but I want to relate before I forget much of it what transpired yesterday. Dean Burch called me early in the morning. As I mentioned I didn't go to the office, knowing I would be besieged by reporters. Anyway, Dean told me to be sure to wear a suit, so I knew then that something was up. About noon Earl Eisenhower drove me out to Dean's house and shortly thereafter Dean and Al Haig arrived, and Pat Burch served us a delicious lunch.

I was told that the president wanted me, John Rhodes and Hugh Scott to come to his office at 5:00—this was yesterday afternoon, August 7th—to lay on the table the exact situation prevailing in the House and the Senate. Scott and Rhodes were being asked because they are the respected Republican minority leaders in the Senate and the House, and I imagine I was called because of our friendship, and because I was a presidential candidate, the once titular head of the Party.

Haig went through the whole drill pointing out that the major problem with the president's resigning was the family, his daughters and sons-in-law, and I think this is going to be one of the dreadful things that will happen to the president when his family realizes that he lied to them as well as to the rest of the world. But that's beside the point. Haig explained that the president had been weighing his options, namely, whether to stand trial for a certain defeat in the Senate or to resign in the best interests of the country. Haig stressed that this was the dominant thing on the president's mind—as I well knew it to be.* After thoroughly briefing me, we left Dean's house and I was taken back to the Senate in a White House car where I immediately conferred with Hugh Scott and Bob Griffin. Hugh and Rhodes had been briefed by Bill Timmons of the White House, so they knew what was going on. I no sooner got back in the Capitol when the rumors started to fly.

Earlier that day, not to mention the night before, NBC had falsely reported that I had tried to gain entrance to the White House but was refused. About one-half hour after my return to the Capitol, ABC's Bob Clark, whom I have always considered an honest man and a friend, went on national television and said that Senator Goldwater had said the president would resign. I don't think ever in my life have I been so furious, and the longer I thought about it the madder I got. Finally Bob Clark called me so I gave him holy hell, something I practically never do, and he promised a retraction and did it. ABC called the White House and apologized, but NBC hasn't done a damn thing about it yet, so they will stand at the bottom end of my barrel.

Late yesterday afternoon I met with the same group of senators who had asked me to go to the White House, and I made as complete a report to them as I could without definitely committing the president to anything. Then I drove to the White House a little before 5:00 PM with Hugh Scott; we parked and went up to Bill Timmons's office and

---

* But as Goldwater made clear in private conversations later, Haig impressed on him that it was a delicate situation. Nixon seemed to be heading for resignation, but everyone needed to let him reach that conclusion on his own. To force this issue would likely have caused Nixon to fight. But if the president knew the end was inevitable, Haig thought he would do the right thing.

met with John Rhodes, Al Haig, Dean Burch and Bill Timmons. We didn't discuss much, just passed the day, but in a short while—which actually seemed like a long time—we went down to the president's office. I will never, as long as I live, forget that thirty or forty minutes we spent there. At one point I was literally on the verge of tears and I could see the glistening in the others' eyes as well.

The president was superbly serene; in fact, he acted as though he had just shot a hole-in-one and was enjoying that thought. I have never seen him so relaxed, his feet on the desk, just talking. We didn't talk about resignation. He asked about the situation in the Senate and Hugh asked me to relate it. I told him I doubted if he would get as many as fifteen votes and that most of those would be older southerners. John Rhodes then related the situation in the House, which looks as though there may be only 10 votes staying with him in that entire 435 member body. The president stressed that whatever decision he made, and it was very obvious that he had made up his mind to resign, he would do it in the best interests of the country and he asked us to stress that point as we appeared before the press assembled on the front lawn.

We reminisced about past campaigns, and how he and I had campaigned together for over twenty years, and how fast that time had passed; he talked about Lyndon Johnson (he was not a Nixon favorite), and how much love he had for Eisenhower. It was little more than a chit-chat among old friends, and when the meeting broke up, we shook hands, said good bye and walked out the door.

We returned to Bill Timmons's office as the press gathered, and then shortly went out the front of the White House onto the lawn where I guess every press man within five hundred miles of Washington was gathered with television cameras, microphones, etc. I had been asked to be the spokesman so I related what had gone on.

Goldwater's comments and responses to questions are from the White House transcript of press conference, 5:42 EDT, on the North Lawn of the White House; he did most of the talking.

SENATOR GOLDWATER: Congressman Rhodes and Senator Scott and I have just concluded a visit with the president. He invited us down this afternoon to disclose with him what we feel the actual conditions in the House and the Senate are relative to his situation.

We had a good, thorough discussion, and I think I speak for my two colleagues when I say that we were extremely impressed with the uppermost thought in his mind, which is that whatever decision he makes, it will be in the best interest of our country.

There has been no decision made. We made no suggestions. We were merely there to offer what we see as the condition on both floors.

. . .

Q: Did any of you recommend that he resign?

SENATOR GOLDWATER: No, that subject didn't even come up.

Q: Senator Goldwater, what about a report today that you had been telling the members on the Hill that the president was about to resign and to stick by their televisions?

SENATOR GOLDWATER: Well, I am not allowed to swear, but it is the biggest lie I ever heard in my life. This is the first time I have been at the White House in over two weeks, and the last time was to visit with Dean Burch.

The last time I saw the president was flying out to Arizona with him back in early May, and furthermore, NBC stated that I came up here last night and found all the gates bolted and was not allowed in. That also is a G.D. lie. I went home and cooked my dinner, had five or six drinks and went to bed. [Laughter]

. . .

Q: Did you gentlemen request this meeting?

SENATOR GOLDWATER: No, the president invited us. I said that at the outset.

Q: Senator, did you discuss possible immunity for the president if he resigned?

SENATOR GOLDWATER: No, that subject was not touched on.

Q: Senator Goldwater, do you think the president will be convicted if he is impeached?

SENATOR GOLDWATER: If he is impeached by the House?

Q: Yes, will he be convicted by the Senate?

SENATOR GOLDWATER: I have no way of knowing, and we have no way of making nose counts. I myself have not made up my mind, and I think I can speak for most of the Senators that they haven't made up their minds as to the three articles or the fifteen points contained therein.

Q: Did the president say when he would make his decision and announce it?

SENATOR GOLDWATER: No, that wasn't even discussed.

Hugh drove me back to the Senate and I went to my office, sat at the desk and picked up the phone because Judy had arranged a conference call with the Arizona press, radio and TV and then for about forty-five minutes I answered questions from every Arizona newsman and after that KTAR called, and I went on for about another twenty minutes. So I had a quick drink in the office, and went to the Quinns' place, where I met up with my beautiful daughter-in-law, Susan, and then took her to the Iranian embassy where we attended a dinner in honor of the ambassador of Morocco.

I forgot one thing that happened in the afternoon before I went down to the White House; it was prompted by those two lying efforts of the television people, and I literally blew my stack. I went over to the Senate floor and I asked unanimous consent to have thirty seconds on the floor, which was granted. Then I related the incidents that had brought on my anger, so looking at the press gallery, looking them right in the eye because they were pouring into mine, for the press gallery was full, I said in a loud voice, "You are a rotten bunch." Well, I have never heard such a spontaneous outburst of applause and cheers from the rest of the Senate gallery, and even members of the Senate on the floor applauded. I mention this because I am, in fact, concerned about the press of my country. Don't they realize that the American people are holding them in lower and lower regard? Why can't they be honest? Why can't they try to be level?

A last thought on this remarkable last visit with Nixon as president. As I sat in the president's office in the White House I thought to myself, here is the first time that such a major event like this ever happened in the history of our country and who is sitting here witnessing it? Three members of Congress, two of them from one of the smallest states in the Union, Arizona.

Journal Entry (August 12, 1974)

On August 8, 1974, Nixon resigned, effective noon the following day, and Gerald Ford became president. Under the 25th Amendment to the Constitution, which had been employed by Nixon when selecting Gerald Ford as vice president, now Ford as president would have to select a vice president. That selection would have to be approved by a majority of both the House and Senate, which was controlled by the Democrats.

Well, it's August the 12th and yesterday, August the 11th, I flew in from Easton, Maryland, to visit the White House and meet with President Ford, who had requested I do so. The president was detained a few minutes by a telephone call, but finally we sat down together enjoying a glass of iced tea. The conversation quickly focused on the reason for the meeting; he wanted to discuss the vice presidential situation [and filling the post]. I told him I thought two things had to be considered: First, of course, who could do the best job and, second, in the doing of that job, I thought he had to consider a man who in six years would be ready to run for the top office.* Because of that I explained that it would practically remove two people: Governor Rockefeller, although I told him I could live with Rockefeller, and myself, because I would be seventy-one at that time. I suggested the name of George Bush, a man just fifty years old of proven ability and a man I think would make excellent timber for the following elections. Ford asked me about blacks, and I told him, yes, if he could find a competent black Republican, but I did not think Senator Brooke [of Massachusetts] represented the typical black, so I hope he does not consider him. We talked about a woman and I told him what I've always thought, that women are excellent in politics but didn't know

---

* *This, of course, assumed that Ford would run for reelection and win a full term of his own.*

whether this country was ready for a woman president at this time. Neither did I know of anyone off hand, I could think of no Republican woman who is nationally known enough to take on the job. We discussed a few governors, some members of the Congress.

Finally he asked point blank if I would take it. I said, certainly, I'll do anything you want me to do; I'll do anything to serve my country but I do not want the job. I did not say this in an arrogant or conceited way, for I think I could do a good job for the president and the Republican Party at the same time. I think the Party is important because we cannot lose any more strength in the Party and remain a viable part of the two-party system. I wound up by telling President Ford of the operation I must have on my knee, which I thought would soon lay me up for at least two months and probably three. He said he had knee troubles too and to prove it, he pulled up his pants and showed me his scars. So I pulled up mine and showed him my scars, and as we compared them, I told him I thought mine were a little neater than his. With that I departed, stopped to talk to the press as I left, and then got in my car and drove home.

Letter (August 24, 1974)

In this letter to an Arizona constituent, Goldwater hints at advance knowledge of President Ford issuing a pardon of Nixon.

Dear Betty:

If things go as we think they will go, Mr. Nixon can forget his troubles. Of course, there are some of those in Washington and in the Congress who aren't going to be happy until they hang and quarter him, but more and more people are beginning to realize that the punishment he inflicted on himself by resigning is the greatest punishment that could ever befall him.

I am inclined to agree with you that as time goes on and history is written the accomplishments of Dick Nixon will far outweigh the misfortunes that befell him because of his unfortunate selection of those around him. Betty, you have no idea of how we tried to get him to realize what was happening to him by the very people who were supposed to help him, but as close as we have been for twenty-five years, it was rare that I even had a chance to see him and never alone. That day that John Rhodes and Hugh Scott and I went to see him was the saddest day of my life, and I never want to live through it again or even think about it.

Letter (September 25, 1974)

To Arizona constituents after Nixon's pardon.

Dear Mr. and Mrs. Applegate:

Thanks for your note and the article relative to Watergate. It is my feeling that there is no worse punishment that any man can receive than to resign under pressure from the presidency of the United States. He is going to live with this the rest of his life and not only that, but he will have to live with the memory of the fact that he was dishonest with his own family.

I think that the pardon was the proper thing to do, although it may have been done too early. Instead of cementing the country together, it has been dividing it again, but I think eventually it will head the other way.

Letter (November 1, 1974)

To an Arizona constituent.

Dear Mr. and Mrs. Hegarty:

Many thanks for letting me know of your strong opposition to the granting of any money to former President Nixon.

Congress chopped President Ford's request for benefits and expenses for ex-President Nixon from $850,000 to $200,000, and this cut had my full support.

There are always some emoluments that go by law to an ex-president, and I have felt that these were sufficient to take care of any pursuit that an ex-president cared to engage in. I feel that Mr. Nixon is entitled to what is granted by law to any former president.

Letter (November 6, 1974)

To an Arizona constituent.

Dear Mrs. McNally:

Thanks for letting me know your concerns. President Ford has done some things that I can agree with, but more sadly he has done more things that I do not find myself going along with. He asked no advice on the Nixon pardon. He merely told us, so we have no responsibility in that matter even though I told him that I thought he was wrong—that it was premature.

Frankly, I'm getting very tired of seeing nothing but extremely liberal appointments, and I've told the president my opinion, and I hope that it will do some good.

1975 AND 1976

Journal Entry (January 23, 1975)

After Nixon returned to San Clemente in disgrace, he became hospitalized. Goldwater may have lost his trust in Nixon but not his compassion for an old friend in failing health, so he sent him a "get well" note and something to cheer him up. On December 18, Nixon responded, explaining that "one of the most gratifying aspects of a time like this is to receive such warm expressions of concern from one whose friendship and loyalty I shall always treasure." Nixon added in his own hand, "The next time you are out this way I hope we can get together for dinner." That happened on this date, which Goldwater recorded for his journal.

I visited with Richard Nixon at San Clemente on this date. Leaving Phoenix on the Hughes West morning flight I arrived at Orange County Airport around noon, Pacific time, picked up a Hertz car and started down the coast highway to San Clemente. Fortunately I remembered my way and turned into the main gate of the estate only to be told that I was supposed to go through the other gate guarded by a marine. I approached that gate, was recognized by the marine who very courteously saluted me and directed me down through the inside

road to the inside gate and I pulled up in front of the house around
1:00 PM.

What a strange comparison to the last time I visited, what was
then the Western White House. No helicopters, no jeeps, no dozens
of little golf carts, no people walking around confused with papers in
their hands, just quiet, almost desolate quiet. There was one guard
at the door, a young Nixon aide who I knew, and we reminisced for
a second and he told me that Mr. Nixon was awaiting me inside, so
I walked through the front door, walked around the patio, didn't see
any sign of life anywhere, walked about the back porch and around
to the swimming pool, saw no one, so I returned through the house,
through the patio, outside and hailed the guard again and told him
I could not find Mr. Nixon. He apologized for not letting me know
that Mr. Nixon was probably upstairs in his study, so he escorted me
back in and lo and behold, stretched out on a chair was the former
president.

Nixon greeted me very warmly, put his arm around me and we
walked around the patio and into the living room. At one time in
our lives Peggy and I had looked at this house, not exactly with the
thought of buying it, but with the thought of looking at, and I'll have
to admit that what the Nixons have done to it is absolutely fabulous.
You can see everywhere the touch of Pat's hand for she had turned it
from a beat-up, broken old adobe house into one of the most beautiful
homes of its kind I believe on the Pacific Coast.

Dick, I will call him that instead of Mr. President, escorted me into
the kitchen where I met his Philippine chef and then we went back
into the living room and talked a little bit before lunch. Naturally, the
main theme of the conversation was how Jerry Ford was doing. I told
him I thought Jerry would do all right if he would quit compromising
and quit listening to the advice of the members of the House that he
had lived with—people who had never had to make a decision in their
lives. The president thought that he was right on what he was doing
about oil, and I agreed with him. He deplored the political use of oil
by Senators Ted Kennedy and Scoop Jackson and others, and he was
very hopeful that President Ford's veto could be sustained if he vetoed
the Kennedy-Jackson measure, as Ford has promised he will do.

At lunch we talked about the tax cut and he agrees with me that he doesn't think it will do much good to the economy, rather that the damage will result from increased inflation due to the spending of money we don't have, thus far offsetting any good that might come from the tax cut. Nixon showed a keen awareness of the makeup of the new Congress and the great danger it poses to the future of our Republic, and because of this, he kept insisting throughout the conversation that I convince the president that if there is a vacancy on the Supreme Court that he fill it with a conservative. Nixon said he didn't care whether he was black, white, brown, a woman or whatever, as long as he or she was conservative and could back up Burger and the other conservative members of the Court because with this Congress, the only protection the Constitution will have will be the Court. I promised him that I would get in touch with Jerry on this immediately and I will do this.

After lunch we went upstairs to his little study, which Pat has fixed up for him and I must say it is a delightful place, very small, not over fourteen or fifteen feet square with a fireplace lined in old Spanish tile with a giant wall window overlooking the Pacific Ocean. He sat down, as I did, and he lighted a pipe and for the first time started talking about what had gotten him into trouble. We talked about the CIA and he was very pleased that I was on the Senate's special intelligence committee, and I urged him to write me or call me anytime he had any questions he wanted asked relative to what might come out in the hearings. He said he had absolutely no knowledge of the ten thousand people that the CIA had under surveillance, but said that if they had not had such a list that he wouldn't think much of the organization, and I agreed with him. He admitted that the mistakes were all his, that he actually didn't know these things were going on at the reelection committee, but when he did find out, he waited too long to do anything. He didn't blame anyone in particular of his staff; he was surprised at Mitchell, of course. Nixon then wanted to tell me something he felt was very, very secret, and I knew immediately what it was going to be, because I had investigated it for the Armed Services Committee. It was the source who was leaking material out of the National Security Council. This was, as I knew, the young navy yeoman, Charles Radford, who had been leaking this material to the Joint Chiefs of

Staff but more particularly to Washington columnist Jack Anderson. Nixon told me that he could have court martialed the yeoman, and he could have put Jack Anderson in jail because of this, but in doing it he would have disgraced Admiral Moorer's position as the head of the Joint Chiefs, and it would probably have caused his resignation and disgrace. I told Nixon, very briefly, that I had investigated this matter and everything he told me I knew. But he added something that I had felt right along, namely, that John Ehrlichman had a hand in it as well. In fact, that was one of the reasons I played this investigation down as low-key as I did when Senator Stuart Symington (D-MO) and I were asked by the Senate to investigate it. I didn't want anything more being heaped on the Nixon White House [after Nixon's resignation] even though this instance was one that could also be laid, I believe, at the door of either Henry Kissinger, for certain purposes, and to the Joint Chiefs of Staff, who didn't feel they were getting the right information out of other members of the National Security Council.

We talked politics and I told him that I really thought he had a place in the 1976 election, that by that time the things that have happened would have been forgotten and he still had hundreds of thousands of friends in the states across the country and he probably, if he wanted to, could get back, in a small way, into helping, but I'd have to leave that up to him. He said he wanted to get back but he didn't know when it could be done. By the way, his health seems excellent, he had a very ruddy complexion, he has lost some weight, but it is very obvious that he is still in pain from the phlebitis in his legs. He told me that the last time he was in the hospital he didn't think he was going to pull through and neither did the doctors, but he said that rumors to the effect that he didn't care was a lot of "bull shit," because he, like everyone else, wanted to live. Right toward the end of our conversation, and I believe I could have stayed all afternoon with no trouble, he wanted to know if he should go ahead with his memoir, and I said yes, by all means, write it, tell the truth, tell everything and this would be another important chapter in the whole affair that we have been through and could go a long way toward clearing up his name and possibly exonerating him, although I told him frankly that might be beyond doing.

I can't think of anything else right now that transpired; he seems to be a very lonely man and I'm going to report to the Senate Republicans next week on this visit and ask them to individually from time to time to contact him by letter because getting him by phone is a most difficult thing. I said goodbye to him about 3:00 PM, after spending two hours; he seemed sorry to see me go, he was very solicitous, followed me to the door, backed up his little golf cart so I could get my car around it, gave me a salute and I went off, again, thinking about this poor, lonesome man in that desolate house that is so beautiful.

I stopped by to see Little Peggy who was in Hoag Memorial Hospital with a bad back and then on to dinner with old friends, and an all night flight back to Washington. We were not able to land at Dulles, so we landed at Friendship [between Baltimore and Washington], which is the only airport in the world for which there is no excuse, and I took a cab back to the apartment, arriving at 11:30 AM.

Addendum: On December 19, 1974, President Ford had signed into law the Presidential Recordings and Materials Preservation Act, which had taken Nixon's secretly recorded conversations and his presidential papers and made them the property of the United States. After making his entry of January 23, 1975, Goldwater recalled that the subject of Nixon's papers had also arisen during their conversation. Accordingly, he added the following comments.

The subject of his papers and the decision of the Congress that they belong to the government and not to Nixon came up and he is going to fight that clear to the United States Supreme Court if necessary. He feels, and I certainly agree with him, that any personal papers are his property; for example, he told me that included in these papers were probably 100,000 sheets of yellow scratch paper that he used to make notes on, and he wants to retain these, he wants to eventually give them to some institution, although the Nixon library seems to have gone by the board as the effort is being abandoned. He doesn't want to give them for tax deduction purposes, he just wants to have these papers for his property, and I agree that they should be his and I would hope that he would chase it through the courts as all of us who have served in public life will be faced with the ownership of things like his tape or papers.

Letter (January 30, 1975)

In this letter to Nixon following their visit in San Clemente, Goldwater, who was untrained in the law, does not appreciate that the type of criminal proceeding he was suggesting was not possible. Courts do not have moot or mock proceedings and Nixon's pardon had forgiven his crimes. Nixon, who was trained in the law, surely understood the fact, not to mention that he had tremendous exposure to liability under the law, and would not likely have participated in such an undertaking whether real or mock. Needless to say Nixon did not act on the suggestion. Nonetheless, this letter is included because it shows that Goldwater continued to feel that Nixon must somehow come clean in a meaningful way and test the claims of his innocence.

Dear Mr. President:

Last Thursday was a very pleasant experience for me and I hope that as your health improves and you are better able to get around that that meeting can happen again.

It was gratifying for me to see you looking so well and it was particularly pleasing to find that you are completely abreast of everything that is happening in our country and around the world.

This suggestion that I am going to make to you has come after quite a bit of arguing with myself, first one way, then the other, but I feel I would be remiss in my friendship with you if I keep it locked up in my mind. The suggestion will be made to you and there will be no copies of this letter.

As the situation now exists and will exist to a lessening degree in the future, you sit rather alone in the world feeling as many people do, that you were the victim of extremely unusual circumstances and charges. Nothing that your friends can do or that the world will do is going to erase from the people's minds that which haunts you the most, namely, that you did something wrong.

Here is my suggestion then. Even though you have a presidential pardon I would, when your health is sufficiently good, waive your pardon and offer to appear before any court in the capital city to, in effect, stand trial for whatever charges might be brought against you, keeping in mind that none have.

This would accomplish several things; it would show you as a man of courage, as a man of decency, as a man of respect for the law and as a man who is determined to allow justice to clear his name. As I said, this suggestion is made to you and is for your eyes only.

Letter (February 25, 1975)

To David Broder, the Washington Post *columnist.*

Dear Dave:

Thank you for writing the piece you did this morning on Nixon. It is a funny thing, but after reading that I sat perfectly still for an hour and thought back through the many years of our association, not yours and mine, but Nixon's and mine, and practically everything that man has done in those years has been for his own advancement, only I was too damn dumb to realize it.

Letter (April 9, 1976)

In this letter to an Arizona constituent Goldwater mentioned the moment he realized that he was through with Richard Nixon. Clearly, he had been moving toward such a break a year earlier, as he suggested to David Broder. In a journal entry a year later, he elaborated on this breaking point mentioned in this letter to his constituent, Louise. Goldwater, when being interviewed for a February 25, 1976, broadcast, had responded to a question about Nixon, who had arrived in China to considerable American media fanfare. "I don't think Mr. Nixon's visit to China did anything, and if he wants to do this country a favor he might stay over there. He is violating the law," Goldwater pointed out, referring to the Logan Act, which prohibits unauthorized persons from entering into foreign policy negotiations on behalf of the United States.

Dear Louise:

I said a half an hour after I made my remark [on national television] on Nixon staying in China that I would never mention his name again, but because you brought it up let me explain it.

When the question was asked me [by the show's host] about Nixon, all of a sudden—like a lightning flash across my mind—came the nearly thirty years that the two of us have worked together, won together and lost together and suddenly I realized that in all of that time, that man was doing one thing and that was to try to get Richard M. Nixon a step ahead at the expense of anyone; and frankly, I don't ever want to hear of him again or talk of him again. He is a part of my life I'm sorry I had anything to do with, and I'm going to get along very well without him.

Journal Entry (April 4, 1977)

The other morning while enjoying the luxury of a hot shower before getting dressed and going to work for some reason the words came to me that I had heard many years ago from an old Chinese priest. He said, in essence, a country that can grow to sophistication then lose that sophistication but once again regain it is the country that will live forever. Why that thought comes to me at the particular time I do not know except I do know the condition of my country, its sophistication, particularly its institutions have been on my mind a lot lately, above all the Congress and the Senate with which, of course, I am best acquainted. So it has prompted some rambling thoughts I want to get down.

We are a country two hundred years old. We have grown into a great sophisticated nation and have produced a remarkably sophisticated system, not to mention untold thousands of complicated gadgets and products, which have all made our lives easier. Now maybe this sophistication that has made life so easy, maybe that's the reason that the old Chinese saying has caused the downfall of nations and civilizations before ours. The question arises then, in my mind anyway, are we at the crest of our sophistication, or have we already passed the peak and started down the other side? Are we starting now to do as other great countries and civilizations and governments have done before us, literally go down the tube by losing our sophistication? If this is so, then the next question that follows is whether we can regain it; find anew and develop sophistication for this fast moving world, so that our country, unlike those who have failed to do so, can live?

Our country, of course, was born on the very simple idea that freedom is our only cause, and that freedom was not given to us by government, it was given to us by God and the government was created by men to enable us to protect those God-given freedoms. Now when all this problem began I can't tell, but I feel very strongly having spent sixty-eight years living on this earth and in this country for which I have nothing but devoted affection. I sense that it began maybe with Woodrow Wilson and if not then certainly during the time of Franklin Roosevelt. What began to happen was—and we saw it develop more following World War II than any of the time before, even though the time before might have produced some symptoms that we have not understood yet—that instead of elected officials running our governments, more and more the academic people took over the operations, particularly of the Congress. For example, when I first came to the Senate I think we had less than four thousand clerks working on Capitol Hill and if my figures are correct, we now have some twenty-four thousand. When I first came to the Senate, senators did their own work. Of course, they were aided by their administrative assistants and by people on their staffs who were supposedly experts in certain fields. The committee staffs were not large and they were generally very expert in their work, but slowly these staffs began to enlarge and the senators' responsibilities in these changing processes of government grew to be so heavy that it is virtually impossible for a senator to say that he takes care of what he was sent here to take care of, namely, his own people's business, the protection of our system of government, and the preparation and passage or non-passage of laws. For example, today I serve ex-officio on every subcommittee of the Select Committee on Intelligence. In addition, I serve on three subcommittees of the Armed Services Committee and three subcommittees of Commerce. Now every morning I get here about 7:30 and starting at 9:30 I am confronted with a schedule calling from three to four committee meetings and, of course, it is absolutely impossible for any man to take care of that many assignments. What we see, and I'm using now as an example in the Aviation Subcommittee of the Commerce Committee, of which I am a member, where we are holding hearings on whether the airlines should be deregulated; yet I haven't found a president of any airline who says that he was asked about the proposition submitted by the General Accounting Office—and which has great weight in what is said on these matters—or by any of the academicians who prepared this particular piece of legislation for three different senators. What I'm trying to say is that the Senate and the House now turn out legislation that very few members understand, which very few members had any hand in developing, and these matters become law without the affected persons really having much to say about the matter.

You might now ask, what has this to do with the declining sophistication of our country? I think this part of it was planned. I think when the academicians began to really move into government during the early days of the Roosevelt administration that everything, if not every step, was made according to FDR's master plan and I suspect that even the universities were picked from which these gentlemen would come. As this has occurred we have watched a change in the type of government that we have under the Constitution. We have watched our institutions in the economic fields deteriorate because making money became the sole determiner of whether success was present or not. Conglomerates were formed with men who headed them who couldn't name the products made by their own company. All they could quote would be the amounts of money they made or lost. As a result of this, we have developed a decreasing number of really good executive heads for business in this country and, at the same time, the academic people who put words into the mouths of members of Congress have been chastising American business until American business, on the whole, is frightened to speak out in its own defense.

Are we going down the road that that old Chinese priest talked about? Are we declining now? Are we going to reach the point where the very purpose for which this country was founded, freedom of the people who live in the country, will disappear, and then the challenge will be, do we have the strength to once again begin and build what we so laboriously, intelligently and honestly built only to watch it be destroyed by people who actually didn't want to destroy it but whose work has brought on this deterioration.

Now let me at this point suggest that maybe because I am older, and maybe because I've lived through the greatest depression this country ever had, the greatest war this world has ever seen, and troubled times in our country too many to mention, and a world that seems to be teetering on the edge of self-destruction, maybe I have grown too old to realize that maybe things have changed and that all of these things that I see are really not happening for the worse but for the better. I must think about this.

Journal Entry (February 26, 1977)

In February of 1975, just after President Ford made his first trip to New Hampshire for the primary, and the day or two after President Nixon made his first return trip to Peking, I was appearing on either the "Today Show" or "Good Morning America," I forget which, and I was asked the question about what I thought of Nixon going to Peking the very day that Ford's news of his visit to New Hampshire would be making the headlines. I can't exactly describe how this happened because it never has happened to me before, but in the instant or two that you always have to answer such a question, your brain is working more rapidly than a computer trying to come up with something, when all of a sudden mine sort of exploded, and in that one, short hundredth of a second or so, the whole past of Nixon down through the years of our association together came before me and I made a remark, "He can stay in China," and I was not externally mad nor really internally angry either. All of a sudden it had come to me.

When I got back to the apartment Peggy said, "Why did you say such a thing?" I said, I don't know why I did, it just came out. It came from my brain; it came after all of those years of watching Nixon use everybody else for his own advantage, including me. I have never gotten over that feeling, even now. I feel sorry for the man but in a different way than I felt before. He has always been obsessed with power, a desire for power probably brought him down, and only time and Nixon's willingness to someday tell the truth will ever solve all the mysteries of Watergate that remain to this day.

THE 1976 PRESIDENTIAL ELECTION

Much to the chagrin of Ronald Reagan and his followers, Goldwater—after months of internal debate—gave his support to President Gerald Ford. Goldwater believed that the country had suffered from the wrenching of Watergate and that it would be best for the nation for there to be continuity at the White House. A few of the senator's musings in his journal tell the story.

Journal Entry (October 23, 1975)

This is the first of several notes I will probably make on this one subject, namely, the presidential candidate of the Republican Party for 1976. I believe I should be ready to expect some pressure from the candidates for the presidency from our Party, but only recently has any serious pressure begun from the Reagan and Ford camps.

Governor Reagan has called me twice this past summer, and again just about two weeks ago. In none of the calls did he indicate that he had made up his mind to seek the nomination, but it's almost impossible to fail to detect that this desire is his and that in all probability he will run. He has made no overt requests for my help, although I do recall that in 1968 I told him that if he desired to seek the presidency that year I would help him and, of course, he didn't. Whether or not he still attaches veracity to that promise made seven years ago I don't know, but I suspect that he does and I suspect he is expecting my assistance.

About three months ago a Ford committee was formed by Dean Burch, whose relationship to me is well known, and a short while later another Ford committee was formed by [former Georgia Congressman] Bo Callaway. Bo retired from the office of secretary of the army to chair that committee. Both of these men are strong Goldwater supporters, so I knew that it wouldn't be long before some overtures came from President Ford himself seeking my help.

Now with that background, let me make my position clear at this stage. Some 27 million people voted for me in 1964. How many of them still would, how many of them are still alive I have no idea, but I do feel a responsibility toward those people. I don't believe these 27 odd million people voted for me merely because I was conservative, so I would have to think they would be divided in their support of Ford and Reagan, but I feel the majority would go with either man that the Party selects.

Now I must add to this particular problem one of a larger nature, namely, my son, Barry, who is thinking of running for the Senate in California but has not yet made up his mind, although I think he will run. His problem, of course, in California will be whether to openly back Reagan or openly back Ford or to walk as gingerly as he can between the two of them if that can be done, and I think we can develop ways for that to happen.

As background for my White House meeting today, I arrived about a half an hour early and sat in the sun room, which is up on the family floor waiting for the president and Bryce Harlow. They finally came and we sat down to a nice simple luncheon of vegetable soup, three lamb chops apiece, asparagus and sherbet. Afterward we got into a long conversation about the president's election chances. I pointed out to him that I thought he would lose New Hampshire and Florida, but he told me that he was committed to both states and would not back out and I agreed with him on this. However, I suggested that he not only concentrate his time in the White House, but that during these two primaries that he concentrate more of his time in the White House with the understandable excuse that there is more important work to do in the White House than in either of those two states.

I pointed out to him that in all probability he would lose a number of primaries, but he would likely carry every large state with the exception of California and that nine states have the ability to nominate a Republican candidate and also to elect him. He agreed. California cannot be handed to Reagan at this time even according to my private poll numbers, but it leans slightly in that direction. We discussed the things that will probably go in the president's favor, which will be a decreasing rate of unemployment, an increasing gross national product, and an economy that in my opinion, his opinion, and the opinion of our economists, will improve to a remarkable degree during the rest of this year, as well as 1976 and, in my opinion, probably for 1977 at the end of which, or the beginning of 1978, we will see tough times again caused again by inflation. I reminded him that the poll numbers showed little interest in inflation but concerns with unemployment, energy, etc., so that it cannot be scrubbed as a national issue and he agreed. He feels that foreign policy will be in good shape, although I disagreed with him. What the meeting boiled down to was an obvious desire on his part to ask me to openly participate in his campaign but I explained to him my position relative to my son. I told him this and that I would not do anything to hurt him, which would include my not coming out for Reagan, and that if the chips got down and the hair got short I'd do what I thought was best because what's best for my country is a damn sight more important to me than what's best for Ronald Reagan or even Gerald Ford, but I also told him that I thought the country had to have continuity of government and I questioned whether we could have that with Reagan coming in and having to organize an entire new administration.

We all agreed that it would be impossible for him to work at all with the Congress while the president has been somewhat successful mostly due to his close association in the House and also, to some extent, with the Senate. My own position is probably the most ticklish one I have ever found myself in because I have a reputation of saying what I think, making my mind up but here is one where I may seem to appear rather weak walking down the middle but, as I say, it becomes obvious that something has to be done to pull the whole thing out.

One really pleasing thing occurred during our conversation. A note was delivered to him from his wife Betty, which said her examination today revealed completely negative results, no recurrence of her cancer and, of course, that's a blessing. It's going to be interesting to watch the developments because I have no question that Reagan will announce and he will run strongly in many of the primaries, even defeating the president in some of them, but I believe when it gets down to the nut cracking stage that the president will win the nomination and it will be about that time when I will have to take a position this way or that. But at this time, a year before the election, I have a lot of time to think about it and to help wherever I can, and I told the president that if I could help him in any way that would be more or less behind the scenes to count me in, so with that the meeting broke up.

Journal Entry (June 6, 1976)

During the presidential primaries, Goldwater made the following observations.

My reaction to the campaigns so far, after watching [California Democratic Governor Jerry] Brown and [Georgia Democratic Governor Jimmy] Carter, is that they are not talking at all about what is wrong with America. And my impression up to this point is that at this time in our history when we are in the most trouble, we do not have honesty among people who have been elected or people who want to get elected to high offices. I think back to my presidential campaign when I told the American people the truth, like the need to sell the TVA [Tennessee Valley Authority] to private industry or to the states, like the need to be strong militarily and what was needed to do that, like standing up to explain how things really are—and none of these candidates is doing it. So I am convinced more than ever that it is virtually impossible to be elected in this country by telling the truth. The people only want to hear what makes them feel better.

I have just been listening to [former Alabama Democratic Governor] George Wallace and, ironically, he is the one who has been telling the people what the government should do relative to unemployment, but it is not the kind of talk that the American people want to hear. It is strange, but here is Wallace, who cannot get elected president and in my opinion should not be president, and he is the candidate who is telling the truth. On the Republican side, I think both our men—Ford and Reagan—do a much better job of telling the truth, but I am becoming more and more convinced that it is the biggest liar who wins these nominations.

Journal Entry (June 25, 1976)

Here we are just a month away from the nominating convention of both national parties and I'm in bed getting over a hip operation, which has given me a brand new, stainless steel hip to replace the nice, clean boney one God gave me. I have a lot of time on my hands just stretched out like this, so I thought I would put down some things particularly in view of recent happenings within the Republican Party, the conservative movement and as they reflect on me. . . . People, I suppose, may some day argue whether I was a conservative, ultra-conservative, middle-of-the-road or what not. I think when the history of the country is written and if there is any place in it for a word or two about me they will call me a liberal.

Had you asked me at the time I first ran for the Senate to define a conservative, I would have used the same definition as today, namely, the conservative does not want to try anything that has been a failure in government or business before unless, and this is important, unless they are convinced they have found a way that the approach can be made to work. But normally, I'd say 99 percent of the time, history has shown the repeated failures of the attempts of those who would do things outside of this conservative pattern, and we true conservatives are not tempted to repeat their mistakes.

For example, I am a complete and firm believer in our Constitution. I believe our Constitution was designed by brilliant men who envisioned the days ahead when that Constitution would have to be changed, and they provided for ways to change it. Ironically, though, every time we've changed it, we've made a mistake. They designed it so that it would be flexible and its flexibility has been tested and it's been proven to be of value, but I do believe implicitly in the Constitution and everything that it says and particularly everything that it means. To understand its meaning I have read the Federalist Papers, many times, and books about its background, together with all of the material that I can gather on the actual writing of the Constitution: why these words were used instead of others, why one approach was taken instead of another. This is the core of my political philosophy.

My economic philosophy is based on personal experience. I was raised by a father who was extremely diligent in his work, and yet, I never knew a man to enjoy life more than he did. He got up early, walked to work, usually came home for lunch, changed his clothes after a nap and went back to work and later on in the afternoon would wind up at the Arizona Club playing poker. I went to work part time at the store when I was in about the seventh grade, and to work permanently in 1929. From my many years in business [1929 to 1952] I learned to respect, with complete confidence, our free enterprise system, and I learned in my formative years that the American economic system could only work well, and at its best, when it was unhampered by government and was allowed to be controlled only by the market-place. I'm not saying that in the years since I first became a merchant that American business has remained the kind of pure, decent ethical thing that I always looked on it as, but that is another discussion. In fact, what I see today in American big business, or some parts of it, is absolutely revolting, disgusting and frightening because I am able to understand at times why colleagues of mine in the Senate want to nationalize some of our major industries, but it is not this view of their reasoning that disturbs me, it is their absolute lack of knowledge of how this system works that causes me to wonder whether or not this country will operate under a free economic system in the years ahead. Thus, the core of my economic philosophy is the free market system—when it is working as it should.

I apply the term conservative to both of these core beliefs. I confess to the fact I have set down these matters because of my rather belated, though not surprising, discovery that many of my friends who call themselves conservatives are, in fact, so radical in their approach that I have to look upon them as people almost as dangerous to our way of life as those fanatics on the left. This revelation really came home to me during these current primary campaigns, which I have tried my best to keep out of. Nonetheless, it became necessary for me to be critical of Ronald Reagan's stand on the Panama Canal. As a result of what I said publicly concerning Ron's position, I received literally thousands of vitriolic letters and hundreds of telephone calls of such a nature that I instructed my staff to hang up rather than listen to the four-letter words, and it has even reached the point where old friends who wrote on my staff, such as Lee Edwards, and maybe one of two others, have not only come out publicly criticizing my position relative to Reagan, but casting extreme doubts as to whether I was a conservative or not, or whether I merely used the term to achieve what I achieved in 1964, the nomination.

I must state that I did not want the nomination. I had been chosen to be chairman of the Republican Senatorial Campaign Committee in my second year in the Senate and I believe I served a total of seven years in that job, but in doing that job I was required to visit every state in the union, almost every district and precinct, not once, but many, many times, raising money, or helping to raise money, and

helping to get people interested in running for office and then helping them get elected. I think I can safely say that I have raised more
money for the Republican Party than any other single person. I think
I can honestly add that I have helped more people get elected to office
in the Republican Party than any other person. But those points are
not important. The first I heard that there was interest in having me
run for the office of president came during the spring of 1963 when
I learned of efforts started by my friend, Clifton White, who wanted
to put together a Draft Goldwater movement. I actually thought so
little of this prospect that I paid no attention to it and I was, frankly,
shocked at the size of the first meeting of the Draft Committee, which
was held in Washington, around July the 4th of 1963. Well, one thing
lead to another and as they say the rest is history, but I want to reiterate, I didn't want to be the Republican nominee. I actually said no
three or four times but I was looked upon then as a conservative and
yet, today, twelve or thirteen years later, I am looked upon by many
of these same people who thought of me as a conservative then, but
now as a socialist, a communist, a traitor—someone who has turned
against his cause. Yet, and this must kill them, I continue to get the
highest ratings from the Americans for Constitutional Action on my
voting record and that's where the judgment should be made.

Journal Entry (November 5, 1976)

Gerald Ford has just lost his bid to be elected president.

It's strange that a man who once sought to live in the White House,
and from that position, help run his country should have so many
unhappy experiences, or maybe I should say memories, connected
with the White House. I remember the sad days of Jack Kennedy who
never really felt that he had a hold of things and would occasionally
expose his feeling to me. I remember the last night Lyndon Johnson
was president when he called me up and asked that I just drop by
and have a drink and after quite a few he had unburdened his soul to
me. Then there was that never-to-be-forgotten day when I had been
chosen by my colleagues in the Senate to inform President Nixon in
a very gentlemanly, nice and mature way that he had just "bought the
farm" and had better quit.

Today, I called President Ford to see if I could come by and just chat with him, hoping to cheer him up a bit. As I walked in the office, I have to admit that a tear came to my eye because here was a man close to me for twenty-seven years in politics, a man with the weaknesses all of us have, but a man with strengths that should have been sufficient to elect him president. He is physically strong, he is honest, he is mentally and morally clean; he is a Christian and he is a natural leader. If he ever had one fault, it was a common fault shared by all leaders of the Republican Party in the House of Representatives: John Rhodes, Melvin Laird and others who, through years and years under the domination of irresponsible Democrats, had to compromise instead of making decisions.

This was the trait I feared when he moved into the presidency, and even though he did overcome it to some extent he was, to the very end, reluctant to make a decision. But that's all beside the point now. This man had lost the election for the presidency. He lost it by a fraction of a hair; he lost it because a man named Jimmy Carter had put together the old formula of Franklin Delano Roosevelt: organize the minorities, promise them everything you can promise them, and you'll get elected. I still think that action of Roosevelt is what started the decline of America and, if continued by Carter, it will contribute to the downfall of this country within a relatively few years.

Ford and I didn't talk long. Under the circumstances it was hard to talk with a man with whom I feel so close. He played center on his college football team, and so did I. He was elected from a small district and I was elected from a small state. He is a conservative and I'm a conservative. He has a gorgeous wife and so do I and we both have wonderful families. So we have a lot in common and I've been close to him through the years and I didn't want to stretch out the sad feeling I had.

I told him that I thought Mr. Carter had an awful challenge ahead of him. I told him I thought Mr. Carter had conducted a very dishonest campaign and both of us agreed that when the people he had made promises to—including the labor chiefs, the blacks, the Puerto Ricans, the Jews, the Catholics, all the other groups—when those promises had to be kept, he might be able to keep the promises but our Republic would cease to exist. . . . On the other hand, I was heartened. The election was so close there is no mandate for Jimmy Carter to do the stupid things he has promised. I hope I am wrong in my judgment of this man. I hope he will realize that his love of country, which he certainly must have, having graduated from the Naval Academy, should teach him that what is good for America is good for every one of us, and what is good for any one of us doesn't necessarily mean it's good for America.

I guess the president and I spent half an hour together. He drank a cup of tea; I fidgeted with my cane, which I'm still using; and finally I stood up and wished him well, and told him that I was proud of what he had done and I would help him in any way that I could. And, to emphasize once again something I have repeatedly said to him, I said, in a laughing way, Mr. President, you still have a couple of months, why in the hell don't you give that Solar Energy Research Institute to Arizona? He looked at me, and laughed, and said he would certainly think about it because he said Arizona did more for him than any state in the Union. In fact, it did more.

PART V

※ ※

ON THE ISSUES

NOTE

During our research we came across a letter that Goldwater received on June 23, 1973, at the height of the unfolding Watergate scandal. It was a handwritten note, dated the day before, from Erwin N. Griswold, the former dean of Harvard Law School and a Democrat who had been appointed Solicitor General of the United States (the man who decides which cases the government will take to the U.S. Supreme Court and then argues many of them before the high Court) by President Lyndon Johnson, but had been asked to remain in that post by President Richard Nixon during his first term. Dean Griswold—a man who passed out many diplomas but few compliments—wrote the following note as he was clearing out his office to leave government service:

Dear Barry,

As I leave this office, I would like to write you something that has been on my mind for a long time. These are difficult and indeed bizarre times, but of course the Republic will survive. But it will take good work by strong men in many public offices. And that leads me to the point of this letter.

Of all the people in public life here in Washington I do not believe there is anyone who has come up as much in my estimation over the past several years as you have. For better or worse I took a rather dim view of you back in 1964. . . . But since you have returned to the Senate [in 1969], you have constantly made good sense. You have spoken well and wisely on a number of important public questions. I have learned that though you are probably more conservative than I am, you are a thoughtful conservative Senator who is often helpful in moving matters along and bringing them to a solution. And I have learned too that you are thoroughly reliable and honorable and straight forward. I would trust Barry Goldwater's word on any issue, and that is quite a lot to say these days. I hope you won't mind my being so bold. I have wanted to communicate this to you, and this seemed to be a good time to do it.

After returning to the Senate, Goldwater would remain for three terms, debating as each term came to its end whether to stay or retire. During these eighteen years he would address countless issues, many of which remain relevant to this day. We have selected a number of those issues where we found "pure Goldwater" material, and we have done so with Dean Griswold's observations in mind that Goldwater had "spoken well and wisely on a number of important public questions." They are collected in the following pages. Some of the speeches we have included, and statements of the floor, had some staff input, but they are issues that the senator addressed on many occasions, often with no staff suggestions at all—they have been included as "pure Goldwater" for that reason.

CHAPTER 15

AMERICAN FOREIGN POLICY

W*hen campaigning for reelection to the Senate in 1968, Gold-water's increasingly sophisticated worldview was evident to more than Arizona voters. During this period, he gave a number of addresses on which he worked intently and personally. They reflect his experiences on the national stage, along with his travels and studies of issues throughout the world when out of office. The following speech on Vietnam and American foreign policy in the Pacific (the only speech we have included in the book) is one such example. His observations still ring as correct and his policy recommendations as sound.*

ON VIETNAM AND THE PACIFIC FOREIGN POLICY

Speech (October 4, 1968)

Ladies and gentlemen, before proceeding I would like to dispose of two preliminary matters: First: The foreign policy which I will present tonight is not meant to be a statement of doctrine binding upon anyone other than Barry Goldwater. Second: I hope you will forgive me tonight for presenting a speech devoid of jokes and nifty one-liners. The serious nature of the topic simply does not permit the luxury of a light-hearted, go get 'em political speech.

To be allowed to discuss American foreign policy before this august group is at the same time an honor, a privilege and an opportunity. The first two you will probably recognize immediately as the required statements of a politician. However, the third—opportunity—might for a moment confuse you. I hope the confusion doesn't last because

I have some grave misgivings about American foreign policy, particularly in the Far East and the perimeter of the Pacific, and have had for some years.

I have chosen tonight to primarily direct my remarks to the Pacific Basin. I do not mean, by this self-imposed limitation, to suggest that Europe and Africa and the Middle East and the sordid invasion of Czechoslovakia, the effective collapse of NATO and our future relationship with Europe are necessarily less important, but I do feel that the future of the United States—indeed of the whole world—is dependent upon developments in the vast, mysterious area of the Pacific.

Before we can develop a foreign policy for the United States, a basic political and psychological question must be answered: Do we in this country wish to relinquish the mantle of world leadership which became ours at the conclusion of World War II?

Many Americans, and I suspect some in this audience, have a nostalgic yearning for the world of the '20s and '30s when the world was a giant globe with oceans conveniently located to separate our continents from one another; with mountains and rivers located so as to separate one nation from another; and when what was done in Australia was not immediately known in Flagstaff and when the sun never set on the British Empire and we were Fortress America. However, technological and industrial strides have left that era behind.

If we are to continue world leadership, I must remind you, we have responsibilities; responsibilities entail courage; courage entails strength; and strength, whether we like it or not, is what the world respects. I think I am standing on firm ground if I say that all of us would like to be loved, but I think I am on equally firm ground if I say we would rather be respected; not for warlike characteristics, but for a desire for peace; not for a willingness to forego our honorable treaties with other countries, but for a desire to keep our promises. Respect can't be earned by a reversion to isolationism—an isolationism which at best would provide an illusory feeling of safety. If we refuse the responsibilities of leadership, so necessary in these critical times, a void will be created, a void that will be filled and, in all probability, by a power not friendly to us or the free world. These then, are some of the considerations that we mush keep in mind as we consider our future course in the world and our continued battle with Communism. And let me make it clear at this point that when I speak of Communism I do not speak of a monolithic organization. I use the term Communism to describe the lump-sum total of dictatorships, monarchies, the neo-Communism of Russia and Cuba, the classic Communism of the mainland of China, all of which are, in my opinion, dedicated to the subjugation of freedom.

As to the Pacific itself, its importance to our total policy has never, in my opinion, been fully understood or appreciated by a good many Americans, including some of those in national leadership. Just over a hundred years ago a Secretary of State named Seward recognized that a great deal, if not all, of the future of our country rested in the Pacific and the countries comprising the perimeter of that body of water. He recognized also that without land possessions offshore from the United States, any wars developing in the Pacific would probably find their way to the mainland of the United States through California, Oregon and Washington. He brought about the purchase of Alaska and the subsequent acquisitions of the Midway Islands and Hawaii. The concept of protection of the mainland of the United States was proven true in World War II.

Around the perimeter of the Pacific we find countries achieving rapid industrial and technological advances such as South Korea, Japan, Taiwan and the Republic of China, Hong Kong, the Malaysian countries, Australia, New Zealand and, coming back to our own side of the Pacific, including South America, Central America and Mexico. Remember, Mexico, Central and South America will by the year two thousand have a population of half a billion people; people who have close economic, political and cultural ties to the United States; people with whom we are "simpatico."

Also, as my liberal friends love to point out, you can't ignore the seven hundred million people living in Communist China. This reminder is even more pointed now when you're dealing with a Red China with missiles, nuclear weapons, and the proven technique of wars of national liberation. My answer to these liberal friends is, you're dead right. We, in this country, can never be secure until all of China is returned to the community of peaceful nations.

No discussion of the Pacific can start anywhere other than in Southeast Asia. This, the current critical area, including Vietnam, has a most important role in this Pacific concept, not only in an economic sense, but in a strategic sense.

After explaining the strategic importance of this country, he continued.

Perhaps a brief review of our history in Vietnam will help illuminate the problems involved and the possible solutions. The American presence in modern-day Vietnam began in 1954 with the assignment, by President Eisenhower, of military advisers to assist the South Vietnamese. The real beginning of what we face today, however, was President Kennedy's order, through Secretary of Defense McNamara, in 1961, that our advisers "shoot back." That was the beginning of war in South Vietnam; war whether declared or undeclared.

This incredible decision to deploy some sixteen thousand advisers into South Vietnam and order them to shoot back meant placing ourselves as active participants in an Asiatic land war with a pitifully tiny force. To make this decision even more incredible, we took this action after having, through the Geneva conferences of 1961 and 1962, handed Laos to the Communists and opened up the key strategic entry points into South Vietnam. The consequences of these decisions have been established.

Besides the "incredible decision," there was another culprit—perhaps the key culprit in the whole Vietnamese situation. This was the doctrine, enunciated by the United States in 1961–62, of "graduated deterrence." This was the reaction of the new administration to the Dulles doctrine of massive retaliation. The general idea of graduated deterrence was that if small forces were deployed quickly to a trouble-spot, little brushfire wars, as they were called, would be quickly stamped out and the campaign won in the first round. It was kind of a contemporary version of gunboat diplomacy, greatly sophisticated by the use of new terms and jargon by personnel within the new administration.

But in Vietnam we were not dealing with some petty, sporadic, ill-organized insurrection with an unsophisticated doctrine. Instead, we were dealing with one of the most sophisticated doctrines of war as yet known to the human species, and with a nation that had the most skilled guerrilla army in the world. To assume that graduated deterrence could handle this situation was like fighting fire with gasoline, or entering a boxing match with Cassius Clay and planning to beat him with a tricky blow the first second after the opening bell and taking no account that the fight might go for another fourteen rounds.

Graduated deterrence or, if you prefer, graduated escalation, however, held something worse than even this for the United States: By escalating gradually, the escalator, i.e., the USA, actually conditioned its adversary and trained him as to our operational methods. It allowed the adversary to call the shots and decide when he would escalate. The cost of graduated deterrence, which failed to work, became truly enormous, not only the cost in money but also in lives and morale. A factor relative to graduated deterrence, which nobody foresaw, was the tremendous psychological impact that this has had on the people at home.

Clausewitz has noted that each war has logic of its own. One can fight for limited objectives, but even these demand deployment over time and space of forces sufficient to do the job. This deployment cannot be spread out—graduated, as it were over lengthy periods—without the gravest possible risks. Indeed, the opposite is the case: The deployment must be sudden, swift, and ample. Of all culprits resulting in the present dilemma in Vietnam, I would rank the doctrine of graduated deterrence as the chief contributor.

The Communists, true to their theory of "Wars of National Liberation," and in response to our graduated deterrence, stepped up their guerrilla activities to more than counter match that provided by the Americans and South Vietnamese. We all know the spiraling series of tragedies since then. It can hardly be expected that Communist leaders in Southeast Asia and others in similar areas around the world can do other than continue to embrace this doctrine of success. How far, though, and how real the extended doctrine of "Wars of National Liberation" can be exploited on a global scale is debatable. We should, however, take note of four things: (1) The original doctrine of the Liberation wars has been tremendously successful in Asia. (2) The aspirations of contemporary Chinese Communist theorists tend now no translate the doctrine into global terms. (3) A new left in the United States and Europe is oriented toward the Chinese Communist doctrine generally. And (4) power is always relative; incidental power can become dominant if it is not effectively opposed. We must agree, however, that the doctrine has been successful in Asia and it has been successful because of our doctrine of "graduated deterrence," whose ineffectiveness has been so graphically demonstrated in Vietnam.

If we were to unilaterally withdraw from South Vietnam without having achieved our objectives or without having been successful at the negotiating table, we could certainly expect that the hopes and aspirations of the Far East Communists would be to translate the doctrine into global terms. In addition, let's not be fooled into thinking that unilateral withdrawal would instantly restore internal peace to the United States. If the United States should withdraw from Vietnam or fail to take positive action, its critics would not go away, nor would criticism subside.

On the contrary, critics and criticism would, in all probability, become more vehement. Critics both at home and abroad could then rightly say, "We told you so. We have told you for half a decade that the government of the United States is not only stupid, but it is run by a bunch of villains. Look at what happened in Vietnam."

Upon our unilateral withdrawal, the oft discussed Domino Theory would become a reality. While the Domino Theory could perhaps be doubted before U.S. intervention, it cannot be doubted after an intervention that has failed. Thus, instead of a friendly, prosperous and valuable Pacific Basin we would be faced instead with an area taken over either gradually or quickly by forces in opposition to peace in the world and to freedom in any place.

To further compound this problem we cannot forget the forty-odd mutual Security Agreements to which we are presently bound. These treaties obligate us to find a solution to problems of the Vietnam type. What, then, is the way out? What is our course of action?

I would offer two proposals: A broad policy for the future and a necessarily responsive proposal for the present.

The broad future foreign policy for the United States must rest on the premise that power being relative, a greater power must always be used by the United States. This is true whether in the field of economics, politics or the final instrument of national policy, war itself. This policy must be oriented toward the proper use of our strengths, rather than a makeshift reaction to a last minute emergency. This doctrine will be understood by our enemies regardless of who or where they may be.

I cannot offer you any quick solutions to our Vietnam dilemma. After seven years of total blundering, miracles come hard, and we and our allies must now pay the price for the blundering of the past. What then are our possible solutions?

(1) Unilateral withdrawal—and I do not believe any honest American could seriously embrace that course.

(2) A negotiated settlement. All of us hope and pray that the seemingly endless "draggings" and "haltings" in Paris will result in a satisfactory end to this national torment. If not, however, we must be prepared to pursue our third option, which is an application of our doctrine of relative power. This would require, at least, the following steps: (A) We must fully exploit our air and sea power to strike those targets in the north, which will most rapidly impair the enemy's will and capacity to fight: such targets as the dock facilities at Haiphong and, if necessary, the dikes of the Red River. Let me state at this point that I do not here suggest, imply, hint or advocate the use of nuclear weapons in Vietnam. (B) We should immediately review tasks and equipments required by American ground forces with the object of giving greater effectiveness and especially tactical, organizational and strategic freedom to the ground commander to break the enemy's capacity to fight in the south. (C) The shockingly delayed rearming and retraining program for the South Vietnamese Army should be stepped up as an emergency measure.

And lastly, (D) that much misunderstood Pacification Program must be dramatically changed. Here we cannot expect quick results. Again, we have to pay for the tragedy of theorists being involved in the reality of war. Community development programs satisfactory in Wisconsin do not meet the needs of a Vietnam under attack. In this new Pacification Program the primary aim must be to provide security to populated areas including the peasant in his village and on his farm. An even more difficult dimension is to provide better services to the population and better administrative and government programs for Vietnamese war veterans; to revive the village councils; to train police and administrators; to endeavor to provide better markets for farm products; but all of these vital measures can only pertain where security exists. We simply can't expect the Vietnamese to worry about the subtleties of democracy until they are convinced that they will survive the night.

We must never again respond with the tragic Vietnam tactic. We must assess our interests and those of our allies and, as a situation demands, be prepared to use the power that is necessary—economic, political, psychological and military.

So much for the use of power in a hostile environment, but what of this use of American power in an environment of peace in the Pacific—especially relative to our friends and allies? What after Vietnam?

For several decades now we have tried foreign aid as an instrument of U.S. policy. Along with the new approach suggested earlier to the use of our power relative to hostile nations, we must as a matter of urgency, totally realign our economic aid relative to our friends. These are measures I suggest.

Only in the rarest of cases should we ever give money. The consequences of giving money to nations with unsophisticated economies can be disastrous because:

(1) Giving money "without strings" often leads to misuse and graft, which, in turn, requires Americans to apply all kinds of controls. The final result, as one Vietnamese diplomat remarked is, "one dollar of aid wrapped up in one pound of red tape." As a Laotian leader has observed about foreign aid, "we have Americans breathing down our necks as no French colonial administration ever did." This situation produces neither the goods nor the friends.

(2) Even this wealthy nation simply cannot give away enough resources to materially effect change in an Asian economy without killing the goose that lays the golden egg. This is especially true relative to recipients who, often through no fault of their own, simply do not have the techniques to make their operations economically viable. There is, I believe, a better way of providing aid—aid which is not only economically sound, but which will not alienate friends. This is the old but totally effective practice of making loans in accordance with bankers' criteria.

By all means let these loans be long term and low interest. Regional banks where local skills and knowledge can be directed to regional problems might be a good vehicle for dissemination of funds. Loans in accordance with bankers' criteria have many assets.

In the long term, we can lend much more money than we can give simply because, like a bank, funds will grow—not disappear. (Incidentally the record of Asian countries in terms of loan repayments has been very good.) Also, by using bankers' criteria, money is spent on the projects that are economically viable—those which can produce equivalent monetary returns.

Perhaps most important of all, loans give greater independence and sense of responsibility to the recipients than do gifts. Let the recipient borrow from the United States of America and hire a Japanese firm or if he hires an American firm, let the recipient fire that firm if it does not do its job. This ought to be the American way. It will, as well, not only help build viable economies but also strong independent allies.

I wonder what would have been the outcome if in the nineteenth century, the British, instead of lending us money had, overcome by guilt relative to their colonial past in America, financed our railroad construction by gifts and then sent over their inspectors and bureaucrats to probe, pay and dominate American enterprise.

I believe the time has come for a new U.S. policy in that area of vital concern, the Pacific and Asia. And let's not continue to neglect Central and South America and Mexico in that policy. Despite the obvious desirability of close ties with the countries to our south, our aid program in Latin America has, in the past, been strictly cut-rate. Turkey, India, Iran, Israel, Jordan, Pakistan, Cambodia, Indonesia, Laos and Thailand have each received more aid than any Latin American nation. We have given more aid to Afghanistan than to Brazil, more to Liberia than to Chile, more to Iraq than to Mexico, and more to Nepal than to Panama.

We can no longer afford any such short-sighted policies. The new U.S. policy must make more effective use of economic aid and stop the stupid paradox of alienating our friends with conditional gifts. We must strive to improve our political influence. This will be a slow and difficult process, but it can be done. We can greatly develop the general area of psychological impact. Must we ever be on the one hand

Goldwater had an elaborate ham radio station, which patched over 200,000 phone calls from servicemen in Vietnam to their families in the United States.

the best educated nation in the world with incredible skills in communications and yet fail to sell ourselves and fail to expose our enemies?

To summarize, a meaningful foreign policy for the United States must encompass three new directions: (1) We must renounce forever the tragic doctrine of graduated deterrence and replace it with a policy of the proper use of our strength. (2) Foreign aid must be restricted to do away with the conditional gift and replace it with regional banks making loans based on bankers' criteria. (3) We must always, in the future, remember the vital nature of the perimeter of the Pacific. Only then will we be able to preserve peace, not only in the Pacific and Asia, but peace throughout the world—a priceless gift that only our great country can bestow.

CHAPTER 16

DOMESTIC ISSUES

W*e have selected issues that continue to resonate in American political debate. They are arranged by the date they first arose for Senator Goldwater. (And because some were recurring, we continue with the subject once we open it.)*

PRESIDENTIAL WAR POWERS

Statement on Senate Floor (April 6, 1972)

During the congressional debate on the War Powers Resolution (whereby the Congress placed strictures on the president's powers to commit troops without congressional approval), Goldwater expressed his views—and those of other conservatives—that such action by Congress was unconstitutional. The core of his argument is found in the following excerpt.

I might start by recalling that the Constitutional Convention rejected a clause giving Congress the power "to make war" and substituted for it only the power "to declare war." From brief records of the debate, it is quite clear that the framers at least had a purpose of "leaving to the Executive the power to repel sudden attacks." How much else the Founding Fathers meant to leave with the president is not specified in this debate, but it is significant that they had a difference in mind between the two terms and left the making of war with the president.

Next, I believe we should review the many passages of the Federalist Papers focusing on the safety of the people. That the ultimate decision over when to act for the safety of the nation was left with the president, rather than Congress, is apparent from the writing by Madison and Hamilton in the Federalist No. 19. Here they state that the Constitutional Convention expressly rejected as being too weak the then-current political model of the Germanic Empire in which the Diet, or legislative body, was vested with the sole power to commence war. In any emergency, they wrote, "military preparation must be preceded by so many tedious discussions . . . that before the Diet can settle the arrangements the enemy are in the field."

While the focus of these writings was on the purpose of protecting the national safety, it is also important to consider Madison's instruction in the Federalist No. 37 that the framers intentionally had removed the direction of the military forces from Congress, where it had been deposited under the Articles of Confederation, because it is "particularly dangerous to give the keys of the Treasury and the command of the army into the same hands." Thus, we should observe that the Founding Fathers not only were concerned about depositing too much power with the executive office but also were watchful that they did not enable congressional usurpation to occur.

Moreover, we must remember the setting of the times in which the framers ratified the Constitution. Professor David Watson, who wrote a two-volume textbook on the Constitution, found that of all the explanations of why the Constitution should make its president commander in chief:

> none seems more reasonable than the fact that during the Revolution Washington experienced great trouble and embarrassment resulting from the failure of Congress to support him with firmness and dispatch. There was a want of directness in the management of affairs during that period which was attributable to the absence of centralized authority to command. The members of the Convention knew this and probably thought they could prevent its recurrence by making the president commander-in-chief of the army and navy.

The power of the chief executive as commander in chief has long been interpreted by constitutional authorities as being free of the policy directives of Congress. In 1862 William Whiting wrote a book on war powers in which he declared that "for the military movements and measures essential to overcome the enemy—for the general conduct of the war—the president is responsible to and controlled by no other department of government." Whiting added that the Constitution "does not prescribe any territorial limits within the United States, to which his military operations shall be restricted."

Numerous constitutional writers have shared the same conclusion. Voluminous citations on this subject can be found in two law review articles that I have inserted in the *Congressional Record*, one on February 9 and the other on February 15 of this year. The first is a short quote by Professor Willoughby, who wrote a three-volume work on constitutional law. He observes that the president's power to send troops outside the country "as a means of preserving or advancing the foreign interests or relations of the United States" is a "discretionary right constitutionally vested in him, and, therefore, not subject to congressional Control." The other is a reference to the statement by William Howard Taft, who wrote in the *Yale Law Journal* that "it is clear that Congress may not usurp the functions of the Executive . . . by forbidding or directing the movements of the army and navy."

Added to these writings is a remarkable chain of precedents that presidents have forged over the years. There have been at least 197 hostilities in America's history and only 5 of them have been declared. Almost 50 percent of these military actions lasted more than a month and well over one-half took place outside the Western Hemisphere. Though these undertakings have been questioned as precedents for full-scale modern warfare overseas, they have in fact always involved whatever amount of force presidents have deemed necessary to accomplish their national defense objectives. The military activities of the past twenty-five years cannot be omitted from this list simply because it would suit the purposes of those who challenge presidential power. When these recent incidents, such as the Korean War and the Cuban naval quarantine, are fitted in with the military actions that preceded them, we can notice the development of a consistent line of precedents in which presidents have always adapted the degree of their military actions to accord with the military technology and capabilities of the times.

Another point about these 197 presidentially authorized hostilities that we should notice is the fact that Congress has never once passed a law blocking or ordering a halt to one of them. The question has come up many times, and Congress has taken many votes on the issue since the birth of the nation. The fact that Congress has never before prohibited any presidential hostility should be given heavy weight in reading the construction that history itself has put on the constitutional allotment of the war powers. For anyone to say that this long continued arrangement may now be overturned by a sudden reversal of interpretation demands that he should bear the burden of proving his case by far more extensive evidence than has been offered to date.

Statement on Senate Floor (September 28, 1983)

A decade after first expressing his opposition to the War Powers Resolution (passed in reaction to Vietnam over Nixon's veto), Goldwater provided specific examples of the problems with Congress trying to control the commander in chief. In 1983, when American troops were being killed in Lebanon and Congress sought to employ the War Powers Resolution against President Ronald Reagan, Goldwater opposed the action—notwithstanding his early opposition to President Reagan's decision to send troops to Lebanon. Thus, while he disagreed with the policy, he did not think Congress should try to substitute its judgment. So when the debate commenced, Goldwater returned to the subject of the ill-advised War Powers Resolution.

I would like to discuss the general subject of the war powers and the folly of congressional efforts to tie the president's hands in making military decisions. Look at what happened in 1975 when President Ford asked Congress to join with him in the decision to evacuate Americans from Saigon. As you will recall, Congress never granted his request. Caught between the choice of strict adherence to the 1973 statutory prohibition on U.S. activities in, over, or off the shores of Indochina and his duty to uphold the lives and interest of his countrymen and women, President Ford ignored the legislative restriction and took into his own hands the protection of Americans.

Weeks later, while Congress was still tied up with its debate on the matter, President Ford announced that the Indochina evacuation was completed. Then, he pleaded for funds to pay for purely humanitarian assistance and transportation of refugees, but Congress rejected this request the very next day.

This episode reveals all too clearly the inability of Congress to act decisively in time of need. Last Tuesday I mentioned an earlier moment in history when Congress also neglected its duties. It was a time when only the strong actions of President Franklin Roosevelt, taken independently of Congress, enabled this nation to aid Great Britain and thereby defend our own security before Pearl Harbor.

The point is that the president had the vision to see that democracies avoid disasters only by confronting the obvious threats to their survival. Yet if the war powers resolution had been in effect in the early 1940's President Roosevelt could not have landed and kept troops in Greenland; he could not have sent and reinforced several thousands of marines on Iceland; he could not have escorted British shipping in the Atlantic; and he could not have done the many other things, several of them held secret at the time even from the State Department, which prevented a total collapse of resistance to Hitler. The war powers resolution would have brought about a complete disaster in the 1940's, and it may well bring about a catastrophe of similar proportions in the future if it is not repealed.

The fact is that the United States, as the strongest free nation in the world has a stake in preventing totalitarian conquest. The president has a duty to resist challenges in the early stages and cannot wait until the challenge is so clear that the cost of resistance is prohibitive. The danger in the war powers resolution and any other legislative effort like it, which is intended to restrict the president's defense powers, is that it takes away all flexibility to deal with unforeseen events. The failure of Congress to approve even humanitarian legislation to support the evacuation of American citizens from Saigon offers convincing proof that Congress cannot be counted on to deal quickly with future problems as the need arises. Unlike the president, an assembly of 535 Secretaries of State does not rush to a decision.

Anyone who reviews history will know that presidents have always exercised independent defense powers, whether or not their statutory authority was clear, and occasionally in the face of direct congressional restrictions. In fact, presidents have used force or the imminent threat of force on more than two hundred occasions without any *congressional* declarations of war. George Washington settled this issue, when, as our first president, he ordered his secretary of state, Thomas Jefferson, to threaten Spain with military force if she would not open the Mississippi River to navigation by American citizens. When he became president, Thomas Jefferson sent a squadron of armed ships into the Mediterranean without any congressional authority, with orders to sink, burn and destroy vessels that may threaten American commerce. Only half a year after he issued military orders and four months after a naval blockade and battle had occurred did Jefferson inform Congress. Jefferson gave an indication of the principle that guided his decision making, when he wrote on September 20, 1810, that: "A strict observance of the written laws is doubtless one of the high duties of a good citizen, but it is not the highest. The laws of necessity, of self-preservation, of saving our country when in danger, are of higher obligation." Jefferson's concise statement summarizes why the Framers vested the president with independent powers to act for the safety of the nation. The majority of Framers had served in the army of militia during the War of Independence and they were intimately familiar with the restrictions which the Continental Congress had imposed on General Washington's activities, restrictions they knew had nearly lost the American Revolution. It was in order to correct this known weakness of the Articles of Confederation that the Framers made the president the "commander in chief" under the new Constitution. . . .

Note: Goldwater was unsuccessful in getting Congress to repeal the War Powers Resolution. Even in retirement, he offered to raise money for a lawsuit to take it to court, but that did not happen either.

ABORTION

On January 22, 1973, the U.S. Supreme Court issued its ruling in Roe v. Wade, holding that state and federal laws prohibiting women from having an abortion violated a constitutional right to privacy under the due process clause of the Fourteenth Amendment. The ruling, one of the most controversial in the Court's history, made abortion a hot political issue. Like all members of Congress, Goldwater received a steady stream of mail on the subject, and over time he prepared a series of sample letters for his staff to respond to the avalanche of mail he received. These letters show he took an increasingly nuanced stance on the issue, although after leaving the Senate he became decidedly pro-choice, which appears to have been his feeling all along. Unlike many issues, on this subject he was not as blunt as he was on others. We have gathered the core points in the evolving responses.

Letter (February 27, 1973)

This letter contained Goldwater's initial response to the Supreme Court's ruling on Roe v. Wade.

Each State has the right to adopt laws giving a woman a right to an abortion and the Supreme Court decision, while I don't agree with the length to which it went, nevertheless made some specific boundaries in such a power.

I know you want my opinion in this and while you may disagree with me, I think that abortion should be legalized because whether it is legal or not, women are going to have it done. If it is legalized and done with a doctor's consent, the woman will not run the risk to her own life that she does now of having to sneak off to Mexico or England, or have it done in some clandestine way.

Letter (March 19, 1973)

In this letter, Goldwater slightly modified his wording when responding to those who opposed the Supreme Court's ruling on Roe v. Wade—dropping his politically inflammatory suggestion that abortion be legalized.

The Supreme Court has now ruled that each state has the right to adopt laws giving a woman a right to an abortion and its decision, while I don't agree with the length to which it went, nevertheless made some specific boundaries in such a power.

This leaves the issue squarely up to each state legislature to define and, as it is currently before the Arizona legislature, I recommend you contact your local representative about this.

Letter (October 4, 1974)

When a movement for a Constitutional amendment overturning Roe v. Wade developed, Goldwater said he was willing to study it. Efforts to make abortion more difficult did not trouble him, however, and when his office was barraged by supporters of amendments to laws that barred the use of federal money to pay for an abortion, he embraced them.

It is my opinion this law does not interfere with any Constitutional right of choice, which the mother holds, but goes to the question of how federal funds shall or shall not be used. As a Constitutional matter, Congress is not compelled to appropriate funds for specific [federal] projects involving abortion. Congress does not prohibit women from obtaining abortions; nor take away any other benefits should they obtain abortions.

The great majority of Arizonans who have voiced their opinions to me on this subject have registered their strong objection to having their tax monies used for abortion and I am supporting this view.

Letter (July 8, 1976)

Goldwater rejected a Constitutional amendment overturning Roe v. Wade.

Thank you very much for the petition supporting the Supreme Court decision on abortion. You may be interested to know that when a proposed Constitutional amendment putting a total ban on abortion was brought before the Senate recently, I voted to table the measure, which had the effect of returning it to Committee. While I think abortion involves a basic moral consideration about human life, I don't think its complete prohibition should be the subject of a Constitutional amendment.

Letter (February 8, 1978)

This letter summarized his position until he left the Senate in 1987.

My position is that I personally do not think that the Congress of the United States or the federal government has any business deciding the wrongness or rightness of a woman having an abortion. While I think abortion involves some rather basic moral considerations, I don't think its complete prohibition should be the subject of a Constitutional amendment. On the other hand, I don't think the government should support it with federal funds either.

AMERICA'S ENERGY POLICY AND VENEZUELA

Statement on Senate Floor (March 22, 1973)

With every passing day, the specter of an energy crisis in this country looms larger and larger. The privately owned sector of this country's energy industry states flatly that there is a problem, that it is continuing to worsen and that the nation will soon be on a collision course with a major energy shortage. Despite claims by some environmentalists that the industry sources are over-emphasizing the problem there is now general agreement that the domestic supplies of natural gas will begin running out in ten years, oil in thirty years, and uranium-235, the basic fuel for nuclear power, in thirty years. When this happens, the United States will become totally dependent upon foreign sources for these fuels. We would be at the mercy of foreign powers who would be in a position to jeopardize our way of life, our industries, and our national security.

This being the case, I suggest that it is long past the time when this country should begin improving its relations with nations of the Western Hemisphere. Nations like Canada and Venezuela, both producers of oil, will become vitally important to the United States should anything happen to our sources of supply in the Middle East. And I'm sure everyone in the Congress understands how explosive and tenuous relations always are in that section of the world. The handwriting is already on the wall as far as I can determine. Only recently, Canada moved to control its petroleum exports and in Venezuela there is now an open debate over whether that country should sell its oil today or wait until a shortage develops and a higher price can be obtained.

It is well for us to remember that Venezuela is presently the world's fourth largest oil exporting nation after Saudi Arabia, Iran and Kuwait. Currently that nation ships about half of its 3 million barrels per day exports to the American east coast. But what becomes important about Venezuela, in light of the developing world energy crisis, is the enormous deposits of heavy oil in the Orinoco belt, which have been bypassed until now for economic reasons. The 375-mile-long Orinoco belt holds to 300 billion barrels of what is largely heavy oil.

If ways can be found to develop this reserve it could be the answer to the entire energy problem in the Western Hemisphere. And if we are to benefit adequately from such a development we'll have to look to our good-neighbor attitude in that part of the world. And we cannot get to this too quickly. Latin America is still smarting from the high promise and lousy performance of what the Kennedy Administration labeled the Alliance for Progress. And, of course, since that time we have been paying so much attention to Indochina that many hemispheric problems went largely unattended.

ILLEGAL ALIENS AND IMMIGRATION REFORM

Goldwater's statement relating to the problems of illegal aliens and immigration policy show how little has changed in all the decades that have since followed.

Statement (Undated, 1978)

America is by the far the wealthiest and freest nation in the world. It is like a magnet that draws people from other, perhaps less-fortunate countries, and many of these countries are in close proximity to the United States. With the incentive of a better life, people will brave laws and obstacles to come here. Thus, this is a complex problem with no easy solution.

There have been many proposals as to how to address this dilemma. Two of the ones that have been floating around for a while are not to my liking. The Carter administration has proposed granting amnesty to illegal aliens in this country who have established "equity." This might take the form of working, length of residence and the like. The Congress has viewed this plan with little enthusiasm and so have I. What amnesty would do in effect is reward people who knowingly break our laws. Beyond that, it would be inequitable and unfair to those who have applied for legal immigration and may often wait years for approval. Another proposal penalizes an employer who knowingly hires illegal aliens. These employer sanctions are inevitably discriminatory and could raise possible violations of civil rights of potential employees. It is the government, not the employer, who should bear the main responsibility of determining who is here legally and who is not.

My recommendations: Expansion of the temporary worker program. I am the cosponsor of legislation that would establish a temporary worker program under which Mexican nationals could enter the United States. This type of program could be extended to other primary sending countries of illegal aliens. It addresses labor market needs and needs for seasonal agricultural workers in a regulated fashion. American workers would be protected under my bill. Visas would be good for 180 days, not necessarily consecutive. This "Bracero"-type program would control the number of workers coming in, provide monitoring and channel the flow of illegal aliens through a legal mechanism.

It should be noted that illegal aliens come from a variety of sources. Often people come here on a legal non-immigrant visa, such as for a student or visitor, and never return home. There is little follow up on the holder of a legal non-immigrant visa. One suggestion to help assure the individual's return upon the expiration of the visa is to require a non-refundable return airline ticket to the national's homeland. In addition, better inspection, detection, surveillance and manpower capabilities for our Immigration and Nationalization Service, Border Patrol and Customs Service. Our personnel do an admirable job under often trying circumstances, but they need more funds, improved equipment and more manpower. We need a clearer U.S. immigration policy that is actually enforced. We need increased cooperation with the countries that are sending illegal aliens. Help providing economic incentives to encourage residents to remain in their native lands. I am not talking about foreign aid, which is something that I've never voted for, but, rather, some kind of joint American private industry/host country ventures (manufacturing, construction, textiles, etc.) that would provide employment within the host country.

America's capacity to absorb more and more people is not limitless. I understand and am sympathetic to the reasons why people wish to come to the United States. But the hard reality is that America cannot be a lifeboat to all who wish to come aboard.

SENATE PROCEDURES

From time to time, as Goldwater became one of the senior members of the Senate, he chastened his colleagues about the way they were running the place, saying to them on the Senate floor what he was writing in his journal. The following two examples are typical.

Statement on the Senate Floor (May 21, 1982)

Although I have known, or at least thought I knew, that the *Congressional Record* could be checked by the Senators, or their assistants, for the purpose of correcting grammatical errors, punctuation and so forth, I never dreamed of the extreme to which this has gone and the way the *Record* is being abused. I learned, to my utter surprise and my complete disgust, that Senators are not only allowed to correct grammatical errors, and correct other such mistakes made during debate, but I was told that entire pages and, indeed, entire speeches were crossed out of the *Record* before the *Record* was completed and handed out the next morning.

Now this is going too far. I was so shocked by this that I began to realize that the only way we are going to keep a permanent, accurate, dependable record of every word that is said on the floor of the Senate is if we allow television to record the actions of the Senate. Never before have I backed or supported a move to televise the Senate, but, I feel that in view of the abuses of the *Congressional Record*, and in the interests of keeping the American people accurately informed as to what we said and what we debated and decided, I must remove myself from the list of opponents to television. I will support the television move when it comes back to the floor.

Statement on the Senate Floor (June 12, 1984)

The following exchange took place on the Senate floor concerning whether to adjourn at 9:00 PM or to continue to vote on proposed amendments to the military authorization bill, which was then pending. Although Senator Goldwater, chairman of the Senate Armed Services Committee, was clearly "pissed" and the Senate rules precluded him from saying so, he managed to convey his message.

> Sen. Goldwater: Mr. President, [referring to the presiding officer of the Senate in the chair], if this Senator may make an observation, we are not going to finish this by July 4. And when you talk about staying late, I can remember when we stayed all night. I had three amendments ready to offer.
>
> Sen. Howard H. Baker, Jr. [Republican of Tennessee, and the majority leader]: If the Senator will yield. . . .
>
> Sen. Goldwater: I have not finished. I will finish in just a short order because I am a little bit you know what.
>
> Sen. Baker: I am ready and waiting for the Senator to finish.
>
> Sen. Goldwater: We sit around here day after day and never do a dog-gone thing. If we want to get this bill passed, we ought to get down to work. It is only 9:00 PM. Every one of us can miss whatever we had planned for tonight. I do not know why people think we have to quit so early. I have been here since 7 o'clock this morning. This place is getting to be like a cookie factory.
>
> Sen. Baker: Mr. President, I do not know whose cookie factory the Senator is talking about.
>
> Sen. Goldwater: Yours.

CAMPAIGN FINANCE REFORM

Statement on Senate Floor (March 22, 1983)

Goldwater's concerns about the rising costs of campaigns for all elected office-holders, delivered twenty-five years ago, could have been given yesterday. His warnings have been coming too true, and his recommendations remain valid. Throughout his Senate career he addressed this problem, for he was intimately familiar with it as one of the Senate's best fundraisers. But he believed the increasing, and unregulated, costs were the "road to anarchy," and if we were walking on that road in 1983, we are running down it today toward the inevitable disaster ahead.

The time has come when the Congress and the American people must face up to a fundamental defect in our political structure. Our election campaigns are too expensive and too long. It is a shocking, but unavoidable fact, that the cost of getting elected in the United States to all offices—state, local and federal—now exceeds one billion dollars in a presidential campaign year.* The burden of raising funds to finance a political campaign has become so great that many office holders neglect their public duties in order to pay off past debts or run for future elections. Candidates for public office must spend so much time appealing to major donors that they ignore their regular responsibilities or lose touch with the ordinary citizen.

This massive spending means that the general person loses interest in voting because whoever gets elected is perceived as being bought and paid for by one or another special interest group. What does it matter who you vote for if you believe the winner has already committed his position in advance to whichever group gave the most money? The average voter, who did not make a large contribution or gave nothing at all, feels his or her vote means nothing in deciding public policy.

The situation has become so bad that I believe the stability of our political process is at stake. Citizens are discouraged from voting. The effectiveness of government operations is impaired. And the reputation of elected officials for the honest performance of their duties is put at question by the massive and growing cost of getting elected. We must correct the course of events and do it now.

My recommendations are that we put a firm limit on total spending in all Federal campaigns, shorten the length of the campaign period, and require timely and more complete disclosure of campaign gifts. . . . I would ask my colleagues to consider this question: What is the most fundamental purpose of the Constitution? Is it the expansion of commerce? Is it the defense of the nation against foreign dangers? Is it the security of each person's life and property? Each of these are important goals that the Framers had in mind; but underlying all the

---

* *The Associated Press reported than for 2004 those expenses were $4 billion. See http://www.msnbc.msn.com/id/6388580/. Goldwater is relying on 1980 figures, which adjusted for inflation would be about $2.5 billion. Thus, the escalation in costs are far exceeding inflation. When viewing the problems he raises, because of this escalation, the problems must be doubled.*

other purposes is the idea that the Framers believed they were setting up a system of self-rule by the people. The Constitution provides a complex system of institutions by which self-government is made possible. Liberty, and human rights, and equal opportunities for all citizens are made possible by the successful functioning of self-government. It is self-rule that makes the other freedoms and privileges of our people work in practice.

The plain meaning of self-rule is that the people shall assert their sovereignty and control over government at regular, frequent elections at which government by consent will be constantly replenished. As Samuel Adams wrote to his cousin, John, about the new Constitution in 1790, "the *whole* sovereignty . . . (is) essentially in the people." He added: "*We the People* is the style of the Federal Constitution: They adopted it; and conformably to it, they delegate the exercise of the powers of government to particular persons, who, after short intervals, resign their powers to the people, and they will re-elect them, or appoint others, as they think fit." [emphasis in original]

But to be successful, representative government assumes that elections will be controlled by the citizenry at large, not by an elitist group of big givers. Of equal importance, citizens must believe their vote counts. And elected officials must owe their allegiance to the people, not to narrow factions who speak only for the selfish fringes of the whole community. When the power of determining the winners of elections is lodged in the hands of a few rich persons or groups, who are independent of the people and of their representatives, and who are not accountable for their actions, no way is left to control them. This is the road to anarchy.

Instead of achieving an intimate relationship between the public and their government, this distorted election process leads to a system in which the force of government will be imposed on the people in the course of their daily lives for the advantage of selfish interests who are removed from the general public. It is important to notice that the Framers wanted elections to be free of the corruption that was then so widespread in England. The Founders of our Constitutional Government were disgusted at the deluge of corruption that overwhelmed eighteenth century British Parliamentary elections. When John Dickinson was a student of law in England, he wrote of his shock, beyond all expectation, at the decay of the election process. Dickinson wrote home that the starting price for the purchase of votes in one borough was two hundred guineas. "Bribery is so common that it is thought there is not a borough in England where it is not practiced," he reported.

The Framers knew that corrupt elections undermine the foundations of liberty. They believed that politics festered in corruption and that this corruption was destroying the prime requisite of constitutional liberty, an independent Parliament free from any influence other than that of the people.

I warn today that if we do not find a means of controlling and limiting the runaway costs of being elected to public office, the faith of the American people in our modern election system will be reduced to the same dismal view held by informed Americans at the birth of our Republic. Our elections will be totally distrusted. Our actions in the Congress will be constantly suspect because the public will believe that each and every member of a legislative body is the creature of special interest groups.

I firstly believe that this nation is facing a crisis of liberty if we do not check election costs. We must prove that the Oval Office is not a prize to be auctioned off to the highest bidder. We cannot allow the belief to persist that elected officials at all levels of government are the paid agents of rich benefactors, rather than being what James Madison intended us to be, agents of the sovereign people.

There are three steps I propose we take to stop the subversion of the political process. First, I propose that we put a ceiling on campaign spending by or for candidates to Federal offices in primary and general elections. Second, we should shorten the length of time of presidential elections. Third, we should have fuller and faster disclosure of who donates to political campaigns.

Goldwater proceeded to spell out a possible formula for placing ceilings on Senate and House races based on the number of voting-age citizens in a state or congressional district. As for presidential races, he would place a flat ceiling.

We should put a spending lid not only on direct campaign expenditures, but on "in-kind" spending or activities, such as telephone banks, volunteer services, and so forth. Also, we should put separate ceilings on overall spending by the candidates and by individuals or groups who spend for the election of a particular candidate, whether the spending is subject to the direction of the candidate or not.

I also believe a reasoned campaign spending limit should be linked to a shortening of the campaign period, at least for presidential candidates. If the time span of election is reduced, the spending during that period will automatically be reduced as well. What period do I recommend? Well, I would like to see us require that the national conventions for choosing presidential candidates begin on Labor Day, the first Monday in September. The election campaign would start two weeks later. The general campaign would last no more than six weeks. The British conduct their Parliamentary campaigns in three weeks, and we should be able to schedule our national elections in no more than twice that time.

Next, the reporting rules should be tightened. Immediate public disclosure of campaign expenditures should be made in the late stages of each election in the form of public press releases. By the time the Federal Election Commission gets around to processing its reports, the election is over. Immediate public statements should be required whenever a candidate loans or gives to his own campaign. Political Action Committees should identify clearly whether or not they are the political arm of another group. Reports should disclose the name and legal address of contributors, using a uniform definition of legal residence so that the same donors cannot give multiple addresses.

Now, I know that some will feel these ideas run afoul of the Constitutional safeguard of free speech. I am well aware of the ruling by the United States Supreme Court in the case of Buckley against Valeo in January of 1976, which held that a congressionally mandated limit on spending in Federal elections is unconstitutional. The Court held that such a campaign lid is an invasion of the opportunity of individuals and organizations to exercise free speech, the communication of arguments and opinions supportive of one political cause or the other. My answer is that we should try again. In my opinion, the argument was not made forcefully enough to convince the Supreme Court that what is at stake is the integrity of the entire political process. The success of our national experiment with self-rule is on the line.

As vital as free speech is, I believe a reasonable and rationally drawn restriction on Federal campaign spending that allows for ample, but not unlimited, spending will be upheld by the courts, when the statute is plainly designed to implement congressional findings that the survival of free elections, the purity of our election process, and the effective performance of government duties are endangered by unlimited expenditures.

One very drastic change has occurred since the Supreme Court made its decision in early 1976. Campaign spending has skyrocketed. Total election spending in the nation has doubled and the end is nowhere in sight. And, in my opinion, at least a third and probably as much as one-half of all the money raised and spent is wasted.

After citing a number of examples, he continued.

It would be a calamity if we just sat back and allowed this spiral of political spending to continue forever. It will feed on itself. It will dominate the election process. It will allow the voting process to be manipulated for private gain, rather than the public good, by political merchants who are enriched with money collected from the special interest groups and wealthy individuals who seek to control their country's political agenda.

If the Supreme Court will not allow us to put a limit on political spending, or even a boundary on the length of the presidential campaign, then I say let us ratify a constitutional amendment to empower Congress to act in this area. I am not proposing that we eliminate all spending for the communication of views and opinions. I am only recommending that we reach a fair balance between the protection of the political process and the ability of candidates or anyone else to communicate opinions.

We should also include whatever provisions are necessary to offset any serious advantage an incumbent may enjoy over his opponent. We have already taken action in Congress to curb the use of the frank [the free congressional mailing privilege] for mass mailings during election periods. If there are other steps that we must take to make the contest fair between incumbents and their opponents, we can incorporate that feature in any spending limit statute.

Now, I know that the weight of political thinking at this moment is running against what I have suggested. Defenders of the present system claim that campaign spending is minor compared with private commercial spending for advertising purposes. Toothpaste, deodorant and soap powder vendors are said to spend more each year to advertise their products than politicians spend to get elected. But this comparison exposes the great flaw in the thinking of those who support open-ended campaign spending. In their minds, there is no difference between a candidate and a detergent. They are both products to be merchandised. This is exactly what is wrong with the trend of American political campaigns. Candidates should not be packaged and sold in the simplistic manner of a consumer product. Candidates must be more than caricatures who front for donors with the most money. Candidates should reach the public on the human level. They should communicate honest principles and values of interest to the entire public and demonstrate their personal qualities of leadership. They should not be the paid hands of any vested interest groups, nor appear to be so.

The most prevalent ideas now circulating in the nation would call for higher and higher spending. It is suggested, for example, that the potential influence of Political Action Committees could be offset by increasing the importance of individual contributors. So, we are told, let us raise the ceiling, double or triple the ceiling, on political donations by individuals. Others propose we remove entirely the ceiling on spending by political parties. It is also suggested that the income tax credit for political donations might be expanded and that contributions be encouraged within the taxpayers' own congressional districts or states by creating a special tax credit for that purpose. These alternatives are worthy of consideration, but only if we adopt the view that it is all right to continue doing business as usual. These changes would merely allow the spiral of spending to go on and on. They would increase the danger to our political system.

Also, it is suggested that both presidential and congressional elections be funded with money obtained from the Federal Government.

Needless to say, I am totally against that approach because it could lead to the loss of all freedom, with the government gaining power to manipulate elections. I know there are many variations to the proposal I have made. I am open and receptive to altering it. The important thing is not the specific law we enact. I don't care whether the spending is set at "X" dollars or "Y" dollars. The critical thing is that we do agree on setting some limit. We must call a halt to runaway campaign spending. We must regain control of the election process for the people. We must assure the people that elections will be honest, that elected officials are not bought, and that each citizen's vote does count. With the bicentennial of our Constitution fast approaching, I can think of no better way of restoring our democratic Republic to the first principles that guided the Founders than to cleanse the political process of the taint of exorbitant spending and control by vested interest groups.

FISCAL COURAGE REGARDING DEFICIT SPENDING

Statement on Senate Floor (January 24, 1985)

About forty years ago, during the first term of Franklin Roosevelt in the midst of the Great Depression, we first started to spend money that we didn't have to try to help the economy. Even at that time, I began to worry and to speak out about the spending of money that the Federal Government did not have. I was greatly concerned because, regardless of how much money Roosevelt spent, we did not come out of the depression. We did not cure the depression until World War II started and that, finally, brought the depression to a close.

Let us not misunderstand, we don't want any more wars, whether it ends a depression or not. However, I am worried today more than I have ever been about our country being in a state of economic trouble that not even a war could produce or cure. When World War II ended, there was every reason to expect that the vast amount of money that we had spent during that war would come to an end. For a short time, it appeared that would happen. But then, we went through the experience of the Cold War, Korea and the experience of Vietnam and, all the while, we continued to be in a war economy.

But, even when peace came, our deficits continued to mount and mount and mount. I will say, without any particular fear of contradiction, that it was not the spending related to Korea and Vietnam that produced the major part of our deficit that we are confronted with today. Our problem has been the spending, during war and peace, on what we call welfare and government support spending.

At the outset of President Reagan's first term and even during his campaign for that first term, he continually called attention to the deficit, the increased interest we had to pay on it, the accompanying inflation and the accompanying high interest rates. Even then, he pledged to do everything in his power to get it down.

Just the other day, President Reagan started his second term of office after having been elected by the highest plurality ever enjoyed by a president. But, what are we looking at? The deficit is higher than it has ever been. The budget is going to be higher.

Yet, a strange thing has been happening during this period of increased deficit. During the last half-year, prime interest rates have

Senator Goldwater with President Reagan.

gone down three times and the indications are growing that they will go down some more. This leads me to believe that a new source or new form of capital is being created in this country. I will not argue for this nor against it nor for the reason or against any reason. But, nevertheless, it is happening. If this trend continues and our economy continues on at an increasing rate of growth, the deficit problems will be relieved greatly. But, and this is a great big but, if it does not do that and we are merely going through a temporary increase in our economy and then the interest rates start to go up again and the deficits persist, then the people of this country are going to have all manner of hell to pay along with all kinds of economic trouble. The possibility of national bankruptcy is a distinct reality if we persist in unabated spending across the board.

As Chairman of the Armed Services Committee, I will not make the flat statement that we can not decrease the money spent there. Already, I have suggested that we close the unneeded military bases in this country and I am going to introduce legislation to accomplish that. Secretary of Defense Weinberger has already done a very commendable job on not reorganizing the defense establishment, but in de-organizing it. I mean by that, that he has been putting men who were in uniform back into the field and then reducing the civilian staff that is no longer needed. There is much more that can be done in this field and the secretary knows this, but he's going to need the help of the Congress to get this accomplished.

The other day, I picked up a book written by John Kennedy before he became president. It was called *Profiles in Courage* and it dealt with those men in the Senate whom he had judged to be the great ones. Their common attribute was one of personal courage. While I did not re-read the book completely, as I skimmed through it the thought hit me that everyone should read that book now. If there ever was a time in the history of our nation when we needed individual and collective courage, starting with the president right on down through every elected official including the citizenry as a whole, it is now. We must take a hard look at the deficit that is going to grow. We will have to look at tax rates that will have to be raised. We must look at an economy that is good now, but might not be so good in the future. And then, we begin to look at the problems and possible solutions.

I mention the need for courage because we are looking at things that are pretty close to people. We are looking at things that influence votes. As a result, the question that keeps coming to my mind is, "Do we have people of enough courage to take a hard look at the problems that face us and to say no to those things that need to be said no to?"

As much as I don't like to say it, we are in a welfare state, whether anyone cares to admit it or not. I have tried to get the last four presidents to talk to the American people about this and to warn them what would have to be done to get us out of this situation, but none of them have faced the issue. A lot of people will say, "what's wrong with the welfare state?" Well, as a matter of history, no country in the world has ever gotten out of one. All of the welfare states that I can remember wound up as a dictatorship and most of them wound up broke.

It could be that this country of ours can find a solution that would enable us to go on with uncontrolled spending in the welfare field and, at the same time, take care of our defense needs. If we can, we should start trying to do it without trying to go along under the pretense that we don't have to do anything but continue on our present path.

Let us face up to this one truth. Let us tell the American people about the actual condition of this country and of the very difficult, if not impossible, task of getting us out of it. Let me remind my colleagues that it is not enough just to say, "let's cut the defense budget." We could eliminate the entire defense budget and still not get out of the trouble we are in. And, I would remind my colleagues also that the first charge to us in the Constitution is to defend our country. But that is irrelevant. What I am worried about is that the fiscal situation we can find ourselves in can lead to the fiscal bankruptcy of our country and the end of our dream of freedom.

Now, what is it going to take to get us out of this? First of all, the president has to go to the American people in very understandable language and simple terms to explain to them that Social Security is in bad shape, that Civil Service Retirement is in trouble, also Railroad Retirement. The retirement funds of all the military personnel stand in jeopardy and there are many, many welfare performances we are funding today that need to be cut down or eliminated completely. Also, there are many government financed programs of no use that are relics of a bygone era. I believe completely in the statement of

Abraham Lincoln that it is the duty of the Federal Government to take care of those people who cannot take care of themselves, but we have gone past that point. What these expenditures are, in total, I cannot tell you. But, what all of this means is that we have to go to people and tell them that the way they live may change.

The wage earner, the wealthy, the middle class, the retired people and particularly the people living on the wages of others have to know that everyone is going to have to make a change in life. It is not going to be easy and I recognize that. It is not easy to tell someone to lower their sights and lower their way of living. But, if we don't, then we had better pray that the American people with their eternal courage will say, "let's do what we have to do and not get this country into more trouble."

All of us could say that we will not allow this country to get into deeper trouble and that we will strive to maintain our individual pride and collective freedom. What it means, ultimately, is that the time for speeches has passed and it is now time for some courageous action.

RETIREMENT YEARS

Whitext{hen} *Goldwater left the Senate he remained active in public affairs while teaching at the University of Arizona, overseeing The Goldwater Institute, and speaking out on issues of interest and concern to him. In addition he maintained regular correspondence with friends (new and old) and former associates. As the elder statesman of the Republican Party he was frequently interviewed on the issues of the day. But as always, he refused to toe any party line; he spoke his mind instead.*

PICKING, AND PROBLEMS WITH, A SENATE SUCCESSOR: JOHN MCCAIN

Letter (December 5, 1985)

Goldwater prepared the following fundraising letter for John McCain, in which he made clear his choice for his successor.

Dear _____:

When I leave the United States Senate at the end of 1986, I know I will be leaving with mixed emotions. But, when the time comes for me to take leave of the Senate, I hope that I can take comfort in the knowledge that the person who takes my seat in the Senate will be someone who shares my ideals and philosophy.

It is my belief that Representative John McCain is the man for that job. John was born into a family long on military service with a history of honor and tradition. Following in his family's footsteps, he graduated from the United States Naval Academy in 1958 and entered active duty as a navy fighter pilot. It was in 1967, while on a bombing raid over the city of Hanoi, that John was shot down and later awarded the Bronze Star and the Silver Star for bravery and conduct in the highest traditions of the navy.

Retiring from the navy after a twenty-two-year career, John moved to my home state of Arizona. Soon after, he ran for and won a seat in the United States House of Representatives vacated by Congressman John Rhodes. In Washington, he was elected president of his class and was assigned to the House Interior Committee and the House Foreign Affairs Committee. In 1984, he was re-elected with an impressive 78 percent of the vote.

Last March, John announced his candidacy for the U.S. Senate race in 1986 and asked me to serve as chairman of his campaign. The reason I agreed to help his campaign is my strong belief that he will be an excellent Senator. His firsthand knowledge of military matters is exactly what the Senate needs if our country is to make rational decisions on national defense and international politics. John is committed to the principle of peace through strength.

When it comes to the United States of America, there is no greater patriot than John McCain. He is a staunch defender of President Reagan's policies in Central America and was credited with playing a key role during the recent House vote on aid to the Contras. In short, I am convinced that his contribution to our nation has just begun.

But, to get to the Senate, he needs your help. Running for state-wide office has become expensive—too expensive in my opinion. But, the fact remains that the outcome of the contest for my seat could well determine which party controls the Senate for the rest of this century. Given that importance, you can be sure that John's opponent will receive full backing of the national Democratic Party organizations, organized labor and various special interest groups.

I know you're probably asked to support a lot of different candidates. But, I hope you agree that John is special and, therefore, worthy of your support. Most importantly, the country needs him in the Senate. I hope that I can count on hearing from you soon and that you will agree to help me get John McCain elected as my successor in the United States Senate.

Note: McCain was elected in November 1986, and for years the two men had an excellent relationship. When McCain became embroiled in the "Keating Five" scandal, Goldwater's feelings toward McCain began to cool. Initially, he tried to ignore McCain's questionable behavior and judgment, but soon found he had to stop McCain from using his good name.

Letter (May 18, 1992)

On May 16, 1992, Goldwater received a letter from an old friend who had been invited to a "salute to Barry Goldwater," which he had planned to attend until he discovered it was "nothing but a fund-raiser for John McCain." Goldwater was advised that he was "being used by McCain, who has brought such discredit on himself and the party that he now must use your name to get people to come to his party." The friend went on: "McCain doesn't care about this state, or the party—only McCain. Why else would he [apparently] take money from the likes of Ivan Boesky and Jim Fail, and take more money from Keating than any of the other Keating 5, and be the only one to spend time in the Bahamas with Keating. We understand McCain is worried sick that Keating will distribute photos taken in the Bahamas. If I were you, I'd come down sick with something, and not show up, and salvage your reputation." Goldwater sent McCain the following note, pulling him up short:

Dear John:

The other day in Washington, I told you that I thought that the so-called salute to Barry Goldwater, turning out to be a fundraiser, should have some of the money raised given to the Republican party.

I propose that one-half of the money raised be given to the Arizona Republican Party, and let me tell you why. I thought this should have been a salute to you. I don't think this should be salute to me. John, the last thing in the world I need is a salute. I've done my damnedest to help my state, and my country, and I don't need any special thanks for it. Because you went to so much trouble, I won't turn it down, but I do insist that we divide the money with the Republican Party.

On top of that, when I got home this afternoon, I found copies of letters that you had mailed asking special friends of mine, to join in this effort. John, this is not the way I've operated in my political life, and I don't want to start it in my retired life. So, you agree to give half the money to the Republican Party, and this thing can go along. If you don't agree to it, then I'm going to have to give it a lot of good hard thinking.

Letter (September 25, 1992)

Remarkably, after agreeing to attend the event for McCain which was made a salute to President Reagan that would benefit the Arizona Republican Party, Goldwater himself had to dun McCain to pay the Arizona GOP its share of the proceeds.

Dear John:

This has to be a letter because you're in session in Washington, and urgency is a matter out here. You will recall during my speech at the dinner for the president in Phoenix, I announced that you were going to give half of the funds you raised to the State Republican Party. I am told by the Party, that you still owe them $35,000, and unless you pay all of it, or most of it, they cannot meet their payroll next Wednesday.

If this is true, I would urge you to make this payment immediately, in the interest of Party harmony, and your own campaign. Don't ignore this. Please pay attention to it.

Letter (December 8, 1992)

The following letter from Goldwater to McCain is about as chilly as a relationship could get with the senator. That McCain would send him a form letter, and again misuse information about him, prompted this not too subtle rejoinder.

Dear John:

Thank you for the Form Letter. However, I must tell you that the president never called for my help, in fact the president never called period. Good luck in the coming New Year.

SUPPORT FOR KARAN ENGLISH

When Goldwater's hand-picked successor in the Senate, John McCain, got himself in trouble with his mentor in 1992 he had reason to worry, for Goldwater had no hesitation to break rank when the circumstances called for it. There is no better example than when Doug Wead, an evangelical activist, ran as the Republican candidate for the congressional seat in Arizona's Sixth Congressional District against Democrat Karan English, calling himself "a Goldwater conservative." Goldwater stated:

Doug Wead does not know or understand Arizona, and his record in Washington, DC, is not the best. If I lived in the Sixth District, I would vote for Karan English. She has lived in the state long enough to know its problems. With her extensive Arizona background, she is well qualified to represent the Sixth District in Congress.

Note: Karan English won.

GAY RIGHTS

Goldwater, after consulting with colleagues with expertise in matters military, and finding no security risk whatsoever among homosexuals, spoke out to lift the ban on gays in the military in June 1993. As the former chair of the Senate Armed Services Committee, he spoke with some authority when he pointed out "that you don't need to be 'straight' to fight and die for your country; you just need to shoot straight." A year later, he expressed his disapproval of all discrimination against homosexuals and lesbians.

Statement (June 1994)

When I look back at the history of our country and the crises we have faced, it's clear to me that without sticking to the principles of the Constitution and the American work ethic, we would have lost our edge a long time ago. Unfortunately, prejudice is chipping away at those principles—and we're all paying the price.

Last year, many who opposed lifting the military's gay-ban gave lip service to the American ideal that employment opportunities should be based on skill and performance. They said the armed forces were different and they'd never condone discrimination in civilian life. Well, now is their chance to put up or shut up!

Yesterday, a bipartisan coalition in Congress proposed legislation to protect gays against job discrimination. Congress is waking up to a reality already recognized by a host of Fortune 500 companies—including AT&T, Marriott, and General Motors. These successful businesses have adopted policies prohibiting discrimination based on sexual orientation because they realize that their employees are their most important asset. America is now engaged in a battle to reduce the deficit and to compete in a global economy. Job discrimination excludes qualified individuals, lowers workforce productivity, and eventually hurts us all. If we are to outdo the Japanese and the Europeans, we have to seize all the talent that's out there. Topping the new world order means attracting the best and creating a work place environment where everyone can excel. Anything less makes us a second-rate nation. It's not just bad—it's bad business.

But job discrimination against gays and lesbians is real and it happens every day. Cracker Barrel, a national restaurant chain, adopted a policy of blatant discrimination against employees suspected of being gay. Would anyone tolerate policies prohibiting the hiring of African Americans, Hispanics, or women? Today, in corporate suites and factory warehouses, qualified people live in fear of losing their livelihood for reasons that have nothing to do with ability. In urban and rural communities, hatred and fear force good people from productive employment to the public dole—wasting their talents and the tax payers' money. In these tough economic times, we need to draw good people in—not drum them out.

Gays and lesbians are a part of every American family—including mine, Phyllis Schaffley's, Colin Powell's and yours. And in America, they should not be shortchanged in their efforts to better their lives and serve their communities. As President Clinton likes to say, "if you work hard and play by the rules, you'll be rewarded"—and not with a pink slip just for being gay. It's time America realized that there was no gay-exemption in the right to "life, liberty, and the pursuit of happiness" in the Declaration of independence. Job discrimination against gays—or anybody else—is contrary to each of these founding principles.

Some will try to paint this as a liberal or a religious issue. I am a Conservative Republican but I believe in democracy and the separation of church and state. The conservative movement is founded on the simple tenet that people have the right to live life as they please, as long as they don't hurt anyone else in the process. No one has ever shown me how being gay or lesbian harms anyone else. Even the 1992 Republican Party platform affirms the principle that "bigotry has no place in our society." I am proud that the Republican party has always stood for individual rights and liberties. And the positive role of limited government has always been the defense of these fundamental principles. Our party has led the way in the fight for freedom and a free market economy—a society where competition and the Constitution matter, and sexual orientation should not.

Now some in our ranks want to extinguish this torch. The radical right has nearly ruined our party. They do not care enough about the Constitution, and they are the ones making all the noise. The party faithful must not let it happen. Anybody who cares about real moral values understands that this isn't about granting special rights—it's about protecting basic rights. It is for this reason that over one hundred mayors and governors, Republicans and Democrats, have signed laws and issued orders protecting gays and lesbians. In fact, nearly half the states have provided some form of protection to gays in employment.

Progress has been made, but not nearly enough. My grandchildren and great-grandchildren are growing up in Arizona. Some of them are gay, some of them aren't. But because Arizona doesn't have a law barring discrimination based on sexual orientation, they may not all get a fair shake. And fairness is the most basic family value. It's not going to be easy—I know first-hand. The right wing will rant and rave that the sky is falling. They've said that before—and we are all still here. Constitutional conservatives know that doing the right thing takes guts and foresight, but that's why we're elected, to make tough decisions that stand the test of time.

My former colleagues in Washington have a chance to stand with civil rights leaders, the business community, and the 74 percent of Americans who polls show favor protecting gays and lesbians from job discrimination. With their vote they can help strengthen the American work ethic and support the principles of the Constitution.

HOW HE WANTED TO BE REMEMBERED

During this June 11, 1993, interview with CNN's Bernard Shaw were hints that Barry Goldwater would become a Bill Clinton supporter on an array of issues, to the utter consternation of other conservatives. Shaw closed the interview with a question on the news media, and after the camera had stopped rolling, he asked Goldwater how he would like to be remembered.

Bernard Shaw: Let's discuss one of your favorite subjects, the news media. How do you evaluate the way the news media have covered President Clinton during his first six months in office?

Sen. Goldwater: I wish somebody could tell me what the hell is wrong with the news media. It's no good. When Bush and Clinton were running against each other, they tore Bush apart. Every time you listen to a television show, every time you heard the radio or read the newspaper, it was how bad Bush was. Now they're tearing the president apart, and my question is why? Why are they making a rag doll out of him now? Why not help him? Here's a young man that is the president of the United States, he was elected by a majority, which is a lot more than any magazine has ever run by, and have the media help. Let them join in. I don't think the media of this country are doing much of a job in promoting America.

Shaw: When we concluded our conversation last night, I asked Barry Goldwater how he wants to be remembered. He replied, "As an honest man who tried his damndest."

EPILOGUE

We close with a few personal thoughts and observations. We believe that the material we have gathered shows precisely the type of person that our nation's founders hoped would represent the American people at the seat of government. Listen, just briefly and incompletely, to the remarks from a few of those who knew him well and were very aware his service and character, as they paused to reflect on his passing.*

Minnesota Democratic Senator Paul Wellstone (author of The Conscience of a Liberal) shared these impromptu remarks with colleagues on the Senate floor:

As a senator, I suppose, on the other side of the ideological continuum—if that is, in fact, even relevant; sometimes I don't think it is. I don't think politics has that much to do with left to right to center; I think it has more to do with trying to do well for people, and we have all reached different conclusions about how to do that. But it is about public service. I just want to say . . . that I think Barry Goldwater really set a standard, especially when it comes to personal integrity and intellectual integrity and political integrity. And I think people in our country really yearn for that. His outspokenness, and especially his courage, and especially in recent years his willingness to speak out,

---

* Comments made in tributes to Goldwater on the floor of the Senate and House of Representatives in early June 1998, following his death. Tellingly, so many sitting and former members of the Senate and House wanted to attend his funeral that the air force had to charter two 727s from Washington, DC, to fly them all to Phoenix. Those in charge of protocol said there had never been so many requests for a funeral. The family had to limit the private service to three thousand VIPs. No doubt Senator Goldwater looked down on it all with pleasure but thought everyone should get back to work doing the people's business.

even after no longer being in office, to continue to serve our country I think really is inspiring for all of us.

South Carolina Republican Senator Strom Thurmond said,

When [Barry Goldwater] announced he was going to run for president, I changed parties that year because I wanted to support this particular man on account of the high principles for which he stood. I did support him. Whether he had a chance to be elected or not, I wanted to have a part in supporting a man who stood for values, who stood for America, and who stood for the good things of life. Senator Goldwater served here for about thirty years. I enjoyed serving with him. . . . I knew a good man when I saw one—that is the reason that I supported him for president. . . . I was sorry he was not elected. He would have made a great president of the United States.

Arizona Republican Senator John Kyle explained,

It is clear that for many of us, particularly my generation, [that Barry Goldwater] was an inspiration for us to become involved in politics and to approach it from what he called a "commonsense conservative point of view." . . . He understood human nature. How did he come to that understanding? Part of it is because he really liked people and he liked to be with people. He learned from them what it was that was the essence of the character of man.

As evidence of his keen perception, Senator Kyle pointed to Goldwater's photography, which we have only provided hints of in these pages. Kyle noted,

The photographs he has taken, particularly in his early life, frequently are commented upon as remarkable for capturing something very special, some inner quality of the people he photographed. . . . He was somehow able to capture the essence of people through his photography. . . . He was able to capture that essence of humanity that I think most of us miss. We are all too busy, too busy with the big important things in life. . . . He found beauty in places that many of us would have passed over because we were in a hurry. . . . I think if more people understood human nature as Senator Goldwater did, . . . that all of us in this body and in the other body would be much better representatives of the people for whom we work, because we would better understand their desires, their hopes, their needs, and perhaps would better be able to reflect those hopes, needs, and desires in the kind of policy that we help to set here in Washington, DC.

New Mexico Republican Senator Pete Domenici noted,

Senator Goldwater was obviously an unflinching patriot whose life, in many ways, mirrored the American experience: He was rugged, independent, and unarguably his own man. . . . He never shied away from honestly stating his beliefs; and as a politician, he led by example, not by polls.

Alaska Republican Senator Frank Murkowski added,

Senator Goldwater was a man who never minced words. He was honest, open and forthright. After his 1964 presidential hopes were completely vanquished, he observed "When you've lost an election by that much, it isn't the case of whether you made the wrong speech or wore the wrong necktie. It was just the wrong time." In fact, Barry Goldwater was far ahead of his time and had the opportunity to see his beliefs vindicated when Ronald Reagan was elected president.

Virginia Republican Senator John Warner reported,

I had the privilege of serving with the distinguished Senator Goldwater for many years and worked with him diligently these years as an understudy, if I may say with great humility, on the Armed Services Committee. He was truly a man who left a profound impact on this humble senator, as he did many others.

Mississippi Republican and Senate Majority Leader Trent Lott, who spoke for the entire Senate, shared his observations about his former colleague:

He loved his work. He loved the people he represented. He spoke his mind. In many ways, he owed nobody, but he loved everybody. He was a winner, not just in the sense of winning elections—with one rather major exception—but in the most important sense of having his ideas vindicated by the course of history. In his one losing election, the presidential race of 1964, he was subject to more falsehoods, in my opinion, than any candidate should ever have to bear. In losing with honor, he did more than encourage others to stand up for their beliefs. I was one of those young people that was fresh out of college and working for my alma mater, the University of Mississippi, and casting my first vote ever in a presidential election for Barry Goldwater in my hometown of Pascagoula, Mississippi, and watching the election returns that night from Pensacola, Florida. I remember how I had been inspired by what he had to say. I think that was the moment I decided I would spend a good portion of my life involved in trying to be a representative of the people in government. Along with then-Governor Ronald Reagan, Barry Goldwater energized the grassroots of American politics, fostered the growth of modern conservatism, and thereby transformed the Republican Party and the nation. . . . The conservative movement has had many heroes, but Barry Goldwater remains preeminent, even though he came to disagree with conservatives on some issues. That disagreement has belatedly won him some new admirers, even some liberals who fail to see the difference between his reasoning and theirs.

Former Senate Majority Leader Howard Baker, whom Goldwater had encouraged to take the leadership post, gave a speech on July 14, 1998, which he titled "On Herding Cats," and explained,

Barry Goldwater and I were also personal friends, as well as professional colleagues and members of the same political team. Even so, I could not automatically count on his support for anything. Once, when I really needed his vote and leaned on him perhaps a little too hard, he said to his majority leader, 'Howard, you have one vote, and I have one vote, and we'll just see how this thing comes out.' It was at that moment that I formulated my theory that being leader of the Senate was like herding cats.

This is not to say that Goldwater was not a loyal party man, for the preceding pages show that he was loyal to the party even when it was not loyal to him.

Arizona Republican Representative Jim Kolbe told his colleagues,

I was just ten years old when I met Barry Goldwater at an old-fashioned political rally in the little town of Elgin, Arizona. At the time he was running against an incumbent Democrat senator and Majority Leader Ernest McFarland. Nobody thought he could do it, but he won. The rest, as they say, is history. Six years later Barry nominated me to become his Senate page, and I served in that capacity for three years. That is when I got to know, really know, this extraordinary man. He always said what was on his mind. He never shaded the truth. Barry Goldwater did not spend a lot of time worrying about whether he would be elected or not. He worried instead about principles and about America. He did not change his principles, but America changed. In an era of cynicism and distrust of public officials, Barry Goldwater's life stands as a reminder of values that are lasting and eternal—honesty, integrity, patriotism. We will miss him, for in our hearts we know he was right.

CHRONOLOGY

This chronology has been developed over a number of years by a number of people, ranging from the *Arizona Republic* newspaper to the senator's staff and the staff of the Arizona Historical Foundation. This prior work has been revised and updated for this book to provide a summarized timeline of the significant events in Barry Goldwater's life.

Jan. 2, 1909   Barry Morris Goldwater was born at 710 N. Center Street (now Central Avenue), Phoenix, Arizona Territory. He was the first-born son of Baron and Josephine (JoJo) Goldwater. (Barry had a sister, Carolyn, and a brother, Robert.)

1920   At age eleven, Goldwater's father gave him his first crystal radio, which resulted in a lifelong involvement with ham radio—and an endless fascination with gadgets both electrical and mechanical.

1922   At age thirteen, he assisted in setting up the first commercial radio transmitter in Arizona, KFDA, which was the thirty-sixth station licensed in the United States.

1923   Graduated from eighth grade at Kenilworth Elementary School in Phoenix and enrolled at Phoenix Union High School, where his poor performance in ninth grade prompted his parents to send him to private school.

1924   Enrolled at Staunton Military Academy in Virginia. Played football (center), ran track, was captain of the swimming team, and excelled in his academic studies.

1928   Graduated from Staunton, named outstanding cadet of his senior class, took his first flying lesson, and attended the University of Arizona during the fall semester.

March 6, 1929   Goldwater's father died at age sixty-two, which caused Barry to leave college and take his first job in the family's department store. Started to learn the business as a salesman in the piece-goods department and worked his way into management.

1930   Commissioned as a Second Lieutenant in the United States Army Reserve. Registered to vote for the first time and, like his mother, registered Republican. Made his first solo flight after ten hours of instruction, and flying becomes another lifelong passion. Won the San Marcos Invitational Golf Tournament in

Chandler, Arizona. In December, twenty-one-year-old Goldwater met Margaret "Peggy" Johnson, who was visiting Phoenix with her mother.

1931   Made his first cross-country flight to Los Angeles from Phoenix. (During his lifetime, he clocked 12,000 hours of flight time in 270 different types of aircraft, including helicopters, sail planes, and gliders.)

1933   Promoted to first lieutenant in the U.S. Infantry Reserve. Proposed marriage to Peggy Johnson, daughter of industrialist R. P. Johnson.

Sept. 22, 1934   Married Peggy Johnson of Muncie, Indiana.

1935   Entered in his first photographic art exhibit at the First Annual Salon of the Arizona Pictorialists. Became a serious photographer, exhibiting his work in over three hundred juried shows nationally and internationally.

Jan. 18, 1936   Daughter, Joanne, born. Organized winter relief flights to the Navajo Nation.

1937   Named president of rapidly growing and successful Goldwater's Department Store chain.

July 15, 1938   Son Barry, Jr., born. Started his private journal.

1939   Created a national fad with "Antsy Pants"—men's underwear printed with large red ants. *Women's Wear Daily* described him as "a creative merchandising dynamo." Sold first photograph "Coalmine Canyon" to the prestigious photographic journal, *Arizona Highways*.

1940   Published first book of photographs *Arizona Portraits*, which becomes the basis for his induction into the Royal Photographic Society. Took first trip down the Green and Colorado Rivers, running the rapids for forty-two days in a wooden boat and becoming the seventy-first known person to travel the full length of the Colorado River. Recording his journey with photographs and a film entitled "Shooting the Rapids," toured throughout Arizona giving a talk about his trip to packed theater audiences. Third child and second son, Michael, born March 15, 1940.

1941   Named chairman of Military Affairs Committee of Phoenix Chamber of Commerce. Goldwater's Department Store reached the million dollar annual sales mark. (Adjusted for inflation that is the equivalent of almost fourteen million dollars today.) With World War II raging, at age thirty-two, enlisted for active duty in Army Air Corps; served as group commander, 90th Air Force Base Squadron and chief of staff, Fourth Air Force; and was chief pilot of Air Transport Command in Azores, Casablanca, and India.

1942   Transferred to Yuma, Arizona, where he oversaw construction and requisitions of supplies for an advanced flight school for

combat pilots. Served as an aerial gunnery instructor and perfected a technique that increased target accuracy. Participated
in training programs for Chiang Kai-shek's Nationalist Chinese
pilots, which began a lifelong relationship with the Republic of
China (Taiwan).

1943   Transferred to the 27th Ferry Squadron and selected as one of
the first ten pilots to ferry P-47 Thunderbolts across the North
Atlantic to Europe. Awarded the Air Medal for meritorious
achievement while participating in aerial flight.

1944   Served in the Asian Theatre and flew three major supply routes:
Snowball, Crescent, and Fireball. He is assigned to fly "The
Hump" (the eastern end of the Himalayan Mountains) for the
last leg of a ten thousand–mile run. Promoted to major and
then lieutenant colonel. Fourth child, Peggy (Margaret, Jr.), is
born (July 27, 1944).

1945   Mustered out of the U.S. Army Air Corps as a lieutenant colonel. Arizona Governor Sydney Osborn assigned him as head
of the Arizona Air National Guard, which, through his efforts,
became the first national guard to open its ranks to African
Americans.

1946   Campaigned for Arizona to become a "Right-to-Work" state in
response to major strikes nationally. (Over President Truman's
veto, in 1947 Congress adopted the Taft-Hartley Act, which
permitted state laws that prohibit trade unions from making
membership or payment of union dues or "fees" a condition of
employment.) Appointed by Governor Sydney Osborn to the
Arizona Colorado River Commission (later renamed the Inter-
state Stream Commission). One of his photographs was selected
for the cover of the first all-color issue of *Arizona Highways*.

1947   Joined the Phoenix Chamber of Commerce Thunderbirds.
Phoenix Mayor Ray Busey appointed Goldwater and thirty-
nine other leading citizens to a committee to study city government and suggest charter revisions and reforms. They became
known as the Phoenix Forty.

1948   The Phoenix Charter Revision Committee announced its findings and recommended the appointment of a professional city
manager who would be immune from political pressure. Goldwater was asked by supporters to run for city council.

1949   The Phoenix Charter Revision Committee reorganized to
become the Charter Government Committee, which provided a
platform for reform-minded candidates who swept the election.
At age forty, won a seat on the Phoenix city council. Named
"Man of the Year" by Phoenix Advertising Club.

1950   Goldwater served as campaign manager (and chief pilot) in a successful gubernatorial bid by John Howard Pyle, a Republican,

	former journalist, and program director of a Phoenix radio station where Goldwater provided public affairs talks.
1951	Reelected to Phoenix city council.
1952	Opened his campaign for U.S. Senate, and defeated Democratic incumbent Senator Ernest McFarland, the Senate's Majority Leader, by 6,500 votes.
1953	Gave first major speech in Senate and appealed for an end to federal price controls. In another early debate in his Senate career, criticized France for its failure to move Indochina (Vietnam) toward independence.
1954	The senator's first bill was signed by President Eisenhower. The bill authorized the secretary of the interior to convey certain land to the City of Tucson, Arizona, and to accept certain other parcels of land in exchange.
1955	Asked to serve as chair of the Republican Senatorial Campaign Committee, which launched him into a GOP leadership role as one of the party's best fundraisers and a spokesman for the growing conservative faction within the party.
1956	Collaborated with Stephen Shadegg, his Senate campaign manager, on the script for the documentary "For Freedom's Sake," which described the dangers of communism. Campaigned to reelect President Eisenhower to a second term.
1958	Won a second term to the U.S. Senate, again defeating Ernest McFarland, who had become Arizona's governor, by a 56 percent majority.
1959	Promoted to brigadier general of the U.S. Air Force Reserves. Agreed to meet Clarence Manion, dean of the Notre Dame Law School and a conservative activist, who had assembled a group of conservatives in Chicago who wanted to draft Goldwater as the GOP presidential nominee. Told Manion he did not want to be president or vice president and sought to dampen their efforts.
1960	Nominated by Arizona Governor Paul Fannin for president at the GOP National Convention in Chicago. Arizona U.S. Congressman John Rhodes seconded the motion. Immediately withdrew his name and campaigned for Richard M. Nixon. Published *The Conscience of a Conservative*, which became a best seller and fueled growth of the conservative political movement.
1961	President Kennedy asked Goldwater for his advice during the Bay of Pigs invasion. The senator responded by advising him to order an air strike immediately or the mission would fail. (No airstrikes were ordered and the mission failed.) Received an honorary doctor of laws degree from Arizona State University. Goldwater's Department Store was sold to Associated Dry Goods.

1962	Prompted by the Bay of Pigs debacle, and the resulting Cuban Missile Crisis, wrote *Why Not Victory*, which became a best-seller. Called for a foreign policy based on military strength. Promoted to major general of the U.S. Air Force Reserves.
Jan. 3, 1964	Formally announced candidacy for GOP nomination for president.
July 15, 1964	Won GOP presidential nomination at convention in San Francisco.
July 16, 1964	Delivered acceptance speech that included famous comment: "I would remind you that extremism in the defense of liberty is no vice! And let me remind you also that moderation in the pursuit of justice is no virtue!"
Sept. 3, 1964	Officially opened presidential campaign.
Nov. 4, 1964	Defeated by Lyndon Johnson by 16 million votes.
1965–1969	Was out of office; traveled the world with his wife.
Dec. 17, 1966	Mother died.
1967	Retired from the U.S. Air Force Reserve as a major general.
November 1968	Reelected to the Senate; defeated Roy Elson 274,607 to 205,338.
1973	Presented with the Wright Brothers Award for service to aviation.
Aug. 7, 1974	With House and Senate leaders, including John Rhodes, visited President Nixon and told the chief executive he did not have the votes to avoid impeachment. Nixon resigned on August 9.
November 1974	Elected to fourth term in Senate; defeated Jonathan Marshall 320,396 to 229,523.
1974	Presented with Aviation Space Writers Distinguished Service Award.
1977	Named to the board of regents of the Smithsonian Institution.
November 1980	Narrowly defeated Bill Schulz for fifth and final term in Senate. Vote count: 432,371 to 422,972.
November 1982	Underwent triple-bypass heart surgery.
Sept. 22, 1984	Celebrated fiftieth wedding anniversary.
Dec. 11, 1985	Wife, Peggy, dies.
May 7, 1986	In a vote described by Goldwater as the proudest moment of his political career, the Senate passed his sweeping military reorganization bill, named after him and Representative William Nichols: "The Goldwater-Nichols Act."
May 12, 1986	Awarded the Presidential Medal of Freedom, the nation's highest civilian award, by President Ronald Reagan.
Sept. 2, 1986	Barry Goldwater High School, 2820 W. Rose Garden Lane in Phoenix, was opened.
Jan. 5, 1987	Senate career came to an end.
February 1987	Elected to the board of directors of National Education Corp.

March 1987	2.7 million-acre bombing and gunnery range near Gila Bend renamed the Barry M. Goldwater Air Force Range.
March 4, 1987	Began lecture stint at Arizona State University. Told ASU students that Governor Evan Mecham was "hardheaded" and needed to change his style.
April 1987	Underwent knee surgery.
August 1987	Agreed to serve as honorary chairman of group seeking to make English Arizona's official language.
October 1987	Endorsed property-tax increase to fund controversial Rio Salado development project.
Oct. 8, 1987	Said Governor Evan Mecham should resign, sparking uproar within state GOP.
Sept. 24, 1987	Honored by West Point with the 1987 Sylvanus Thayer Award.
April 1988	Site dedication for Barry M. Goldwater Center for Science and Engineering at Arizona State University.
July 1988	Published the co-authored autobiography *Goldwater*, which took Ronald Reagan to task over Iranian arms sale.
August 1988	Declared the Phoenix Indian School land swap "probably the stupidest thing that's ever been suggested by the Interior Department."
Aug. 15, 1988	Honored by delegates at the Republican National Convention in New Orleans.
October 1988	Told George H. W. Bush and Michael Dukakis to "quit calling each other names."
November 1988	Awarded the Arthritis Foundation Marriott Lifetime Achievement Award.
February 1989	Said the Republican Party had been taken over by a "bunch of kooks," a reference to forces supporting TV evangelist Pat Robertson and former Arizona Governor Evan Mecham.
February 1989	Awarded the Arizona Medal of Honor by the Legislature in a resolution signed by Governor Rose Mofford.
Feb. 20, 1989	Five Goldwater's stores changed their name to Robinsons, a subsidiary of the Associated Dry Goods chain, ending 128 years of Arizona having a store with the name Goldwater.
April 1989	Honored by the Arizona Senate.
July 1989	Underwent hip surgery.
October 1989	Nominated by President George H. W. Bush to serve on the board of directors of the Communications Satellite Corp.
May 1990	Said "it's time this old Republican quit hiding behind the bush" (referring to himself) and admitted that he gave $500 to Democratic Representative Morris K. Udall's last reelection campaign.
June 1990	Signed onto the Arizona Citizens for Education initiative to increase state spending on education.

Oct. 13, 1990	Endorsed Proposition 302 to create a state holiday honoring the Reverend Martin Luther King, Jr.
Nov. 3, 1990	Joined former Governor Bruce Babbitt and Representative Morris K. Udall (D-Ariz.) in pushing for the Arizona Heritage Fund, which set aside state lottery funds for state parks and wildlife.
Nov. 4, 1990	Barry M. Goldwater Terminal opened at Sky Harbor International Airport in Phoenix.
September 1991	Urged the United States to send money and other aid to the former Eastern European republics emerging from the collapse of the Soviet Union.
November 1991	Honored by the Phoenix Urban League as one of the group's founding members.
Feb. 9, 1992	Married Susan Shaffer Wechsler, branch manager of a home health care agency, at a private ceremony in Scottsdale.
July 1992	Joined Arizona Public Service Co. President Mark DeMichele in urging Phoenix city council to reverse an earlier decision to put a Phoenix gay rights proposal on the ballot. Otherwise, he warned, "all hell is going to break loose."
August 1992	Predicted that President George H. W. Bush would lose the election unless the GOP dropped its strict anti-abortion plank, reflecting his own belief that women should have the right to make their own choice.
October 1992	Appeared in television commercials urging Arizona voters to oppose anti-abortion ballot measure.
October 1992	Shocked state GOP by endorsing Democrat Karan English for Congress over Republican Doug Wead, a favorite of the religious right who called himself "a Goldwater Republican." English went on to defeat Wead.
Nov. 5, 1992	Said President George H. W. Bush had run "the worst campaign I have ever witnessed, whether it be for president or precinct committeeman."
December 1992	Some Arizona Republican Party activists considered a resolution removing Goldwater's name from state GOP headquarters in response to Goldwater's Karan English endorsement.
January 1993	Efforts by some GOP activists to strip Goldwater's name from party headquarters failed and was dropped.
June 1993	Declared that the military should lift its ban on gays.
July 1993	Honored by the Arizona Human Rights Fund, the state's top gay and lesbian rights organization.
August 1993	Said in an interview with the *Advocate*, a national gay and lesbian news magazine, that he viewed concerns about gays in the military as pointless and stupid. Added that the GOP's stance on gays is "dumb."

Nov. 9, 1993   Appeared on "The Tonight Show with Jay Leno" and proclaimed he planned to get a tattoo "right on my ass." Also recalled Hillary Rodham Clinton as a 1964 Goldwater Girl: "I remember her going around in a gingham dress trying to get people to vote for me. Trouble is, she didn't get around to enough of them."

September 1993   Joined opponents of a proposed bridge at the landmark Red Rock Crossing near Sedona.

Jan. 22, 1994   Honored by Planned Parenthood for his decades-long commitment to the right of privacy and a woman's right to choose.

February 1994   Became chairman of a petition drive to raise the sales tax for a pack of cigarettes by forty cents.

March 16, 1994   Horrified Arizona Republicans by calling on the GOP to get off President Clinton's back over the Whitewater affair. "I haven't heard anything yet that says this is all that big of a deal," he said.

December 1994   Received the 1994 Civil Libertarian of the Year Award from the Arizona Civil Liberties Union.

January 1995   Urged state lawmakers to kill a bill that would have funneled tobacco-tax money into the state's general fund to be spent as lawmakers see fit.

March 1995   PBS aired documentary salute to Goldwater's hobby—photography.

May 1995   Threw his support behind Scottsdale's preservation-minded Proposition 400, saying that "it would be a sin" to build on the McDowell Mountains.

February 1996   Described himself and Bob Dole as "the new liberals of the Republican Party" during a meeting with Dole at Goldwater's home in Paradise Valley. Despite Goldwater's support, Dole lost state GOP presidential primary to wealthy publisher Steve Forbes.

March 1996   Led several Arizona Republicans in urging the GOP to abandon a law that requires the military to discharge service members who carry the virus that causes AIDS. "Our revolution is about creating hope and opportunity and a better future for our children and grandchildren," Goldwater said in a letter to GOP members of a House-Senate conference committee debating whether to repeal the law. "It is not about throwing 1,049 patriotic Americans out of the armed forces because they happen to be HIV-positive. That kind of senseless sideshow only distracts our attention and reduces our credibility."

July 1996   Agreed to become an honorary member of Republicans for Environmental Protection, a fledgling nationwide organization.

September 1996   Suffered a minor stroke and was hospitalized at Barrow Neurological Institute at St. Joseph's Hospital and Medical Center. His stay was a busy one, with visits from President Clinton;

	GOP presidential challenger Bob Dole; and Colin Powell, former head of the Joint Chiefs of Staff. Goldwater did not suffer any paralysis and was released after a two-week stay.
October 1996	Hillary Rodham Clinton, a former "Goldwater Girl," made a surprise visit to Goldwater's Paradise Valley home.
September 1997	Family members said that Goldwater might have been showing early signs of Alzheimer's disease but cautioned that even his physicians had a difference of opinion over the diagnosis. They also corrected a *Tribune Newspapers* article that suggested Goldwater was infirm and imprisoned by his wife, Susan, characterizing the article as "bizarrely off-base" and "inappropriate."
May 29, 1998	Goldwater died in his own home, in his own bed, with his family at his side, overlooking his beloved Arizona mountains and landscape, at the age of eighty-nine, from complications from a stroke.

ACKNOWLEDGMENTS

Publishing this book at this time means that Senator Barry Goldwater's voice can be heard in the pivotal 2008 election year, not to mention in the years that will follow. But we think it is important that it be heard now, and that has only been made possible because of the efforts of a number of people who have provided us great assistance.

First, Linda Whitaker of the Arizona Historical Foundation, the archivist who is most familiar with the Goldwater papers, was vital to locating information in the senator's collection. With both of us frequently traveling, she has been indispensible in assisting with our digging. In addition, Washington attorney David Dorsen tracked down materials relating to the *Goldwater v. Ginzburg* trial in New York by locating former Ginzburg attorney Stanley Arkin, who in turn thoughtfully provided us with his personal and pristine copy of the trial transcript that contains uniquely "pure Goldwater" material. Jack August, the former head of the AHF and now executive director of the Barry Goldwater Center for the Southwest, considerately provided material on Goldwater's continuing relevance in American politics, but because we ran out of room we did not use his excellent material. We hope he will use it elsewhere (or we will borrow from it when discussing this book). Susan Irwin, acting director of the AHF, made the administrative tasks of obtaining permissions painless. Rebekah Tabah is one of the few practicing photographic preservationists in the country, and she works at the AHF, where she has catalogued over 10,000 of the senator's slides, movies, and photographs, no small task.

Special thanks to two people with very exceptional knowledge of the subject of this book, who expressed interest in our undertaking. We sincerely appreciate their taking the time (many hours, and days) to read the manuscript as we were assembling the material, and for their suggestions based on their first-hand knowledge of the events recounted in these pages: Mike Goldwater, the senator's youngest son (we view him as the innocent son), and Judy Eisenhower, who was hired as a mere child by the senator in the late 1950s and proceeded to make his political career her own. We could not have had better fact-checkers, for none exist. We urge you to unfairly blame Mike for all errors (of any nature) because he is our junior, he is accustomed to taking our static since our days together at Staunton Military Academy, and because he once was so foolish as to kiss one of his big brother's favorite girlfriends for which he has been sentenced to a lifetime of undeserved punishment.

As hefty as this book is it was once even stouter. Accordingly, we imposed ourselves on the good will and incisive judgment of a couple of professional historians—one seasoned and another getting seasoned fast—to suggest places to trim the material, and both offered helpful thoughts. Much of the material that we would have liked to include is now on the cutting room floor. So for the material that you might have wanted to read but now will never know about you must look to Stanley I. Kutler, an emeritus professor of law at the University of Wisconsin, whose works on Vietnam and Nixon have long defined the scholarship of the period, and who had no trouble finding the historical nuggets scattered throughout these pages. Needless to say, he did not suggest cutting those. In addition, Thomas Long, a newly minted PhD and assistant professor of history at California State University (San Bernardino), who is now writing and teaching about the period we address in this book, provided his thoughtful views from his fresh perspective.

Matching a book with a publisher is an art form in itself, so allow us to give a tip of our hats to our literary agent extraordinaire, Ms. Lydia Wills, who knew exactly where to take this unique project. Lydia waltzed this through the world of books she knows so well to place it in the proper hands. In turn, this book has had the benefit of being a personal project of Airié Stuart, senior vice president and publisher of Palgrave Macmillan. Had this not been Airié's project, it might have been another election cycle (or two) before we completed it. But notwithstanding our interest in procrastinating, Airié was determined that it be published this election year. She is correct, of course, for this is the time to remember this man's approach to politics and government, so she drove this project onward, not with a whip we must add, rather by removing all obstacles (and excuses) that would slow it down. She believes, as we do, that regardless of one's politics, this is timely information for all, and therefore it was worth the extra effort to assemble the book at warp speed. The team at Palgrave is highly professional, and it has been our pleasure to work with them from start to finish. As they have pressed this book forward it occurred to us that maybe Senator Goldwater learned of this project and provided all the folks at Palgrave with "antsy pants." Whatever the case, we have no doubt he would be extremely pleased with the efforts of Airié and her team, as are we. Words of wisdom buried in an archive serve no purpose, but together we have hopefully gathered a few of them in *Pure Goldwater*, making them accessible to all.

For those interested in the senator's remarkable photography, the Goldwater Family Foundation maintains a Web site we encourage you to visit: http://www.barrygoldwaterphotographs.com. In addition, we would suggest those interested also visit the Goldwater collection at the Arizona Historical Foundation: http://www.ahfweb.org/collections_bmg.htm. Finally, we call attention to the terrific film documentary that the senator's granddaughter, CC Goldwater, produced with Home Box Office. For more information please visit http://www.hbo.com/docs/programs/mrconservative/index.html or http://www.zeitgeistvideo.com.

INDEX

A

abortion, xiii, 346–48, 385. See also *Roe v. Wade*
Adams, Samuel, 355
Adams, Sherman, 99, 214
Agnew, Spiro: Nixon, Richard, and, 257, 273; scandal and, 273, 275–92; Scott, Hugh, and, 243; Southern conservatives and, 236
Ahrens, Les, 236
Air National Guard (Arizona), 148, 197, 381
Albert, Carl, 285, 286
Alliance for Progress, 350
Alsop, Joe, 207
American energy policy, 349–50
Anderson, Bob, 282
Anderson, Clinton Presba, 90–91
Anderson, Jack, 277, 311
anti-ballistic missiles (ABMs), 221, 227, 244
anti-Semitism, charges of, 106, 144, 159–62, 167
Antsy Pants, 6, 380, 391
Arends, Les, 286
Atomic Energy Commission, 222

B

Babbitt, Bruce, 385
Baker, Howard, 243, 282, 353, 376
Ball, George W., 223
Barkley, Alban, 89
Baroody, Bill, 217

Bay of Pigs, 118–19, 132, 135, 381, 383
Bayless, A. J., 46–47
Benson, Ezra Taft, 93, 205
Blue Book [*of the John Birch Society*], 169
Bork, Robert, 292
Bowles, Chester, 135
Bozell, L. Brent, 106, 108, 111
Brandt, Willie, 251
Brezhnev, Leonid, 279
Brock, Bill, 272, 299
Broder, David, 143, 314
Brown, Jerry, 322
Buckley, William, Jr., xi, 106, 357
Burch, Dean: Early Bird program and, 215, 216; Nixon, Richard, and, 272; Watergate and, 296–97, 299, 300–301, 303, 319
Busey, Ray, 381
Bush, George H. W.: 1988 presidential campaign, 384; 1992 presidential campaign, 372, 385; Republican National Committee and, 272; Watergate and, 280, 282, 297–98, 305
Buzhardt, Fred, 289, 290
Byrd, Harry, Jr., 224, 225

C

Calhoun, John, 283–84
Callaway, Bo, 319
Camp Little, 45, 47
campaign finance reform, 353–60
Carmen, Jim, 130

Carter, Jimmy, 322, 326–27, 350
Case, Clifford, 230, 232
Casey, Bill, 268
Casserly, Jack, 72, 120–21, 141–43, 222, 286
Castro, Fidel, 118, 121, 134, 145
Chamberlain, Neville, 24
Chandler, Harrison, 204, 380
Chiang Kai-shek, 179–80, 381
Childs, Marquis, 207
China, 13, 65, 97, 117, 126, 179–82, 185, 235, 252–53, 257, 314, 318, 333
civil rights, 171, 206, 236, 351, 371
Clark, Bob, 301
Clark, Ramsey, 265
Clausewitz, Karl Von, 161–62, 335
Clements, William, 269
Clifford, Clark, 142
Clinton, Bill, 370, 372, 386
Clinton, Hillary, 386, 387
Community Chest drive, 20–21
Connally, John, 239, 268–69, 273, 276, 285, 288
Connally Amendment, 203, 205
Conscience of a Conservative, The (Goldwater), 106, 111, 172, 382
Conscience of a Liberal, The (Wellstone), 373
Conservatives and Radicals (McGovern), 112
Cortines, Adolfo Ruiz, 87
Cotton, Norris, 299
Cox, Archibald, 292
Cracker Barrel, 370
Craswell, Hop, 50
Cuba, 118–19, 123, 132–34, 333, 348, 383
Cuban Missile Crisis, 119, 132–34, 383
Curve of Pursuit, 64

D

Dalrymple, Jim, 88
Dean, John, 276, 277, 279

deficit spending, 83, 360–64
DeMichele, Mark, 385
Dent, Harry, 235
Devine, Sam, 236
Dewey, Thomas, 81, 99
Dirksen, Everett, 72, 82, 199, 232
discrimination, 350, 372–74
Dole, Bob, 236, 241, 243, 264, 272, 386, 387
Domenici, Pete, 375
Domino Theory, 336
Donaldson, Teddy, 64
Douglas, William O., 176
Drummond, Roscoe, 207
Dukakis, Michael, 384
Dulles, John Foster, 99, 202, 334

E

Early Birds program, 216
Edison, Thomas, 3–4
Edwards, Lee, 324
Ehrlichman, John, 261, 277, 277, 311
Eisenhower, Dwight: Bay of Pigs and, 119; foreign policy, 334; Goldwater and, 103–4, 169, 198, 382; Goldwater's early Senate career and, 93, 98; Goldwater's initial Senate run and, 75, 78, 81–82, 84; Kennedy, John F., and, 115–16, 123–24; Miller, William E., and, 135; Nixon, Richard, and, 203, 205, 208–9, 213–16, 222, 224, 226, 236; Republican Party and, 129; Rogers, Bill, and, 199; Warren, Earl, and, 163; Watergate and, 268, 302
Eisenhower, Earl, 300
Elson, Roy, 193, 383
Emerson, Terry, 245
English, Karan, 369, 385

F

FACT magazine, 144–45, 150, 154, 165, 174–76
Fair Deal, 79, 95–96, 204, 207
Fannin, Paul, 4, 124, 128, 214, 382
Federal Aid to Education, 112
Federalist Papers, 323, 344, 373
Fellers, Bonner, 113
Flannigan, Peter, 223–24
Fleeson, Doris, 207
Ford, Gerald: Clements, William, and, 269; Douglas, William O., and, 176; foreign policy, 346–47; Goldwater and, xiv; Watergate and, 285, 292, 298, 305–7, 309, 312, 318–19, 322, 325–27
Forrestal, James, 162
Fortas, Abe, 142, 226
Freeman, Orville, 216
fund-raising, 20, 103, 127, 131, 367

G

gay rights, xiii, 369–72, 385
Ginzburg, Ralph, xii, 146–80
Goldwater, Barry, Jr., ix, 15, 48, 146, 160, 218, 223, 260, 277, 380
Goldwater, Morris, 21–22
Goldwater's Department Store, 3, 6, 7, 75, 146, 153, 379, 380, 382
Goodell, Charles, 230–32
Gore, Louise, 220, 232
Griffin, Bob, 299, 301
Griswold, Erwin N., 329, 330
guest editorials, 17–19
Gurney, Ed, 236

H

Haig, Alexander: Connally, John, and, 268–69; Watergate and, 278–79, 281, 284–86, 296–301

Haldeman, Bob, 256, 277
Hall, Leonard, 198–99
Halleck, Charlie, 163
Halperin, Morton, 214, 220
Hargis, Billy Gene, 166–67
Harlow, Bryce: Nixon, Richard, and, 216, 218–19, 224; Scott, Hugh, and, 243; Southern conservatives and, 236; Watergate and, 282–90, 320
Harris, Bucky, 10
Hart, Jeffrey, 141
Hayden, Carl, 75, 88, 127, 132, 134–35, 143, 193, 260
Helms, Dick, 274
Hendrickson, Robert C., 120
Herman, Ab, 80–81
Hess, Karl, 191–93
Hickel, Walter, 237
Hitler, Adolf, 24, 147, 167, 177, 179, 347
Hoover, Herbert, 5, 117
Hunt, H. L., 75

I

illegal immigration, 350–51
immigration reform, 350–51
Indian reservations, ix, 82–83
Indochina, 346–47, 350, 382

J

Jarwoski, Leon, 296
Javits, Jacob, 210, 226, 230–32, 262, 281, 399
Jefferson, Thomas, 107, 348
Jenkins, Walter, 142–43
John Birch Society, 166, 169
Johnson, Abbott, 75
Johnson, Annie, 61
Johnson, Lyndon: 1964 presidential campaign, 141–45, 383; Freeman,

Orville, and, 216; Goldwater on, 138, 325; Griswold, Erwin, and, 329; holdover appointments from administration, 220, 234, 237; Nixon, Richard, and, 213, 232, 268; press and, 277, 302; Strauss, Lewis, and, 222–23
Johnson, Mack, 12
Johnson, Ray, 10, 78, 202
Johnston, Vic, 205
Jones, Tom, 251

K

Keating Five scandal, 366–67
Kefauver, Estes, 80
Kelland, Clarence Buddington, 80, 104–5
Keller, Millette F., 187
Kennedy, Basil, 190
Kennedy, David, 239
Kennedy, John F.: Alliance for Progress and, 349; Bay of Pigs and, 118–19, 362; Cuba and, 132–34; foreign policy, 117–19, 124; Goldwater and, 164–65, 172; legacy, 228, 234, 237; New Frontier and, 114–16, 123; political aftermath of assassination, 137–38, 143, 201; press and, 277; *Profiles in Courage*, 362; Vietnam War and, 98, 223, 334
Kennedy, Robert F., 135
Kennedy, Ted, 222, 227, 309
Khrushchev, Nikita, 134, 202
Kilgore, Leonard, 43
King, Bob, 38, 40
King, Martin Luther, Jr., 385
Kissinger, Henry: ABM and, 244; Goldwater and, 234; Halperin, Morton, and, 220; McNamara, Robert, and, 217; Nixon, Richard, and, 255–56, 257; SST program and, 251; Strauss, Lewis, and, 222; Vietnam War and, 261–62; Watergate and, 311
Kitchel, Dennis, 142

Kleindienst, Richard, 126, 214, 223, 246, 277
Kline, Herb, 205
Korean War, 83, 117, 215, 333, 346, 360–61
Krock, Arthur, 234
Kyle, John, 374

L

labor unions, 17, 95–96, 116–17, 129, 210, 229, 381
Labor-Management Act, 208
Laird, Mel, 214, 217, 220–21, 237, 256, 269, 280, 326
LaRue, Fred, 223, 265
Lindsay, John, 230
Lippmann, Walter, 207
Lott, Trent, 375
Luke, Frank, Jr., 5

M

Manion, Clarence, 104–5, 109, 113–14, 382
Mansfield, Mike, 122, 268
massive retaliation, 334
McCain, John, 365–68
McCarthy, Joseph, 75, 85, 99–100, 119–20, 121, 162
McFarland, Ernest: as Arizona governor, 103; Goldwater on, 173; Goldwater's initial Senate run and, 71–72, 75, 77–79, 84–86, 377, 382
McGovern, George, 112, 242, 262, 267
McGregor, Clark, 263
McNamara, Robert, 334; Cuban Missile Crisis and, 119; effectiveness operation, 227–28; Goldwater on, 119, 215, 217; Nixon, Richard, and, 232–33; Vietnam War and, 223
McSparron, Cozy, 28–29

Mecham, Evan, 125, 130, 134–35, 384

Miliken, Roger, 206

Military Industrial Complex, 252

Mill, John Stuart, 112

Miller, William E., 127, 133, 205, 241

Mitchell, John, 212, 227–28, 240–41, 250, 267, 310

Mofford, Rose, 384

Momyer, William Wallace, 184, 185

Mondale, Walter, 7

Montgomery, Russ, 32

Morris, Paul, 46–47

Morris, Wayne, 95

Morse, Wayne, 131

Morton, Rogers, 205, 271

Moyers, Bill, 141

Murkowski, Frank, 375

N

NASA, 241

National Review, 106, 140

NATO, 332

Nevills, Norman, 39

New Deal, 79, 82, 95–96, 98–100, 122

New York Times v. Sullivan, 144, 175

Nichols, William, 383

Nixon, Richard: 1960 presidential campaign, 113–15, 124, 382; 1968 presidential campaign, 199–214; Agnew, Spiro, and, 256–57, 273; Burch, Dean, and, 272; Eisenhower, Dwight, and, 203, 205, 208–9, 213–16, 220, 222, 224, 236; first presidential term, 213–54; Goldwater and, 109, 193–94, 383; Griswold, Erwin, and, 329; gubernatorial campaign, 143; Harlow, Bryce, and, 216, 218–19, 224; Johnson, Lyndon, and, 213, 232, 268; Kissinger, Henry, and, 255–57; McNamara, Robert, and, 232–33; second presidential term, 255–74; War Powers

Resolution and, 346; Watergate and, 275–327; Welch, Robert, and, 173

O

O'Donnell, Pete, 211

Oppenheimer, Harry, 190

Orinoco oil belt, 349–50

Osborn, Sydney, 381

Otepka, Otto, 219–20

P

Pacification Program, 337

Packard, Dave, 271

Paris Peace Talks, 220, 229, 233, 253, 261, 337

Patch, Alexander, 64

Pearson, Drew, 207

Pentagon Papers, 252

Percy, Chuck, 210–11, 282

Petersen, Henry, 285

Pitts, Bill, 179

Political Action Committees, 357, 359

Powell, Colin, 371, 387

presidential war powers. *See* War Powers Resolution

Proxmire, William, 232, 242

Pulliam, Eugene, 105, 109

Pyle, John Howard, 67, 70–72, 79, 84, 126, 381

Q

Quinn, Bill, 223–24

Quinn, Sally, 291

R

Reagan, Ronald: 1976 presidential election and, 318–22, 324; budget, 362; Casey, Bill, and, 268; Goldwater and, 361, 375–76, 383; Iranian

arms deal, 384; McCain, John, and, 366, 365; Nixon, Richard, and, 210–12, 218–19, 268, 282; War Powers Resolution and, 346
Reed, Thomas C., 211–12
Reedy, George, 141
Rehnquist, William, 259
Reuther, Walter, 91, 155, 156
Rhodes, John, 126, 300–302, 306, 326, 366, 382, 383
Rhodesia, 191–92, 235
Richardson, Elliott, 257, 283, 285, 292
Richardson, Sid, 75
right-to-work laws, 83, 199, 381
Robb, Roger, 145–46, 150, 151, 165, 170
Rockefeller, Nelson: 1960 presidential campaign and, 109, 113–15; 1964 Republican National Convention and, 140; 1968 presidential campaign and, 212; Ford, Gerald, and, 305; Goldwater on, 155–56; Nixon, Richard, and, 198–99, 210, 231, 243, 266, 285, 288; Republican Party and, 286
Rockwell, Margaret, 82
Roe v. Wade, 341–43. See also abortion
Rogers, Bill, 199, 204, 262, 268, 271
Romney, George, 210–11
Rooney, Judy, 143–44
Roosevelt, Franklin, 79, 116, 122, 239, 294, 316, 317, 326, 347, 360
Roper, R. D., 5
Rosenzweig, Harry, 13, 67, 125
Ruckelhaus, William, 292
Rusk, Dean, 223

S

Saufley, Bill, 38
Schaffley, Phyllis, 370
Schlesinger, Arthur M., 159, 171

Schlessinger, James, 271, 274
Scott, Hugh, 241, 243, 272, 278, 299, 301, 302, 306, 385
Scranton, Bill, 210
Senate procedures, 351–53
Shadegg, Stephen, 63, 75, 81, 83, 84, 109–11, 118, 122, 125, 132, 141, 201, 382
Shaw, Bernard, 372
Shorrey, Gregg, 206
Smith, Dean, 45
Smith, Gerald L. K., 167–68
Smith, Ian, 192
Southern conservatives, 96, 235–36
Soviet Union, 134, 239, 244, 249, 256, 385
Spellman, Francis Cardinal, 120
Sperling, Godfrey, Jr., 289
Spivak, Lawrence, 170–71
SST program, 239–40, 242, 244, 248–52, 259
St. Clair, James, 299
Stans, Maurice, 203
Staunton Military Academy, xi, 45–46, 64, 96, 149, 379
Steinberg, Harris B., 165, 172, 174
Stevens, Ted, 129, 130
Stevenson, Adlai, 99, 133
Strauss, Lewis, 222
Symington, Fife, 128
Symington, Stuart, 97, 311

T

Taft, Robert, 80–81, 82, 98, 101, 381
Taft, William Howard, 345
Taft-Hartley Act, 84, 100, 381
Tennessee Valley Authority (TVA), 322
Thornburg, Jack, 5
Thurmond, Strom, 236, 374
Tidelands debate, 95
Timmons, Bill, 269, 301–2
Tower, John, 240, 299

Truman, Harry: Civil Service and, 268; Eisenhower, Dwight, and, 236; Fair Deal and, 79, 132; Goldwater on, 170; Goldwater's initial Senate run and, 80, 85–86; leadership, 116, 228; Taft-Hartley Act and, 381; views of, ix, 99
Turner, Pappy, 52, 57
Tyler, Harold, 146

U

Udall, Morris, 112, 384, 385
Unander, Sigfrid Benson, 130, 131

V

Venezuela, 349–50
Vietnam War: attempts to end, 260–62, 272; budget deficit and, 360–61; Goldwater's 1967 visit to, 181–91; Goldwater's speech on, 331–40; Hess, Karl, and, 191–92; McNamara, Robert, and, 223; Nixon, Richard, and, 229, 234, 239, 241, 252–53, 267; nuclear weapons and, 158; origins of, 97, 382; Paris Peace Talks and, 220–21, 253; political opposition to, 210, 227, 245, 249; troop withdrawals, 229, 255; War Powers Resolution and, 346
Vietnamization plan, 239, 253
Volpe, John, 237

W

Wallace, George, 322
War Powers Resolution, 344–46, 348
Warner, John, 375
Warren, Earl, 163, 226
Watergate, 275–327; beginnings of, 199–200, 263; Burch, Dean, and, 296–97, 299, 300–301, 303, 319; Bush, George H. W., and, 280, 282, 297–98, 305; Eisenhower, Dwight, and, 268, 302; Ford, Gerald, and, 285, 292, 298, 305–7, 309, 312, 318–19, 322, 325–27; Haig, Alexander, and, 278–79, 281, 284–86, 296–301; Harlow, Bryce, and, 282–90, 320; impeachment, calls for, 180, 283, 285, 287, 292, 296–99, 383; Kissinger, Henry, and, 311; Nixon, Richard, and, 275–327
Watkins, Arthur V., 120
Watson, David, 344
Wead, Doug, 369, 385
Weinberger, Casper, 382
Welch, Robert, 168, 170
Wellstone, Paul, 373–74
Wetherill, John, 31, 32
White, Clif, 140, 211
Whitehead, Ennis, 64
Whiting, William, 345
Williams, Eddy, 119
Wilson, Bill, 32
Wilson, Bob, 133, 205
Wilson, Katherine, 33
Wilson, Woodrow, 316
Wolfson, Louis, 226